MW01097377

Thomas Mann's "Joseph and His Brothers"

Studies in German Literature, Linguistics, and Culture

Edited by James Hardin
(*South Carolina*)

William E. McDonald

THOMAS MANN'S *JOSEPH AND HIS BROTHERS*

WRITING, PERFORMANCE, AND THE POLITICS OF LOYALTY

CAMDEN HOUSE

First published 1999
by Camden House

Camden House is an imprint of Boydell & Brewer Inc.
PO Box 41026, Rochester, NY 14604–4126 USA
and of Boydell & Brewer Limited
PO Box 9, Woodbridge, Suffolk IP12 3DF, UK

ISBN: 1–57113–154–x

Library of Congress Cataloging-in-Publication Data

McDonald, William E., 1940–
    Thomas Mann's Joseph and His Brothers: writing, performance, and
the politics of loyalty / William E. McDonald.
        p.   cm. – (Studies in German literature, linguistics, and
culture)
    Includes bibliographical references and index.
    ISBN 1–57113–154–X (alk. paper)
    1. Mann, Thomas, 1875–1955. Joseph und seine Brüder.   II. Title.
II. Series: Studies in German literature, linguistics, and culture
(Unnumbered)
PT2625.A44J7848   1999
833'.912—dc21   98–32148
                                                          CIP

This publication is printed on acid-free paper.
Printed in the United States of America

Photographs by the kind permission of the Thomas-Mann-Archiv, ETH Zürich.

Contents

Illustrations

Preface

IN 1961 *THE AMERICAN SCHOLAR*, ONE OF mid-century America's most prestigious journals, marked its thirtieth anniversary. Led by Hiram Haydn, its editorial board overflowed with high-ranking public intellectuals: Jacques Barzun, Loren Eiseley, John Kenneth Galbraith, Alfred Kazin, and ten others of similar stature. To mark the occasion the editors invited a number of "distinguished writers, scholars and critics" to join them in choosing "The Outstanding Books of 1931–1961" and to write a paragraph or two justifying their selection. The final group of sixty-four comprised a Who's Who of North American culture; Daniel Boorstin, Eleanor Roosevelt, W. E. B. Du Bois, and Archibald MacLeish are representative of those who agreed to participate. Together they formed a panel of cultural arbiters rarely, if ever, assembled in our century.

Their choices appeared in the Autumn 1961 issue, and covered a wide range. Only five authors received two or more nominations: Hannah Arendt, Kenneth Burke, James Joyce, Lewis Mumford, and Thomas Mann. Only one book received three votes: *Finnegans Wake* (Northrop Frye, Harry Levin, and Thornton Wilder). Mann's *Doctor Faustus* received two nominations (Gore Vidal and H. Stuart Hughes) and *Joseph and his Brothers* one (Gladys Schmidt); both books were also named runners-up by another panelist, John Gassner. This puts Mann's work at or near the top of the list. Schmidt, whose novel *Rembrandt* was nominated by Hiram Haydn, wrote of *Joseph*:

> . . . the masterly qualities of his prose are there — its classical precision of statement, its urbane poise, its ability to move from homely concreteness to poetic or philosophical flight. When Flaubert and George Eliot reached into the past for material, they were unable to evoke the reality present in their contemporary novels, but Mann creates characters with the same intimacy in ancient Egypt as in modern Germany.
>
> It was through Mann that I first found my own voice, and rereadings have never failed to bring back that old heady sense of release.
>
> (*The American Scholar*, Autumn 1961, 624)

A fine tribute from a fellow artist, and representative of the high place Mann's work held in America six years after his death. *Doctor Faustus, The Holy Sinner*, and the final novel in the *Joseph* tetralogy, *Joseph the Provider*, had all been Book of the Month Club selections, and his popularity as a principled German artist persisted despite the Red-scare accusations of his final years in the country. Schmidt's admiration led her to celebrate two things in particular: the intimate sense of reality of *Joseph*'s "ancient" characters, and the discovery of her own artistic voice in and through its prose. Her gratitude reminds us of the spoken roots of all storytelling, and directs us both to the oral effects in Mann's prose and to the freedom from, presumably, artistic and temporal constraints she found in that voice. Readers of her *Rembrandt* may well detect Mann's narrating voice in her book and take added pleasure in the intertextual echoes her praise encourages them to hear.

In the years following that *American Scholar* tribute, Mann's popularity in America receded. Like many writers, he passed through a different sort of "generation gap," the period of neglect that so often seems to follow the death of an artist famous in his own time. Now, however, John E. Woods's new translations of several novels, the University of California's new edition of Mann's correspondence with his brother Heinrich, and the three new biographies published since 1995 signal a Mann revival in the English-speaking world. This revival, together with the sea changes that have taken place in literary theory since 1961, invite new critical approaches to his texts.

Like Gladys Schmidt, though of course in a much more modest way, I write out of a long-standing love of and loyalty toward *Joseph and his Brothers,* and I hope also to celebrate its "precision, poise and intimacy" in what follows. Like her, I also want to honor Mann's voice and his love of intertextual play. Among the many fresh ways of reading afforded by recent theory, these two interconnected subjects seem particularly fruitful for understanding Mann's tetralogy. Specifically, I take up the intertextual relationships between the *Joseph* project and several of the lecture-essays that took shape in and around its making. I interpret these connections in light of Mann's "voice," not only the oral qualities of his narrative but his love of performing all his texts in public, of making his voice heard. Generally, the first half of the book foregrounds the essays and weaves its account of *Joseph* through them; the second half reverses the order.

Intertextuality and especially performance have been much discussed in recent literary theory. An intertextual reading commits me to writing in good part about the half-known arts of the texts' production. This means I must consider equally what Mann did deliberately and what occurred in his writing as a result of subliminal textual and cultural pressures. In doing so I implicitly claim to recognize more than Mann did about aspects of his creations, but always with the goal of honoring his achievement. Reading with oral performance in mind foregrounds the texts' political and ethical dimensions, illuminates their form in surprising ways, and situates the "timeless" Joseph story in the specific cultural circumstances of Mann's retelling. While speech-act practitioners, film studies scholars, feminists, queer theorists, and interpreters of the "politics of theatricality" offer many new perspectives on performativity, perspectives I hope other readers of Mann will develop, I concentrate more narrowly on how the exigencies of his own actual performances figured directly in his literary practice. I am, throughout, interested in how all these involved, sometimes penumbral interactions lead to a fresh understanding of *Joseph*. I have also minimized potential debates with Mann's many excellent critics; I admire and refer to a number of them, but concentrate on developing my own reading as fully and directly as I can. I hope to illuminate Mann's public achievements even as I trace the subliminal threads of his craft.

Readers unfamiliar with the *Joseph* tetralogy and its satellite essays, or long removed from their encounter with Mann's narratives, can still read this study with pleasure because I concentrate on some fifteen short sections of Mann's text and include detailed accounts of the featured essays. In doing so I happily imitate Mann's own practice in *Joseph* of giving the reader what he termed "representative" conversations among the many others he claims he might have recorded. In this way I hope to make a somewhat technical, tightly focused book interesting to readers in and out of the academy. Toward the same end I also make liberal use of what William Ian Miller in *The Anatomy of Disgust* calls the "invitational 'we.'" Neither royal nor the voice of some cadre of expert, all-knowing readers — Mann satirizes such voices in the "we" narration of the angels in *Joseph the Provider*'s "Prelude" — the invitational we "is the voice of attempted sympathy and imagination" that invites readers to "entertain" for a time views different from their own (xiii).

My use of English and German require a brief comment. The Joseph text — arguably best seen as a single novel but typically referred to as a set of novels or a tetralogy — consists of *Die Geschichten Jaakobs (The Tales of Jacob); Der junge Joseph (Young Joseph); Joseph in Ägypten (Joseph in Egypt); and Joseph, der Ernährer (Joseph the Provider)*. The German publication dates are, respectively, 1933, 1934, 1936, and 1943; the English dates are 1934, 1935, 1938, and 1944. For all citations of Mann's texts I give first the 1990 *Gesammelte Werke* (*GW*) reference, then the English translation (*JHB*). Since the *Joseph* volumes in the *GW* (IV and V) are numbered consecutively, I omit the volume reference. I also omit the volume reference when citing a sequence of passages from a single work. Citations from Mann's *Tagebücher* (*Diaries*) are abbreviated as *TB*. Since this book is intended mainly for an English-reading audience, I will, after an initial citation, use the English titles of Mann's works, chapter titles, and so on. I also use the English spellings of names and places. Titles of critical works appear in their original language.

The nuances of Mann's prose easily disappear in translation, of course, especially in several passages central to my argument. So at a few important junctures I will give the original, then my translation. This method may seem arbitrary — German for some passages, not for others — but it yields the compensatory advantage of limiting interruptions. I am using the newest reprint of Mann's *Gesammelte Werke* (1990) and the standard English versions published by Knopf. The pagination of the 1990 *GW Joseph* differs slightly from earlier editions; the other volumes are the same. Readers seeking quoted passages in the English version will inevitably encounter a small frustration. I have made alterations, and often wholesale revisions, in the Lowe-Porter translations (John Woods has not yet undertaken a new translation of the tetralogy). This means that virtually all the citations of the English text, when consulted, will seem "wrong"; no such English quote actually appears on the page. The alternatives, however, of giving English readers no citations or of simply letting the Lowe-Porter versions stand seem much less attractive. I have also used the original Freud texts, especially *Totem und Taboo*, but have made few alterations in the Strachey and Reviere translations.

After an opening chapter on *Joseph*'s many beginning points in text, biography, and theory, I turn to the lecture-essay on Kleist's play *Amphitryon* (1927). This major text from the first years of the *Joseph* cycle contains complex intertextuality, enactments of performance, and a specifically literary modeling of the psyche that exert, I argue, a powerful influence on the texts that follow it. I then show how the ongoing *Joseph* project fashions — and is fashioned by — the 1929 "Freud" essay's startling combination of *Totem and Taboo* and political responsibility. Next I take up narcissism in *Young Joseph*, a subject closely bound up with *Amphitryon*, with Freud, with Mann's biography, and with performance itself. Chapter V considers Freud's *Civilization and its Discontents*'s ubiquitous presence in the opening of *Joseph in Egypt* — and beyond. Finally, I show how Mann's 1936 lecture, "Freud and the Future," in tandem with the last two *Joseph* novels, both affirms and supersedes psychoanalysis's drama of development. It does so by interweaving a literary, performative model of personal identity with Freud's construction of an archetypal Oedipus to produce a richer understanding of right human, and political, identity. In

Mann's retelling, we are not simply condemned to be Oedipus; we are also chosen to be performers of our own harrowing yet open-ended constructions of selfhood. *Joseph and his Brothers* fabricates a counter-story to Freud's narrative that lightens the past and enlightens the future. In all this I follow the *Joseph* narrator's advice concerning the right reading of "the original story;" only those succeed who " . . . make their way precisely into its forms of expression and know how to read between the lines" (V, 1755–56; 1165).

I have been blessed with both institutional and personal support for this project. First are the several groups of talented, dedicated Proudian honors scholars and Johnston Center students who read the *Joseph* novels with me over the past seven years. Our hundreds of conversations about the tetralogy have interwoven themselves with my writing in ways I can no longer distinguish, but which are more than fitting for a book about intertext and performance. One of these friends, Patrick Harrigan, read the entire manuscript with great care and made hundreds of invaluable suggestions on everything from comma placement to points of theory. Herbert Lehnert, one of Mann's finest readers and scholars, generously invited me to his home for conversation, provided reprints, answered e-mail inquiries at length, and read a draft of the manuscript with extraordinary patience and care. He remained supportive of a project somewhat removed from his own critical interests and temperament. My friend of nearly fifty years, philosopher Stanley Bates, read several versions of the manuscript with acuity and kindness. Dr. Thomas Sprecher and staff members Cornelia Bernini and Martina Peter of the Thomas-Mann-Archiv in Zurich responded promptly and most helpfully to my requests. The Faculty Review Committee of the University of Redlands granted me a year-long sabbatical during which the manuscript took shape, as well as a research award that supported my initial work. The university's Wilcox fund helped to defer other costs; my gratitude to Dean Nancy Carrick for her support. My colleagues in literature at the university read portions of my early drafts and offered me steady encouragement as well as a lighter teaching schedule for the final months of the project. Professor of religion Bill Huntley and Egyptologist Doug Bowman supplied me with helpful details, and librarian Sandra Richey tracked down many an obscure article. My colleague and Germanist Dora Van Vranken deserves special thanks. She spent hours with me discussing my translations of Mann's rich and subtle text, helping me to capture shades of meaning or delicate ironies. She took phone calls at odd hours, traced down unusual usages, and interlaced her critical advice with heartfelt encouragement. I am also very grateful to Professor James Hardin of Camden House for his straight-to-the-point recommendations about both content and style, and for his broad support throughout the project. And my wife Dolores, herself a long-standing admirer of the *Joseph* novels, offered not only commonsensical advice about style and strategy but — even more important — the intangible, invaluable support and succor that made this project possible.

1: Beginnings: "Jacob and His Sons"

God made man because he loves stories.

— Elie Wiesel

But what a simple-minded idea most people have about "confessions"! When I deal with an artist, or even a master, I do not mean "me," I am not asserting that I am a master or even an artist — only that I know something about artistry and mastery. Nietzsche says somewhere: "To understand something about art, make a few works of art." And he considers the artists of the day as intermediaries between us and the great masters; they somehow catch and conduct the heat rays of the great masters of the past. When I examine myself thoroughly, I see that this and nothing else has always been the goal of my creative work: to achieve the consciousness of the masters. It has been a game, just as I played "prince" as a boy in order to acquire the princely sensibility. In working as an artist, I acquired knowledge about the existence of the artist, even the great artist, and can therefore say something about it.

— Thomas Mann to Paul Amann, 10 September 1915

Perhaps educating the nation is the mission of all German men of the spirit who have progressed, like Goethe, from a loving self-absorption via autobiographical confession to educative responsibility.

— Thomas Mann, "On the German Republic" (1922)

I

JOSEPH AND HIS BROTHERS BEGINS AT MULTIPLE points and in multiple ways. A large and varied number of events in Mann's life led to its writing: a request to draft an introduction to a portfolio of illustrations of Joseph's life; the early memory of hearing the tale read from the family Bible; the rereading of the story in that same Bible, with its faded underlinings made by his ancestors as they reread; the sudden recollection of a chance remark of Goethe's; plans for a group of three novellas to form a religious-historical triptych; a journey to the Levant and especially to Egypt, a country that had fascinated him since childhood. It began also in the struggles and political demands of the Weimar Republic, in scores of books on the ancient Mediterranean, in *Totem and Taboo*, in the face of a lovely boy, in the imperatives and

momentum of Mann's artistic life. It began in ways that Mann understood deeply and in ways he only half-consciously intuited. The text
itself begins by demonstrating, in the kaleidoscopic speculations of its
"Prelude," the impossibility of establishing authoritative beginnings. Its
dramatic narrative begins with an adolescent's narcissism and a father's
loyal love, and ends with a father's mythic narcissism and a son's loving
loyalty. Viewed ethically, it begins with the Hebrew word *Chased*,
meaning "steadfast love," which interlaces love and loyalty and which
occurs some dozen times in Genesis (e.g., 20:13, 32:10, 47:29). It begins again in each of its four separate volumes. It begins in the full
awareness that it is yet another retelling of the Genesis story that has
"been told a hundred times in a hundred different ways. And now today it is passing through another retelling, in which it as it were gains
consciousness of itself and remembers how things had actually been
once, both in detail and in actuality, so that it simultaneously pours
forth and examines itself as it pours" (*GW*, 827; *JHB*, 553). The power
of narration is such that, impossibly, the tale becomes a self-knowing
agent in the same way that an analysand comes to knowledge through
repeated renarrations of the past.

The psychoanalytic echo in this passage from *Joseph in Egypt* points
toward another set of beginnings. *Joseph and his Brothers* begins in the
writings of a pantheon of well-known and oft-discussed patriarchs:
Goethe, Schopenhauer, Wagner, Nietzsche, Tolstoy, Turgenyev.
Freud's name also usually appears in this assemblage of fathers. Yet he
is different in one material way. He is a living compatriot: a father, perhaps, or an older brother. Of all Mann's major essays — the thirty
pieces in *GW* IX and the sixteen translated in *Essays of Three Decades* —
only the two "Freud" lectures ponder a contemporary. Freud and
Mann corresponded fitfully, though quite revealingly, and met several
times. Even though Mann thought Freud's scientific methodology
made him indifferent to his wider cultural heritage — a main theme of
the 1929 lecture — Freud in fact recognized patriarchs of his own in
this pantheon.

Joseph and his Brothers begins also with the love of names and never
tires of the associations that name-play produces. Every major figure,
divine and human, has at least two names, and several have four or five.
Pharaoh rewards his new vizier Joseph with a full dozen (1475–77;
976–78) and takes up his mentor's idea that one's name should suit
one's circumstances (1441; 953). This plurality marks a dispersed and
alienated figure occasionally, but more commonly a character of en-
riching multiplicity and many-sidedness. The novel itself oscillated for a
time between several names. More than three years into its writing

Mann still seriously entertained the title "Jacob and his Sons" because it honored the patriarch's dominating presence in the narrative.[1] The complex relationships between fathers and sons indeed lie at the heart of the tetralogy's action. Jacob's life occupies the first novel, and his death closes the last; each of the twelve brothers, right to the final page, fundamentally understands himself as a son. Willa Cather once aptly remarked that without Jacob, *Joseph and his Brothers* would be just another young man's success story (Cather 1936, 118: see also 121–22). Mainly for these reasons I have reclaimed Mann's abandoned title for my chapter.

Further, in the spirit of *Joseph*'s name-play and unending interest in the half-known, "Jacob and his Sons" offers other, subliminal associations. To begin, Freud's own father's name was Jacob. Nothing more than an entertaining coincidence, of course, yet young Siegmund, in a rough approximation to Joseph, was himself a younger brother born late to Jacob Freud's third, "true" wife. Both left their homes for foreign lands, cosmopolitan careers, and fame. Sigmund's uncle was one Josef Freud, a much-traveled con man and trader in counterfeit rubles, who appears in the childhood dreams later recounted in *The Interpretation of Dreams*. More important, Freud's account of patriarchs, both personal and mythic, plays a prominent role in my study. His story of fathers and sons in violent psycho-sexual competition both appears and undergoes transformation in Mann's narrative. Narratives of patriarchy also connect directly to the central political and ethical issues of the novels, and to Mann's own political engagement during their writing. Seen in this light, the phrase "Jacob and his sons" invites comparison with "Germany and its sons," that is, with the Aryan youth that Mann repeatedly tried, during the early *Joseph* years, to woo away from the Austrian pseudo-patriarch Hitler and fascism's own myth of Germany's beginnings.

The *Joseph* tetralogy has another, less scrutinized beginning point: an ancestor whose drama of love, loyalty, and identity quietly shaped its ethical vision. Heinrich von Kleist's *Amphitryon*, and Mann's passionate lecture on the play, anchor a mythic counterstory to Freud's Oedipal drama that Mann would reorient and elaborate ceaselessly in both the *Joseph* and a number of the essay-lectures that accompanied its making. This leads to more subliminal name-play. Mann's oft-chronicled stormy relationship with his older brother, Heinrich, rightly takes center stage in biographical accounts of his art. Like Freud, Heinrich von Kleist functions both as a humanist forebearer and fellow artist for Mann in his struggles with his too-liberal sibling and with the too-conservative fascists. So Kleist and Freud — Prussian playwright and cosmopolitan

Moravian Jew, a dead and a living compatriot — form a contending and complementary patrimony for Mann's re-creation of the Joseph story.

Looking in the other direction, *Joseph and his Brothers* itself can be named as an unacknowledged ancestor of several more recent thinkers. The tetralogy uncannily anticipates a number of contemporary theorists of ethics and psychology. Heinz Kohut, Julia Kristeva, Emmanuel Levinas, Stanley Cavell, Martha Nussbaum: the ideas and worldviews of any one of these putative descendants, each different from the others, could sponsor a powerful account of the novels. I have chosen to background these lines of indirect inheritance, but readers familiar with their writings will notice Mann's fatherly anticipations.

My subtitle puts forward the central group of subjects that shape my reading of *Joseph*: intertextuality, self-influence, public performance, the politics and ethics of loyalty, narcissism. They are, in a nutshell, what this book is about. Each chapter considers all of them in varying proportions. This opening chapter concentrates on the first three. The second chapter takes up the *Amphitryon* essay-lecture, principally to explore ethics and identity. Mann's first "Freud" essay (1929) and its uses in *The Tales of Jacob* occupy most of the third chapter. Narcissism dominates the fourth chapter, both Freud's version and Mann's literary revision in *Young Joseph*. All these subjects then come together in the final two chapters: on *Joseph in Egypt* and on Mann's 1936 "Freud" essay and *Joseph the Provider*, respectively. These subjects interweave both in Mann's devising of them and in my account of their significance. "Weaving": an enabling metaphor ever since *The Odyssey* for the twice-told tales of epic, and equally empowering for this revisionary account of *Joseph and his Brothers*.

II
Intertextuality and Self-influence

The living utterance, having taken meaning and shape at a particular historical moment in a socially specific environment, cannot fail to brush up against thousands of living dialogic threads, woven by socio-ideological consciousness around the given object of an utterance; it cannot fail to become an active participant in social dialogue.

— Mikhail Bakhtin, *The Dialogic Imagination*

The one text is . . . an entrance into a network with a thousand entrances . . . the networks are many and interact, without any one of them being able to surpass the rest; the text is a galaxy of signifiers, not a struc-

*ture of signifieds; it has no beginning; it is reversible; we gain access to it
by several entrances, none of which can be authoritatively declared to be
the main one.*

— Roland Barthes, *S/Z*

Nearly thirty years of theorizing have made "intertextuality" a familiar
and increasingly more useful concept, and I presume that history in
what follows. The epigraphs from Bakhtin and Barthes locate, for me,
intertextuality's particular force. The term includes a spectrum of possible relations between intertext and focus text, from the deliberate use
of other texts or systems of signs all the way to the independent, unrecognized operations of textual forces. Intertextuality has expanded
from its initial critical task of undermining claims of textual unity to the
more inclusive investigation of how multiple voices and systems of signs
within texts create meaning. Once sharply contrasted with source and
influence studies, theorists of intertext have moved past that binary to
emphasize the constructive interplay between these two critical methods.[2] Following Bakhtin, I see intertexts as more liberating than unraveling, and as entailing "active participation in social dialogue."

One of the most intriguing and least explored aspects of intertextuality is self-influence. It includes writers' deliberate use of their own
writings, past and contemporaneous, in a new project, as well as the
more subliminal, text-driven ways in which these productions shape
one another. The concept of self-influence is especially useful in understanding writers who carry on several projects simultaneously; the web
of textual connections across manuscripts can produce enlightening
parallels and surprising disjunctions. So Virginia Woolf, for example,
may in a review of another novelist explore technical problems that illuminate, consciously and intuitively, her own work in progress. Others — John Fowles in *The Aristos* or Mann himself in *Betrachtungen
eines Unpolitischen (Reflections of a Non-political Man)* — may use
nonfiction as a kind of safety valve for ungainly or half-formed philosophical material that might well sink the novel already under way.
That speculative writing may then be used profitably to reread its fictional sibling.

So understood, self-influence complements another kind of "influence" study, one that forms a broad current in Mann criticism: the
ways in which his famous cultural precursors molded his intellectual,
artistic, and even political career. In this study the weight falls rather on
how Mann's own writings, the particular productions and performances
themselves, shaped each other. This sets self-influence apart from
Mann's more general cultural knowledge without opposing the many

fine interpretations that long tradition has produced. (My commitment is to negotiation between readings, not to "wars," textual or cultural.) Self-influence highlights how the specific revisiting of Kleist's *Amphitryon* that Mann dramatized in his 1927 essay plays a role in shaping the *Joseph* tetralogy. Hence I have retained the established word "self-'influence'" for the particular kind of intertextual study I have in mind, one that partakes of writers' conscious, demonstrable manipulations of their own archive, and the continuities which that archive generates in and through the artistic performances that follow it.

Thomas Mann was a deliberate but steady, and therefore prolific, writer. Like Wagner before him, he created all his longer works in multiple, intertextual layers.[3] Other novels, novellas, short stories, essays, lectures, reviews, newspaper and radio interviews — not to mention his voluminous correspondence and meticulous diary keeping — regularly interleave with the major manuscript under construction.[4] More than twenty important texts were produced during the long drafting of *Joseph and his Brothers* (12/1926–1/1943), from a major novel (*Lotte in Weimar*), a minor novel (*Die vertauschten Köpfe: The Transposed Heads*), and a classic antifascist tale ("Mario und der Zauberer": "Mario and the Magician") to several of Mann's most significant cultural essays: four on Goethe, two on Wagner, and single pieces on Lessing, Storm, von Platen, *Don Quixote*, Schopenhauer, and Tolstoy, as well as the "Kleist" and the two "Freud" lectures that will particularly concern us. Each of these contributes to the tetralogy that surrounds it and is in turn shaped by its gravitational force. Also of note are the many political essays, articles, interviews, and lectures, particularly the "Deutsche Ansprache — Ein Appell an die Vernunft" ("German Address — An Appeal to Reason") of 1930, the "Achtung, Europa!" of 1937 [Nice Conference letter], the outraged reaction to the Munich appeasement "Dieser Friede" ("This Peace"), and "Vom kommenden Sieg der Demokratie" ("On the Coming Victory of Democracy") of 1938, and several others that followed it into the war years.

As even this abbreviated catalog makes clear, the greatest difficulty in a study of Thomas Mann's intertextual self-influence is setting limits on the inquiry. After a time, a single text's associations can seem inexhaustible to a careful reader. Multiply this by what Mann calculated to be, in mythic round numbers, the "seventy thousand lines" of the *Joseph* (XI, 670; *JHB*, v) and then by the number of ancillary texts, and the subject can quickly overwhelm both interpreter and audience alike. Choosing the proper beginning point adds another layer of inexhaustibility; plausible cases can easily be made for launching this study not as

I do with the "Kleist" essay but with the "Lübeck" essay of 1926, or the 1925 version of "Goethe and Tolstoy," or even *Reflections*. So however worthy it might seem, a one-volume study of *Joseph* and its companion texts remains unattainable; even a survey of all the writings would require a length surpassing that of the tetralogy itself. Mann himself quickly came to the same conclusion when he started to catalog "all the critical escapades and marginalia for *Joseph*" (672; vi). It is also less necessary because of the considerable number of excellent critical studies, particularly on Mann and Goethe, already available to readers of *Joseph and his Brothers*.

Having said this, it is still a dramatic step to omit from this study all of Mann's other fictions of the period, and to use the great Goethe, Wagner, and Schopenhauer essays only in supplementary roles. But dramatic gains more than compensate for doing so. The two "Freud" essays, especially when read with and through the earlier "Kleist" essay, are both relatively underappreciated and (to use Mann's own metaphor) "colored" in especially absorbing ways by the novels' development (672; vi). The "Kleist" essay and the two "Freud" essays also best represent, respectively, two principal kinds of intertextual self-influence at work in the *Joseph*: the continuous, half-conscious return to a relatively unappreciated German precursor; and the more deliberate struggle with a powerful contemporary whose ideas both enable and threaten his writing and public performances. Mann's passionate reconstruction of the *Amphitryon* appears and recedes in his conscious meditation on the *Joseph* story as it unfolds, while his wrestling with Freud becomes increasingly self-conscious and confident. But Kleist's subterranean influence will prove just as decisive in the climactic scenes of *Joseph and his Brothers* as Mann's more conscious readings — and misreadings — of Freud. So while nearly all of the major essays make appearances below, I concentrate on these three and the tetralogy.

Complexity would again be multiplied by examining every linguistic repetition and echo at the phrase, sentence, and paragraph levels, and by making a treatment of these myriad linguistic repetitions and deviations the center of the study. I will do some of this in what follows, dipping into paragraphs that seem especially revealing, but for the most part I intend to read at a slightly more general level. My thesis requires reading a number of passages carefully — there is no other way to make it persuasive — but I will not concentrate on specific linguistic repetitions. Limiting the subject in these ways should make this study more manageable, informative, and pleasurable to read.

III
Autobiography and Self-influence

Mann was well aware of his penchant for the intertextual, and his most notable account of the subject during the *Joseph* years offers us an excellent place to begin. The passage comes from *A Sketch of My Life*. Mann slyly layers his description of textual layering; beginning with a description and a cheerful complaint, it modulates into celebration and playful self-quotation, and then repeats the entire process.

> *Der Zauberberg* (*The Magic Mountain*) was flowing again, but the work on it was accompanied by the composition of critical essays of which the three most extensive in range — "Goethe and Tolstoy," "On the German Republic," and "An Experience in the Occult" — were direct offshoots of the novel. I shall probably never be able to guard my creative work, however much more "rewarding" it may be, from wicked interruptions and delays caused by my propensity for essay, even polemical, writing. This tendency goes back a long way and is clearly an inalienable element of my personality. Perhaps in yielding to it I partake more keenly in Goethe's self-confidence in being "a born writer" than when I am spinning a tale. For that reason I do not like the popular distinction we make in Germany between a creative writer (Dichter) and an author (Schriftsteller). Surely the border between the two does not run outwardly and between the manifestations, but within the personality, where it is entirely fluid. "An art," as I said in my Lessing speech in 1929, "whose medium is language will always bring about a high degree of critical creativity, for language itself is a critique of life: it names, it defines, it hits the mark, it passes judgment, and all by making things alive." And yet, shall I confess that I typically feel that "writing" — as distinct from the free composition of the epic poet — is a sort of passionate truancy and a self-tormenting theft from happier tasks? There is a very artless sense of duty and "categorical imperative" in play here, and one could speak of the paradox of asceticism with a bad conscience, if it were not that a good deal of pleasure and satisfaction were bound up in it — as is, incidentally, the case with all asceticism. In any event, it seems that the essay, as a critical overseer of my life, shall remain as an aspect of my productivity . . . . Thus, out of the meeting between inner necessity and the needs of the time arose the addresses, discussions, introductions, rejoinders . . . . of these, especially the speeches beginning with "The German Republic" . . . represent, above and beyond the literary, elevated moments in my personal life (XI, 129–31; 55–57).[5]

Mann's playful, and serious, sense of his affinity for the intertextual appears everywhere in this passage. First, he laments that he cannot protect his work from these intrusive essays because, like his fiction, they arise from a fundamental part of his character. Yet precisely because these allegedly victimizing texts, these unwanted intrusions that retard his artistic output, have their roots in the depths of his personality, they make him feel more the "natural writer," more like his self-confident master, Goethe. This amusing reversal leads to the heart of the passage. Mann wants to show that an analogous opposition — the oft-discussed critical division between the lofty Dichter and the workmanlike Schriftsteller — all but disappears under scrutiny. It should not be looked for in the texts themselves, and even within the character of the writer, its actual locus, the membrane between the two is shifting and permeable. Then he swiftly supplements this claim with a broader argument: the interlacing connections between Dichter and Schriftsteller inhere in the critical, mediated nature of language itself. This larger truth adds a second layer of inevitability to their complex connectedness. Mann is alert to the entertaining irony of affirming language's indirection in the most transparent prose.[6]

To establish this claim about language Mann does not cite a philosopher or a linguist, or even Goethe. Instead, he resorts to self-quotation, the most overt form of self-influence. This citing of one's own text as full authority for one's present argument makes for a wry *mise en abyme* of self-influential writing; by interweaving his critical and autobiographical writings Mann reincarnates the very dissolving of borders between types of writing he has claimed earlier in the passage. The quotation itself, taken from his recent Lessing essay ("Rede über Lessing," 1929), concerned exactly the same subject: the stereotypical, "dull," and "provincial" divisions between Dichter and Schriftsteller. "Our conventional criticism simply lives on it." The real enemy, both here and in the Lessing essay, is "simplification," reduction; the "provincial" binary of Dichter and Schriftsteller is dissolved in both argument and textual practice.

A reading of the Lessing lecture shows that the *Sketch* sentence on "personality" is also, one pronoun excepted, a direct quote from that essay ("weil ja die Grenze . . . der Persönlichkeit verläuft": IX, 232; *Essays*, 191–92). This concealed citation accounts for the condensed, slightly jerky quality in the *Sketch* passage; he had surreptitiously already begun copying out his own earlier work before he acknowledged doing so. So Mann, in effect, used self-quotation to mask self-quotation: a small private joke, and of the sort he loved to practice. He has also managed to bring Lessing, who is " . . . der Klassiker des dichterischen Verstandes, der Erzvater alles klugen und wachen Dichtertums" ("the archetype of creative intelligence, the patriarch of all clever and alert

writers") into the argument as proof of the artistic personality's inte-
grative powers (232; 191). Lessing and Goethe, the classical intelligence and the "natural born writer," are now both enlisted in the cause
of dissolving this hierarchy. Mann admired this sentence enough to use
a close paraphrase of it again two years later in his lecture "Goethe's
Career as a Man of Letters." He attributes any insistence on the distinction between "Dichtertum und Schriftstellertum" to a "fruitless
critical mania."[7] This layering, both theorized and practiced in our passage, keeps the reader constantly alert for the nuances of uneven surfaces and intricate connections. It also underscores the literal
inexhaustibility of Mann's texts.

But after having exposed the unreality of the distinction, Mann
subtly reinstates it. Returning to the questions of choice and compulsion with which he began, he speaks of the suspect freedom, the heady
dereliction of duty, that his essay writing alone produces. Writing that a
few lines earlier was compelled by his artistic personality now becomes
an expression of freedom from artistic duty. And the suddenly announced "pleasures of asceticism" — yet another playful paradox —
perpetuate writing that is both duty-bound and a theft of duty. Mann
then draws together his inner compulsions and the demands of his political position in post-1918 Germany to justify the three volumes of
essays and speeches that he produced during that time. The paragraph
ends with a final surprise, declaring that the performance — not simply
the drafting — of the 1922 essay "Von Deutscher Republik" was the
first in a series of high points in his personal experience "above and beyond the literary." The importance of that performance — Mann's first
address to the entire nation — can hardly be exaggerated. Such "geho-
bene Augenblicke" also occur in the "Kleist" lecture, and in both
"Freud" performances as well. This sentiment on behalf of a lecture is
not what we expect to hear from a Nobel Prize-winning novelist.

So Mann's carefully crafted self-examination begins with a mild lament about the impositions of essay writing on literary production,
proceeds to dissolve the distinction among kinds of writing upon which
that lament depends, and ends by reaffirming a convoluted reseparation
that credits essay writing with experiences of freedom and of elevated
feelings which are independent of those that literature provides. Playful
indeed, but also serious: only in complexity, not in reduction, can a
writer be rightly understood. That this is also a brief *ars poetica* for the
contemporary "Epiker" and his *Joseph* novels, with their persistent interweaving of the "essayistic" and the "poetic," will come as small surprise. As we shall see repeatedly, the artistic, moral and political

concerns of the tetralogy extend deep into the fabric of every satellite text that accompanied its making.

IV
Thomas Mann: 1918–1926

Biography has added a new terror to death.

— Sir Charles Wetherell (1869)

There is a more or less standard story about Mann's career between the publication of *Reflections of a Non-political Man* in 1918 and the opening pages of the *Joseph* novels in 1926. It is "standard" in that it is the story most commonly told and retold by scholars, German and Anglo-American, each bringing some new information or a more subtle angle of vision to the narrative.[8]

Thomas Mann emerged from the First World War as a leading representative of his defeated nation's cultural integrity and conservative political thought. This representation was not simply verbal; Mann literally embodied for many of his embittered countrymen the value and the mystique of the German spirit. He remained a voice on the Right during the early days of the Weimar Republic, scorning the new, floundering democracy with Nietzschean hauteur and exalting the integrity of German Kultur against the shallow Enlightenment partisans of the West.[9] The vengeance-driven blockade of the fatherland reconfirmed the thoroughgoing hypocrisy of Anglo-French humanism. So he sought other allies: the lecture version of "Goethe and Tolstoy" (1921) made common cause with the "pagan divinities" of Germany and Russia against this enemy; if Western humanism is indeed morally bankrupt, then it must be replaced.[10] With what? Mann was a little vague, but his audiences at Nordic Week Kulturfests in the early 1920s would not have been puzzled: "der völkische Mythus" was the only possible answer (Reed 1974, 286).[11] But when Mann saw the incarnation that "der völkische Mythus" was in fact assuming, most dramatically in his beloved Munich, his wholehearted commitment to the conservative worldview began to change. The June 1922 assassination of foreign minister (and Jew and homosexual) Walther Rathenau was crucial to this unraveling. What followed was Mann's fitful transition from the aristocratic, nationalistic conservatism of 1918 to the liberal democratic opposition to Nazism of the late 1920s and beyond.

Here our standard story splits into two versions, each of which has energetic and thoughtful defenders. The first, still popular account emphasizes discontinuity between the Mann of the war years and the emerging social democrat of the 1920s. These discontinuities include the Nazis' cheapening glorification of Nietzsche's "blond beast," who was not his "bourgeois" Nietzsche (XI, 110; *Sketch*, 23). Next, new cultural voices endorsing liberalism included Mann's first, rapturous encounter with Hans Reisiger's translations of (for Mann) the "exotic" bard of democracy, Walt Whitman. The first of the strong antifascist speeches, "On the German Republic," followed shortly; it was delivered in Berlin the following October.[12] Then, in the 1925 version of "Goethe and Tolstoy," Mann confirmed another *echtdeutsche* humanist tradition. The elaboration of this more ancient practice, no longer grounded in the deceitful French Enlightenment (or in the politics of his brother and rival Heinrich), provided the intellectual floor for an entire reassessment of his political and cultural position. Western rationalism reemerged as an ally sprung from a common root, while romantic mystification, especially in the form of cultural mythmaking, came in for ever-sharper critique, and Mann launched a new career as *praeceptor Germaniae* (Reed 1974, 296). Irony that once unmasked the stupidity and pathos of life was now redirected to the less corrosive task of mediating between oppositions. On the political front Germany must mediate between the poles of European politics and at the same time mediate its own political binaries ("our socialism . . . . will not truly rise to the height of its national task until . . . Karl Marx will have read Friedrich Hölderlin").[13] More allies were found in the reshaped tradition: Kleist offered a tragicomedy of personal identity that rescued the mythic for reason ("the blitheness of its mysticism, the warmth of its humor"); Lessing offered a sturdy defense of classicism and the place of the rational in art; and Freud emerged as a surprising follower of the ethical (not the "pagan") Goethe. Mann cast Freud as the latest German thinker to venture into the underworld of our individual and cultural psyches, not to celebrate or even humbly acknowledge their power (as the "Freud" of "Death in Venice" had done), but for the sole purpose of bringing them under the control of the ego and its enlightened reason.

The second and arguably more coherent version has been forcefully articulated by Herbert Lehnert (1963a, 1973, 1991: see also Koelb 1984). It claims a strong continuity between the Mann of *Reflections* and the notably aristocratic "democrat" of the middle 1920s and beyond. A few "exaggerated" portions of *Reflections* aside (1963a, 282), Lehnert maintains that the main conceptions of that long book of "confusing national partiality" in fact made possible Mann's advocacy of more republican, liberal views (1973, 1157). "Mann's *Betrachtungen eines Unpolitischen* and his war-essays are 'nationalistic' in a very special way, that cannot be confused with the ordinary German nationalism of the time. Mann had a generally cosmopolitan attitude, considered German culture quintessentially European and opposed democracy that he [initially] confused with ideology. His anti-National Socialism is not a reversal, but a continuation of the *Betrachtungen*."[14] Examples multiply: he takes his defense of Germany as a mediator in European culture and politics directly from his wartime book rather than some "new" perspective. The same holds true for his defense of the vital artistic freedom arising from the German artist's position as mediator. Mann used the phrase "new Humanism" as early as 1913, and equated it directly to democracy in his praise of Whitman nine years later (1973, 1156–58). And during the years of writing *Reflections* Mann drafted more than a few expressions of liberal optimism: "I can feel something of the Europe to come: an exhausted Europe, but full of youthful hope, sensitive, refined, and blessed by common suffering . . . undoctrinaire, undogmatic, for all the earlier antitheses and slogans will be obsolete."[15] The "rediscovered" German humanism had in fact been there all along, "combining a spiritualized conception of progress with a tendency to mythical romanticism. As a result the *Joseph* structure reflects the peculiar German tradition, the desire to have it both ways, to be progressive and spiritual, to have social justice and the preservation of elitism" (1973, 1148).

Despite these important differences, both versions agree on several things: that a number of Mann's contemporaries believed, rightly or wrongly, that he had indeed abandoned his earlier views; that Mann self-consciously "made adjustments" in his views to meet new circumstances; and that he deliberately became a more public figure (Lehnert 1973, 1159). I have no wish to resolve this debate — though I think Lehnert's "continuity" reading is more persuasive — because it will be material in what follows to keep both of these accounts of Mann's development in mind.

So Thomas Mann, in his own well-known formulation, moved from a loving self-absorption to autobiographical confession to educative responsibility ("Goethe and Tolstoy" and "On the German Republic"). Even as political events gradually outstripped his opposition, he persevered. Over the decade his pro-democratic ideas solidified and his speaking engagements multiplied. In effect, he took to the road against the Nazis. Believing that he continued to have a special hold on the minds of young German males, he concentrated his lectures on that audience. He knew that Romantic conservatism was a powerful force in German education, and that its irrationalism fanned the flames of anti-

Semitism and nationalistic fervor among its students. By 1930 and the "German Address" Mann's opposition was theoretically complete and for a time politically forceful. And from 1926 on, Mann was writing the *Joseph* novels, texts typically viewed as far removed in time and space from the political and cultural violence of the late Weimar period. The novels were seen, sometimes even by Mann himself, as a refuge whose comedy and cheerful sanity gave protection and a strong sense of order against the madness of Hitler's rise.

Flight and exile came in 1933. The last chapter of the standard story harbors complexities and fissures: for all his defenses, public and private, of the political ideology Weimar sought to embody, Mann retained an allegiance to aspects of the old cultural agenda and to the ironic detachment he felt necessary for art. One sign of this was the chronic indecision that backlit his hatred of the new mythology: he waffled on the defense of anti-Nazi political figures; his son Klaus's editorship of an antifascist periodical was tepidly supported, then withdrawn; in his desire, for both pedagogic and financial reasons, to keep hold of his German readers, he permitted a sales campaign for the first of the *Joseph* novels filled with conventional nationalistic phrases of the day.[16] And deeper traces of the now suspect allegiance to the values of the *Reflections* appear in nearly all of the newer writings.[17] But despite these crosscurrents, Mann's commitment to his elevated notion of democracy, a carefully redefined "classical" humanism, and political engagement remained firm throughout the Nazi years. The accompanying novels came to reflect that commitment in the synthesis of politics, commerce, and the artist in the figure of Joseph (e.g. Mayer 1980, 364–66).

So to reformulate my purpose in the wake of this biographical material, I am making two basic claims. First, the essays and novels interweave at levels that Mann consciously manipulated, and at levels of which he was only — could only be — partially aware. The excerpts from *A Sketch of My Life* and, shortly, from the "Foreword" to the 1948 one-volume edition of the *Joseph* model this interplay. Following their examples, the rest of this book explores the many encounters between our three representative essays and the retelling of the Genesis saga. The interpretations this premise engenders, though grounded in more recent theories of the text, connect firmly to more traditional and familiar interpretations. My second, related claim is a little less familiar: this self-influence and textual interplay shape, and in turn are shaped by, Mann's penchant for public performance.

V
Intertextuality and the "Foreword" to the *Joseph* novels

By "intertextual reading" I mean reading two texts in both directions simultaneously, and foregrounding family resemblances between open texts rather than cause-and-effect sequences between hermetically sealed works.[18] This way of reading encourages us to see how, for example, the Esau narrative in the fourth chapter of *The Tales of Jacob* works out aspects of the servant Sosias's tale in Kleist's *Amphitryon* in such a way that deepens our understanding of both. It allows us to see both texts in relation to one another and to privilege neither. Intertextual reading here does not seek to dominate or erase more traditional interpretations; it supplements them in order to investigate subjects easily overlooked or awkwardly handled in established readings.

Some of the crossings empowered by writing's momentum will be easy to see: interwoven patterns on or near a text's surface. These will also be closest to more traditional thematic and sources studies. Textual interweavings are also, of course, linguistic: from deliberate self-quotation to more associative junctures; from the phrase and sentence level to larger structures. Detecting these echoes is a familiar task in stylistic studies and will play an occasional role in what follows.[19] But this approach is most productive for the difficult, penumbral areas of textual crossings: places where evidence, traditionally conceived, is ambiguous or largely absent. I'm especially interested in these shaded points of contact that writing produces, sites of mutual molding that are latent yet detectable. To paraphrase Bakhtin, because writers know so well the central place of intuition and inspiration in their work, they always intend for their performances to mean more than their consciously intended meanings. As Mann remarked of Wagner, "Artists do misunderstand themselves" (IX, 519; *Essays*, 365).

Several kinds of practice mark self-influence's presence. For example, textual incongruities — surprises and misfits — in the essays and the *Joseph* sometimes derive from their intertextual interlacing. Incongruities may be of argument, of narrative flow, of unexpected or subtle swerves from an established narrative direction. These counter–threads move at or below the threshold of immediate perception, a sort of textual preconscious, and like the preconscious exert a persistent sway across the texts in question. Condensation and displacement, the critical terms of dream-work, may also signal textual encounters. Further, the momentum that an essay or novel generates shapes its companion in constantly evolving ways. Self-influence over longer stretches of time — from, say, the 1927 "Kleist" and the 1929 "Freud" essays to the writing of *Joseph in Egypt* several years later — involves ideas and formulations that are "forgotten" yet leave measurable traces in the succeeding text. Finally, the terms and range of self-influence alter smoothly with the texts in question. So when the tetralogy is read with and through its accompanying essays, the outcome resembles, yet importantly differs from, accounts which foreground only individual textual integrity.

The danger — one common to any method that reads beneath the surface — is that claims for self-influence may be capricious, or arbitrary, and/or better described in more traditional terms. Protection against the first two pitfalls always has to do with the reasons offered, and with the overall persuasiveness of the interpreter's eye for color traces and ear for barely detectable sounds. "Described in more traditional terms" is especially tricky; I risk knowledgeable readers muttering, "But that's really taken from Schopenhauer (or Nietzsche or Goethe or Hegel or . . .)." I too recognize, and happily affirm, the importance of those many connections — and the value of the literally thousands of essays that have already described them in great detail. Those studies drive toward settled conclusions about sources and meaning; I hope instead, by reading in this somewhat different way, to highlight other threads in the text's inexhaustible weaving.

Another of Mann's accounts of intertextuality comes not from the early years of the *Joseph* novels' creation but from their aftermath. His 1948 "Foreword" to the English version of the tetralogy, written eighteen years after our passage from *A Sketch of My Life*, is also an autobiographical essay. Written primarily for an American audience, the "Foreword" returns to the relationships between Dichter and Schriftsteller, pure art and literary essay, and gives us a second take on this complex pair. Ostensibly an account of Mann's artistic and political life from 1926 to 1943, the "Foreword" is also from first to last a self-study in the intertext.[20]

Mann devises a situation to begin his "Foreword." He has just received the definitive one-volume edition from his loyal publisher, Alfred A. Knopf, that at last brings the separate novels together under one roof as they were meant to be. This is part dramatic ploy, since the "Foreword" he claims to be drafting would already be in the published book before him.[21] The *Joseph* project has at last attained its definitive form; once a seemingly unfinishable project, it has become a monument, a "monstrous" black rectangle gilded by a pretty dust jacket (XI, 669; *JHB*, v). "Monstron" suggests to him a second metaphor, "pyramidenhaft" ("pyramid-like"), and the essay develops within the subtle frame of figuration and mood created by this playful-yet-melancholic conceit. Knopf's latest bookmaking marvel humorously rivals the pyramids themselves as a technical achievement. Mann tries to amuse himself and his audience with the hyperbole — this new pyramid differs from its Libyan Desert counterparts only in requiring the patient labor of a single man, not the lives of "hecatombs" of slaves — but a somber mood overtakes him. The enlivening and agonizing labor of sixteen years has been reduced to one large, geometric black object. This sense of finality produces "a certain autobiographical pensiveness" (XI, 670; v) which colors all his reflections. It had indeed been a pensive year for Mann; his last great "pyramid," *Doktor Faustus*, had just appeared the previous October, and he intuited that he had no major work left in him. The charming America of Roosevelt had vanished, and the growing conservatism and Red-baiting that replaced it reminded him all too sharply of the Germany he had fled. He even faced a new physical problem: trying to write with a broken collarbone. He had been "agitated and sad" the day he finished the *Joseph*, and these emotions seem to return here (*TB*, 4 Jan. 1943).

The inaugural trope of the "Foreword" is, then, pyramidal, or more broadly, archaeological. Opening and excavating the one-volume pyramid his publisher has placed before him, Mann uncovers the tomb of the past even as his reader has just entered his "monstrous" book. He bypasses several of the traditional subjects of an introduction; he tells the reader comparatively little about the novels' story or other contents and gives few reading instructions. Instead he writes, as the builder, about the ancillary structures that accompanied the main project. Equally, he writes about the builder himself; the archaeology is also of a person and a creative life, not only a monumental work. So the smooth external surface of the book-pyramid is now shown to contain, and conceal, many chambers or narratives: those that prompted its construction, those of the genocidal time of its crafting, and the many memory-rooms of its maker. The book is, in these ways, "pyramidenhaft," with a trace pun on "Haft"; the pyramid is also a "prison" for the past, for the dead. This takes Mann — as he loves to be taken — in contrary directions. On the one hand the pyramid is a gravestone, a monument to a process and an era now definitively over. It seems plausible that Mann's "pensiveness" comes from such a thought; this well-crafted tomb marker both obscures and brings to mind the years of fighting and exile that accompanied its making. Perhaps slaves did not perish to build it, but a way of life, many friendships, indeed a whole culture passed away during its construction. Yet, as Mann writes eloquently elsewhere, death also preserves and sanctifies because it renders the past beyond change.[22] His autobiographical reflections can now aid that preservation by bringing to light all the surviving tales and events, both those published and those known only to himself, that made up the "tumultuous" *Joseph* epoch. He had written in a similar spirit twelve years earlier, saying that he saw the *Joseph* not so much as an objective work of art as "a track of my life which it would be almost dishonest to retouch" (*Briefe* I, 429).

The argument of the "Foreword" initially takes the same form as the paragraph from *A Sketch of My Life*. Unlike the legendary pyramid builders, Mann originally set out in 1926 to build three small monuments: a novella on the *Joseph* story and two related tales of the Reformation and Counter-Reformation. But, once again, the monument grew beyond its planned borders and eventually occupied the entire site. And as he did in 1930, Mann views these almost countless interruptions of *Joseph*'s long construction as "irritations" and at first belittles their importance. He uses the same word — "Ableger" ("offshoots") — to describe them (XI, 129 and 672) and, if anything, is even more derisive: they are "critical escapades and marginalia" ("kritischen Seitensprüngen und Randzeichnungen") "which often were prompted and demanded only by the outside world, but basically had no other purpose but to strengthen me in the former (main task)." This is virtually an anti-intertext view; the offshoots are sealed off from the main building by origin and motive, and their only real value is to fortify the architect. But the reader, also launched on an archaeological expedition, soon becomes suspicious; if the offshoots mean so little, why does Mann devote all the rest of the "Foreword" to their careful enumeration? This initial belittlement shows several cracks in its edifice almost immediately. In the same paragraph Mann terms "Mario and the Magician" a "self-interruption." He also introduces a more welcoming metaphor to describe the interplay between his texts: these "escapades" not only "belong to, but are colored by the *Joseph*" ("Was alles an solchen kritischen Seitensprüngen und Randzeichnungen zum 'Joseph' gehört und von ihm gefärbt ist" (672). The image of the *Joseph* project shading, and brightening, the essays that accompany it dilutes the sharpness of Mann's dismissal, and suggests that we look for those hues and interplays as we read.

Indeed, every time these sharply denigrating statements appear in the "Foreword" — and there are none sharper than the first example —

Mann quickly qualifies them. The rhythm and organization of the presentation seem to repeat the reception of each "outside" task: first irritation, then interest, and finally self-praise, even celebration. This same pattern appears in the metaphors Mann uses to advance, after the initial dismissal, the actual ways in which his texts connect. From "escapades" and "coloration" we move to the "amorous analysis" of Kleist's *Amphitryon* that further "equipped" him for the "journey into the mythical land" and helped him discover the right "voice" for the passage.[23] The tone is again light. Mann wonders why he needed such support, given the sixty pages of the *Joseph* "Prelude" devoted to the same task, but he did need it. And as we shall see, the "Kleist" lecture's "verliebte Analyse" proved invaluable not only for the opening but for the entire project. The Lessing essay enters not into the "pyramid" but "zur Sache," the "business" of *Joseph*: "Moreover, even the casual reader will find that the mythicizing introductory sentences of my lecture on Lessing prove that it, too, belongs in this business, or let us rather say that it has been brought into the business by gentle pressure" (vii). And so with all the others: Mann performed the 1933 Wagner essay, requested by "several cities in several countries, . . . before a thoroughly sympathetic audience at the University of Munich." It also led to his comments, later in the "Foreword," about the central role of *The Ring* in *Joseph*'s making (677; xi). "Achtung, Europa!" created "a considerable sensation" in Nice in 1935, even when it was read — in French — by someone else before the League of Nation's Permanent Committee on Letters and Arts.[24] "On the Coming Victory of Democracy" was well received in the fourteen American cities of his 1938 tour. The letter to Bonn replying to the revocation of his honorary doctorate "was translated into many languages." The longest "interruption," for *Lotte in Weimar*, is one that Mann plainly does not regret or even pretend to find irritating.

As his catalog of satellite texts acquires its own weight, and as he seems to rediscover the importance of these "marginalia," Mann writes his way into a second, more congenial theory of the intertext. In *A Sketch of My Life* he had argued for the permeable membrane between Dichter and Schriftsteller; now he takes a slightly different tack. Smaller works are "interpolations" ("Einschaltungen") into the main project, and then still smaller "improvisational" pieces occur within them; the pyramid metaphor opens up to reveal its complex interior. The side projects still cause labor and exhaustion, but also figure as part of the "*totality*" (*das Ganze*: italics in original: 676; x) of an author's work; every writing, major and minor, is now a "burden" — or another locale of triumph.

Yet another metaphor takes us further into the pyramid's interior. In writing of *Lotte in Weimar*'s interpolation between *Joseph in Egypt* and *Joseph the Provider* Mann uses the phrase "Verschachtelung der Aufgaben." "Verschachtelung" suggests "compartmentalization": the root is "die Schachtel," "box." He immediately connects this metaphor for the intertext to both economics and psychology: "This compartmentalization of tasks, apparently inevitable in certain cases of productive economy, is no small psychic burden" (675; x). So Mann at once keeps his several tasks in separate compartments, in order to do justice to each, then goes on to suggest connections between the compartments. On this account the "Foreword" unpacks the many boxes or pyramidal chambers that accompanied *Joseph*'s making and finds them integral both to the text and to a writer's "productive economy." Mann's "verschachtelte" archaeology leads him to reassemble his novel and reassess the *Joseph* years, to rediscover that "patience" and "steadfastness" are "everything" for the artist (676; x). So Mann resees the *Joseph* project not as an isolated, uniform pyramid but as a unified yet chamber-filled, interlocking intertextual site: not only the essays and lectures, but Wagner's *Ring*, the "Klassische Walpurgisnacht" of *Faust*, and any number of other texts enter its confines freely. And even though *Joseph the Provider* suffers from more interruptions than any of the others — hard to imagine, given Mann's catalog for the earlier volumes — he recasts those interruptions as ones "to which I always yielded reluctantly and yet with all my heart" (678; xii).

By the end of the essay Mann takes the final step: the nonfiction demands of the war claimed center stage as necessary expressions of the unmediated seriousness and passion that only life can call forth from us. The defense of Western civilization was at stake. In an overreaching metaphor that evokes the unself-conscious patriotic feelings of 1941, he compares America's entrance into the war to Achilles' emergence onto the field after the death of Patroklos.[25] (There seems to be an autobiographical "emergence" in this too, though even the high-flown feelings of the period don't quite permit him to don the armor directly.) His "fifty-five radio speeches" and the many war-connected essays necessarily take time away from the *Joseph*, that is, from the "humorously exact realization of the unreal by staging and discussion" (679; xii). The pyramid has metamorphosed into a theater, one that is at best of equal importance to the worldly demands that the essays and lectures struggle to meet. We have come full circle. At the opening *Joseph* was the duty which the "irritating" essays interrupted; now Joseph is the site of freedom and play while the lectures and public performances summon Mann the warrior to the more solemn and important duties of the battlefield.

In a corresponding move, the primary metaphors for unveiling the *Joseph* intertext shift from architecture to its fluid counterparts: language and music. In the second half of the "Foreword" Mann makes much of the musical qualities of the *Joseph*, particularly its debt to the Wagnerian Ring-structure ("Motivbau"). He terms his tetralogy "Märchenopern," or "fairy-tale operas" (XI, 677; xi). He affirms that, after the lengthy interpolation of *Lotte in Weimar* and its companion texts, he could only recommence work on the series when he recovered "the keynote tone" of his humorous epic (678; xii). Now the pyramid, that is the "spirit of the tale," has become a "success story" (English phrase in the original [679; xiii]), one whose melodic, polyglot interweavings put forward one of the novels' central achievements: "The spirit of the narrative, if anyone wants to hear my mythical opinion, is one of spirit unrestrained to the point of abstraction, whose medium is language in itself and as such, language that regards itself as absolute and so inquires very little into dialects and local linguistic divinities" (680; xiii). In writing this, Mann is specifically defending himself against the charge that the German of *Joseph the Provider* is so "colored" by Anglo-Saxon that it is "no longer German" (680; xiii). But the counter-claim takes us past refuting Mann's purist Aryan critics to the *Joseph*'s practice of a polyphonic yet universal speech, a language that incorporates the local, and even the national, in a text in which every sort of language from the most primitive to the most modern can be found. To emphasize, Mann's "universal speech" is not a single speech, but a speech that incorporates, brings into play, every speech. It is a kind of interlinguistic intertext, merging as many linguistic masks as its hero does god-roles. So each of the new integrations he has mapped in the "Foreword" — "coloration," "Verschachtelung," "polyphony" — carefully preserves the presence and independent voice of the individual texts. The speech of the "Foreword" has its own polyphonic qualities, embodying as it does evolving attitudes toward its own intertexts, both conscious and hidden. The archaeological dig ends by re-presenting the pyramidal text in all its many-voiced variety.

Naturally, Mann does not announce a theory of the intertext that matches those of recent theorists. But nearly all his writings do contain reflections on intertextuality such as those we have just discussed. From *Buddenbrooks*'s treatment of Schopenhauer and antecedent Scandinavian merchant novels to *Doctor Faustus*'s obsessive compilation of hundreds of other texts, Mann's fictions advertise their intertextual weave. Every major essay written during the *Joseph* years, especially those on

Kleist, Lessing, Goethe, Wagner, Don Quixote, and Freud, contain both explicit reflections on and continuous practice of intertextuality and self-influence. *Joseph and his Brothers* itself contains dozens of similar reflections, some amusing and campy and others in Mann's favorite configuration: comic, and very serious indeed.

By the time we reach the end of the "Foreword," the metaphoric shift from architecture to speech and music reminds us that time has been a concern all along: time to write; time to lecture; time to finish. And in the final paragraph time opens out in order to return us to the question of this intertextual pyramid's own durability and significance. Once again Mann sees the *Joseph* in its pyramid-like unity, its interwoven intertexts once again concealed within its smooth exterior. Will it only be a curio for antiquarians, as so many smaller Egyptian pyramids are, or will it be a great monument? That question of course must remain open, but Mann can affirm, with considerable emotion, that the "Qualität" of the novel gives him hope for its future. Just as this mammoth English edition displays the "Treue" (loyalty) of its translator, Helen Lowe-Porter, so the "Joseph-Lied ist gute, *getreue* Arbeit" ("the song of Joseph is good, loyal work": 681; xiii-xiv: italics mine) whose quality and sympathy give it, modestly, "a measure of durability." Mann's specifies his own loyalty as a "Kaufmannssohn," a son of a businessman faithful to the craftsmanship of his burgher heritage. Like his work, he too has shown a measure of durability that his forefathers, whom he only appeared to desert by becoming an artist, would recognize and approve. The book, finished and monumentalized, preserves the heritage of the "best Germany," one that Mann has honored in fiction and public performance throughout the years of war and exile. It is a pyramid loyally constructed in honor of that heritage. It served as its refuge, even its grave, during the war years, and now yields up its contents to a future full of new promise. In short, the making of the *Joseph* replicated the career of its hero, who too became an exiled "Osarsiph," a pyramid-like repository of many narratives and values beneath the smooth surface of his revamped selfhood, and who constructed a God-play and an economics that provided a future for his people.

The shift from the arts of space to the arts of time in the "Foreword" also marks another of our central subjects: the relationship between writing and performance, twin poles of Mann's artistic practice. It expresses a favorite Mann distinction; published, pyramidal texts preserve but entomb, while performances enliven but leave small trace. The "Foreword" deliberately honors and preserves not only the silent intertextual play within the novels, but also the loud adulation and exhilaration of the performances that accompanied its making. Mann's attitude toward those performances shifts, as he writes, from a high modernist disdain for distractions from his monumental art-making to warm celebration of their public triumph. This recapitulates both his lifelong suspicion and his lifelong attraction to the performance of his work.

In the midst of the "Foreword" Mann surprisingly tarries over an entertaining but apparently inconsequential tale. When he was on his way to America just after the outbreak of the war, London airport authorities detained him because they viewed with much suspicion his hand-drawn sketch of the seating plan of a Goethe dinner party (676–77; xi). Yet an artist from an enemy country, whatever his status, should hardly be surprised by such treatment, and the purpose of the anecdote continues to puzzle. For Mann readers, however, the story invokes a familiar intertext, one anchored in a real-life event: city authorities interrogate his fictional character Tonio Kröger because he resembles an escaped Munich con man, and Lübeck police once interrogated Mann himself on the same charge during an incognito visit to his home city. Neither had any official papers to prove his identity — something each wished to keep secret — and so showed the proof sheets of a recent story. "The policeman arranged the work on the desk and began to read. The proprietor came nearer and joined in the reading. Tonio Kröger looked over their shoulders and noticed which part they read. It was a good moment, a point and effect he had worked out splendidly. He was pleased with himself" (VIII, 317; *Stories of Three Decades*, 118). The scene tellingly models the subtle, sub-conscious pressures of self-influence. Innocent of the manifest charge but guilty of the latent one — disloyalty to family and class and cultural traditions — both Tonio and his creator offer an ironic substitute, an artful, "perfect" scene, as testament to their oblique loyalty. *Lotte in Weimar* and especially *Joseph and his Brothers* are, Mann again affirms, loyal both to the sense of craft and the burgher tradition that engendered them. Looking back, Mann reaffirms the central place of loyalty and sonship, art and the ethical, the essay and the tale in *Joseph*'s making. These will be among our principal subjects in the two chapters that follow: on his literary precursor Kleist, the great artistic explorer of identity's mysteries; and on his psychological precursor and contem-porary, Freud, the archaeologist of human depths and of sons' problematic relations with their fathers.

VI
Performance

Joseph read, with his feet drawn up under him or standing at a sort of liturgical reading desk. He read capitally; was fluent, exact, unaffected, moderately dramatic, with such natural command of words that the most involved literary style had a happy conversational ease. Literally he read himself into the heart of his listener; and when we seek to understand his swift rise in the Egyptian's favor, we must by no means leave out of account these reading hours.

— *Joseph in Egypt*

[Adrian Leverkühn was entirely lacking in] *the gypsy blood of the concert artist, who may produce himself before the public through music . . . the desire for a loving exchange with the crowd, for garlands and bowing and kowtowing to the clatter of applause.*

— *Doctor Faustus*

If you had seen Macready last night — undisguisedly sobbing, and crying on the sofa as I read — you would have felt (as I did) what a thing it is to have Power.

— Charles Dickens to his wife Catherine,
after a reading of "The Chimes"

Ever since *Buddenbrooks*'s success in the early years of the century, Mann had been a tireless, even obsessive performer of his own work.[26] Every year he gave lectures and public readings by the score.[27] Naturally he did it for money (frequently for very good money) and, like so many orators and poets from the classical world forward, to promote sales of written copies. Such performances were more common in the 1920s and 1930s in Germany, with its plethora of clubs and literary organizations, and with its traditions of the artist as cultural and national spokesperson.[28] But his motivations ran deeper. He read when exhausted and ill; he read when money was plentiful or when the fees were negligible. He went alone on many long lecture tours in Germany, leaving his family and the sanctuary of his writing room. Like Tolstoy, he read his novels in progress to family and friends at virtually every opportunity. In 1929, the year of "Mario and the Magician," the first "Freud" lecture, and new lecture-essays on Lessing, Hofmannsthal, Knut Hamsun, the theater, German literature, and "burgherdom," a year in which he described himself as so overwhelmed with correspondence that he could make no progress on his novel or even write to his children individually, Mann also gave fourteen formal public readings from the nascent *Joseph* novels.[29] Seen in this light, his portrait of Jacob earning his way eastward to his uncle Laban's house by constantly re-telling exaggerated versions of his "robbery" by Eliphaz acquires an autobiographical shading (218–19; 143–44).

It is also easy to show how Mann's writing lends itself to quasi-theatrical performance at the sentence and paragraph levels. Any good reader can demonstrate this immediately, and there are many testimo-nies to Mann's skill in reading his texts, dramatizing characters with voices, and/or lending urgency to his political addresses.[30] The advent of the microphone removed his main weakness as a public performer — a soft voice — and with it he could enthrall crowds of several thousand. Donald Prater summarizes: "Recordings in later years of such readings illustrate vividly his virtuosity in maintaining, as he once said, 'clarity and total speakability' in his texts: the drawbacks of his style on the printed page — over-long sentences, and humor often obscure or con-trived — seem to show to positive advantage" (1995, 47). Prater (1995, 125–26) credits this obsession to "his unfailing care to keep himself before the public eye . . . and public relations exercises": un-doubtedly true but not the end of the subject.[31]

Accounts of his performances fill Mann's letters and diaries. Some of these exaggerate his reception and impact, another sign of their high importance to him. But he did not confine his enthusiasm and self-praise to his private writing. As we have just seen, Mann repeatedly re-calls his performance triumphs in his "Foreword." Most affecting is his account of the "extemporaneous" (*improvisierte*) speech he made in Budapest in early June 1936 before another meeting of the League of Nations committee. He spoke "against the murderers of freedom and on behalf of the necessity for a militant democracy" (XI, 674: *JHB*, ix). His "tactless" remarks gave offense to the Nazi representatives, and the Hungarian public's sustained applause gave him great pleasure. Most memorable, his performance produced an "enthusiastic embrace" from his fellow artist Karel Capek. That applause and embrace encapsulate the rewards of performance for the isolated novelist: tangible, sustain-ing recognition not from silent readers but a vocal audience, and the admiring public friendship of a peer.

Although he was not an improvisational performer — even the "extemporaneous" denunciation that won Capek's affection probably relied on some prepared text — Mann valued the feeling of spontaneity that oral performance creates. Like many other writers, he particularly prized the interpretive control public readings permitted. A printed text may freeze words in a certain order, but it also gives the reader a free-dom to interpret which the intonations and emphases of an onstage reenactment actually restrict. An oral performance may also be better suited to conveying both the subtleties of comic irony and the rousing emotion demanded by the author's pedagogy or politics, intentions which a hasty or careless reader might overlook. There's no skipping or skimming in a public reading. Instead, its slower pace compels attention to detail, invaluable for appreciating a motif writer such as Mann. At the same time it can make even weighty prose more lively; "See, I'm not really long-winded or boring" is the unvoiced claim of every intellectual artist before an audience. Joseph, reading to Potiphar, "was fluent, exact, unpretentious, moderately dramatic, with such natural command of words that the most involved literary style had an improvisational lightness and happy conversational ease" (916; 610). Mann's slightly idealized self-description? Almost certainly.

The podium itself evokes contrasting vitalities. It offers the dignity and authority of a haute-bourgeois cultural occasion, which Mann frankly loved, and at the same time the very different dignity and authority of ancient narrative enchantment and oracular magic. Modern oral performance imitates the spontaneity, the once-for-allness, of traditional epic without the unpredictable risks of a rhapsode's invention. The podium also approximates a position that Mann always prized: the musical virtuoso conducting a score before his enraptured fans. He spoke "admiringly" — which for him meant lovingly — of Wagner performing his own poems and sundry other texts at soirées in Zurich, in Bayreuth, even as an old man in Venice.[32] Here is Potiphar, every novelist's ideal listener, absorbing his young slave Joseph's performance: "And Potiphar listened to the words as they were shaped by Joseph's lips, as one listens to music which one knows by heart" (917; 610). The performer can interpret every nuance of the score and lead his audience to the thrill of its climactic moments. Performance also brings alive the formal qualities of the script: structural nuances and motivic repetitions can appear before an audience with just the right emphasis.

Highlighting the performative in Mann's work also sharpens our sense of his audiences and his rhetorical virtuosity.[33] At one level, of course, Mann "wrote for posterity," that is for an ideal German, or European, or even world audience that would love and preserve his art long after he could perform it in person. But "posterity" is a fickle congregation, notoriously unpredictable in its tastes and frankly unhelpful when facing the blank page, the insistent deadline. Better to foreground more concrete narratees: the family circle, friends (even individual friends), confused German youths, the more literary electorate. Each of the three essays we shall closely consider projects a different audience, or rather plays to different qualities of each audience, with noticeable effects on its structure and pace. None of them is identical with the imagined narratees for the *Joseph* tales, which themselves shift continuously as the tetralogy unfolds. Now singular, now plural, the narrator's audience includes everyone from the most sober and objective persons to, on one funny occasion, Jacob himself (1517; 1004). The narrator may "look around at the faces of his hearers" and address them directly with rhetorical questions (for example, the opening of the "Tamar" chapter [1533; 1015]), or he may speak in seemingly private meditation which we happen to overhear. But the hypothetical audiences for hearing and reading his texts largely overlap.

A lifelong passion for drama also links Mann's political and aesthetic performances. Though he wrote only one full-length play, Mann thought constantly about drama, from his much-treasured childhood puppet stage of the 1880s to his 1955 plans for a play on Luther's marriage.[34] In his 1940 autobiographical essay "On Myself," he anchors his art in the "games of my childhood" and traces artistic talent in writers and actors to the "primitive and playful . . . instinct of copying and imitation . . . [that comes] earlier than experience or emotions" (XIII, 128, 131). His mother was a hypnotic dramatizer of novels and fairy tales, and the Mann children regularly reenacted scenes from Homer. Thomas's ear was so good that his father had him mimic the voices of Lübeckers. He wrote plays in childhood and performed them with his siblings before relatives and guests; "You Can't Poison Me" is one provocative title.[35] He would clamber up onto a little red table — Zeus on Olympus — and crush the rebellious Aloadai. "I hopped through the room as Hermes, with paper shoes that were wings" (XI, 329). Zeus and Hermes: prophetic of his love of Kleist's *Amphitryon*, in which they play leading roles. Shy and inattentive in school, Mann devised a disguise: when teachers called on him for answers he assumed a thoughtful air that, if nothing else, gained him a reputation as an actor. Sometimes he would silently adopt a role for the day — an eighteen-year-old prince named Karl, for example — and encounter teachers and family "proud and happy in the secret of my dignity" (XI, 328). His first adolescent literary production was a drama, "Aischa," and one of his first major essays (written in early 1907 and published a year later) was on the theater. In a 1902 letter to Paul Ehrenberg, complaining about the new policy of forbidding curtain calls at the Munich opera (especially for his beloved *Tristan*), he wrote: "too much dignity is inartistic . . . I at least have enough of the artist, actor, entertainer, clown, in me to feel: *there must be applause*" (italics in the original).

Though not a gifted musician, his passion for musical performance is well known. He loved opera and went often to performances. He did not, however, attend many readings by fellow artists; that was the public art *he* excelled at. Nor did he read others' work aloud, though he did know many poems by heart, especially Platen and Goethe, "and when the occasion arose he loved to quote them" (Katia Mann 1975, 79). The fact that his brother and rival Heinrich did not share his compulsion for public readings no doubt made them even more attractive.

Mann constantly entertained his children with readings and stories, some in stage-conscious Plattdeutsch or Yiddish accents.

> Father would shut the door behind us — there was a book in his hand: a volume of the *Arabian Nights,* or Grimm's *Fairy Tales,* or Tolstoy's *Popular Tales.* He read beautifully; the figures came out of the stories and filled the room; the funny ones made us all laugh till we cried. We were moved, thrilled, saddened or shocked, according to the story . . . . we knew, too, that he could have gone on the stage if he had wanted to. He was passionately fond of the theater, and would often talk about what it would be like the first time he took us there (Erika and Klaus Mann 1947, 60).

It is easy to hear the same voice reading Grimm's "Märchen" to his children, and performing the "Märchenopern" of the *Joseph.* The children thought him a magician of the podium. Monika Mann playfully recalls how her father, on walks or even at the lunch table, would "ham" his way through lieder by Schubert or Brahms, "with chin and eyebrows slightly raised, eyes full of sweet recognition" (1960, 119, 120–21). In a lecture at the University of Redlands in 1952, Erica related that her father used to read Dickens regularly to the children and then translate the story into German.[36] Erika and Klaus devoted much of their lives to cabaret and political theater; Erika especially was also a great mimic, and playfully termed both herself and her father "monkeys." Thomas's performances sometimes went forward even at the price of causing pain to his family: his readings of "Wälsungenblut" ("The Blood of the Walsungs") and, later, "Unordnung und frühes Leid" ("Disorder and Early Sorrow") embarrassed and even angered his audiences.[37] But he loved performance, at which he excelled right to the end of his life. In an E-mail message of April 2 1998 Herbert Lehnert vividly recalled one of Mann's final public appearances, in Lübeck:

> It was the Spring of 1955. I was teaching at the Katharineum at the time. Mann, accompanied by Katia, visited the school in the morning, and said a few words to the assembled students of the upper classes in the Assembly Hall ("Aula") to the effect that he knew how different

the school was from what it was in his days. This obviously was a reference to Hanno's school day in *Buddenbrooks*. The reading was in the Stadttheater in the Beckergrube near where the house had been in which Mann grew up. It had been bombed with much of the rest of the street in 1942. The ruins had been cleared, and nothing was left. The reading was introduced by the orchestra playing the Overture of Wagner's Lohengrin (compare Hanno in *Buddenbrooks*). When he entered the stage, he appeared healthy and relatively vigorous. I believe I read somewhere that he had chosen the music. But he acted as if the choice was a surprise to him, thanked the orchestra for its playing and said a few words how much he loved the music. This caused applause.

He read sitting on a small table [see photograph]. He read first Tonio Kröger's walk on the ramparts with Hans Hansen, then "Das bunte Kleid" ["The Coat of Many Colors" from *Joseph*], and finally the circus chapter from *Felix Krull*. He read with a strong sonorous voice, distinguishing between the speeches of the characters. It was a dramatic, but not overly dramatic reading, just right, near ideal. There was a long applause. Three months later he was dead.

During the same year I heard the Schiller speech on the radio. This was a very similar, lively performance.

Next, Mann's many narrative passages are self-conscious performances that, to the exasperation of some readers, sometimes seem of lecture length. His characters prefer long speeches, even alternating monologues, to succinct conversation. Less than 10 percent of the tetralogy involves rapid-fire exchanges between characters, and few of these are sustained for more than half a page without a longer speech intervening. But whatever their alleged limitations on the page, longer utterances by narrator or character nearly always make for excellent platform delivery. Length eliminates the interruptive "he said" and "she said" that make public readings of dialogue awkward, and lets the performer develop the voice of the character and hence the illusion of presence that storytelling requires. Mann's wishes to be exhaustive about a subject and to perform his discoveries perfectly coincide.

Mann consistently thought about, and even evaluated, his productions in terms of how they would sound to an audience. Representative is this excerpt from a letter to Bermann Fischer in August 1933: "I recently read that chapter (Rachel's death) aloud in the garden: my audience consisted of some twenty persons, and the little terrace outside my room served as a platform. Everyone seemed much taken with it. Even the dreaded 'essayistic' prelude is not so bad, in its fashion. The sore spot is at the end of the first chapter. But I do not know how to improve it" (*Briefe* I, 334–35). Mann also wrote ceaselessly about playwrights: from Kleist and Lessing, Schiller and Goethe, to Wagner and Hauptmann and, in different keys, Nietzsche's *isolato* monologues and Freud's closet dramas. It is hard to name a Mann work that does not contain some self-conscious performance before a real or projected audience. His account of Joseph as he enters Potiphar's house has an autobiographical echo: "Joseph played with a potpourri of imitation and blinding self-metamorphoses, knowing how to make an impression with them and win men over to him, if only for the briefest moment" (825; 531).

Joseph and his Brothers obviously thematizes performance; nearly all the main characters are playwrights, stage managers, and con men who know how to serve their antecedents and their god by performing his works. Theatrical metaphors and performances appear throughout the tetralogy. They dominate *Joseph in Egypt* and *Joseph the Provider* — nearly two-thirds of the whole — which include several full-blown script narratives. On literally hundreds of narrative occasions, characters more or less consciously "assume roles," "play parts," and "stage events," and they do so more or less against their will. Curtains and veils repeatedly rise or fall, and ritual feasts play themselves out. Characters — and God — watch plays, plan plays, and understand themselves theatrically. Tragedy, comedy, satire, farce, black mass, melodrama, opera, mime, postmodern camp: few subgenres of theater suffer neglect. From the mythic drama of the Fall to Jacob's death-bed "sacred play" and the novels' climactic "Great Progress," performance reigns. Both the lengthy interpolated fictions between the third and fourth volumes have theatrical qualities; in an interview with the *Neues Wiener Tageblatt* Mann labeled the opening of *Lotte in Weimar* "the first act of a comedy [*Lustspiel*]" (*Frage und Antwort*, 229). Even Mann's stories of *Joseph*'s beginnings in his imagination are performative (and intertextual); he notes that the young Goethe "dictated" the Joseph story to a friend, and in doing so "spun it into a broad narrative" (XI, 654; "Theme," 5).

Mann organized his tetralogy with at least half an eye on its own performance. The short sections (two to six pages in the *GW*) make for excellent reading scripts. A page in the *GW* averages about 330 words, which take two and a half to three minutes to read. Take, for example, "Die Prüfung" ("The Testing"), a representative chapter section from *The Tales of Jacob*. It requires about twelve minutes to perform by itself — a nice hors d'oeuvre — and when read with the two succeeding sections that complete the father-son "duet," the little group form a coherent half hour. Beginning a little earlier with "The Monkey-land of Egypt" and reading to the end of the chapter yields an excellent full-hour program. The narrator even provides a pronunciation guide for Joseph's r's and e's (89; 55). Some entire chapters fit that time template as well: in *The Tales of Jacob*, "Jacob and Esau" and "The Story of Dinah"; in *Young Joseph*, "Thoth," "Joseph and Benjamin," and even "Abraham" (fewer pages but denser material that requires slower reading, like the unhurried expansiveness of Midrash that it imitates). The longer later novels have wonderful set-piece chapter sections that stand by themselves: "Huia and Tuia" entertains enormously when done "in character," as does the full-blown drama "The Painful Tongue: Play and Epilogue," which must be heard to appreciate fully the interwoven mock-innocence and degradation in Mut's lisp-language. Mann added most of his section and chapter breaks after the fact, and their almost universal congruity with oral performance suggests the part his public readings played in shaping *Joseph*'s final literary organization.

Reading straight through the *Joseph* novels with oral performance in mind, it becomes apparent that virtually every section lends itself well to reading (though a few, "Joseph visibly Becomes an Egyptian" for example, would probably not play particularly well). Nearly all of the tetralogy can be performed in coherent segments that do not exceed an hour. For a full evening's reading this time could of course be extended, though it was Mann's audience-pleasing habit on such occasions to read from two different works — say, an essay and a fiction. Narrational repetition, for example the thrice-told account of the relation between Eliezer and Abraham in the opening pages of *Young Joseph*, also benefits auditors. That the short sections and repetitions have specifically textual functions as well is of course true, but their happy alignment with the requirements of the reading platform is not coincidental. Neither is their inherent orality. The form of individual sections is shaped as much by sound as by its place in the larger architecture of the novel. Sections such as the operatic "Duet" in *The Tales of Jacob* are virtually meant to be sung. More telling, even the allegedly slow sections gain dramatically from performance. Take, for example, "Seventy of Them" in *Joseph the Provider*, sometimes singled out for its tedium and narrative retardation, and try reading it silently, then out loud. The section does seem sluggish on the page, but read aloud (in German, or even in Ms. Lowe-Porter's much maligned English) its playful scholarly parody, and self-parody, becomes very funny, a real crowd-pleaser. That Mann's popularity could survive translation and the silence of the page is in part a tribute to the narrative voice readers hear as they read.

This leads directly to another important consequence of reading Mann performatively: his treatment of his narrators. They are nearly as versatile a set of performers as his characters; we hear their multileveled voices spinning us each tale even as Mann's contemporaries heard him do the same "in person." One might expect his essays' narrators to be more univocal, more consonant with Mann's own voice. This is to some extent true of the two Freud pieces, which gave him a short holiday from irony. But the narrator of "Kleist's *Amphitryon*" takes on the roles of the play's major characters and shifts his tone to dramatize now his youthful enthusiasm, now his mature reflection on the drama. Similar complexity and role playing can be found in many other essay performances, from the "Chamisso" of 1911 to the dramatized opening of the 1955 Schiller lecture delivered just months before his death — in Katia Mann's opinion "probably the most successful performance he ever gave."[38]

The *Joseph* narrator is more kaleidoscopic still. Like any seasoned performer, he assumes many different personae during his lengthy script: Talmudic scholar, playful parodist, empathetic observer, intertextual mimic, impassioned moralist, on-site tour guide, comedic playwright, mock-serious reprimander of his own excess emotion or moral shortcomings, even "Thomas Mann" the Egyptian traveler and raconteur. From the beginning he calls himself a "storyteller" (53; 32), but he is really an amalgam of storytellers; his ego opens at the back to include narrative voices from Midrash to *Tristram Shandy*. At points he seems a fully rounded character in his own right, at others a barely locatable, fragmented voice: one minute a familiar singularity, the next a collage.[39] He moves easily among these voices, a professional liminalist in *Joseph*'s "feast of storytelling" (54; 33).

By the same token, the Mann of the lectures and the *Joseph and his Brothers* performances made deliberate use of the permeable borders between the flesh-and-blood author and the authorial persona that published books and staged readings create. The two figures, performer and writer, are neither identical nor complete representations of each other. In what follows, therefore, I deliberately elide the small differences between *Joseph*'s chameleon narrator and "Mann" in his various guises in order to mark this ever-shifting intimacy between the narrative voice and the writer. In other words, I intend throughout the book for the name "Mann" to appear in faint quote marks, or if the reader can imagine this, as a kaleidoscopic image; Pharaoh gives Joseph a dozen names in *Joseph the Provider*, and "Mann" takes on at least that many himself. No performer's voice embodies all of Mann's character, and from time to time he deliberately exploits the gap between them. Joseph's appearances before his brothers in Egypt actually dramatize these mixed figurings of the authorial, with Joseph re-presenting virtually the whole gamut of options in his extended God-play.

This leads us to a more recent theoretical binary, that between speech and writing, the performance and the text. Patently, "oral" and "performance" become critical concepts only after we portray "writing" as different and a cultural competitor; there could be no such conflict in preliterate societies. Derrida's attempts to undo speech's alleged privilege in philosophical discourse could well have its inverse counterpart here; *Joseph* might be read as a struggle between the forces of a dominant, written literary modernism and those of a suppressed orality rooted in Genesis and Mann's own predilections to perform. But reading for tension or conflict in the tetralogy turns out, I believe, to be less productive than reading for interconnectedness. The differences between speech and writing still matter, but they are sufficiently interwoven in the text, interchangeable as background and foreground, that the binary becomes more complementary than oppositional. Left with only the written text, the reader must listen a little harder for its orality, or (hopefully) take the time to read at least a few sections aloud. For the writing in *Joseph* does not erase the oral but rather insists on its importance. The novel repeatedly dramatizes responses to its many performances, underscoring the significance of the oral even when mediated through writing. So while Derrida cleverly trades upon the paradoxes of the written repression of writing ("Plato's Pharmacy"), *Joseph and his Brothers* seems to privilege speech in order to enrich writing's possibilities.

Another aspect of performance links Mann's productions to their nineteenth-century antecedents. Like his precursors, Mann not only performed his works in progress but published segments of his novels in journals long before the manuscripts were completed. This made for a more interactive form of literary creation; family, friends, and critics had countless opportunities to offer comments. Katia Mann (1975, 79) records that her husband was "receptive to minor criticism" after a family reading: he would respond to suggestions with "Perhaps that's not quite right . . . . Well, I'll think it over; yes, maybe I'll change that." During the *Reflections* years he and Ernst Bertram read chapters of their books in progress out loud to one another and discussed what they heard. The many reviews of the *Joseph* novels as they appeared in sequence undoubtedly left some mark on Mann's devising. Reading aloud also compelled him to rehear every line, a process that inevitably affected subsequent writing. To my knowledge, no firm evidence exists to show that Mann changed an already written text in accordance with unsolicited advice, but such opinions surely had, at the very least, subliminal effects as the work progressed.[40] The notion that Mann, once launched on a work, was hermetically sealed from any external forces seems even less likely when his welcoming attitude toward criticism, his intertextual practices, his ongoing correspondence with helpful scholars, and his widespread use of montage are taken into account.

More speculatively, it seems plausible that Mann derived real psychological benefits from his performances. His journals and notes from as early as 1897 show his preoccupation with what he terms "nervous strength" and its constant companion, nervous exhaustion.[41] He often felt himself on the edge of collapse, worn down not simply by effort but by the complex, unstable, irony-laced territory in which an artist like himself must reside. Comparatively brief, complete, and unambiguous, public performance offered temporary respite from the high-wire act of suspended convictions and the nervous toll of irony's endless reflections and rebounds. It wasn't only the applause or the eagerness of upturned young faces, though both were important; performance also offered relief from, counterpoint to, the exhausting craft of the writing desk. The sheer performance of the equivocal text was, when compared to its production, blessedly unequivocal.

At the same time, public performance as an art form was for Mann highly ambiguous. It conjured darker aspects of his life and art; several of the early tales, notably "Der Bajazzo" ("The Clown"), explore its superficial, dilettantish, and destructive sides. Performers seen in this light are frauds, not serious artists, and the seductive deceptions of acting appear throughout Mann's narratives. The constant repetition of theatrical performance also risks self-parody, ho-hum iteration. There were also political implications. Mann knew that his performances risked aestheticizing politics as much as those of the Nazis, and that no performer, however high-minded, could escape entirely from its distorting temptations. His nemesis-performer, Adolf Hitler, who had found his own voice as a spontaneous orator after the Munich Soviet of 1919, epitomized both the power and the corruption of public theatrics. More obscurely, exposure of the role, the cracking of the public facade, always held terror for Mann the closeted bisexual and composer of fictive selves. Darkest of all, the suicide of his sister Carla was intimately interwoven with her failure as an actress, and with all the seductions and artificialities of the stage.

This dual attitude is interlaced with a further ambiguity of performance: it is both narcissistic and selfless. On the one hand, Mann performing is Mann the self-centered player, taking all roles and all applause unto himself. At the same time performance effaces the speaker; other characters and voices speak through him. This touches on the ancient, oracular qualities of the storyteller, mesmerizing and enculturating his listeners. And when this latter experience is coupled

with the idea of political and cultural service — that the narcissistic artist in fact has a pedagogic mission for his country and even European
civilization — then such personal effacement can be put to ethical uses
which rescue, even redeem, narcissism. Paradoxically, self-abnegation
can even let the full humanity of the performer show through — "there
is something honest, warm, and good in me, and not just irony"[42] —
and make even his on-stage concealments and role playing seem intimate, unproblematic, selfless.

All this makes Mann's devotion to performance exceptionally fruitful for understanding his productions. Even as his performances gratify
his much-discussed narcissism, his suspicions and fears about the stage
strengthen his self-critique of that same narcissistic drift. Disappearing
into the voice of another is one way of containing this critique. Even
more important is the emphasis on the ethical necessity for performance that gives narcissism a goal beyond itself.[43] Mann's constant interest in dramatizing the effects of a performance on its audience, and his
interest in the intricate relations between the teller of a tale and the tale
itself, keep the oral in the forefront of his texts.

Performance shapes the performer; Mann's identity as a writer-
performer grew out of his frequent public appearances and in turn
molded not only his texts but his self-understanding. Inevitably, critics
of his readings had their say. Some earlier reviews complained about
the density of his text or chided his "North German accent," but most
reports were favorable (e.g., Katia Mann 1975, 21). Newspaper summaries of any lecture or reading concentrate on content, making empirical evidence about performance style difficult to acquire or assess.
Only the outlandish typically merits attention. But what family, friends.
and reviewers praised he persisted in, gradually forming his public character and the scripts that promoted it. Mann the performer became as
self-shaping and dynamic a figure as Mann the novelist.

In sum, Mann's prose was always written to be heard, and the conception of a live audience as well as a reading public played an important part in shaping the contours of both his fiction and his essay-
lectures. This in turn led him to write in rhythms and lengths that did
not simply coincide with reading performances but actually enabled
them. His later habit of writing lengthy essay drafts that he and Erika
would then edit for performance and publication shows once more the
importance of the public world, and public responsibility, for his
imagination. Further, the wish and need to perform led him to assimi-
late others' texts — Kleist's, Freud's — in ways that form a second basis
for unpacking the subtleties of self-influence. It isn't just that Mann
wrote an essay about Freud that he then happened to perform; argua-

bly from the beginning, and increasingly after 1921, he wrote in order to perform, to persuade. His history with performance in turn led Mann to become the political public figure he had once disparaged. It is in the preparation for, and act of, performance that Mann's aesthetic and political texts draw together in ways that supplement more traditional thematic comparisons. When Mann resolutely finished every word of his October 1930 "German Address" in the Beethoven Hall in Berlin, despite heckling and interruptions from Nazi sympathizers (see photograph) and despite the whispered urging of his nervous friends to finish quickly, he preserved both the form and the content of the speech.

So while the distinct requirements of his different genres and the obvious contrasts between the biblical novels and the political lectures seem to keep his texts discrete, they are drawn together by intertextual connections and by the demands, conscious and otherwise, of performance. Even his most writerly fictions, allegedly aloof from such ephemoralities in their high modernist devotion to form and monumentality, were immediately made public in performance. Publication and readership followed afterwards. Mann's political performances were very literary, and his literary productions were shaped by the environment and "heavy applause" of public readings and recognitions. In all these ways foregrounding the desire to perform rather than simply to write a text expands and enriches our understanding of Mann's art. We can now see another Mann, the performer who takes his meticulously crafted scripts on the road. In performance he makes public the personal and ethical Mann he wishes to be, and he does so before audiences that in turn can, like the biblical promise of blessing, create a humane, open future both for him and for his beloved Germany. In performing, Thomas Mann was reconstructing Thomas Mann for the demands of the day.

So, to borrow a phrase from Bernard Williams (1991, 10), I want "to get a certain kind of reading going" that will illuminate this extremely complex and exciting subject. Reading with performance and the performative in mind reveals how the elaborate structures of Mann's texts are organized and paced to serve oral performance. Reading in this way keeps our attention on the telling of the tale as well as the content of the telling, and offers a fresh angle of vision on Mann's penchant for intertextual play, parody and montage. It clarifies Mann's insistence on narrative's pedagogic and ethical value in the *Joseph* novels, and on the necessity for creating German, and European, audiences that are artistically, politically, and morally self-aware. Such reading also helps us hear the narrative's in/famous expansions and elaborations as Mann plausibly did — oral performances slowly unrolling in his imagination — and so connect them directly to his public appearances. It urges us to see the *Joseph* novels' lengthy exploration of narcissism as an ethical as well as psychological subject, and to see Mann's long-standing interest in the fluid borderlines of selfhood as having political as well as artistic consequences. Seen as an aspect of public performance, Mann's self-influence is not merely an account of a writer's subliminal life, it is another path into illuminating his ethical imagination.

Notes

[1] *Lebensabriss* (*A Sketch of my Life*: XI, 138; 69). Mann was not the first artist to struggle with the right title for the story. He owned a German translation of Etienne Méhul's 1807 comic opera *Joseph and his Brothers, or Jacob and his Sons* (Lehnert 1965, 520).

[2] Susan Stanford Friedmann offers an insightful recent account of the genealogy of the intertext. "Intertextuality was born under the guise of influence . . . Refusing the influence of influence, intertextuality is a concept that denies its filiation to its precursor, influence . . . . Intertextuality was born of an anticolonial resistance to the concept of hegemonic influence . . . the influences of influence on the generation of intertextuality . . . the discourses of influence and intertextuality have not been and cannot be kept pure, untainted by each other" (Clayton and Rothstein 1991, 146, 150, 153–54). Friedmann succinctly summarizes the development I have sketched: from rejecting the "filiation" of the intertext entirely to acknowledging that the two discourses are inextricably interwoven. See also David Cowart's excellent *Literary Symbiosis*, chapter 1; he suggests "auto-symbiosis" for the particular phenomenon of self-influence I describe.

[3] For *Buddenbrooks* "layering," see Prater 1995, 2. This novel was delayed not by essays but by Mann's time-consuming editing duties at *Simplicissimus*, his social life, and in small part by his already familiar habit of reading his work in progress aloud to various friends. Mann acknowledges that his early essay on the relation between the writer and reality, "Bilse und Ich," was written in the aftermath of *Buddenbrooks* (XI, 130; *Sketch*, 56). Especially insightful on Mann's imitation of Wagner are Hans Vaget (1975) and Eckhard Heftrich (1993).

[4] Mann sometimes referred to his essays and other "direct speech" writings as "one-dimensional," in contrast to his "three-dimensional" fictions. This view has made its way into the critical literature as well and is in some respects true. At the same time, I argue that the relations between the two are much more complex, and the essays considerably more "dimensional," than Mann and his readers have sometimes termed them.

[5] Compare this to Mann's earlier acknowledgment that he had begun his *Reflections of a Non-political Man* to spare *The Magic Mountain* from "an intellectually impossible overloading" (Letter to Paul Amann, Mar. 1917: cited in Prater 1995, 108).

[6] Compare the *Sketch* formulation to this passage from the first of his "Letters from Germany" in *Dial* (November 1922): Contemporary readers want a "fusion of criticism and creation, which was inaugurated by our romantic school and powerfully furthered by . . . Nietzsche . . . and the novel of intellect" (*GW* XIII, 265). The passage emphasizes the role of the audience in shaping artistic practice; the *Dial* piece is also a discreet advertisement for *The Magic Mountain*. One of Mann's earliest formulations of this synthesis occurs in his 1912 essay on *Fiorenza* (*GW* XI, 564), where he announces the "dritte Reich" of art in which the opposites that have haunted German aesthetics and artistic practice achieve "reconciliation" ("Versöhnung"). He will extend these arguments in "On the German Republic" and in the "Kleist" and "Lessing" lectures. His interest in the Dichter-Schriftsteller debates is at least as old, though developed most fully in his correspondence with his friend Josef Ponten after 1919. See Wysling (1988).

[7] "Goethes Laufbahn als Schriftsteller" ("Goethe's Career as a Man of Letters": IX, 334; *Essays*, 44).

[8] T. J. Reed's remains the authoritative version in English. In German, Hermann Kurzke's account is representative and sharply focused (213ff).

[9] "I hate democracy, and so I hate politics, which amounts to the same thing" (*Letters to Paul Amann*, 25 Nov. 1916, 79: translation slightly altered). Yet even at this early date there were small fissures of accommodation in his politics. In January 1919 his contribution to the social democratic *Vorwärts* — a contribution which followed his brother Heinrich's celebration of revolution — allowed that the "social people's state" was a logical and fitting outcome of Germany's "development," though it needed a middle-class "spirit of morality" to survive (Prater 1995, 121).

Mann's brief attraction to Spengler's pessimism in 1919 had emphatically dissipated by 1922 (see Koopmann 1988). It especially outraged Mann that Spengler "instructed young people" in his reductive, apocalyptic vision ("On the German Republic": XI, 841). See also "On the Teachings of Spengler" (1924), which groups Spengler with "the moderns who, in a detestable manner, teach what they have no right to teach" (X, 180). Mann's entanglements with pedagogy and its political consequences were already in full force. Spengler also plays a small part in the 1929 "Freud" essay.

[10] As Clayton Koelb (1984) has shown, the pedagogic "center" of the fully realized "Goethe and Tolstoy" essay (1925) already appears in his earliest notes for the project.

[11] Mann's evocative phrase was "das Mythisch-Wurzelhaft-Volkstümliche," the "myth-rooted nation of the folk." The delivery of the lecture in his home city of Lübeck takes on a posthumous dark irony after 1992 because of the

several racist and anti-Semitic acts of violence that have struck the city in the past several years (*L.A. Times*, 19 Jan. 1996).

[12] There is little doubt that Mann's youthful audience perceived the speech as political in spite of its lyrical language; in a postcard to Heinrich (20 Oct. 1922) Mann wrote that his auditors thought he was campaigning for the republic's president, Friedrich Ebert (*HM/TM Briefwechsel*, 180; *Letters of TM and HM*, 129).

[13] "Goethe und Tolstoi" (IX, 170; *Essays*, 173). On the sources of irony, see the final chapter of *Reflections*, "Irony and Radicalism" (especially XII, 571–4).

[14] Letter to the author, 22 Mar. 1996. See also Lehnert and Wessell 1991. Mann's letter of 19 Feb. 1943 to Reinhold Niebuhr is representative: "If I had remained at the level of *Reflections of a Non-political Man*, which was finally not an anti-humane book, I would still have taken a position with the same rage *and the same justification* against this horror as I do today — *sit venia verbo* — as a 'democrat'" (*Briefe* II, 301: italics in original).

[15] Letter to Paul Amann, 25 Feb. 1915 (qtd. in Prater 1995, 103).

[16] See Hayman 1995, 373, 408; Prater 1995, 211–14; and Ridley 1994, 39.

[17] Koelb 1984, 11ff. gives a representative account of this continuity. On the other side, as noted above, a careful reader of *Reflections* can find ample sources for these "new" views. Mann's account of a performance of Siegfried's funeral music in Rome in the late 1890s offers a dramatic example. The crowd divided loudly, even violently, along nationalistic vs. European lines, and a near riot ensued as the dogged conductor, Maestro Vessella, labored to the finish. The incident both aroused Mann's own nationalism and empowered him to hear in Wagner's music "not the German-national, German-poetic, German-Romantic element in Wagner's art ... it was much more those powerful all-European charms that emanate from it ... I was not German enough to overlook the deep, psychological-artistic relationship between Wagner's methods and those of Zola and Ibsen ... " (XII, 82; *Reflections*, 56). The notes for the "Goethe and Tolstoy" lectures contain such fragments as "individual and social morality [are] not to be differentiated" and "every intellectual achievement, every work of thought and of art, is social" (Koelb 1984, 49).

[18] Owen Miller's essay "Intertextual Identity" ably theorizes these relationships. His marking out of common ground between the poststructural intertext and the more traditional coherence presumed in the word "identity" has been especially useful to me.

[19] Readers especially interested in a more traditional account of this subject should consult Gert Bruhn's valuable 1992 thematic study of self-quotation in Mann.

[20] The "Foreword" appeared first in March 1948 under the title "Sechzehn Jahre: Zur amerikanischen Ausgabe von *Joseph und seine Brüder* in einem

Bande" in the *Neue Schweizer Rundschau* (XI, 669–81; *JHB*, v-xiv). Inter-
estingly, two paragraphs which rehearse the writing and reception of *Reflections* — including the insightful remark from "a Swiss critic" that the work
was an "essayistic adventure and cultural novel" — were deleted by Mann
from the *Rundschau* version (see *TB*, 1946–1948, 221f.). It seems likely that
Mann did not want to, once again, stir up his German readers by defending a
book they were determined to regard as reactionary. The Zurich version appeared in March 1948; the one volume was issued in June 1948, in part to
honor his seventy-third birthday.

[21] *Dichter über ihre Dichtungen* 14: II, 327–28. It was submitted in English
to Knopf in late February. The German one-volume edition came out from
Suhrkamp in July 1948 (*DüD* 14/II, 329).

[22] See, for example, *The Magic Mountain,* chapter 2: "Of the Baptismal Bowl
and of the Grandfather in Two Forms."

[23] In the "Foreword" Mann is hazy about a few dates in the early *Joseph* years.
He places the "Kleist" essay in 1926, not 1927, and locates his first "Freud"
essay (1929) in the later period of his journeys to America (1934ff). See
chapter 2, i.

[24] At the time Mann, fearing to alienate even further the Nazi government
that controlled his access to German readers, did not want the essay read
publicly. He wanted it shared only with members of the organizing committee (*TB,* 23 Mar. 1935).

[25] A similarly hyperbolic intertext is Mann's paraphrase of the 23rd Psalm near
the opening of the "Foreword": "I am grateful to this work, which was my
staff and my stay on a path that often led through dark valleys" (XI, 670;
JHB, v).

[26] Mann's first public reading took place in January, 1901. He shared the podium with Kurt Martens and read from "The Way to the Churchyard." He
gave another performance in November of that year, this time reading both
the school chapter from *Buddenbrooks* and "Gladius Dei" (Prater 1995, 36,
40–41). Ronald Hayman hypothesizes that these readings, and the lively response they produced, made him think more of the novel as an entertainment, which helped him preserve a lighter tone (1994, 150). Dagmar
Barnouw tartly suggests that "The large German republic did not refuse him
love, and the very success of *Buddenbrooks*, which made him experience identity — on a higher level, of course — with his audience, caused him to modify
Tonio Kröger's view of art as *zersetzend* of human feeling, of life itself . . . .
the very reception of the book had assured him of his readers 'unzersetzt,'
whole, strong feelings for those expressions of himself, that is, for him, the
author" (1988, 127). Mann's first visit to Berlin in February 1903 was in response to two invitations to read. He earned praise for his "dry humor" and
the nuances of his cadences, "somewhere between rapture and roguishness."
Hedwig Fischer heard him there for the first time and loved the performance.
In 1904 Mann gave a highly successful reading to a rapt audience at the Göt-

tingen Literary Society. It was followed by a speech in his honor at a faculty dinner, then Liebfraumilch with the students. A definite pattern began to emerge.

There were, inevitably, a few bad performances, with reviews to match. Representative is the columnist for the Essen paper who panned his January 1918 reading from chapter 1 of *The Magic Mountain* and, after intermission, from "Felix Krull." The writer judged the *Mountain* excerpt dull and without action, and its reader as pretentiously aristocratic and obsessed with "psychology." The reviewer preferred the "Krull" reading, but by then, he tells us, "the hall was already very empty" (Prater 1995, 111).

[27] In 1920 Mann spent what amounted to the fees for upcoming lectures on a new suit and refurbished overcoat so that he could appear at the podium as the Thomas Mann he wished to be.

[28] These clubs included the nearly half million people who sang in workers' choral societies, and the "speech choirs" that gave large-scale performances of texts at festivals and celebrations (Burns 1995, 65).

[29] Letter to Erika Mann, 6 June 1929: *Briefe* I, 293–4.

[30] Mann also admired mimicry. He took his son Klaus to see the impersonator Ludwig Hardt, who did dramatic readings from Kleist and other masters as well as contemporary figures. His "fantastic accuracy" gave TM much pleasure — and perhaps some pointers (*TB*, 11 Apr. 1920). Parenthetically, Hardt also did monologues based on Kafka — hardly a figure we now associate with "entertainment" — which may say something about the early reception of his stories.

[31] My reading is indebted to — but separable from — those interpreters who emphasize Mann's self-construction in and through his writings. In this view, texts rehearse and test solutions to psychic dilemmas. This includes proponents of the "production aesthetic" (Susanne Otto 1982, et al.). Rolf Renner (1985) offers a sophisticated and far-reaching version of this mode. Hugh Ridley claims (1994, 158ff) that in the 1920s and 1930s Mann evolved from a self-protective writer to one who became "less embodied," a "spirit of the story" (*Der Erwählte*). This new voice replaced the revealing/self-concealing neurotic of the earlier texts. I prefer to see performance as an incarnation of the text before an (admiring) audience of what, in writing, seems free-floating and disembodied. As Ridley points out, the "production aesthetic" risks endorsing, uncritically, the much-contested idea of the unified self.

[32] "Richard Wagner and *The Ring of the Nibelung*" (IX, 502–4; *Essays*, 353–54).

[33] Readers interested in pursuing questions of audience would very much enjoy James Phalen's excellent *Narrative as Rhetoric* (1996), esp. chap. 1 and pp. 138–46.

[34] Coincidentally, one of the plays which came with that little theater from his grandmother Elizabeth was Kleist's *Das Käthchen von Heilbronn*. She actually gave the theater to Heinrich, but he eventually lost interest; Thomas did not.

The fact that Goethe had first seen a version of Faust in such a puppet theater made another pleasing continuity in Mann's sense of tradition. He even theorized on the "remarkable role" played by puppet theaters in the lives of other writers (XIII, 131).

[35] All of this more or less well-known biographical information is taken from Mann's letters, the little essay "Kinderspiele" ("Children's Games"), "A Sketch of My Life" (esp. 18, 21) and "On Myself." "On Myself" contains self-quotations from "Kinderspiele."

[36] Recalled by professor of English emeritus Fritz Bromberger.

[37] "Wälsungenblut" (1905) notoriously uses his bride Katia, her twin brother Klaus, and their opulent Munich family home as models. After hearing the story performed Klaus Pringsheim affected to be "flattered," and Katia appeared unruffled (59), but it is hard to believe that these were their only reactions. "Disorder" so disturbed Klaus Mann that he retaliated with a story of his own, which included a grotesque Thomas descending passionately on poor Katia.

[38] Letter to Alfred A. Knopf (qtd. in Prater 1995, 508).

[39] Heftrich carefully situates the *Joseph* narrator in Mann's fictions, and in the history of realism (1993, 42ff).

According to Ridley (1994, 100), Jürgen Peterson makes the interesting claim that "Mann's narrator's voice is not heard as that of an observer, concerned with an accurate description of his subject, with reality. Instead the narrator opens out a horizon of meaning and makes the story he is telling pass through its lens" (192). Peterson primarily discusses Mann's early fiction, but the idea illuminates *Joseph* as well. Peterson's Cologne dissertation is entitled *The Role of the Narrator and Epic Irony in the Early World of Thomas Mann*.

[40] After reading part of the "Research" chapter of *The Magic Mountain*, Mann received some corrections and advice from a medically trained fellow writer (*TB*, 1 Mar. 1921), but it is not clear how much, if any, he used. Mann did give the in-progress manuscript of *Doctor Faustus* to his adviser and mentor Adorno, and he edited the "final" manuscript of that novel — with, as always, Erika's help — in the interests of readability. He also discussed problems in all his works-in-progress with Katia (*Memories*, 79–80).

[41] See "Notizbuch #2" in *Notizbücher 1–6*. Lehnert (1973, 1152, and 1965, 53) discusses the subject briefly.

[42] A much-quoted phrase from Mann's letter to his brother Heinrich concerning his love for Paul Ehrenberg (13 Feb. 1901: *Briefe* I, 25).

[43] Mann develops these ideas in a dramatic way in the section of the "Schopenhauer" essay (1938) on ethics and the *principium individuationis* (IX, 547–556; *Essays*, 386–92).

2: "Kleist's *Amphitryon*" and the Beginning of the *Joseph* Novels

The writer [Schriftsteller] may be defined as the educator who has himself been raised in the strangest way, and for whom education always goes hand in hand with his struggle against himself: it is an interweaving of consciousness and experience, a simultaneous wrestling with the self and the world . . . . But this wrestling with the larger self, that is with the nation, this insistence upon self-discipline and self-control, this pedagogic solidarity with the outside world and with people which one practices, may, of course, look like aloofness and the coldly critical attitude and sternness, as we know them from the words and judgments of all great Germans, especially in Goethe and Nietzsche. And yet how much more binding such an attitude is, compared with the bawling of loud-mouthed patriots, asserting their own importance and that of the "folk!"

— Thomas Mann, "Goethes Laufbahn als Schriftsteller"
("Goethe's Career as Writer")

I see the hosts of German youth today, pricking up their ears, for it is to them I have something to say.

— Thomas Mann, from the opening paragraph of
"On the German Republic"

I believe that I only need to speak about myself, and the times, in order to let the general public speak as well, and without this conviction I could give up the labor of writing.

— Thomas Mann, "On Royal Highness" (1910)

I

To BEGIN, A BRIEF CHRONOLOGY HELPS US locate the "Kleist" performance in *Joseph*'s production. Mann first mentioned the *Joseph* project in February 1925.[1] In March of that year he made his first tour of Egypt and other eastern Mediterranean countries. He began compiling his bibliography and browsing in its contents; however, preparatory work did not begin in earnest until November. In July 1925, he visited his children Golo and Monika at Schloss Salem, their state boarding school on Lake Constance, where he gave a reading to the students. One of their schoolmates, a boy "of Spanish ancestry" with "exotic good looks," probably provided one source for the young Joseph (Monika Mann 1960, 57–58; 52). Reenacting both his own history and several of his famous fictional scenes, Mann gazed at the boy but did not speak to him.

Research continued throughout 1926, a year filled with other writings and many lectures. The drafting of the *Joseph* "Prelude: Descent into Hell" did not begin until December 1926.[2] But after finishing the "Prelude," Mann set the novel aside for yet other projects and performances. His own indefatigable research contributed to the postponement; he kept encountering fresh information that suggested new fictional possibilities.[3] He most probably wrote the opening scenes of *The Tales of Jacob* in July 1927.[4] Just how far he had proceeded by August is not certain; Prater (1995, 169) claims that he had finished only the "Prelude" before leaving on 10 August for a vacation on the island of Sylt. So the opening scenes of the novel were either in progress or just under way when another, now-famous opening scene took place in life. During his holiday Mann met and became infatuated with Klaus Heuser, the seventeen-year-old son of the director of the Düsseldorf art academy. On his return to Munich he arranged for Klaus to visit the Mann family for two weeks at the beginning of October; they also met several other times over the next few months. Mann composed "Kleists *Amphitryon*: Eine Wiedereroberung" [literally, "a reconquest"] immediately after his return, during September and early October 1927.[5] He began the project, in other words, when Heuser was absent but keenly remembered, and then continued it in his presence. He first performed the lecture version of the essay, "Die Grosse Szene in Kleists *Amphitryon*" ("The Great Scene in Kleist's *Amphitryon*"), on 10 October 1927, preceding the festival production of the play in the Munich Schauspielhaus, with Heuser directly before him in the audience.[6] Further, Mann's affection for Heuser was itself a kind of "reconquest" or reenchantment. The scene repeats an event of March 1919 in which a "Hermes-like dandy . . . with a slight, youthful figure" whom Mann had first glimpsed several weeks earlier attended a reading (*TB*, 30 Mar. 1919). It also recalled for him his earlier, even more passionate attachment to Paul Ehrenberg (*TB*, 6 June 1934).

In this charged sense "Kleist's *Amphitryon*" is as much love lecture as critical commentary. Kouros-muse, half-hidden subject and audience all at once, Heuser is both an inspiration for and recipient of Mann's performance. Mann wrote to Erika and Klaus on 19 October, saying that the high point of Heuser's visit had been when he gave his *Amphitryon* analysis in "Kläuschen's" presence "as a treat," and noted wryly that it "was not without effect" on him. He concluded with a sly moral: "the secret and almost inaudible adventures of life are the finest."[7] This may have been the love that dared not speak its name, but Mann was obviously not troubled by mentioning it to his elder children. Was there a small family performance of some or all of the "Kleist" essay during Heuser's two-week stay? Quite plausibly, given Mann's predilections, but any record of such a gathering disappeared when Mann destroyed his diaries. Regardless, work on the first dramatic father-and-son scenes of the *Joseph* novels continued under the stimulus of this "amorous analysis" (XI, 672; *JHB*, vii); this included the crucial sections "The Testing," "Of Oil, Wine and Figs," and "Moon-grammar," as well as the first portraits of Jacob and Esau.

The rhetoric of the "Kleist" essay strongly suggests that Mann deliberately planned for its public performance, rather than silent reading. The writing persistently mimics and enables speech. Mann knew that "direct from the manuscript, my lectures and stories are five times better and more gripping, more winning and enthralling, than when they are simply read."[8] He wished he could perform the entire essay at the Kleist festival, as the two introductory transition paragraphs he inserted for the lecture make clear (*Essays* III, 1926–1933, 64). He complains politely about the time restrictions he faces, which allow him to perform only a fragment of what he might do to honor such a playwright.

Mann confused the dates of the "Kleist" lecture, giving 1926 rather than the correct 1927 in his 1948 "Foreword" to the one-volume edition of *Joseph*.[9] Even the sixty pages of the "Prelude," he claims, "were not enough to equip me for the journey into that mythical land and to put me in the mood" for the novelistic task ahead (XI, 672; vi-vii). He also needed the "amorous analysis" of the "Kleist" project. The error seems to proceed from his feeling of strong connection between the "Amphitryon" and his *Joseph*, a feeling still strong five years after the novels were completed. It is hard to quarrel with the intuitive insight of his artistic memory even if his chronology is slightly skewed.

With this frame in mind we can now explore, generally and in detail, Mann's "recapitulation" of Kleist's *Amphitryon* (1807) and its intertextual affinities with the *Joseph* tetralogy. In what follows, I have deliberately not evaluated Mann's reading of Kleist or compared it to other critical accounts for the simple reason that another layer of analysis would distract from my main focus. The play formed one of the crucial beginning nodes of the *Joseph* novels. Mann termed *Amphitryon* one of the "great old books, the ones toward which one has special personal relations of love and insight" (IX, 188; *Essays of Three Decades*, 203). He wrote as early as 1921 that *Amphitryon* was "the play of my soul" and termed it "my favorite stage play" in a September 1927 letter to Ernst Bertram, when the essay was already under way.[10] His rereading

of *Amphitryon* provided, after the relatively cool "Prelude" to the tetralogy, both inspiration and reinforcement for the novel's charged
opening scenes between a seventeen-year-old boy and a loving father.
At the most general level, his rereading and essay performance put the
larger questions of selfhood, substitution, and ethical affirmation into a
particular lyrical form shaped by, and shaping, the biblical retelling just
under way.[11] Kleist's subtitle for the play, "Ein Lustspiel nach Molière,"
helped place the metaphysical playfulness and self-conscious intertextuality of the *Joseph* project in a welcome tradition.[12] Kleist had himself
theorized the effects of performance and spontaneity on art in his essay
"Über die allmähliche Verfertigung der Gedanken beim Reden" ("On
the Gradual Formation of Thoughts while Speaking").

Mann's rereading of *Amphitryon* also helped shape his use of
Freud's texts in the *Joseph* novels. Indeed, the long resonance of *Amphitryon* in Mann's life roughly parallels Freud's fascination with Oedipus. Just as Freud made his youthful encounter with the Oedipus
drama a beginning point of his universalizing theory, so Mann at the
beginning of the *Joseph* series found a long-familiar play consonant with
his universalizing fictions. The play and its re-creation perform a kind
of dream-work for Mann, one that helps give him the "easy, natural,
organic power, utility and technique" that will sustain the entire project
(IX, 189; Essays, 204). Its obvious affinities with the *Phaedrus*, which
Mann had used so tellingly in "Death in Venice," and especially with
the *Symposium*, in which Socrates' "ego" opens to reveal the Dionysian
Silenus, the flute-playing Marsyas, indeed Eros itself beneath his elderly
appearance, anchor his performance even more firmly in Western erotic
pedagogy.

The "Kleist" essay's study of love and identity begins with a barely
veiled love confession. The oft-cited first paragraph proclaims the high
value of the lover's "loyalty" ("Treue") to his beloved's face (187;
202). "Treue" has stronger connotations of faithfulness, of constancy
and steadfastness than does "loyalty" in contemporary English usage.[13]
Defining loyalty as "loving without seeing," Mann praises its triumph,
for a time, over our inevitable forgetfulness of the beloved's image,
over love's fading and loss. These first sentences smoothly transpose
Joseph's opening, Wagnerian chord — "Deep is the well of the past.
Should one not call it bottomless?" — into an attendant key and composition. The many "provisional stopping points" of the "Prelude's"
descent into the bottomless past are replaced by the historical, well-
remembered stopping points of the beloved's image, anchoring and organizing time. The transposition includes the "certainty" that, should
we see the beloved — or his likeness — again, our love will be renewed.

The opening of *The Tales of Jacob* then superimposes the face of Joseph over the frightening "unsounded abysses of the past" (53; 32). The essay repeats this move as well, subtly substituting for the face of that impossible beloved, Klaus Heuser, a loyalty to another kind of vanished image, namely Kleist's play and its politically enabling construction of identity (187; 202). As proof of that loyalty to both fading image and play, it contains the most sustained close reading of another's text in any of Mann's essays.

Over the next few pages of the essay (and the next sixteen years of his life as well) Mann will elaborate "Treue" in such a way as to supply moral and psychological grounds for upholding both the foundations of German humanism and his forward-looking pedagogy and politics. He does this first by interlacing one of his stories' most obsessive images — the isolating, silent *Tristan*-gaze of lovers set against society — with the gaze of public recognition and acknowledgment that makes selfhood and loyalty possible within the social world. The interplay between these two gazes runs throughout the *Joseph*, now threatening, now empowering ethical selfhood.[14] Next, he interlaces his powerful emotions of love and steadfastness toward one young German youth with an expansive loyalty toward all the German youth who need his guidance and inspiration. Heuser, and all his comrades, must be won to loyalty to authentic German humanism, and away from the competing version of "old Germany": the jingoistic myth-obscurity of the Nazis that makes a knowing, philosophical loyalty impossible. So the Kleist performance of loyalty marks a dramatic point in Mann's work, a point at which "nonpolitical" art and highly political democracy self-consciously enter the same libidinal and textual space. It is a many-layered territory for the unveiling of another beautiful boy in the fiction and for attempting, via sublimated seduction, the rescue of all German youths for humanism and democracy.[15] The performance brings together an "almost inaudible" passion and an increasingly dangerous political resistance in a set of writings that are seemingly about neither, yet refigure both. It gives a further grounding to Mann's conviction, from at least "On the German Republic" of 1922, that all politics must draw energy from ideas and myth, and that a government divorced from these libido-enriched forces will fail. And his own artistic loyalty to Kleist will extend from the *Joseph* novels' beginning to the "Freud" essays of 1929 and 1936, to its explicit extension in the 1940 short novel *The Transposed Heads*, all the way to the tale of Mai-Sachme's loyalty to his reappearing beloveds near the end of the *Joseph* cycle.[16] This "law of our nature" (187; 202) gives us grounds for hope and for continuity, one that sustains when the vital image of a beloved or of a true Germany have faded. So Mann's own "amorous analysis" of Amphitryon turns out to be indispensable, I believe, for the ways in which the *Joseph* tetralogy develops.

II

The dead depend entirely on our loyalty.

— François Villon

Was Mark Twain a great actor who wrote, or a great writer who could act?

— Gore Vidal

Like a great actor, Thomas could find his way instinctively to equilibrium between self-exposure and discretion.

— Ronald Hayman, *Thomas Mann*

Criticism that is not confessional in character is worthless. The really deep and passionate critique is poetic in the sense of Ibsen: putting oneself on trial.

— Thomas Mann, "Geist und Kunst"

The story of Amphitryon is less well known than that of Oedipus, but the two have several things in common. Like the unsuspecting Oedipus, Amphitryon is a stranger from the Argolid who comes to Thebes. In a burst of anger he accidentally murdered not his father but his father-in-law, Electryon, King of Mycenae, and seeks sanctuary and purification in the Boeotian city. He is appointed Commander (Feldherr) of the city. At the behest of his new wife, Alkmene, he immediately leaves the city for Pharissa to fight a war of honor involving her brothers; she will not respect, or in one version even consummate, their marriage until her family is avenged. While he is away Zeus conceives a passion for her, one consonant with his wish to beget a son who will be helper and defender of both gods and men. The god appears to Alkmene *as* Amphitryon, a perfect simulacrum of her husband, telling her that her brothers have been requited. Their night together is beyond compare but not beyond comparison. Amphitryon returns only to find himself confronted by his mirror image, an "other" Amphitryon who has supplanted him and who is the blood-and-nectar father of his future son, Herakles.[17] Questions of identity and moral responsibility instantly multiply: who "is" the "man" with Alkmene; is she an unfaithful wife if she sleeps with her husband's perfect likeness; where is the self to be located if appearances are identical? To whom should wife and citizens be loyal? An exquisite dilemma for this classical heroine: Penelope had to interpret a beggar who concealed a husband; Jocasta had to interpret a brilliant rescuer who concealed a son. But Alkmene's task — indeed the task of all the human characters in *Amphitryon* — is to detect difference in perfect similarity, to make substitutions where no space for substitution seems to exist. Kleist doubles the drama of substitution by having the royal servants Sosias and Charis duped by Hermes in a similar way.[18] In his performance Mann spins and respins Kleist's tragicomic permutations of these subjects, lingering over the particular agonies and hilarities of many of them.

"Kleists *Amphitryon*: Eine Wiedereroberung" opens with an astonishing three-page introduction whose charged autobiographical tone sets it apart from virtually all the rest of Mann's essays. We have already seen how the essay's first paragraph moves from loyalty to the beloved's image to loyalty to a beloved text, Kleist's drama. When the lover's gaze falls on the *Amphitryon* script again, this same loyalty re-illuminates its "image," that is its stage performance, and reanimates the original reasons for loving it so deeply.[19] But the original cannot reappear unmediated to the narrator, since he knows that he rereads and reimagines. Nor does it appear so to the members of his audience, who as readers either imagine the narrator speaking to them, or who in person saw Mann "himself" on the podium performing his re-creation of the "Great Scene." Acknowledging this inevitable slippage, the artist's task is nonetheless to make for his audience (and himself) a simulacrum of the play even as Jupiter made a "true" simulacrum of the "real" Amphitryon.[20] The goal of both god and man is to draw us via a substitution into loving them, loving the text, loving the performer.[21]

To make his simulacrum the narrator launches us into a recollected paradise of reading and loving. He does everything he can to expunge the space between the "original" and this performance, and between Kleist's sources and his play. He asserts "as if it were true" that the play is new, unread and unseen, and so encountered here for the first time.[22] His loving loyalty to the first encounter gives him the power to overcome, for a while, the time between the two performances. To achieve this he adopts the voice of the naïf, the first-nighter (like Alkmene). He urges us to "hear" and "see" Thomas Mann the youthful reader behind the skilled and knowing performer before us on the page or in the Schauspielhaus. Audience members who know Mann's autobiography readily envision not only the younger persona, but behind it the childhood puppet theater, the father-pleasing mimicry, the juvenile plays. So re-creating that resonant, youthful world is an act of loyalty, and writing and dramatizing become self-narrating acts of loyalty that preserve. In this way Mann's performance incarnates the values he discovers in Kleist's drama.

At the same time we in the audience detect a second palimpsest through the evocation of loyalty and the revival of the play. We see and hear not only a younger but also an ideal or "true" Thomas Mann behind the real appearance before us. In other words, we perceive not only the sensitive youth but the godlike in the performer. We see a Jupiter figure both within and outside *Amphitryon*. And if we readers also know something of Klaus Heuser, we hear that Jupiter speaking indirectly but fondly to his own youthful Alkmene in the Schauspielhaus audience. The godlike performer is veiled from an actual declaration of love, yet a canny beloved such as Heuser may well see through the disguise (the performance was "not without effect"). Further, the entrancing spell of Mann's "reconquest" of *Amphitryon* may capture all German youths within hearing, and form the basis of educating them to their true cultural heritage. And we are subtly urged to one final image: Kleist himself, both intellectual and "child-like" (189–90; 204), writing the "original" text to enchant our feelings and command our loyalty.

This last distinction between the childlike and the intellectual, immediate perception and the mind, returns us to an earlier subject. It represents the dialectic between the Dichter and the Schriftsteller, the poet and the literary man. We have already seen that throughout the 1920s Mann was theorizing ways in which this opposition, and many of the other binaries that had informed and haunted his thought, might be "mediated" by a new kind of literary artist.[23] Both *Joseph* and the essays written around its beginning experiment, at many levels, with that ongoing process of mediation.[24] What sets the "Kleist" performance apart, in this context, is how it mediates this tension. It does so not by lengthy elaboration ("Goethe and Tolstoy") or by tracing a long process of historical development and integration. Instead it celebrates, lyrically, its achievement in Kleist's play. Kleist has already miraculously staged what Mann hopes to accomplish, and Mann, as he performs, invents before our eyes and ears a new genre of essay-performance that pursues a similar integration. Both the play and this performance are, in other words, criticism as literature: Dichter and Schriftsteller in the same skin.[25] Kleist's mediation commands Mann's emulation and his loyalty; we will see both played out in the character of Joseph, moon-struck lyricist and self-conscious critic.

Mann elaborates his new method in the essay's opening paragraphs. At first his essay seems written expressly against intertextuality, self-influence, and historical awareness. Kleist, he says, readily takes his material from nature, fantasy, and earlier texts, and "kindles the spirit" latent in all three in such a way that their separate effects blend into his new creation (188; 203). He seems entirely free of the historical self-consciousness and obsessive reflection of writers such as Mann and his compatriot modernists, who come late in a tradition. So isolated and purified, the play's emotion reaches out for us. Then the narrator immediately adds that Kleist's work is shot through with wit and intellect, and with clever reworkings of the several "Amphitryon" dramas that preceded it. Kleist's seemingly effortless combination of feeling and idea, inspiration and sources, models the narrator's own restaging of the *Amphitryon* that itself smoothly restages at least five earlier versions of the same story. Kleist's version, Mann also tells us, "towers incomparably above every earlier treatment of the subject" (207; 220). *Amphitryon's* achievements make it an especially valuable model for the *Joseph* project.

These remarkable opening pages have their counterparts in what Mann called his "fantastic essay" (XI 671; vi), the *Joseph* "Prelude," and the opening pages of the novel. Mann too affects to be the first teller of the *Joseph* tale, the original witness-narrator.[26] He wants his audience to read as if there were no other retellings, no commentaries; that is, for him, an enabling fiction within his fiction. Yet he is already steeped in the many retellings and in the many elaborations and commentaries, just as his forerunner Kleist knew the *Amphitryons* of Plautus, Rotrou, and Molière, and at least some of the just-scorned "callous stuff" of literary historians and critics that has attached itself to the story (188; 203). Portions of these texts will eventually appear in the essay, just as a much more wide-ranging gallery of sources and precursors appears in the novels. The rhythm is similar: the model of the erudite "universal historical" novel is superimposed on the recovered image of *Joseph*'s "innocent" narrator who lyrically urge us to "See — the moonlight-sharpened shadows cross the peaceful, rolling landscape! Feel — the mild freshness of the summer-starry spring night!" (55; 34). The learned narrator hopes to appropriate and interweave his sources into his novel as seamlessly as Kleist used Molière in his play. So in the "Kleist" essay and the *Joseph*, Mann creates this dialogic moment: even as he draws us into the seamless world of our own primal reading experiences, he celebrates all the erudition — even erudition quite like the recalcitrant "unmoved stuff" of literary historians he said he would not read — that contributes to that world. Originality now includes not simply the artist's pure impressions but his childlike appropriation of the texts of his predecessors as well as his prodigious learning: Dichter

and Schriftsteller together. Kleist's performance reveals a marriage between the naive and the knowing that preserves the power of both.
This consummation raises questions of identity and intertextuality that
occupy the *Joseph* tetralogy for the next sixteen years.

A related interplay occurs in the two audiences the lecture creates.
The lecture's "original" audience could see the palimpsestic performer
before them; his younger, "first reading" self, the isolated artist-god,
and Kleist himself all appeared, as it were, through his image. All later,
reading audiences can envision both that performer, whose ego seems
to "open at the back" (IV, 122; *JHB*, 78) to other images, and the
original audience's enthrallment with his performance. We latecomers,
at our further remove, can in effect watch from both the auditorium
and the page at the same time. This points toward the even more complex position of the audience for the *Joseph* novels. We read of characters watching the performances of other characters, and perceiving (or
sometimes not perceiving) the many voices and figures that appear
through each present action. At once involved and removed, the audience of *Joseph* continually watches the novels' many fictionalized audiences struggling to see everything before them. Like Joseph watching
his father perform the tales of Abraham, we both "wish we were there"
at the original event and gain in knowledge from the fact that we are
not.

This double perspective also has direct social implications because it
dramatizes how any public figure, especially political leaders, should be
heard and interpreted. Entering passionately into a political performance and remaining there is dangerous, while coolly observing from the
"nonpolitical" high ground of cultural superiority has risks of its own.
This is the newly civic direction that the mediation of Mann's lifelong
dualities — Dichter and Schriftsteller, art and life, and so on — takes
during this period of reconception. He seeks to create audiences that
are enthusiastic and scrutinizing at the same time, patriotic audiences
ready to see through demagogues and to read his layered essay-fictions.

The "Kleist" essay explores these permutations in ways that have
lasting consequences for the *Joseph*. Near the end of his introduction
Mann draws these subjects together in a complex portrait of both the
loyal speaker and his text: ". . . and a conservatism of the future, serene,
remote from all crudely sentimental reactionism, with its eye on the
new, plays with old forms of expression in order that they not fall into
oblivion, and may prove to be the most useful attitude for further development" (189; 204). "Playing" with old stories and old language
not only provides material for the artist's new creation, it is also a rescue operation. In this summary account the intertexts remain more

visible in the newest version and retain some measure of their original voices. This version also seems remarkably apposite to his hopes for the *Joseph* tetralogy: some lines of the "low" characters Sosias and Charis are "happy, social commentary vestiges from an earlier version [Molière's], smiling their way into a poetry full of mystical intellectuality and extraordinary feeling" (190–91; 205). The traces of an intertext remain and function ably because they complement the focus text that now embodies them.[27] This refinement of intertext theory may seem superfluous for understanding Kleist's "child-like" following of his precursors, but not if we consider the background presence of the *Joseph* writing. For the "Kleist" lecture's "mystical intellectuality and extraordinary sensitiveness" substitute "mythic playfulness and psychological acuity," and the analogy takes on resonance; Kleist's play offers a model of artistic knowledge and textual interlacing that supports the *Joseph* writing, even as the novels exert their influence on this way of reading Kleist. This positioning, in which the originary voice and image are put in play with other writings, replicates the layers of identity — immediate, historical, mythic — which the Kleist play, and the *Joseph* novels, unpack with "wit and metaphysical warmth." The inevitability of forgetting and recovering, of losing a self in order to regain it, describes the identity crises of the *Amphitryon* — and Joseph's as well.

Mann's essay prelude ends with what is in effect a manifesto, under the banner of Kleist, for the *Joseph* story: "For it is a translation, in the most audacious sense of the word: the actual and incredible transference, abduction, and enchantment of a work from its own sphere into another one originally quite foreign to it; from one century into another; one nationality into another. It is a radical Germanization and romanticization of a masterpiece of the French classical period" (191; 205). To transpose: "The *Joseph* novels are a radical Germanizing and conservative, yet forward looking, universalizing of a masterpiece of ancient Hebrew narrative." The program of the "Kleist" essay and the embryonic *Joseph* novels could not be more succinctly described. It contains an aesthetics of mythic recovery that remains loyal to the original (German and Hebrew) forms of expression, and that can recover that lover-text for all present and future audiences. It offers an aesthetic that can "translate" across time both intellectually and empathetically, without succumbing to the primitive or the traditional. It shows how the tales of Amphitryon and Joseph pass through another retelling and come to know themselves more fully in doing so (V, 827; 553). It depends on the ethics of loyalty, which keep the beloved image and text (loving without seeing) before performer and audience alike. It presents a loyalty interwoven with love and knowledge, one that fosters honoring and honorable devotion, not fanatical subserviences.[28] It insists that the erotic is, at its best, bound up with both the knowledge of inevitable loss (forgetfulness) and with loyalty; desire and the moral are firmly and advantageously coupled.

Just as the essay models the intertextuality that Mann, consciously and otherwise, employs in the *Joseph* tetralogy, it also models our next subject: how the Kleistian construction of the psyche, dramatized in the identity paradoxes of *Amphitryon*, interlaces with *Joseph*'s account of our psychic development and with Mann's rather self-serving account of Freud. That line of descent will lead to a performance of identity that will resist alike the unifying erasures of fascism, the pessimisms of Schopenhauer and Spengler, and the dark side of Freud himself.[29] Seen as an inaugural document, the "Kleist" gives us the *Joseph* identity studies in embryo; seen from within the novel, the essay is like a notebook or sketch sheet from which its final portraits can evolve.

III

Lessing was more radical than he dared to express; but it was precisely in his ambiguity that he was radical.

— Thomas Mann, "Lessing"

Throughout his artistic life, both on the page and at the lectern, Mann was drawn to the borderlines of selfhood, to the mysteries and interpenetrations of identity. This deep attraction is visible not only in the actual subject matter but in the mosaic texts and thematized intertextuality that characterize his production virtually from the beginning. The rereading of *Amphitryon* expanded Mann's vocabulary for liminality, and he first performed it in the white heat of his re-created youthful reading. Even so, the full subtleties — and usefulness — of the Kleistian model of identity emerged for Mann only as he wrote further into the *Joseph* tale. His essays on Freud, readings and misreadings alike, helped to connect that expanding account to a scientific-literary psychology, and so to widen the loom on which the *Joseph* tapestry took shape.

Next, a self-influential reading urges us to see Mann's entire "Kleist" performance as an exploration of identity, rather than singling out the title character as its focus. He does not simply pose Amphitryon as an alternative or counterfigure to Oedipus; this is not simply an archetype-against-archetype comparison. Mann does have an interest in free-standing archetypes, and he will use them in his performances of the *Amphitryon*, the 1936 "Freud" lecture, and of course in *Joseph*.[30]

But he reads *Amphitryon* in a different way than Freud read *Oedipus the King*: as the study of one man's horrifying, heroic self-discovery. Mann's counterstrategy is to take the whole of *Amphitryon*, or more accurately his own refashioning of the play, in which all the characters contribute to the model of identity. This means that his model develops as much around relationships between characters as it does around the isolated inner quest of the hero. So Mann does not simply pose a symmetrical, alternative model to Freud's but rather incorporates the performances of hero and heroine, gods and servants, into a revamped story of identity, substitution, and the containment of narcissism that both his politics and his novels require.

This is confirmed by a surprising fact: the name of Oedipus, in either Sophocles' or Freud's enactments, rarely appears in Mann's writing. He does not mention Oedipus in his diaries for the *Joseph* years or in his published letters. Even his extensive correspondence with mythographer and theologian Karl Kerenyi ignores this hero. No major essay takes up this central figure in the Freudian imagination. *Joseph and his Brothers* entertains any number of Greek gods and heroes, but not this one. Its one seeming Oedipal drama — Reuben and his father's concubine (85–87; 52–53) — turns out to be its clever inversion.[31] In the 1929 "Freud" essay "incest" comes up, but the "Ödipuskomplex – Konzeption" appears only in a brief catalog of Freud's leading ideas (*Essays* III, 1926–1933, 124). Oedipus is absent from the 1936 essay, where other archetypal figures — Cleopatra, Jesus, Napoleon — seemingly fill in for him. Not until the beginning of *Der Erwählte* (*The Holy Sinner*) in early 1948 does Mann make significant reference to the story, on which his new novel is to be a self-conscious "variation."[32] However, because Oedipus is all but silent in the Mann corpus does not mean, as we shall see, that he is entirely absent.

Mann remains loyal, in other words, to his loving rereading and reenactment of *Amphitryon*. The play is not simply plundered for archetypes but brought whole into the making of the *Joseph*. This places a determinedly literary, as opposed to scientific or philosophical, account of selfhood in conversation with Mann's evolving understanding of Freud. That Mann thought of Kleist as a deep spirit worthy of comparison with Sophocles, or Freud, is clear from "Heinrich von Kleist und seine Erzählungen"; his "pre-Olympian, titanic, barbaric character" and dramatic gift "can give us the archaic shudder of ancient tragedy" (IX, 829). The strictly autobiographical or "heroic" reading is complemented by one which supports pedagogic and political consequences. In this way Mann's *Amphitryon* is caught up in, and dramatically enacts, the Goethe-endorsed move "from a loving self-absorption via autobiographical confession to educative responsibility."[33]

Once alerted to its rhythms, the reader finds constant intertextual weaving between the "Kleist" performance and the early stages of the *Joseph* project. Predictably, others have commented on their relationship, led by Mann himself:

> The weeks of loving preoccupation with Kleist's comedy and the wonder of his metaphysical brilliance I will not call a waste of time, *as all sorts of subterranean associations connected this critical task with my "main business,"* and love is never uneconomical . . . . I love that word *associations.* For me, and in however relative a sense, that which is full of associations is, quite precisely, that which is significant.[34]

"Subterranean associations" between the *Amphitryon* and *The Tales of Jacob* indeed abound, as the following examples dramatize.

The doubling and loss of identity that the male characters in *Amphitryon* must endure constitute one important field of self-influence. In Kleist's play, first Sosias, then his master confront their perfect simulacra and are broken by them. Mann's essay-narrator argues that the comic mode of Sosias's doubling protects the audience from the servant's suffering (197; 211); it also softens them for the more affecting parallel trial of Amphitryon. The main figures in *Joseph* face much more complicated, internalized forms of doubling and substitution, but their debt to the Kleist characters remains near the surface.

Joseph's prototype of substitution is Jacob's half brother and chief servant Eliezer, who unreflectively adopts the narrative of "Eliezer," the prototypical attendant of the patriarchs, for his own character. He knows his own person only as he knows the stories of his father-predecessors. His sense of differentiated individuality is so muted that his literal reenactment of the "true Eliezer" is enabling rather than invasive or obliterating: Mann's first permutation on the basic Kleist model. The youthful Joseph watches him raptly, just as we presume Heuser watched Mann's self-conscious incarnations of Jupiter or Amphitryon:

> Joseph listened to all this with a delight unprejudiced either by Eliezer's grammatical idiosyncrasies, or by the fact that the old man's ego was not quite clearly demarcated, that it opened at the back, as it were, into earlier ages and overflowed into spheres external to his own individuality, embodying in his own experience events which, when remembered and related in the daylight, should have been put in the third person, not the first. (122–23; 78)

In the course of the novels this rudimentary type-character acquires a greater sense of individuation, so that his son and successor more or less knows that he enacts a role. But Damasek-Eliezer's self-consciousness ironically renders him incompetent as a servant and repository of mythic lore and ritual (1784; 1184). So from one point of view Eliezer's open ego is a low rung indeed on the ladder of individual development. But from another, Eliezer's performance reveals what individuation suppresses: the indispensable grounding of identity in objective, traditional roles. To know yourself in this context means to know the doubles, the historical simulacra, that give you character.[35]

Joseph's intricate relation with the "Kleist" essay's construction of identity becomes even more evident in the generalizing passage that follows immediately. The passage means to instruct — and unsettle — the reader:

> But just what do we mean, then, by "actually," and is perchance man's ego really imprisoned in itself, a watertight thing firmly sealed in its boundaries of flesh and time? Do not many of the elements which compose it belong to a world before and outside of it, and isn't the claim that each person is himself and can be no other only a convention and convenient supposition, which willfully overlooks all the nuances which bind the individual consciousness to the general? The conception of individuality belongs finally to the same category as those of unity and entirety, the whole and the all; and in the days of which I am writing the distinction between spirit in general and individual spirit possessed not nearly so much power over the mind as it has today, a time we have left behind to narrate the other. It is highly significant that in those days there were no words for conceptions dealing with "personality" and "individuality," other than such external ones as "confession" and "religion." (123; 78)

The narrator's confident rhetorical questions concerning mankind's deep past produce a quagmire of literal self-doubt in his attentive audience. Our very achievement of knowledge and self-demarcation simultaneously reveals its own contingency. Precisely because we now understand Eliezer's expansive character we see the conventionality of our own ego's watertight borders. We claim distance from Eliezer, yet our descent into the past has brought him too close for comfort; an ancient "nobody" mirrors our own unstable foundations. In this sense Eliezer plays Hermes to our Sosias, but in time, not space; he confronts us not with a literal double but with an ancient typological character that undermines our individuation. He shows us that our selfhood is not some triumphant outcome of human development but rather fundamentally other than we imagine. This is the skeptical, unsettling side of the *Joseph* novels; its account of the psyche's development toward modern self-consciousness is always shadowed by the undoing of any uncritical self-satisfaction or erasure of the past. Clearly this amusing yet disturbing deconstruction of the self has Kleistian threads in its cloth.

But within the passage, as within the play, the threat of dissolution is countered by the freedom from the sealed borders of isolation and self-sufficiency (123; 78) that this expansive view of selfhood puts forward. In *Joseph* we soon come to see the self in both ways at once: as a construction vainly attempting to conceal or contain its unbounded origins, and as a liberated escapee from the deceiving sureties of the unitary ego. We are both ourselves and not ourselves; self-awareness both frees us and traps us in its confinements. The delicate balancing act of the phrase "a time that we have left behind us to tell of the other" also enlarges our self-knowledge. It conjures the "other world," of course, but equally the other selves that we have left behind in the strata of our development. The effect of all this matches the double perspective we experienced as watchers of the "Kleist" performance. Seen intertextually, the two performances appear in and through each other; whichever we are focused on, the shadowy presence of the other multiplies our uncertainties and enriches our discoveries. So the scene of the play and the setting of the novels, ostensibly so different, create the same awareness of our ego's permeable edges; each rehearses what the other performs.

With this in mind we can pick up the thread of an earlier discussion. The *Joseph* "Prelude: Descent into Hell" is the "sculpture and mirror"[36] of our descent via rereading and performance into Kleist's *Amphitryon*. Seen literally, both descents are pseudo-epic and comic; the narrator takes no physical risk, any more than his audience jeopardizes a forcible unraveling of its sense of selfhood. Yet seen another way our descent — narrator and audience alike — has heroic qualities. We indeed "open at the back" and lose ourselves in the unsure footing of identity doubling and mythic consciousness so that we may recover "the first and last of all our speaking and questioning and all our concern: the nature of man" (54; 33).[37] In other words, we attend in order to overcome forgetfulness and to recover that past truly seen, truly read. So our induced loyalty to the ancient stories of Genesis both rehearses and expands the loyalty-quest of the Kleist narrator. The times require similar loyalty to the authentic German humanist tradition and its mythic underpinnings in order to compete with the Nazis' counterepic of obscurantism and grotesquely distorted or forgotten faces. Both narrators and both their audiences descend out of love and loyalty, and both explore how, through that descent, loyalty enables love by "saving (the) face," by giving an ethical center to both the present and the future.[38]

We can now see that our narrators are fraternal twins, self-echoing voices who wish to be heard and, ideally, seen. Their common task requires constructing new forms of narrative to mediate between poetry and criticism, emotion and idea, art and politics. Both reject the self-effacing, Flaubertian cool of impersonal modernist narration as well as any attempt to create a countercult to the fascism they oppose. They articulate a political position deeply skeptical of personal and cultural certainties yet insistent on the loyalty that the personal and cultural require. To claim that the *Joseph* novels are "non-political" is to say that the political is confined to the watertight rhetorics of public debate or official negotiation. Instead, our narrators both occupy and illuminate territory that makes humanistic politics possible. They are not characterized fully, or conventionally, but occupy a constantly shifting ground between full incarnation and the pared fingernails of Olympian remoteness. Performers to the core, they also dramatize intertextuality itself in their self-conscious efforts to reweave tales that empower fresh understanding of the past, and ethical action in the increasingly dangerous present.

IV

My real and secret text is the Bible, at the end of the story. It is the blessing that the dying Jacob pronounces upon Joseph: "The Almighty shall bless you with blessings of heaven above, blessings of the deep that lie beneath." When one decides upon a subject there has to be, in the material, a point somewhere that regularly stirs the heart every time it is touched. This is that productive point.

— Thomas Mann to Ernst Bertram, 28 Dec. 1926

Substitutions and blurred identities also structure the life of Jacob. Putative ancestors and actual family repeatedly cross and unsettle his ego's borders: Abel, Abraham, Isaac, Rebecca, and even Esau interfuse, briefly or continuously, with his psychic life. He recognizes many of these crossings, while others are noted by his nimble son Joseph or by the reader alone. Jacob in turn looks through his beloveds. Rachel's adult face always doubles, for him, both the Babylonian mother goddess and the young shepherdess who first greeted him at the well. In turn he constantly sees her features in the face of their shared Damuzi, the true son. When Jacob encounters strangers he typically looks right through them for their representative characters, seeing them as national types or linking them directly to their (inferior) gods. With his beloveds, Jacob sees specific faces, then archetypes; with others (including the more bloodthirsty of his sons), he sees archetypes and then, perhaps, individual faces.

"The Testing" section of chapter 1 of *The Tales of Jacob* ("Die Prüfung": 103–8; 64–67) interweaves with the "Kleist" performance in particularly revealing ways. The section opens exactly as the essay opens — with an elder admiring the beautiful head of a youthful beloved. Joseph of course is no passive Heuser; ever a stage director, he carefully blocks each of his opening conversations with his father (e.g., 91; 56). The father sits on the well's edge, the lad on the ground before him, and their subterranean feelings play in and through their words. Jacob delivers an open-air lecture, admonishing Joseph for his idolatrous near-nakedness before the Ishtar-moon, and then re-creates a tale of identity and substitution for him. The father's hand moves lovingly, if absently, across his son's hair, and he looks through Joseph's lovely seventeen-year-old face to the beauty of Rachel, and even to the problematic goddess Ishtar, whose nickname, "Mami," Rachel bore. The scene opens, in other words, with the "lecturer" speaking generally and ethically, yet revealing his own complicity in the magic of the goddess. The attraction of the father for the son is in the broadest sense erotic, rooted in the passion for the beloved wife and the dangerous-yet-irresistible Ishtar who appeared in her. It is another kind of forbidden love, countenancing rebellion against God's demand that He be loved before all others. The reader of the "Kleist" essay who knows Mann's story sees other faces — Martens, Timpe, Ehrenberg, a "boy of Spanish ancestry," and of course Klaus Heuser — behind the conjured beauty of the transparent Joseph. As the father begins to speak of Abraham, that is to re-dramatize a beloved yet deeply unsettling old story, the boy "becomes" Isaac under his hand. The opening of "The Testing," with its dramatic setting and fluid model of identity, replicates the lecture; Mann self-consciously draws on both the scene and the content of his "reconquest" of *Amphitryon*. The fact that the image of the face, seen and unseen, occurs some forty times in Genesis, makes Mann's interweaving of the "Kleist" ethic into his *Joseph* all the easier.

The imaging of earlier faces continues as Jacob briefly imagines himself at Joseph's age, when he was more "lustig" ("energetic") and not made weary by events both new and recalled. Like Eliezer, but in a much more fugal, less mechanical way, Jacob's ego now "opens at the back" to admit one of the "old events" to which he remains devoutly loyal. He follows a familiar association of ideas: from Joseph's beautiful features to God's mild countenance, then immediately to the Lord's "other face" — the fiery wrath that punished the men of Sodom (an almost inaudible connection) — and from thence to the desire for religious self-purification in God's cleansing fire. From there it is a short leap to scenes of sacrifice: Passover, and especially the original call to sacrifice, that of God to Abraham. Could he, Jacob, also sacrifice the beloved face of the son, or are his love and loyalty too strong? The God that faces him in this "Prüfung" is not the deity of his more abstract speculations, but the terrifying, incomprehensible God of Abraham.

Bowed by the heavy challenge, Jacob sits and begins in his vivid style to retell the testing of Abraham. He interweaves story and criticism, confession and theology, into a spellbinding account of his own dread and religious insufficiency. He begins with a theology of God's greatness, which he figures comparatively. God necessarily can command whatever lesser, more primitive, deities can command. If men must bring their first-born male infants to the god Melech in "secret feast," then God may well require something even greater: the sacrifice of the beloved, half-grown son. To require less would be to be less. Abraham faced this irremediable test, and every man who follows Abraham must measure his faith against that impossible standard.

The test actually comes, of course, from the narrative re-staging of the original drama, and Jacob captures us with his reenactment exactly as the Kleist narrator did. He creates a simulacrum of Abraham, the ideal or "true" Jacob, who judges him unfit to be "Israel," a patriarch of the blessing. Abraham can easily answer Isaac's question about the lamb for the burnt offering, but Jacob is struck dumb by it. Like Amphitryon, he is stripped by the question that the true Jacob puts to him, and in his silence he forfeits his identity as a man of God in order to "keep the child," that is, to keep the identity of Jacob the lover of Joseph (and Rachel-Ishtar). As Sosias "tests" ("prüft": IX, 196) Hermes, and Amphitryon Jupiter, so Jacob the patriarch tests his true self and finds it wanting. At the end of his self-trial he narrates his own imagined prostration; he falls on the ground as "thunder rolled from the place along heaven far and wide" (105; 66). Compare the end of Mann's *Amphitryon* retelling: at the god's departure "clouds roll up, there are flashings and crashings . . . they all fling themselves in the dust — all but one: the man, the beloved and husband, who holds her he never lost in his strong arms" (227; 239).

Now comes Joseph's preternaturally clever attempt to resituate his father before a different double. He seeks to leave Jacob exactly in Amphitryon's final position: the one man standing, holding the beloved

Alkmene he had never really lost. His attempt turns upon the temporal paradox of "reconquest" that the "Kleist" lecture models. Jacob's narrative made the old new, so new it was as if he never knew it. His retelling made the past present, merged his identity into Abraham's, and judged his inadequacy. In effect, the facile Joseph says to his despondent father: "Simply undo the paradox of intense rereading and you are saved. You cannot really have despaired, since you already knew the outcome of the tale: that God would substitute the ram in the thicket for the first-born." Knowing the double, in other words, rescued the father. But Jacob, loving as always a *schriftstellerische* dispute, holds to the paradox of identity that rereading and retelling dramatize: "for I was as Abraham, and the tale had not yet happened." But Joseph again distinguishes: "Ah, but didn't you say that you cried out 'I am not Abraham?' But if you were not, then you were Jacob, and knew the outcome," and so only "acted" as the father of faith. The son's moral is determinedly modern and secular, his notion of identity firm-bordered: "But that is the advantage of these latter days, that we know already the cycles in which the world rolls on, and the tales in which it is fulfilled and which were founded by the fathers. So you might well have trusted in the voice and the ram" (106; 66). Joseph, in his narcissism, sees himself living at the telos of time, when egos are well demarcated and everything that matters is already known. Like the audience both Kleist and Mann wish to unsettle, he calculates rationally, lives by expectation and prediction, and concludes that the future will be only a further working out of an already known set of alternatives. Tales that threaten his superficial notion of progress must be retold so that they accommodate his cheerful complacency. We hear Sosias's voice in his glibness, a boy of the hour who lives by his wits. And like Sosias, he will have many dealings with Hermes — including assuming his identity — before his story ends.

Jacob, aroused from self-abasement, joins the issue crisply — "Your speech is witty, but ungrounded" — and spins out the full implications of his shattering encounter with his double. First, God's actions cannot simply be predicted on the basis of past performance: Joseph's theology is weak. Second, and more important, the kind of expectation and foreknowledge that Joseph evokes would render devotion and faithfulness empty and meaningless. If all trials merely replicate old trials, if all knowledge of the depths is already in "the tales," then there can be no ongoing religious life. What would be lost specifically, says Jacob, is a "God that can make the future go through the fire unsinged and spring the bolts of death and is Lord of the resurrection" (106; 66). God would be a Mechanism who always gives the same Prüfung, not a mysterious Activity known only in the ever-shifting interweaving of story and the open future. So once again Jacob laments that God tested Abraham, who stood firm, but that he, Jacob, has tested himself with the same trial and found that his love was stronger than his faith. Son-sacrifice was utterly beyond him.

Joseph, shifting quickly from theology to narratology, makes one last attempt to simplify his father. He prepares the ground by proclaiming a false, if engaging humility ("and a camel is like to Noah in judgment compared to this mindless lad" [107: 66]). Then he reclassifies his "little father's" trial by fire and holy sacrifice as a mere "amusement." The actual narrator of Jacob's tale, he says, is his father's simulacrum of God himself, who whimsically chose to try Jacob with the trial of Abraham. And as the real storyteller behind this God-narrator, the authorial Jacob knew all along how it would turn out and so never actually put himself on trial. All he narrated was a diverting story about his inability to do what God had already forbidden to Abraham. This spares the father any suffering and "proves" how impossible the sacrifice of the son is in these "latter days." The trial was never a real one, after all. The sheer hypnotic charm of this homogenizing narration, as it flows easily from the very mindful Joseph, tempts Jacob and the reader alike.

Joseph cannot resist the enchantment of his own rhetoric. He gives his God-character a wordy speech, full of entertaining bombast, that turns Jacob's original comparison to the bull-god Melech into parody. On closer look, Joseph's self-absorption appears everywhere in his charming, many-layered story: God's "face" is now not "mild" or "fiery" but "like the face of the moon," whose reflective surface the boy had just been dreamily worshipping (107; 67).[39] God, in Joseph's mythic palimpsest, flows into the moon-Ishtar of his seventeen-year-old imagination, an erotic "Mami" who is stirred by his beauty and mirrors it back to him with uncritical approval. Joseph tries, in short, to make everyone and everything — his father, God, the lore of his people — into his likeness; his narrative practice reveals his adolescent narcissism. He constructs a father who perfectly mirrors his own self-love and who therefore approves his story — and perhaps, then, even his quasi-religious posturing before the moon. Jacob undertook a harrowing tale of selfhood's open boundaries and religion's holy yet impossible demands; Joseph blithely turns it into barely disguised psychodrama of his own well-demarcated ego.

Jacob speaks for the reader as well as himself when he divides the truth between them: "I say that only half of the truth is in your words, and the other half remains in mine, for I proved myself weak in faith"

(107–8; 67). But Jacob's deepest reaction to Joseph's performance is not divided; his love, as it always will, ultimately pushes aside his judgment and even his religious musing, and the chapter ends with his heartfelt yet ominous over-praising of his son's narration. He shows his final loyalty to his love of the mother, and to her "face" in that of the son. "The Testing" turns on religion's claim of steadfastness, and on the several other kinds of loving loyalty — narcissism, the erotic, the romantic — that may challenge that claim.

In all these ways the "Kleist" retelling helps to mold "The Testing." The molding is situational and autobiographical but also, as we saw with the two narrators, formal and even political. The exchanges between father and son in "The Testing" unroll in patterns similar to those the "Kleist" performance wove between Sosias and Hermes, Amphitryon and Jupiter. Indeed, *Joseph*'s whole conception of biblical testing and identity is Kleistian. Most readers, including Mann, regard Joseph's and Amphitryon's stories as universal in scope and appeal. The Kleistian intertext supplements that breadth with a specific cultural and political context: Mann's refounded German humanism and pedagogic responsibility. Mann spoke often of the "escape" writing the tetralogy provided him during his exile. Certainly it provided him with an alternative world to the ever-increasing daily demands of political and social leadership during the 1930s. But it emerged from, and constantly reflected upon, the fundamental issues that enabled his politics and his public performances: political and artistic responsibility to the German people, the reassertion of German humanism in the seemingly impossible circumstances of twentieth-century Europe, the preservation of an authentic German culture against its Nazi destroyers.

Seen this way, the making of *Joseph* is itself a kind of ongoing *Prüfung* of Mann's own loyalty to the best in German culture and politics. So although essay and novel may appear very different, even a little digging among their roots shows their similar formation. The doubling of the narrators' voices also marks their mutual orbiting. While it seems likely that Mann was aware of the beginning connections between the two — the palimpsestic images of the beloved, the lecture format — it seems equally plausible that the impetus of the texts themselves, the proximity of their making, generated subtler shaping forces. Which came first, the head of Heuser or the head of Joseph? Was "The Testing" Mann's way of declaring his erotic weakness before the stern demands of his art, or was it instead his writing-into-being the knowledge of his beloved's narcissism? Answers can only be speculative, but one-way, causal conclusions seem to me less illuminating than the dynamic, shifting web of connections and feelings that this action produced in our two interwoven texts. *Joseph* enables the "Kleist" essay, and the "Kleist," *Joseph*.

A final note: "The Testing" quietly refuses to follow the Freudian scene that it appears to create. In *Totem and Taboo*, the text that Mann praised above all his other writings in the 1929 essay, Freud observes that

> Divine figures such as Attis, Adonis and Tammuz emerged, spirits of vegetation and at the same time youthful divinities enjoying the favors of mother goddesses and committing incest with their mother in defiance of their father. But the sense of guilt, which was not allayed by these creations, found expression in myths which granted only short lives to these youthful favorites of the mother goddesses and decreed their punishment by emasculation or by the wrath of the father in a form of an animal. (*SE* XIII, 152)

This description could almost be called a program for "The Testing," yet Mann skillfully and repeatedly backgrounds it. Joseph's erotic self-baring before "Mami" images not some symbolic attempt to displace the father, but a self-amusing, theological "chicken" — let's see how far I can go without really crossing a line. Any potential Oedipal confrontation swiftly transforms itself into a clever hermeneutical exercise that rescues the father from despair. Nor are we encouraged to read the scene in a Freudian way, letting the Oedipal subtext structure the conversation's significance. The reader may do so regardless, but the resulting interpretation is neither as fruitful nor as persuasive as the Kleistian alternative.

V

Kleist's clever servant, Sosias, and Jacob's hirsute twin, Esau, at first seem unlikely partners. But they are in fact carefully considered preliminary studies for the more radical problems of identity facing the central characters in each work. Esau's portrait owes much to Sosias's, and self-influence urges us to read Mann's account of the servant as an early draft of Esau's fate. As noted earlier, staging the loss of identity first in Sosias lets the audience watch Amphitryon's unraveling with a more nuanced awareness of his dilemmas. Similarly, Esau's comipathetic wrestling with the mythic patterns shaping his fate in "The Great Hoaxing" prepares the *Joseph* audience for the much more sophisticated trickery and substitutions to come. In both productions the weight falls not on the "what" but the "how" of the action: perfect material for performers on stage. More important, the particular mar-gins of identity in these two secondary characters take us further into two of *Joseph*'s foundation narratives. Esau's tale owes much to the story of culture's origins as told in Freud's *Totem and Taboo* (as carefully revised by Mann). Sosias's story also draws on the myth of Narcissus, whose complex elaborations figure prominently in virtually every scene of the play, the tetralogy, and the remainder of this study.

At the beginning of *Amphitryon* Sosias comically substitutes his lantern for Alkmene and then composes lines for his mistress.[40] At once actor and audience, he ignores the patrons beyond the footlights and applauds his own performance. The scene unmistakably echoes Joseph's first self-intoxicated evocation of the lantern-moon and "mistress" Ishtar. Watching characters who themselves stage events, particularly events that involve substitution, is a hallmark of the *Joseph*, and Kleist's clever uses of it provided several strategies for the tetralogy. Sosias's leveling dramatization of Alkmene soon turns against him, however, when Hermes appears as the uppity servant's perfect simulacrum. A metonymic lantern is one thing, but the perfect doubling of the self into an uncontrollable Other quite another. In Ovid's retelling of the Narcissus myth, Narcissus's "others" are split into the silent image in the pond and the rejected voice of Echo. Enlarging on the possibilities of the myth, the *Amphitryon* implicitly entertains several variations on the story. In this scene, for example, these figures combine; the mirroring simulacrum's ironically echoing voice takes vengeance on the self-regarding servant. Sosias will be driven temporarily mad by this "subtle, comic and painful soul-experiment of the most cutting kind . . . and the stations of his suffering are so heart-rending to the listener because the poet gives us to feel them by words and outcries from the depths of the creature's being" (193–94; 207). Mann keeps us removed with hyperbole: the "stations of the cross" that poor Sosias traverses can't help but produce a laugh as well as commiseration.

Sosias must not simply comply with the god, but conform actually and inwardly. His name — here identical with his will to be himself and to have his own future — has been stolen from him. In his agony Sosias has lines that make the connection to Esau's hoaxing explicit:

> So go to hell! I can not negate myself,
> Change myself, step outside my own skin
> and drape it around your shoulders.
> Since the world began, has anyone seen the like? (195; 209)

The play with skin and substitution makes this a speech that Esau and Jacob could easily slip into. The apparently stable border of the self has suddenly become opaque, transferable. Joseph's pedagogue Eliezer, we saw, made this move willingly, entering the "skin" of earlier Eliezers without fear of dissolution. But Sosias and Esau stand at different points in the history of selfhood and so suffer when they are comically flayed, robbed of their borders by a simulacrum and a twin. Sosias goes on to "test" himself ("und er *prüft* 'sich' weiter": 196; 209), to give himself a beating and even to beg for a new identity, but every attempt to remain inside his skin fails, and he finally accedes to the god.

The limits of both self-knowledge and destiny-awareness in Sosias and Esau are clearly drawn. They connect to the precise comic position of the two characters; each text dramatizes the exact sequence in which overconfidence and exultant triumph turn into their opposites. First comes shock, then disbelief, embarrassment, blundering rescue attempts, humiliation, capitulation, and collapse. It makes for a series of calibrated rebounds between recognition and denial, a series in which the audience's distance and empathy also oscillate rapidly. Like Sosias, Esau is comical before he realizes it, oblivious to the laughter of Jacob's entire household as he wildly boasts of the paternal blessing to come. Mann adds a level in the Esau scene, reminding us that a story may have its "honorable hours" even if the ending is "lamentable" and "terrible" (203, 211; 133, 138). But this attempt to promote sympathy for "the hairy one" is simultaneously estranging, another part of the joke. Esau's fate is perhaps lamentable for a time but certainly not terrible, and honorable only in a limited, prudential sense.

This particular comic moment is also ostentatiously tied to class. Both scenes encourage us to enjoy laughing at those beneath us. With Sosias this is obvious, but Esau is the eldest son of the blessing-bearer. Yet in the longer view of the blessing's unfolding he is of lower station, an actor with a smallish part. His position has never been what he thought it was; all the rest of Isaac's people seem to have always known, consciously or otherwise, that he too was only the servant of a greater story. And even he at times "knows" it as well, partially and subliminally. Esau's pretension to the blessing is analogous to Sosias's putting Alkmene's words in the mouth of his lantern; both are instances of overreaching that are punished. Mann may have become a democrat by conviction and political necessity, but never an egalitarian; the claims of "the best" in both art and society were permanent fixtures in his performances and temperament.

There is a second, misery-producing realization that accompanies substitution. Both Sosias and Esau make the unsettling discovery that even the most candid confession may not confirm one's unique selfhood. The spilling of all your secrets does not necessarily have empowering psychic or ethical consequences. "The tortured ego summons itself to the clearest consciousness, it repeats to itself the circumstances of its own life — and has to hear, has to learn to believe, that all of that belongs to the other man, nothing is his own" (195; 209). Hermes, the perfect mimic beneath a Kleistian Tarnhelm, simply recites Sosias' most private thoughts in the first person; "his self-awareness is no guide either externally or within" (196; 209). So even self-loyalty is uncannily rendered impossible, and Sosias becomes the truly superfluous man ("Ein Mehreres scheint überflüssig mir" [196; 209]). *Joseph in Egypt* explores this territory carefully. The endlessly repeated confessions of Huia and Tuia cannot overcome their guilt, and the tragic fate of the "Freudian" Mut-em-enet turns on her repression: her loss of loyalty to the passionate self, and the superfluous life that follows its loss.

In his rehearsal of later events, Esau discovers that shouting and weeping his wrongs to his father's followers earns him only laughter, not understanding (let alone restoration). He finds that he is not "himself" at all but the brother who must be outcast — a Cain, an Ishmael — and that there is no help for it; he cannot be the Esau he thought himself to be, the "chosen one," the "bearer of the blessing." These names have been stolen from him by an impostor. Esau confronts these dilemmas in his conspiratorial conversations with his outcast uncle Ishmael, whose years of exile have made him rather more canny about mythic tradition. Esau hopes to have his uncle slay his brother, the betrayer Isaac, an act from which Esau might draw the courage to slay his own brother in turn. But "wild" Ishmael, for once finding himself in the role of pedagogue, holds up the myth-mirror: he is Hermes in another form before Esau, urging the hairy one himself to undertake father murder.[41] In a wry intertextual joke, Ishmael cites *Totem and Taboo*; he tells Esau that there are indeed stories — stories "that had perhaps been the beginning of everything" — in which the son slays the father himself and afterward partakes of his flesh (215; 141). Not knowing his Freud, the unimaginative Esau had "only the traditional fratricide in mind." Actual father-slaying is too much for him, however, and distracted by Ishmael's beautiful daughter Mahalath, Esau's blood-lust diverts into a more familiar channel. Even when his thinning passion for vengeance rebounds, the best the broken Esau can do is to acquiesce to a substitute, his loyal son Eliphaz, who may slay his tent-dwelling uncle for him and so break the pattern of brother slaughter that would make Esau forever Cain. Like Wagner's Wotan, he cannot compel this action on his son without entangling himself hopelessly in the roles he hopes to evade. The upshot for Esau is that he recognizes inaction as his only small freedom, and the cold comfort of avoiding the fate of Cain as his only inheritance.

Poor Sosias has even less respite. He sees his Narcissus-image full-blown before him, and watches his life simply vanish. But his funny self-alienation will form part of *Amphitryon*'s long afterlife in the tetralogy, just as Mann's early elaborations of the Joseph story affected his take on *Amphitryon*. The complex, deflecting mirrors into which Esau looks are not as immediately stripping as Sosias's double, and in those differences Mann moves from farce to the subtleties of accommodation in Esau. Later, Sosias's fate modulates into Joseph's "disappearance" into Osarsiph, the dead Joseph. Joseph's final attitude toward his impersonations echoes that of Hermes' cool reply to the anguished servant: "When I Sosias longer not shall be, / Then be you he, for my part I don't care" (197; 211). In this same spirit Joseph will leave the husk of Osarsiph behind.

Beyond even this permutation lies the deepest instability of identity doubling, one that Kleist shows to the audience and then contains. Romantic doubles that evoke the buried side of the protagonist's psyche have become cultural mainstays, even clichés. Famous mirroring pairs such as Jekyll-Hyde, Frankenstein and his monster, Wotan-Alberich, or, closer to home, the mysterious, Conradian "Yankee" of Mann's 1934 "Meerfahrt mit Don Quixote" ("Voyage with Don Quixote"), who ventures into the hold of the ship where Mann himself dares not enter — all depend on the externalization of self-division for their drama. But even more anarchic may be the literal doubling of identity itself, since the organizing hierarchies of "self" and "other," of "conscious" and unconscious" or higher and lower class (Don Quixote-Sancho; Amphitryon-Sosias) disappear in their rapid reflections. If there is, even for a time, no "original" and "copy" but only doubling, only simulacra, we can only oscillate between figures, not anchor our understanding in difference.[42] This turn of the screw surpasses even the destabilizing dangers of the artist's magical empathy, of entering so fully into a character that the sense of self disappears. It emerges from the archetypal myth that informs the identity narratives of both Kleist and Freud: the endlessly rebounding, endlessly reflexive gaze of Narcissus.

Esau also differs from Sosias in another important way that distinguishes between the lyric re-creation of the Kleist drama and the epic development of the *Joseph*. The difference is, simply, *Totem and Taboo*. Sosias is not located on any developmental ladder. Committed from the beginning to unpacking the "blessing" of present and future generations that anchors the Genesis tale, Mann found in Freud's anthropology a valuable structure for showing development, and hence the way to the future. This also marks an important difference within *Joseph*. It shows how Esau, "red and hairy" though he is, has already moved from the acted-out violence of *Totem and Taboo*'s "primitive band" of brothers. He intuits that he should kill neither the brother, as Cain did, nor the father, as Freud's enraged brothers did, but seek a substitute instead. This model was sufficient for Esau and lets us see him as Sosias-cum-Freud, as a low comic character who attains a certain temporary knowledge from his deflating victimization. But Freud's anthropology, taken alone, says little to Mann about his major theme: the movement of the blessing into the future — for the patriarchs, and for Germany. Freud's conception of the blessings the future will bring is, as Mann knew well from his own reading, very different: "all our provisional ideas in psychology will some day be based on an organic substructure" ("On Narcissism," *SE* XIV, 78). Mann, despite a lifelong susceptibility to Schopenhauer's metaphysical monism, steadfastly resists this material, determinist position, what Derrida once called "Freud's neurological fable." In the novels, the "low" characters dramatize the evolutionary model of *Totem and Taboo* that will be honored, then superseded as we proceed through the tetralogy. "Provisional" marks success, not inadequacy, in *Joseph and his Brothers*.

VI

To summarize, Mann composed his "Kleist" performance while immersed in *Totem and Taboo*'s account of civilization's emergence from the primitive, and in the nascent anthropology of the *Joseph* series. Accordingly, he read Kleist's play intertextually, as an antecedent literary account of identity and development. Doing so allowed him to play with ideas he then elaborated in the tetralogy; the essay is both a rehearsal and a final performance. For example, Amphitryon undergoes a speedy yet subtle transformation from a macho "low" character quite like Sosias or "a French soldier" Esau to a more knowing figure of identity's dilemmas and permeable borders (202; 217). *Joseph* then takes up the many complicating variations of this pattern — most richly in the Jacob and Joseph of *Joseph the Provider*, but also in Laban as a frozen, "undevelopable" character and in Damasek-Eliezer as parody of such development — that arose from Mann's long reflection on identity and loyalty. Amphitryon's development, specifically around the questions of selfhood and otherness, decisively supplemented both the Freudian version and the established Bildungsroman accounts of naïveté and growth with which Mann was already so familiar.

Kleist made elaborate preparations for his hero's entrance. Sosias opens the play with a witty recitation of Amphitryon's story narrated to his lantern, and the servant's ensuing near-madness at Hermes' hands rehearses the well-known fate of the hero. "Amphitryon" then appears onstage, but in effect as his own double; Jupiter speaks as Amphitryon before the "real" Amphitryon enters. Thanks to Hermes the audience knows this is the King and not the king, yet our unease remains because the god's replication of the hero is so uncannily perfect that it deceives Alkmene. She believes she has just made love with the real Amphitryon, and her wholehearted emotion draws us in even as we shudder at her deception. So when Amphitryon finally does appear, we cannot help in part seeing *him* as the duplicate in spite of what we know. This cannily inverts the Narcissus tale: we see a hero who cannot be fully embodied, who himself seems the echo of the god's perfection.

Mann also adds his own summary of the hero's reputation as a warrior: "His nature is direct, courageous, primitively male" (203–4; 217). Alkmene speaks to the god of "his" violent temper, which she knows well since it led to her father's death; she also knows Amphitryon's gifts for warfare, since she sent him on her mission of family revenge. ("Primitive maleness" and a propensity for violence, in our context, connect quietly with *Totem and Taboo*.) So before the "real" Amphitryon ever speaks, Mann highlights the clever way that Kleist has given us the extremes of his character to date; we know his reputation and we see his ideal. Our points of view are nearly as tangled as the mystery of identity itself.

The first scene of the main action portrays Jupiter's paradoxical attempts to make Alkmene love him, the god himself, even as he has just won her passionate love for his impersonation. To re-create himself in man's image turns out to be more complicated than he had imagined. Jupiter wishes to be fully the human lover — a great reversal for this seducer-god — and to have his beloved's heartfelt gratitude for his own. But he cannot receive her love wholeheartedly precisely because his disguise is complete; no chink of the god behind the mask can show through. Ironically defeated by the perfection of his substitution, his position is impossible from the outset, and he intuitively knows it; the drama lies in how he acts on that half-accepted presentiment. In this first scene he compulsively hints at the gaps between self and substitution, repeatedly drawing a distinction between spouse and lover that seems superfluous to the bedazzled Alkmene. The more she accedes to his domestic plans and distinctions, the more he is "tormented" because their impossibility becomes clearer (199; 213); the more she praises his lovemaking the more frustrated he becomes.

We know how the course of the play will bring him to the full recognition of godhead's limits, and to his decisive action: renunciation of

Alkmene's love. This seems to parallel one of *Joseph*'s great themes: gods can develop their divinity only through their intercourse with men. But Kleist's Jupiter seeks only adoration and approval, not development. His incarnation is finally futile: his curse and blessing is that he can never cease to be Jupiter, even when he appears to be another, and so can only learn to reconcile himself to his nature, not lose it. His character can hide behind a front but never "open at the back." So, for Jupiter, becoming the Other confirms self-knowledge but not a transforming compassion; he learns the limitations of godhead. But for mortals similar incarnations and substitutions can be perilous indeed. Leah's melancholic words to Jacob after her wedding night substitution for the true spouse, Rachel, resonate with this intertextual play. It is the one night in which Leah, in disguise, receives Jacob as both her lover and husband. After the deception unravels, he will only be her legal spouse and her reluctant mate, just as Jupiter feels himself sliding back into his customary, unwanted role of distant deity or overmastering seducer. Leah expresses a despair the deceiving god cannot equal: "Always it was I, and I was yours this night ever since I entered in the veil" (310; 203). "Always it was I": Leah may not have the spiritual range of Jupiter, but she knows the paradise that substitution creates and then bitterly destroys.

In one sense, Jupiter himself did not make love with anyone; his intercourse with Alkmene was actual, yet fictive. He easily simulates both heroic and sexual prowess, yet cannot make them his own; he can act, but he can't become. Gods in disguise are always gods in alienation. This sheds more light on *Joseph*'s view of divinity. If, like Jupiter, all gods insist on the unassailable integrity of their natures, if they lack permeable borders, then paradoxically they will never develop, never become omnipotent. Jupiter can either try to surrender his godhood completely, losing himself in the earthly "matter" of Alkmene's love, or he can openly return, through renunciation, to his unchanging nature. A god such as Jupiter can only take the latter course; his renunciation does not alter his divinity. The dilemma of incarnation remains as insoluble for him as for Leah; the frail human's power to receive unambiguous and honest love becomes an impossible ideal for the Ideal. Jupiter models, in this scene, the traditional conception of Soul and Deity alike as unchanging, perfectly self-contained, and ultimately static entities. Readers of *Joseph* immediately recognize in this account a variation on "Die Roman der Seele," the tetralogy's master myth of God, soul, spirit, and matter, set forth at the end of the "Prelude" and so written just before Mann's rereading of Kleist. The intertextual self-

influence of the "Prelude's" mythic story on the "Kleist" essay is clear
and important.

The tale has two versions (39–49; 23–30). In the first, *Adam qad-
man*, "the youthful being fashioned out of pure light, . . . the prototype and epitome of humanity," falls in love with the beauty of "his
own mirror-image in matter" and gives himself to it. In surrendering to
this "narcissistic image of tragic loveliness" ("narzissischen Bilde voll
tragischer Anmut"), the youth's longing separates him from God; desire becomes interwoven with "culpability" ("Schuldhaftigkeit"). This
parable generalizes into the "romance of the soul," in which the
youth's embrace of matter formed around his image becomes, allegori-
cally, the union of form with unorganized matter. The soul suffers in its
descent, both because it separates itself from God and because matter
resists its attempts to give it beautiful form. God then sends "from his
own substance" a second emissary, the reasonable "spirit," to rescue
the soul from its love affair. At this point an uncertainty about God's
intent leads to the two versions of the tale. In the first, the spirit descends to show the soul that its embrace of matter was sinful, and to
recall it immediately to the upper world. In the second — the one preferred in the *Joseph* novels — the soul had not in fact "sinned" since
God had not explicitly forbidden its congress with its own image, i.e.
with matter. So in this version the spirit comes not to woo the soul
back to oneness with God but rather, as the well-known free shifting of
tenses in mythic narratives suggests, to eventually become one with the
soul and produce a humanity blessed with both nature and spirit. The
reasonable spirit too has its desires, but they point toward a new consummation, not a retrograde return. So the spirit is the "principle of
the future," the soul is the holy "It was," and the spirit's role is essentially pedagogic: to save the soul for the future.

This is Mann's cosmic version of primary narcissism. Narcissism inaugurates creation just as it inaugurates personality, but cannot by itself
complete it. Self-enamored youths always fall into the blindness of the
pit, and can only be rescued for the future by acknowledging the reality
of the other and hearkening to a higher self-knowledge. The soul's embrace of matter cannot and should not be undone, yet by itself it is
"mindless" and therefore incapable of development. The spirit, however, signals a dynamic conception of creation and of selfhood; it is
both anchored and open to alteration. This begins one of Mann's most
interesting revisions of Freud, one that we shall elaborate over the next
three chapters. Mann will both endorse and swerve from his "scientific
psychologist" mentor by working out the implications of the "Prelude's" allegory, and then connecting his revision of identity to per-

formance and political action. The Kleist play figures the dynamic "anchor" of selfhood, and that figuration will play into the crosscurrents of Freudian and contra-Freudian ideas in the tetralogy.

Returning now to the rest of the *Amphitryon*, we can see how that anchor and future orientation of the spirit influence Mann's reconstruction. Amphitryon, like Oedipus, is stripped of everything that constitutes his selfhood: his wife's fidelity; the effectiveness, even the relevance, of his military strength; his heroic honor; finally, like Sosias, his name. The narrator playfully chides him for his limited knowledge of mythic tales; had he known of, say, Callisto or Europa, he would have "known the story already" about gods and simulacra and acted accordingly. But the chiding is superficial; we cannot fathom certain stories until experience has made it possible for us to do so. In this regard Amphitryon anticipates Joseph; without blindness and riddles, there can be no growth and discovery.

Since the entire play is Mann's arena, Alkmene also elaborates the story of identity. Alkmene sees double but has no external double in the drama. The god doubles her husband, both figures perhaps interlacing imaginatively in her mind with the ghostly father she has just buried.[43] Reading *Amphitryon* with the kindred story of Oedipus in mind, however, suggests a literary doubling with Sophocles' hero. She finds that her senses and her recent memories, so clear and moving, are nothing but misreadings, deceptions. Events call into question everything that made her fully herself as spouse and queenly woman: Amphitryon's triumphant return, the gift of the crown, revenge against her brother-enemies, the night of divine love in which her identity opened its borders to another. She reacts as Oedipus does to those who reinterpret his memories; her husband is plainly tricking her for unclear, perhaps malicious reasons, and she will solve the riddle. (Her deception illuminates the wedding-night deception of Jacob, and her denunciation of the humiliated husband helps to shape Mut-em-enet's last attempt to keep her dignity in *Joseph in Egypt*.) The solution comes quickly; the ocular proof of her own unintentioned infidelity lies on the gift-crown that symbolizes her nobility: the *J* imprint of the god. The consequences of her culpability, again like Oedipus, reennoble her as she "mounts through stages of an immeasurably difficult self-testing" ("Selbstprüfung": 207; 220). This is the content of the "Great Scene" that Mann, with Jupiter's own "reverence and longing," re-created before Klaus Heuser and his generation. The scene's "witty and reverent suggestions" apply equally to Mann's performance and to the parallel encounters between humans and the divine in *Joseph*.

Since her misread memories are only of the previous night, not the deep, violent past that rises up before Jocasta's husband and son, both her suffering and her recovery are compressed in time and space. But Alkmene's agony does retrace the steps of Oedipus's self-revelation; she "laments her shocking self-assurance" and becomes "full of distrust of her own nature" (207; 220). Her language is nearly as noble as that of the Sophoclean hero she echoes. Out of this replication Mann will tacitly construct another part of his counterstory to Sophocles', and Freud's, narrative. Freud and Mann agree that "where psychology is, there is already the pathological; the border between the two is close and fluid" (205; 219).[44] "Psychology and pathology": Mann's retelling of *Amphitryon* seems to go through all their "fluid" permutations before he arrives at his own denouement. We can only trace the most consequential of them.

Barely concealed within her regal nobility is the innocent Alkmene, the sentimentalized girl-child of Kleist's (and Mann's) imagination. Especially stirred by her "honest, upright little heart," the narrator creates a "glorious woman" and "wide-eyed child" that he, like the god, both honors and patronizes (206–7; 220). He puts this Alkmene to certain specific uses in the *Joseph*: her "baby-talk" (215–16; 228) anticipates the painful lisping of Mut in *Joseph in Egypt*; her childlikeness colors the portrait of "little" Rachel. But her character, however imbued with male stereotypes, does lead to one kind of authorial self-discovery and revelation that, when combined with those of Jupiter and Amphitryon, create the necessary new "psychology" for both the podium and the writing desk.

In the climactic "Great Scene" Jupiter doubles Amphitryon so completely that even the god himself at times seems willingly deceived by the blurring ambiguities. His yearning and Alkmene's innocent simplicity make him literally idolize her (209; 222). He spins out his suffering in an enchanting vein that revisits Mann's long agonizing, from "Tonio Kröger" forward, about the proximate living and painful remove of the third party, the artist-creator. Mann termed this kind of erotic narcissism "Goethean," since both Egmont and Faust "find a special ecstasy in the bewitching of simple innocence" (IX, 615; *Essays*, 35). Of course Jupiter's goal, like that of all such narrators and other creature makers, remains consummation and surrender of the beloved to the "real" god, even as he knows that the only way he may seduce her is to keep in hiding. The balancing act is perilous even for an Olympian; he comes close to believing his own impersonation, and so ceasing to be Jupiter.

When he finally does, in extremis, reveal himself (thunderclap and all), she can only think him impious and mad, and his revelation ironically silences him. When he can speak again he smilingly offers her the three lines that, for Mann, express the erotic theology and emotional core of the drama:

> Ob du der Gnade *wert*, ob nicht, kömmt nicht
> Zu prüfen *dir* zu. *Du wirst über dich,*
> *Wie er dich würdiget, ergehen lassen.*
>
> (211; 224: italics in Mann's essay)

> Whether or not you are *worthy* of his favor,
> Is not for y*ou* to test. *What you will suffer is*
> *The ennobling he confers on you.* (224)

These words and the silent smile together identify "the witty and heartfelt, iridescent doubleness of the piece, at once social comedy and intellectual play [*Gedankenspiel*], how it is all expressed in the profound smile of this reply, where an inscrutable, higher art mingles with the inscrutability of the heart" (211–12; 224). The smiling-yet-painful interlacing of wit and feeling, high art and the depths of emotion — the phrases echo the sentence that Mann had termed, a few months earlier, the "real and secret text" of the *Joseph* novels, Jacob's blessing on his Damuzi in Genesis 49: 25: "The Almighty shall bless you with the blessings of heaven above, blessings of the deep that lie beneath."[45] "Arbitrary election" on the one hand, and "the whole inclination and painful irony of absolute, uncritical love" on the other, name the spiritual boundaries within which play and novels work. "Here love is the power that confers true worth rather than inquiring about worthiness. It *is* — and this being is sovereign" (212; 224: italics in original). The passage forms the joining point, the most patent umbilical, between the two texts. The lines originate in Genesis but also in the high emotion of Mann's first encounter with *Amphitryon*, and are now reenacted in the two rereadings, the lecture and the epic, that accompanied each other in Mann's imagination, and whose *Geist und Kunst* will silently stay in loyal tandem during the trying years of composition and exile that follow.

This tripartite model of stripping, resignation, and the regaining of self through love and its sustaining loyalty grounds the literary psychology that will carry the *Joseph* project onward, and anchors Mann's pedagogy and politics in an ethics of renewal rather than prohibition. Freud too suggests that our lives are constructed around a set of substitutions that replace, more or less successfully, the inaugural events of our psychic life. But unlike Oedipus, who finds a stranger buried within himself, Amphitryon's ego limits are externalized, ideally doubled in the world, and his identity is constructed on outward relationships rather than repression. What sets this apart from, or at least marks an advance upon, the artist dilemmas of Mann's earlier career is its development. Amphitryon himself offers the last, defining gesture. In a revealing instance of self-conscious self-influence, Mann describes the hero's stripping with the otherwise incongruous Hebrew word *killel*, a "curse," a "making light of" or dismissing that is, he says, the inversion of Jacob's blessing of recognition (218; 230). Amphitryon faces not only banishment now but literal erasure; on this account there could be no suffering-shaped recovery, no "Amphitryon at Colonos." It reminds us not only of Esau and Oedipus, but Odysseus. Treated as a drunken impostor by Hermes, Amphitryon is made a beggar in his wife's palace and told repeatedly that she is sleeping with her suitor. Then in full view of his summoned courtiers and friends he must meet his own ideal self in Jupiter, and see every shred of his self-respect and honor embodied only in the Other. He has "dwelt all too defiantly in the strong fortress of his own consciousness" (220; 231) — the parallels with Joseph's fall thicken — and must be made to grovel. He tries to attack in his "direct, courageous, primitively male" way, but it is useless. Narcissistic mirrorings multiply: his former heroic self is replicated also in the exaggerated "man of honor" Argatiphontidas, who bullyingly denounces him in a manner he himself might well have used at the play's opening. The poor man then asks the assembled Thebans to be his "glass" and show him who he is; they comply by turning to the simulacrum, the god, whom they effortlessly distinguish from this empty outsider. And they are right: the "almighty one is more fully, more essentially, ideally Amphitryon than Amphitryon himself; he surpasses him in selfhood, he outdoes him" (223–24; 235). Even his name is usurped: he is a maddened, Odyssean No-man, a useless "stranger to the story" who deserves banishment. He faints, "senseless from his suffering," and Sosias proclaims him "dead" (224; 235–36).

What awakens him, and begins his restoration, is his decisive line "Der ist's, den seine eigne Frau erkennt" ("He it is, whom his own wife recognizes" [224; 236]). Bring forth my wife, and she will decide who is Amphitryon. Jupiter quickly agrees, since he can only imagine victory for himself. It is the play's finest example of self-regard's self-undoing: because *he* would never be able to greet a mere human "other" as himself, Jupiter thinks the same is true of the smitten bride. He believes that she can only choose the Ideal, the essential, the "true" Amphitryon.

Alkmene is summoned to judge between the god and the debased. Amphitryon submits: without her recognition, he cannot be himself. No-man speaks:

> — If she can claim him as her spouse,
> Then never more will I ask who I *am*:
> Then I will greet him as Amphitryon. (224; 236)

And, of course, she does just that, choosing the "true husband" and scorning the "unworthy, shameless" shell before her (225; 236–37). She curses her own deceiving senses for even considering this "marsh-brood" of a man. By emphasizing Alkmene's disgust with the "un-Treue" husband, the "Kleist" narrator effectively sustains his ground bass of love and loyalty. "He stares across at the other with eyes that are indeed his, but no longer Amphitryon's" (225; 237).

So in extremis, beyond any point of calculation or measured choice, Amphitryon nonetheless remains loyal. About to be "driven forth" like Oedipus, he will accept her naming the Other as Amphitryon, ex-punging his own individual self-awareness. He utters on pain of "sev-enfold death" the impossible line: "That he Amphitryon is, and hers" (226; 238). That line miraculously marks not a moment of madness and vanishing but of epiphany: it reveals the god. Misnaming forces revelation, and Jupiter the praise-seeking lover is unraveled by his tri-umphant substitution. He cannot be the real Amphitryon, only the Ideal; bound to the essential and to his narcissistic prowess, he cannot sustain loyal love. Exposed by his victory, he declares himself to be not-Amphitryon. Alkmene tries to cling to the Ideal, but the god renounces her: "dark, sweet god-words he breathes to her in farewell" (227; 239). And he is consistent: once he has renounced, Jupiter looks at no mor-tal, confers no final love. Forswearing loyalty, he summons Hermes and departs. Like Narcissus, his body dissolves into air, leaving behind not a flower but a name.

The drama ends with Amphitryon again himself. He is restored to his friends and polity, and to his wife, who at last sees, and knows, and simply names him: "Amphitryon." The naming embodies, re-incarnates him. His love and loyalty recover her identity and close the curtain. Naming and recognition: the loving acknowledgment from the other, the loyal one, who has held the image of the beloved's face through absence and loss. This self-constituting emotion remains at the heart of selfhood after all stripping and degradation; it can rename the nameless and even awaken the dead. The overture of Mann's "Kleist" perform-ance returns incisively in its finale. Selfhood begins not in isolation or in a substantive nature, but in relation, naming, calling forth. The beloved's countenance, recognized, exceeds any idea or idealization. In *Joseph* the narrator interrupts his introduction of the lovely girl-child Rachel for an apostrophe to the human face:

> Who can separate out the interplay of those sweet and happy chances to which life, groping here and there among inherited traits, adds the one unique thing that forms the gracefulness of the human face? It is a charm suspended on a knife-edge, it hangs, one may say, on a hair; so that if only a tiny trait, the smallest muscle, were placed differently, though but little were changed yet the heart's delight, the whole haunting miracle, would unravel. (228; 149)

To know that unique face, and then to re-call it into being, requires both love and loyalty; passion attached only to abstract ideas or the myth of the State, or passion free-standing and self-constituting, is inherently and finally self-serving, narcissistic, dis-loyal. So there is, in Mann's reconstruction of *Amphitryon* and Genesis, a point beneath even the most ruthless substitutions, beneath the invasions and erasures that appear to cancel identity itself. That point lets the ethical enter into the so-called "primitive," both its private substitutions and the ego-ideal operations of politics and mass social behavior. The emotion plainly rises in Mann's conclusion, as his own loyalty to the reading of Kleist and to the image of the beloved permeates his reconstruction.

The mainstream reading of the "Kleist" essay places Jupiter's poignant renunciation of ordinary human life and love at the center of Mann's reconstruction, quite rightly likening it to his many earlier fictions in which other isolated, knowing characters faced a similar dilemma. The god's likeness to the "higher being" of the dedicated artist also allegorizes Mann's own struggles with participation in quotidian life: the glad-sorry interweaving of desire and distance in his writing, his friendships, his family. His essay's announced theme is loyalty, especially loyalty in "impossible" situations: the sustained memory of an unwarranted love (Klaus Heuser); the faithfulness to great love, even in the face of the beloved's forgetfulness or rejection (Amphitryon); the passion of a god for a mortal. But Jupiter's ultimate loyalty, despite all his passion and tenderness, can only be to his godlike nature. He offers little compensation, artistic or otherwise, for the suffering he inflicts: a crown with his initial; the memory of his "image" in and behind the real Amphitryon which he hopes Alkmene will treasure (212–13; 225); the "glow of eternal love" that his "immortal countenance" (Antlitz) could — but cannot — reveal (213; 225). (In the myth, of course, he leaves Alkmene pregnant with Herakles, but Mann makes nothing of this in his reconstruction [see 211; 224].) This makes Jupiter's impersonation and desertion both moving and ironic; he asks for loyalty but finally cannot sustain it. Here the tight and fruitful analogy between the god and the human artist breaks down. Jupiter, "his adventure over, his longing healed, and *again entirely himself*" (227; 239: my italics), cannot remember Alkmene the way that Mann can remember Heuser or Kleist's play. Nothing in Mann's retelling suggests that Jupiter will remain privately loyal to Alkmene's face after their one long night together. (In the myth, and by implication in the play's forceful ending, Alkmene is the last of Jupiter's human loves; his withdrawal to godhead is complete, and his knowledge of the impossibility of full human love permanent.) Foregrounding Amphitryon's steadfastness, however, keeps the drama of loyal love of another at center stage; "there rises out of his annihilated being a *Credo*, a faith no longer in himself, no, but in the infallible purity and truth of the beloved's soul" (226; 238).

Both threads make their way in to the *Joseph*, as we shall see, but as questions of loyalty — to family, to German young people, to the best in German culture, to Western democracy — moved to the fore of Mann's public life, they also came to occupy a central place in his tetralogy. In particular, the drama of losing and regaining the self in and through loyal relation to others — not Olympian withdrawal — structures much of the last two-thirds of *Joseph*, and will play a prominent part in our exploration of it.

Mann's performance, however, does not stop with his loyal "reconquest" of *Amphitryon*. Having bid farewell to the players, Mann now steps before a curtain of his own construction to take leave of the play itself. His declaration of love for what has just transpired leads him to honor it one last time; with the "cheerfulness of its mysticism, the warmth of its wit," it is an "entertainment" whose perfect performance would celebrate equally "feeling and intellect" (228; 239). The language gives everything away; loyal love never takes final leave. Mann's rereading and performance celebrate a literary father, an *echtdeutsch* humanist precursor, to whom the son and his text will remain loyal. The play of this beloved father is again firmly established in the mind of his *treues* child, and its images are woven into his emerging epic of gods and men. Literary production, like human identity, begins in recognition and response to the other, not in subjective isolation or narcissistic originality, and continues in passionate *and* mindful loyalty to that relation. And like full human identity, it is ethical from the beginning, not isolated in an empty aestheticism or a self-consuming immersion in mindless, nation-deceiving unities. Loyalty is an activity, a continuous performance, preserving love and animated by it. As such, it promises a future when the beloved will reappear, when "spirit and soul and matter" will reunite in passionate, formal relation.[46]

Read aesthetically, Jupiter at the end of the play, Jupiter returned to glory, can represent a kind of narrator as well as a kind of god: conservative, mock-omniscient, single-voiced. An all-knowing narrator cannot author the tales that need to be told; Kleist's drama and Joseph's story require a more limited yet versatile narrator who can enter fully into their many voices and be changed by them. Even the god's bittersweet longing of renunciation, an emotion that Mann has always prized, now appears suspect. We know that Mann identified this feeling, which accompanied the god's conferral of undeserved favor, as the "heart of the drama." But in his performance he also moves past that point to another center of his own devising. For Jupiter finally has no narrative but autobiography; he cannot move to "educative responsibility." So the familiar equation of Mann with the imperial Jupiter and his renunciation of the beloved is, yet again, only a part of the story. Mann is working out his new artistic path through all the principal figures.[47] In refusing to be only Jupiter or to rest in the security of renunciation, Mann also leaves room for surprising, even anarchic, moments in his storytelling that are beyond Olympian control. His performance embodies, then, his own loyal lovemaking, his enthusiastic intercourse with the play that refigures artistic mediation. His narrating selfhood, unlike the god's, is permeable, spread across the characters; he is no longer only the enigmatic Zauberer but the lover welcomed with his proper name by a beloved.

Like *Amphitryon, Joseph and his Brothers* risks being little read; "everyday theater practice," everyday novel reading, is against it (228; 239). Yet Mann imagines a young director, "with brains and feeling, with the most sensuous intellectuality" (228; 239), bringing the play to life again. He would have "actors who combine the most pleasing physical gifts with an obedient sensitivity for the precise directives" he would impart to them. This aptly describes the characters in *Joseph* as well, or more accurately what the characters in *Joseph* will become. Joseph's "obedient sensitivity" to the demands of the God-story will make him both a playwright and an actor capable of constructing a drama worthy of his forebearers. Just so, Mann replays the Kleist drama (and Genesis and his other foretexts), weaving them into a new production, a revival that is also a "new word" for the future. The rejuvenating pleasure that he has drawn from his retelling, even his appropriation, of Kleist's drama, resonates through this final scene. He too can be the young Mann who restages a great God-story and who makes a political difference in doing so. Mann, now fifty-seven, tacitly imagines for himself the strength of his "youthful director" for what lies ahead, and he also, slyly and obliquely, opens his own ego to embrace the German youths who will be pleasurably instructed by his performance and politically rescued by his loyalty. So, like Jacob in "The Testing," Mann is revitalized by his love and loyalty even as its difficulties age him, and envisions himself among a line of blessing-bearers who will carry the promise of German humanism into the future.

The closing line — that Mann would "travel a long way to see such a performance" — is wonderfully paradoxical. The moon-wanderer's journey of *Joseph*'s creation will indeed be long, one with jarring turns and exiles that he can hardly imagine in 1927. At the same time the performance has been in the here and now, before our eyes, and the journey has in one sense already been completed. Mann's narrators rebuild in language the artful pleasures and authentic vision of lost eras that can still teach us how to live.

Notes

[1] "I shall be traveling in this manner about four weeks . . . . during which time, without wanting to concern myself too much with the humanistic elements, I am primarily interested in Egypt. I shall take a look at the desert, the pyramids, the sphinx, for these can be useful in some of my definite, though perhaps ulterior plans which I have laid in secret" (To Ernst Bertram, 4 Feb. 1925). Precise dating is difficult because, as is well known, Mann destroyed his diaries for this period in 1945 (as Freud, in a parallel attempt to control his historical reputation, destroyed his records in 1877 and again in 1907). The more or less familiar biographical information here is taken from Harpprecht (1995), Heilbut (1996), Hayman (1995), Prater (1995), and Bürgin and Mayer (1969).

[2] Letter to Erika Mann, 23 Dec. 1926 (*Briefe* I, 260–62).

[3] Postcard to Ernst Bertram, 24 Sept. 1927.

[4] Hayman (1995), 369: see also Bürgin and Mayer (1969), 79. Mann wrote to Bertram on 28 July that he had "finished the first section of *Joseph*." Whether this means part or all of the printed first chapter is hard to determine without the diaries for the period. To mark an outer limit, Mann gave a reading from the "first chapter" of *Joseph* in November 1927 (*DüD* 14/II, 99n). By then he had at least arrived at the section later entitled "Der Name" (IV, 89–96).

[5] Mann wrote two essays on Kleist during his career. In what follows I refer to the 1927 piece simply as the "Kleist" essay or the "Kleist" lecture. My few citations of the 1954 introduction "Heinrich von Kleist und seine Erzählungen" use the full title.

[6] Mann also delivered the lecture in Berlin in late October. He responded to Julius Bab's complimentary note about the Munich performance on 18 October, noting that his "comprehensive analysis" was already completed. He was unsure where to send the full essay for publication, since the *Rundschau* was already bringing out "Descent into Hell" in its next issue (*DüD* 14/II, 354).

[7] This passage was cut in the 1961 *Briefe* I but appears in *Ein Appell an die Vernunft: Essays* III, 1926–1933, 391. The full text, including Mann's calling Heuser "Kläuschen" and connecting him briefly to his own son Klaus ("Eissi"), appears in Erika Mann 1984, 16–19.

[8] Letter to Hans Mayer, 23 June 1950 (*Briefe* III, 152).

[9] The lecture first appeared as "Die Grosse Szene in Kleists *Amphitryon*" in the *Vossiche Zeitung*, 16 Oct. 1927. The date (1926) given in Bürgin and Meyer (1969, 79) for the publication of the full essay is an error. This is a popular mistake, since it is repeated in *Essays of Three Decades* and, as noted, by Mann himself.

[10] *DüD* 14/II, 353. See also the one paragraph "Wie stehst du zu Kleist?" (XIII, 828). It is possible that Mann knew of the November 1927 production of the play in Prague, directed by Dr. K. J. Schwarz, in which the same actor played the roles of Jupiter and Amphitryon (Reeve 1993, 58).

[11] Betsy Draine offers a fine formulation of these ideas in a more theoretical idiom: "The texts in dialogue within any given piece of writing come from some place and some time, and they carry their histories with them . . . . The discourses within a writer come thickly or thinly, in short or long strings, crossed and recrossed by others, but always bearing with them the 'passions, humors, feelings, impressions' that sealed them, at some historical time, in the writer's memory. If to bear such historically rooted passions within one's word-hoard is to be authorial, not writerly, then every writer is in some sense authorial, just as every writer is in some sense writerly — driven by the exigencies of language 'itself'" ("Chronotope and Intertext: The Case of Jean Rhys' *Quartet*" in Clayton and Rothstein 1991, 324–25). The internal quote is from Roland Barthes, "The Death of the Author" (*Image, Music, Text*, 147).

[12] Mann and Kleist received similar criticism for their attempts to mix comedy and intellectual seriousness. This American critique of *Amphitryon* anticipates what some German reviewers said of the "Americanized" *Joseph the Provider*: "The more earnest scenes as he wrote them are true to themselves, though unfortunately they do not mix with the lighter. You wish only that the ingredients had been served on separate evenings, not stewed all together" (Reeve 1993, 53, 58). Kleist's youthful interest in what Mann termed "moral pedagogy" reads like a parody of Mann's own efforts and seductions: in his kindly 1954 introduction to an English version of Kleist's tales, Mann describes the young writer wooing his pupil and fiancée by assigning her an essay on "the aims and satisfactions of authentic married life" ("Heinrich von Kleist und seine Erzählungen" [IX, 825]).

[13] "Treue" was Mann's epithet of choice for Joachim Ziemssen in *The Magic Mountain*, and it figures in several of his other texts. His reaction to his brother Heinrich's actions after the Bolshevik putsch in Munich in 1920 offers a particularly revealing example. Heinrich was the butt of political cartoons for his flight from the city's violence; Thomas confined his criticism to questioning his brother's loyalty, comparing this flight to his similar panic during their father's final illness. Thomas, of course, had kept his *Treue* and had earned his dying father's praise for it. Love and loyalty are repeatedly intertwined in Mann's writing to the young during this period; his 1926 Christmas letter to his beloved daughter Erika begins "I must thank you for all your love and loyalty" (*Briefe* I, 260).

[14] Heftrich (1993) offers a valuable reprise of Mann's "private mythology" (245) surrounding "das Augenspiel," beginning with "Little Herr Friedemann" (243ff.). While my reading moves in a different direction, I draw on his analysis in my succeeding comments on "the gaze."

[15] To elaborate Mann's mode of sublimation, here is an excerpt from his diary entry for 26 July 1921, written on a hot day while "reworking" the earlier "pedagogic" essay "Goethe and Tolstoy": "some gardeners busy in the garden, one of whom, young, beardless, with brown arms and open shirt, gave me quite a turn. Spent the remainder of the day thinking out future plans, feeling listless, and somewhat ill from lack of exercise. A wealth of thoughts on education — the importance of enthusiasm, love, dedication. Read in *Wilhelm Meister's Travels*. Astounded at the truly Goethean aura of *The Magic Mountain*. The lecture will in this sense be an appropriate, full-fledged counterpart to the novel."

"Goethe and Tolstoy" contains this description of Goethe's development as a pedagogue, one that Mann plainly reenacted: "Nobody has ever loved his own ego, nobody was ever egocentric, in the sense of conceiving of his own ego as a cultural task and toiling early and late in pursuance of it, without reaping, almost as though by accident, educational influence in the outer world, and the joy and dignity of a leader and former of youth" (IX, 150–51; *Essays*, 160).

[16] That Heuser was the figure in the essay was confirmed by Mann years later (*TB*, 20 Feb. 1952 and 16 July 1950), where he joins the pantheon of Armin Martens ("Tonio Kröger"), Willri Timpe (*The Magic Mountain*), and Paul Ehrenberg (*Doctor Faustus*). As the dates indicate, Mann's personal loyalty to Heuser extended well beyond the *Joseph* years. Ten years after the fact Mann spent an emotional evening rereading at length his 1927 diaries and musing on his "passion" for Heuser (*TB*, 21 Mar. 1937).

[17] The earliest ancient source is Hesiod fragment 195 MW: "The beginning of the Hesiodic *Apsis* . . . narrates in detail the circumstances surrounding [Herakles'] conception" (Gantz 1993, 374). Fifth-century writers commonly credited Amphitryon, not the god, with fatherhood (Herodotus, Bakchylides). The mythic record is most in dispute over the kind of deception Zeus practiced on the couple (Gantz 1993, 375 gives the complex history and citations). Sadly, Sophocles' play *Amphitryon* has not survived, but it is irresistible to speculate about the consequences for psychoanalysis if the young Freud could have read both it and *Oedipus the King* together. The rhyme aside, a few of Kleist's *Amphitryon*'s early lines — confident and direct — could almost come from the *Oedipus*:

Dann werd' ich auf des Rätsels Grund gelangen,
Und wehe! ruf' ich, wer mich hintergangen.
Then the riddle's answer I shall achieve
And woe, cry I, to any who deceive.

[18] Mann goes back and forth, in no pattern that I can see, between the Greek and Roman names for the gods. I have followed his lead with Zeus/Jupiter, and have used Hermes rather than Mercury simply because it is the preferred name for this god in the *Joseph*.

[19] Loyalty thus conceived is a counterforce to the frequently analyzed erotic "visitations" ("Heimsuchungen") that haunted Mann's imagination and ravaged a number of his characters. The Kleist essay is one site where this counterdynamic — love in service of the ethical — is worked out.

[20] In *Essays* III, 391, editors Hermann Kurze and Stephan Stachorski comment that Mann wants to be both himself and the honored, godlike Nobel Prize winner (awarding him the palm two years early). Mann termed Jupiter a "Künstlergeist" who "woos" life, is rejected, and triumphantly learns to be satisfied with his remote godliness. Mann's self-consciousness about the "identity" between himself and the god is important in what follows. While Mann does not cite it, it is worth remembering that the tale of Zeus weaving a mantle for his bride, a mantle which interlaced Ocean and Earth, is one of the most archaic of myths, and that weaving remained a central metaphor in the classical imagination for conjugal and even for political interconnections. See Scheid and Svenbro (1996), passim.

[21] In "On the German Republic," arguably the most erotic political speech of our time, Mann described *Wilhelm Meister*'s view of the theater as "the free, sensuous, erotic sphere." *Wilhelm Meister* is important also in this context because, in Mann's view, it inaugurated the humanistic shift from *Innerlichkeit*, the special German, idealistic mastery of the inner life, to political awareness and responsibility (see "The Spirit and Essence of The German Republic," the 1924 memorial speech for Walther Rathenau, XI, 853–60).

[22] In "Survivre: Journal de bord" (*Parages*) Derrida poses this quest for origin as the "demand" (insistence, order, petition) for narrative finality and truth: "Tell us exactly what happened." For Derrida, you cannot narrate narrative's origin because that too would only be another narrative, but you can return to an originary scene of demand (*Reader* 260). Mann's own writing about narrative is of course more traditional, but his actual practice resembles Derrida's conception closely.

[23] See Wysling 1967, 150, and chapter 1. i above.

[24] Koelb writes of "Goethe and Tolstoy" (1984, 33): "Such an irony is antirhetorical in that it is nonpartisan: it introduces conflicting views and opinions, not to champion one against the other but to play with both. It is . . . a procedure one would associate with the Dichter rather than the Schriftsteller." So while "Goethe and Tolstoy" properly belongs to the persuasive sphere, it remains "playful and sly" in the manner and mode of the Dichter.

[25] Compare Mann's comment on Max Reinhardt in the third "Briefe aus Deutschland" sent to *Dial*: "the most interesting theater that has ever been . . . a theater which profited from appealing to the sense of criticism . . . " (XIII, 285).

[26] To my knowledge, Jonas Lesser (1952, 306–7) was the first to note this parallel. There is an unexpressed poignancy in Mann's reconquest of the play; Kleist himself never saw his play performed. *Amphitryon* did not reach the stage until April 1899 (Reeve 1993, 54).

[27] We saw a related move in the 1948 "Foreword": there Mann initially belittled the ancillary writings to the novel, then gradually reasserted their importance. See chapter 1, v.

[28] In this sense it picks up threads first woven at the end of Mann's novel *Royal Highness*: "But what is it that at last gave you confidence in me, and led me to real-life study of public affairs? Does he who knows love really know nothing about life?" (II, 363; *RH*, 338).

[29] This reading obviously differs from Manfred Dierks's strong account of the *Joseph* novels' (indeed, all of Mann's writing) anchoring in Schopenhauer and Nietzsche, and then diversifying through the "systemic" interrelations of many figures and ideas in Mann's textual web (1972). Dierks portrays Jung, Freud, and Mann as descendants of Schopenhauer, a shared heritage that sanctioned Mann's use of Jung's ideas while maintaining his connection, personal and intellectual, to Freud. In my view, Mann's actual writing generated complementary currents of which he was only partially aware, and which constitute a neglected field of self-shaping.

[30] Susan von Rohr Scaff's interesting paper (1990) on the "historical and flexible" nature of Mannian archetypes complements my discussion here. Scaff reads Mann more as an intellectual and cultural historian, and anchors his view of immanent archetype in Hegel, Eliade, and Cassirer; my reading foregrounds Mann the narrativist and performer.

[31] Reuben's "tomfoolery" ("gescherzt") with Jacob's "current favorite" Bilhah occurs because he set out to humiliate his mother's younger competitor by spying on her in the bath and got carried away (85; 52). Far from supplanting Jacob or desiring his mother, he wanted Jacob to restore Leah to her full status within the patriarchal household. Jacob's attachment for Bilhah was particularly galling to the sons of Leah because Rachel, the true wife, had just died. So Mann's humor and ingenious plotting provides perfect cover; this is no Oedipal substitution, Bilhah for Leah, but its opposite: the mother returned to the father's embrace (336; 222). Jacob's hyperbolic denunciation of his first-born, whom he likens to Ham and to the Behemoth-hippopotamus that "in Egyptian gossip" kills its father and assaults its mother, mainly shows his eagerness to displace his elder sons in order to elevate Joseph. The tale takes its broadly comic tone not from Reuben's alleged rebellion but from Joseph's tattling report of the event to his father.

[32] Letter to Agnes Meyer, 17 Feb. 1948 (*Thomas Mann-Agnes E. Meyer Briefwechsel*, 694). Mann does discuss Oedipus briefly in his 1951 short piece "Bemerkungen zu dem Roman *Der Erwählte*" (XI, 687–91).

[33] Mann returns to this passage yet again in his longest discussion of education and the artist, in "Goethe's Career as a Man of Letters" (XI, 340; *Essays*, 49).

[34] *Sketch of My Life*, 70 (my italics) and 45 (italics in the original). To repeat, Jonas Lesser wrote an excellent early account of this subject (1952).

[35] Richard Lanham's *Homo rhetoricus* offers an apt way to describe Eliezer as both personality and pedagogue. "Rhetorical man" emphasizes "minute concentration on the word, how to speak it, write it, remember it." He warehouses countless narratives, sees other people as mythological types, regards "behavior as performance," loves reciting and reading aloud, and "nourishes an acute sense of a social situation" (1976, 2). Joseph too has many of these traits and owes much of his success to them. At the same time he constantly finds himself in circumstances which require more original thought than *bricoleur* virtuosity: from the "Grove of Adonis" and his two falls all the way to the new God-play he must author at the end. I am grateful to Michael Bissell for the connection to Lanham.

[36] A pivotal phrase from "Death in Venice" (VIII, 490; *Stories of Three Decades*, 412).

[37] Heinrich Mann summarized the tone of the "Prelude" this way: "I have a particular feeling for the eager earnestness in the tone of your dialectics, behind which there appears humor and even travesty, and behind that eagerness once again" (*Briefwechsel* 1984, 212; *Letters* 1998, 153).

[38] Dietmar Mieth explores some of these same issues from a different perspective in *Epik und Ethik* (1976), especially in the sections "Gottvertrauen-Selbstvertrauen" (98–104) and "Person und Interaktion" (204–5).

[39] "Angesicht" occurs three times in his brief narration. The "face" of the beloved is of course the inaugural image in the first paragraph of the "Kleist" lecture. It is worth noting that the Hebrew for confronting the text, "standing before the text," is literally to be "in the face of the text."

While not central to my reading, there is a good deal of fine-grain, "direct" linguistic evidence of mutual self-influence between the "Kleist" essay and the opening scenes of the *Joseph*: Joseph's "Hier bin ich" ("Here am I") and Zeus's "Ich war's" ("It was I"), with their attendant ambiguities, is the most obvious and recurrent example. Jonas Lesser (1952, 303–9) offers a number of linguistic parallels and echoes, particularly those connecting Joseph and Zeus. He argues for *Joseph* as the controlling text throughout, shaping the reading of *Amphitryon* and even the essay's language.

[40] The dramatic situation of Jacob and Rebecca reverses this nicely: in the hoaxing it is the mistress and mother who gives the words and substituted identity to the downcast chosen one, Jacob. In *The Tales of Jacob* Isaac is blind, both in fact and half-willfully in spirit, and Jacob undertakes his doubling amidst much comic trembling and shaking. This gives us a playful, if silent, inversion of Oedipus's self-blinding; the father can see the "true chosen one" only when he can no longer see.

[41] The narrator also tells us that Ishmael has another impediment: he is reluctant to harm Isaac because of their old bond. Ishmael had been expelled for "tomfoolery" with his beautiful half brother and remained loyal to that memory, that face. In this sly reconstruction, gay love saves the blessing (192; 126).

[42] For a strong theoretical exploration of this, see Derrida's *The Post-Card*, esp. "Freud's Legacy" (292–337).

[43] This scene closely follows Kleist's *Der zerbrochne Krug*, where Judge Adam pursues Eve and compels her into submission by threatening to conscript her true love. Leaving her bedroom hurriedly, he accidentally knocks over the pitcher ("Krug"). Eve's mother mistakes Judge Adam for the true beloved and hauls the poor innocent into court to pay for the damages he caused. So Judge Adam presides at the trial of the lover, knowing that he himself is the guilty party. During the trial Eve asks her lover why he didn't confess to the crime even though he knows he is innocent, since to do so would prove his love and loyalty to her. Behind her question is a ghostly other, just hinted in the play, of a divine, incorruptible judge who may or may not have been "present" as well.

[44] This line echoes Freud's "Gradiva" study (*SE* IX 34–37).

[45] Letter to Ernst Bertram, 28 Dec. 1926 (*Briefe* I, 263).

[46] In Eliezer's cosmic theology, the Promise is the Apocalypse, when God shall end the world and begin again (433–34; 288). In the novel's more soul-sized universe, the promise has many intervening fulfillments.

[47] This direction is new but certainly not unique; there are a number of precedents and anticipations in Mann's work. Perhaps most significant is Hans Castorp's hard-won proclamation near the end of the "Snow" chapter of *The Magic Mountain*: "*For the sake of goodness and love, man shall let death have no sovereignty over his thoughts.*" (III, 686: *MM,* 487: italics in the original). Just before he arrives at this epiphany Hans meditates over his long-standing intimacy with the past and with death. He sees that he must "keep *loyalty* to death in my heart" ("Ich will dem Tode *Treue* halten in meinem Herzen"; italics mine) but that such loyalty must be limited, contained. Hans's declaration has several ironic frames within the novel that control its absoluteness and its sentiment: it is emphatically Hans's own claim, and one that he quickly forgets — at least consciously — in the days that follow his great adventure. Seen in this light, the "Kleist" lecture reworks Hans's affirmation; loyalty interwoven with love makes more explicit the "goodness" in Hans's sentence. Similarly, "death," for all its allure and inevitability, finally allies itself with the hermetic narcissism of a Jupiter. So the intertextual connections broaden out; in one sense, at least, it is still "Snowing."

Mann performing at the Prussian Academy for the Arts in March 1932 before a specially invited audience of 300, including the French ambassador. His brother Heinrich is fourth from the left. The photograph captures Mann in full regalia and apparently in mid-sentence, just turning a page as his audience applauds what they have heard. Courtesy of Thomas Mann Archives, Zurich.

Mann reading in the family circle, 1940,
included despite the low quality of the photograph
because it is the only surviving image of him doing so.
Courtesy of Thomas Mann Archives, Zurich.

Mann performing for his grandsons Frido and Toni, 1948.
Courtesy of Thomas Mann Archives, Zurich.

Mann reading from "Goethe and Democracy" at Oxford,
1949, after receiving an honorary D. Litt.
Courtesy of Thomas Mann Archives, Zurich.

The reading at the Stadttheater in Lübeck, May 1955,
described by Herbert Lehnert in chapter 1, part vi.
Mann is probably reading from "Tonio Kröger," with
the Joseph *and* Felix Krull *volumes awaiting their turn.*
Courtesy of Thomas Mann Archives, Zurich.

3: "Freud's Position in the History of Modern Thought": The Containment of *Totem and Taboo*

I endeavor to make heaviness light; my ideal is clarity, and when I write long sentences . . . I make it a point, not without success I believe, to keep each periodic structure completely lucid and "speakable" ("Sprechbarkeit").

— Thomas Mann to Irita van Doren, 28 Aug. 1951

I am gradually coming to see the dangers of history, which obscures through false analogies the uniqueness of a situation and leads a certain kind of youth into madness. I suffer over the distortion of the German countenance [des deutschen Antlitzes]. I am thinking of turning a birthday article on Hauptmann into a kind of manifesto in which I appeal to the conscience of youth, whose ear I have.

— Thomas Mann to Ernst Bertram, 8 July 1921

The process of cure is accomplished in a relapse into love, if we combine all the many components of the sexual instinct under the term "love"; and such a relapse is indispensable, for the symptoms on account of which the treatment has been undertaken are nothing other than precipitates of earlier struggles connected with repression or the return of the repressed, and they can only be washed away by a fresh high tide of the same passions. Every psycho-analytic attempt is an attempt at liberating repressed love which has found a meagre outlet in the compromise of a symptom . . . . in analytic psychotherapy too the reawakened passion, whether it is love or hate, invariably chooses as its object the figure of the doctor . . . .

The doctor has been a stranger, and must endeavor to become a stranger again after the cure; he is often at a loss what advice to give the patients he has cured as to how in real life they can use their recovered capacity to love.

— Sigmund Freud, "Jensen's *Gradiva*"

I

MANN'S HISTORY WITH FREUD IS AN INTRICATE subject. Archival evidence — books bought and annotated — suggests that he did not read Freud systematically, or even very seriously, until the mid-

1920s, when *Totem and Taboo* and several other texts cast their spell over the beginning of the *Joseph* novels.[1] Some earlier contact with Freud — or at least with his ideas — certainly did occur, but it is difficult to determine what Mann absorbed from his own reading, and what he took from discussions with friends and from the general cultural climate in which both he and Freud wrote. For example, there are rough connections between his 1907 "Delusions and Dreams in W. Jensen's *Gradiva*" narrative and both "Death in Venice" and Hans Castorp's dream of Hippe in *The Magic Mountain*.[2] Mann acknowledged in a 1925 interview that Freud had some influence on his most famous novella.[3] On another occasion he claimed, in a generous anachronism, that psychoanalysis had been a general influence on his work "from its beginning."[4] The ambivalent portrait of Edhin (Erwin) Krokowski in *The Magic Mountain* seems to be both a knowing exaggeration of proselytizing Freudians and a critique of analysis's early, reductive claims for power.[5] The portrait reflects Mann's own ambivalence about psychoanalysis. On the one hand, its confident "science" offered him a powerful means of unmasking character. Yet in the hands of an unsympathetic critic it could unmask text and author as well. In that threatening circumstance no secrets would be safe, and no artistic processes privileged. The power and authority of its language could also overmaster literary style. So its "knowledge" had to be set aside in the name of continuing creativity — and privacy. Tonio Kröger and particularly Aschenbach make related renunciations.[6]

This view acquired several complicating overlays during the 1920s as Mann began to read Freud in earnest. Archival evidence again suggests that he knew Freud's work from 1913 forward much better than the earlier writings. The first four volumes of his 1924–25 edition of the *Gesammelte Werke* are unmarked, read (if at all) "without the pencil" as Mann liked to remark, while portions of the remaining six volumes are annotated and underlined.[7] Mann first read *Totem and Taboo* (1913) in this edition — "shamefully late," as he later wrote to Freud (*Briefe* I, 296). During this period he read a number of Freud's later works; "On Narcissism," *The Future of an Illusion,* and *Beyond the Pleasure Principle* are all quoted directly in the 1929 essay. As he did so he may have detected the increased problematizing and caution entering Freud's work in the years just before the war. In addition, Mann's motives for studying Freud expanded; they were now civic as well as literary, and he most probably read pieces such as "Mass Psychology and Ego Analysis" and *The Ego and the Id* in good part for his political lectures.

Yet despite his new enthusiasm and motives, Mann retained his earlier distrust of Freud's method. This double attitude — acceptance and suspicion, trust and distrust — makes for a welter of crosscurrents in both the 1929 essay and the tetralogy. For example, Mann both used and resisted psychoanalytic reduction. Predictably, he continued to connect any single-minded explanations with Freud's medical, positivistic side and to reject them. At the same time he wanted to use some of Freud's more reductive conclusions for his political pedagogy, where confident assertiveness was, he felt, vital to persuasion. So, like many readers of Freud before and after him, he used psychoanalysis's open-ended ambiguities or reductions as his different performances required. But his first wish was to keep Freud's most disturbing insights within boundaries, under control. This meant that he had to check Freud in two different directions: as the authoritarian theorist of process, especially artistic process, whose claims erased ambiguity and disabled creativity; and as the prophet of the unbounded psyche, whose dark and violent recesses threatened to undermine knowledge and political conviction. These contrary impulses play out in remarkable ways in the complexities of *Joseph*'s inquiry into human nature.[8]

The permutations of Mann's rereading of Freud in the 1929 essay and the *Joseph* novels will occupy the rest of this chapter. After a brief account of the lecture's circumstances, I'll make my way through the essay, imitating Mann's own practice of writing glosses on particular passages in Freud, and revisiting passages from the "Kleist" essay and the tetralogy. My central claim is that Mann's reading of Freud, particularly of *Totem and Taboo*, is molded by the "Kleist" lecture's countermodel of identity, by his expanding political purposes, and by the powerful gravitational field of *Joseph*. My claim requires the critical exploration of three interconnected subjects: (1) the rhetorical and especially the pedagogical strategies that shape the essay's organization and performance (including several gaps or sleights-of-hand in its argument); (2) Mann's reading, and half-deliberate misreading, of *Totem and Taboo* and their elaborations in the *Joseph*; (3) the intertextual play of *The Tales of Jacob* in the essay's making, and in turn its influence on the tetralogy. I am, throughout, fascinated by how these involved, penumbral interactions play out, and in the revisions in our understanding of both *Joseph* and the essay that they generate.

II

. . . it is consistent with Mann's conception of himself as an artist in the tradition of Goethe and Tolstoy, those for whom the making public of the private was the foundation of a career. In Mann's case, at least, we observe that this tendency means not only that the private world and private modes of utterance move into the public but that the forms and demands of public expression more and more shape the private world.

— Clayton Koelb, *Thomas Mann's "Goethe and Tolstoy"*

And yet, this is a time and a world where it makes almost no difference what we talk about — we always talk about one and the same thing. Categories crumble, the borderlines between different spheres of human thought become unessential. Everything is connected to everything else — and in truth it has always been so: only, we were not conscious of it.

— Thomas Mann, "The Theme of the *Joseph* Novels:
An Address to the Library of Congress"

The years between the "Kleist" and the 1929 "Freud" lecture were, for Mann, filled with unremitting hard work, demanding schedules, and frequent performances. Even the briefest of surveys makes clear his increasing immersion in political matters. Lectures taken on tour in late 1927 included "Freiheit und Vornehmheit" ("Freedom and Nobility") and "Natur und Nation." An interview in the French journal *Comoedia* blandly urging better relations between the two countries led to preposterous charges that he was "kow-towing to Paris." "Kultur und Sozialismus" ("Culture and Socialism"), of April 1928, promoted a marriage of advanced politics and conservative culture: Moscow and Greece, Marx and Hölderlin. He would bring a similar message to the youthful audience of the "Freud" lecture a year later. They are to be in the vanguard of preserving German self-understanding and tradition in the new democratic future (Burns 1995, 62–63). In July he became embroiled in a distracting controversy over a new, abridged edition of *Reflections*. A partisan reader claimed that Mann omitted or altered its conservative elements to suit his more liberal "new views." One Munich paper even urged him to leave the city, and Heidelberg obligingly offered him a new home. So public reactionary assaults on his character were already a fact of life before he began the "Freud" essay. His heavy performance schedule in late 1928 included several major appearances. In the midst of them he began the "Lessing" essay with the frank intention of unhorsing the nationalists in the literary academy and ending their seemingly endless dispute over the relative merits of the chthonic

Dichter and the cosmopolitan, inferior Schriftsteller. Its publication in January of 1929 offered a *Joseph*-shaped rereading of Lessing as a defender of the true enlightenment, a "patriarchal" founder of a mythical type, and an opponent of "provincial nationalism" and fascism. In sum, there was a crescendo of performances on psychological and political themes leading up to the "Freud" essay.

Without the diaries it is impossible to say exactly how far Mann had progressed in the *Joseph* manuscript by April 1929. Despite the many interruptions his hectic schedule created, he worked as steadily as he could. Various comments in letters place him near the juncture of chapters 6 and 7 of *The Tales of Jacob:* the wedding night and the substitution of Leah; the quarrel between the sisters over the mandrake; the ambiguous auguries preceding the birth of Joseph.[9]

Mann's first performance of the "Freud" essay took place on 16 May, 1929 at the Auditorium Maximum at the University of Munich. His audience was the Democratic Students' Club. It was, he wrote to Ernst Bertram, "an enormous throng of youths" (*DüD* 14/II, 360). Some of Mann's earlier lectures (e.g., "On the German Republic") exhorted patriotic young Germans, but also the educated and nationalistic middle class so suspicious of the cosmopolitan new republic. Here he focused almost exclusively on Klaus Heuser's generation. In 1929–1930 German youth numbered 9 million. Of these, 4.3 million belonged to some youth organization, "and most of those opposed the democratic reforms of the Weimar period and had a marked preference for *völkische* ideas and traditions" (Craig 1995, 25). University enrollments increased 55 percent during the 1920s, and the great majority of these students were aggressively and narrowly nationalistic (Burns 1995, 60). By 1931, 70 percent of the Nazi SA members in Berlin were under thirty. So the club was itself a group already under siege. It was a smallish, minority organization at the university, unsupported by its actual political counterpart, the German Democratic Party in the Reichstag. All the more reason for Mann to tender his support, and all the more reason for his satisfaction at the large turnout and generous reception he received. Even the relatively conservative *Münchner Neueste Nachrichten* reviewed the evening positively (*DüD* 14: II, 360). If the Nazis' goal was indeed to create a "state-dominated youth culture . . . by tying itself to all their favorite ideas" and frustrations, then groups such as this very much needed guidance and support from a figure such as Mann (Craig 1995, 26–27). And by 1929 new, concrete dangers have been added to the suspicions that Mann had always harbored about public performance. He now not only risked the dilettantism of the actor and the disabling memories of his actress sister's suicide, but also vitriolic abuse in the right-wing press and even physical violence against himself and his family.

Mann views his student audience with a combination of condescension and empathy.[10] "Verwirrung" ("confusion," "perplexity") is their hallmark, and Mann uses the term repeatedly in the essay. They are confused by the intellectual crosscurrents in which they must make political choices, and by constant, reductive appeals to their nationalistic pride. In *Joseph* Mann uses "Verwirrung" primarily to characterize the seventeen-year-old Joseph before the angel at Shechem (536; 360), the virginal Mut in the early stages of love with her "pedagogue" Joseph ("Wirre": 1111; 736), and "little Rachel," whose uneducated bravery and child-like readiness for life keep her permanently young (e.g., 321ff, 363; 211ff, 240). All owe something to "die süße Verwirrung" of Alkmene at the end of the "Kleist" performance (IX, 228; 239). As part of his "new pedagogy," Mann justifies his students' confusion with several sympathetic comments. These subjects are indeed paradoxical and difficult, he assures them. Even professional scientists may be duped in the same way that some of them — or their fellows — have been taken in (X, 269–70; *PM*, 184–85). Reactionary forces "disguise" themselves well, and young people must guard against their "cunning trick" of transforming outworn ideas into current "hot" news ("Lebensneuigkeit" [270; 185]). Other reassurances follow: students need not feel ashamed of their mistakes or gullibility; the concepts may be shopworn, but their crafty presentation by conservative ideologues makes them tempting.

Mann's young men seem, in other words, to be the younger brethren of Hans Castorp, the "simple but canny hero" he had come to know very well indeed. Like Hans they are forgivably bewildered fence-sitters, suspended between alternatives: they lean intellectually toward the democracy their organization espouses, yet feel the allure of fascist simplicities and pageantry. If Hans, poised between East and West on a twilit Holstein lake, represented the German spirit, they too are a representative population, Hänschen multiplied (III, 218; *The Magic Mountain*, 152). The pedagogy they require is a cousin of the "alchemistisch-hermetische Pädagogik" that Hans Castorp underwent above Davos: more worldly, perhaps, but definitely a relation. Mann shrewdly tries to isolate them from their high-flying, Icarean brothers, singing reactionary songs and making the Roman salute as they parade through the city streets; such cheap theater "is no longer unfamiliar to us," he says, and he hopes that his charges accept his offer of solidarity and remain detached observers of the Nazis' hollow performances (273–74;

189–90). Mann constructs his audience as simple, puzzled, and receptive.

The Nazis aestheticize politics crudely with rallies and parades, but other conservatives are more artful. The loftiest example that Mann cites is Hans Pfitzner and his *Palestrina*. Mann had honored the opera in the "On Virtue" chapter of *Reflections* a decade earlier, and now in 1929 (though not in later years) he still carefully separates Pfitzner from the Nazis. But he also repeats his conclusion of 1918: honor Pfitzner's achievement but leave him in his backward-looking melancholia and "sympathy with death." His art may thrill, but it is divorced from the ethical and cannot guide us (XI, 423–26).

Nonetheless, the more dangerous dissemblers remain not only the (unnamed) Nazis but all the reactionary intellectuals who disguise their hostility to life in a youthful, future-affirming costume (271; 186–87). Mann explores the disguise image, drawing on the symbolic repertory of his earlier writing: Old, backward men are among you disguised as youths (the loose-toothed "Socratic lover" of "Death in Venice"). Like the hags in Hans Castorp's "Snow" vision who devour the future, they draw energy from a revolutionary spirit they hope to turn to their own destructive purposes. It is a haunting, palimpsestic image Mann urges on his charges: look right through your youthful university comrade in his fascist costume and see the old wolf, the seducer, the dissembler, the devourer at work. The Nazis acknowledge sublimation, but only in order to move beneath it to the primitive, not to advance toward new levels of civilization. And when they succeed they create a new monster: youth in a parody-disguise of its own — brown shirts, swastika armbands — that lends its "biologic charm" to the evils of old age. The fascists offer, says Mann, the "doubtful light of a very early dawn," citing the aphorism from Nietzsche's *Morgenröte* with which the essay began (271; 187). But no young person who embraces the goals of psychoanalysis — that is, who reads Freud and understands him as their pedagogue does — can succumb to these grotesque charades and self-betrayals.

Comparing Mann's conception of his audience to that of the "Kleist" gathering two years earlier reveals his shift in emphasis: the openly erotic address of the former has been redirected to both group representation and an overt political agenda. Yet important continuities remain: youth must still be instructed in authentic loyalty. In both lectures the individual will of each character or audience member must choose the future and reject the glamorized false substitutions. This brings into view another intertextual thread: Mann again places himself, half-knowingly, in the position of the admonishing Jacob urging right loyalties on his Joseph-audience, *ephoebi* tempted by the erotic sympathy with death and the past that cult goddesses and cult politics parade before them. His pedagogy, however sublimated and generalized in 1929, still displays the eroticism and father-love that empowered his performance of the "Kleist" essay. It also contains a thread of anxiety, not unlike that of Jacob before his unruly, tradition-threatening sons at Shechem.

Mann's sympathy for his university students extends to the rigidities of the education system in which they find themselves. The official late nineteenth century curriculum remains that of the "monistic Enlightenment," with the "confusion and narrowness of its specialization" that eliminated all "higher human questions" in the "dreary rigor of its methods of research" (269; 183). Mann knows what students, then and now, complain about: the dehumanized, "irrelevant" regimen of their disciplinary schooling. The competing counter-curriculum proclaimed by the anti-intellectual Nazi pedagogues and their more sophisticated conservative brethren celebrates the primitive and the irrational: a leveling, meta-disciplinary chaos. Mann's "third way" offers a curriculum based on the reunification of science with the arts in which both are seen as "genuine instruments of knowledge" (269; 184).[11] The arts parallel psychoanalysis in that they both traffic in the buried and unseen, and make knowledge claims that don't fit with strict disciplinary criteria. This reinserts emotion and the exploration of the primitive into official learning without succumbing to their excesses. It also suggests that ethical choices may flow from this course of study, as they decidedly do not from the highly disciplinary, objectifying curriculum currently in place. The lecture itself seeks to distill this curriculum, with Freud supplying the wise science, Nietzsche and Novalis the joyful wisdom, and Mann highlighting their commonalities within his moderating pedagogic frame.

Mann seems unaware — whether by design or otherwise — that his arguments for a more open and liberal curriculum have their own small ironies in his performance. His actual pedagogy at this point in the essay is one of inoculation; his Hanses and Josephs need to be vaccinated against the known tyrannies of the monistic Enlightenment, and the counter-tyrannies of the cultic irrationalists. The echoes of Settembrini and Naphta, contending pedagogues of *The Magic Mountain*, are unmistakable, and Mann seeks to supplant them by avoiding their hypocrisies and their hectoring manner. He energetically sets himself apart from the chthonic caesarism of the fascist demagogues that both he and his charges have heard in similar Munich gatherings. But schoolmasterish condescensions remain; he assumes the position of a formal lecturer, and his charges, urged to exercise their free will and ethical loyalty, are kept passive by his authoritative delivery. Were there a few Castorpian headshakings and private demurs in the audience?

III

Psychoanalysis skirts religious faith [the Origin] in order to expend it in the form of literary discourse.

— Julia Kristeva, *Tales of Love*

In its implications the distortion of a text resembles a murder; the difficulty is not in perpetrating the deed, but in getting rid of the traces.

— Sigmund Freud, *Moses and Monotheism*

The 1929 lecture is in nearly every way organized around its projected performance. At heart an essay of containment and artful transformation, Mann sets out to both honor and control Freud's ideas. In this it models (with even greater caution) the tetralogy's careful celebration of the violent and bloody "depths beneath" from which civilization sprang. Its purpose, he explicitly affirmed, was instructional. Two weeks before delivery he described it as "a wide-ranging essay on the problem of revolution, *full of pedagogical intentions* and in fact serving the purposes of those who recognize the psychoanalytical movement as the only manifestation of modern anti-rationalism — which in no way offers a pretext for reactionary misuse."[12] This pedagogy shapes, from the beginning, the view of Freud as a contemporary figure who embodies and continues traditions — often misunderstood traditions — of German *Geistesgeschichte*. Mann places Freud's "revolutionary" teachings in the carefully prepared soil of earlier, more familiar German writers, particularly Nietzsche and Novalis. Specifically, the Nietzschean notion of revolution as both conservative and progressive, and Novalis's commitment to self-transcendence rather than self-immersion, sanction young Germans to see both Freud and the current political struggle in the proper light.[13]

Mann's sympathy with the complexities of Freud's project and his lingering distrust of Freud's analytic power can be seen in the elaborate framing in which the 1929 essay places Freud's ideas. He arranges the essay's sections with this containment policy in mind; dangerous or subversive ideas are carefully handled, like explosive material, and given to his students in well-reinforced packages. More positively, Mann also contains Freud's analysis by modulating some of his ideas into keys more harmonious with his own artistic and political tasks. Intertextuality also plays a role in this policy of containment; *The Tales of Jacob* could well be described as an even more risky struggle for control, with the dispersing forces of the "bottomless past" of the "Prelude" and the reductive, pessimistic sides of Freud's inquiry continually threatening to unseat the novel's own version of chastened humanism and a future ripe with blessing. The essay both reinforces — and rehearses — what the novels require.

Unlike the manuscript of "Kleist's Amphitryon," where we are sure of the portion of the essay used in performance, the two texts of the 1929 essay make the matter less clear. It is an inevitable problem in interpreting Mann, since he regularly altered his lectures when preparing them for publication in a collection. The first version appeared in the May/June 1929 issue of *Die psychoanalytische Bewegung* (and was submitted to the journal before the lecture was delivered). The second version came out later that summer in the August issue of *Neue Rundschau*. In addition to small editing changes, the August version also deletes nine passages of between two lines and two pages from the May/June version.[14] To my knowledge, there is no transcript or detailed account of the lecture that might help decide this, or even a record of how long Mann's performance took.[15] Possibilities abound: the lecture could have been delivered directly from either version, or formed from a composite of the two versions, or even from an independent third ur-version that has not survived. On balance, however, it seems most probable that the lecture was based almost entirely on the May/June version. A well-paced reading of it takes between eighty and ninety minutes. This is long, but not too long, for a performance, and one that Mann happily practiced even at eighty (Katia Mann 1975, 151). It is also a time frame all too familiar to the student audience; the most common lecture period in German universities was ninety minutes. Rhetorically, the first version also seems more lecture than essay; eight of the nine passages under discussion are more oral in mode, and their content seems directed toward a younger, less informed audience.[16] This manuscript was then edited into a rather more adult version that appeared two months later.[17]

The opening pages (*Essays* III, 122–24) recall the "Kleist" lecture in subject matter and, to a certain extent, tone. So far as we know, there was no Klaus Heuser to focus and intensify the sublimated eroticism of Mann's pedagogy. Instead he faced an auditorium jammed full of young men whom he earnestly wanted to engage. Once again Mann is autobiographical in his initial orientation and unrestrained in his praise for the text before him. The Freud he presents in his introduction is pre-eminently the author of *Totem and Taboo*, a text that Mann lauds lavishly on both intellectual and literary grounds. This "rhapsodic and genial work" is a "masterpiece," and belongs to "world literature"; Freud's *schriftstellerische* mastery of the form of the essay is as great as his mastery of clinical and scientific knowledge. Mann also emphasizes Freud's intellectual heroism; the word "bold" is used three times in this brief space. All these qualities — scientific and literary talent, wide range of inquiry, audacity of thought — should make Freud as alluring a figure for the young audience as he is for Mann.[18] Mann abjures summarizing all of Freud's ideas — a sigh of relief may well have been audible in the hall — and turns to his main task: Freud's place in the history of modern thought. This is where the *GW* text begins.

Nietzsche made a cameo appearance in the opening panegyric, and now Mann returns to him at length. Beginning his exposition with Nietzsche allows him both to situate Freud's thought in its proper tradition and to inaugurate the essay's political pedagogy. Nietzsche is not only a resonant figure for his youthful audience, but a contested one between Mann and his reactionary opponents; it is not only Freud whom his charges must learn to read correctly. He begins by summarizing Nietzsche's "decisive aphorism," entitled "The German Hostility to Enlightenment" (256–57; 167–68): German thinkers, historians, and natural scientists of the first half of the nineteenth century opposed the Enlightenment and social revolution, yet were so crudely misunderstood that they were given credit for it. In fact these figures developed a cult of feeling and a consuming reverence for the past that left no room for "future goals and innovations." Although some cultural benefits did come from this period, its main effect was to subordinate knowledge to feeling. But these men and ideas, once dangerous, are so no longer, says Nietzsche, because their innovations — "the idea of history, the understanding of origins and developments, sympathy with the past, renewed passion of feeling and knowledge" — one day all came into the service of the Enlightenment. This incorporation altered history, refiguring the "great revolution" against the eighteenth-century Enlightenment and the "great reaction" to that revolution as mere "wave-play" when compared to the ongoing "great and general enlightenment . . . the flood-tide on which we drift, and want to drift" (257; 168). In the same way, Nietzsche continues, great conservative thinkers such as Schopenhauer corrected the naïveté and broadened the range of Enlightenment thought so that even their critiques became part of a reconstituted humanism's development. To establish this first point firmly, Mann doubles the *Morgenröte* passage with an earlier one from *Menschliches, Allzumenschliches* on "progress and reaction."

Yes, Mann tells his students, we still stand under the "overshadow-ing greatness" of Nietzsche, whose relevance to our own struggles is nowhere clearer than in this aphorism. All of us in the present time — you, and by implication myself and even Freud — are knowingly or otherwise his students, and live out our own "little waves," our "satyr plays," at the feet of his grand style and overshadowing greatness. So Mann continues his lecture by naming a second great teacher and "dominating genius," for whom the speaker at the podium is also an intermediary and ally. He repeats the performative strategy of the "Kleist" lecture, acting as a medium through whom archetypal figures appear for a youthful audience. As we shall see, loyalty and the deci-sions it empowers are again central to the story in these more urgent political circumstances.

Mann's framing material is itself the product of a prudent, and very selective, containment. Section 197 of *Morgenröte* is not representative of the whole, where critiques of selfless service (Book 1) lead to the nascent formulations of the will to power (Book 4), and where the conception of free will, which will prove crucial to Mann's essay, is called into question (section 128). Even the "great flood" that ends section 197 suggests a more unstable psychological and moral world than the one Mann hopes to conjure for his audience. His small sleight-of-hand actually emphasizes the "daily ebb and flow of the little waves" that Nietzsche carries us past, and substitutes for Nietzsche's "drifting" the "gaze into the open future of humanity" (257; 168).

Following this magisterial, if slightly slippery, opening, Mann sum-marizes the paradox he has been unveiling: romanticism and the En-lightenment, reaction and progress repeatedly cross one another historically. Their interconnection has made it possible for thinkers to overcome the simple binary of their opposition, and to value both without privileging either. He devotes the rest of the lecture to helping his charges, under the banners of Nietzsche and Freud, interpret such dichotomies in the right way. Doing so, he says, will lead them on a path that he himself has already traversed. This step clarifies his peda-gogy; he plans not only to instruct but to dramatize instruction, subtly including the history of his own learning even as he tries to bring clarity and simplicity to his pupils. As in the "Kleist" performance, autobiog-raphy creates a common ground that underwrites education. Mann firmly separates Freud from those thinkers, flawed and dangerous read-ers all, who have rejected this revised version of the Enlightenment's connection to romanticism.

Primed with this beginning understanding of how conservative thought may connect to the future, Mann constructs yet another frame before hazarding a specific discussion of Freud. He does so in a way that surely intends a bit of theatrical surprise for his students. Christianity, he says, may be read either as an enlightened critique of earlier religion or as a retrograde, killing "hoar-frost" on the budding fruits of the Renaissance. This is because Christianity itself has always been an indissoluble mixture of the most primitive, bloodthirsty religious sacrifice and cannibalism with the progressive refinements of the human spirit (259–60; 171).

Highlighting the intertextual threads in this passage reveals Mann's style of weaving. Several of Nietzsche's texts — *Der Antichrist* (61); *Ecce Homo*; *Morgenröte* I's relentless scrutinizing of Paul, Luther and Christianity — form the warp, and *Totem and Taboo* the woof. There may even be a self-citation from "Goethe and Tolstoy" (IX, 121; *Essays*, 138–39). But all the elaboration spins out directly, if silently, from the organizing metaphor of the *Joseph* novels. Civilized antiquity can only have seen Christianity as a "hideous relapse and atavistic return" to the primitive, in which — the *Joseph* keynote — "in every sense the bottom of the world had become uppermost" (259; 171). With this move *Joseph*'s central figure of the revolving sphere enters pedagogy and political performance. Mann wisely does not pause here to elaborate the subtle operations of the sphere's rotation for his pupils, but *Joseph* readers can feel its organizing momentum in the undertext of the essay. Just as the sphere revolves in the novels, turning gods into men and men into gods, so towering figures such as Nietzsche "descend" to our present time, both in their textual incarnations and in those figures — Freud, Mann — who consciously or unknowingly reincarnate their truths. Just as Christianity can be seen as passing through both the upper and lower reaches of the sphere's revolution — as spirituality for the future or primitive atavism of the past — so political figures resist or repeat the mindless indulgence in cultic irrationalism that so shocked the civilized world of the Romans and must shock our civilized citizens as well. The three-dimensional geometry of the sphere provides the hidden lineaments of Mann's ruminations; the novels and essay interlace in both idea and structure.

This double understanding of Christianity and its conservative revolution "all came clear to me," Mann tells his class, "as I reread portions of *Totem and Taboo*." Even as Freud — "with the careful, relentless probe of the surgeon" (260; 172) — situated and clarified these primitive roots for me, so I will try to do so for you. We surgically cut away the intervening flesh-time to "analyze and illuminate" those roots with the brave detachment of the committed scientist (260; 171–72). Mann of course has written similar things about Christianity in earlier work — *The Magic Mountain, Fiorenza* — but not, he now says, with the "clarity," that is, with the grounding in a general anthropology, that Freud permits. Mann then spends several minutes cataloging those nineteenth-century precursors of Freud's journey into the night side of life. Some of these figures in effect lacked or refused the surgeon's scalpel, and so fell under the spell of the "hostility to mind" that now bears such bitter political fruit in Germany.

Finally, Mann feels he can risk summarizing those darker portions of Freud's "Meisterstück," *Totem and Taboo*, that are pertinent to the interplay between reaction and progress. Just as he had quickly cataloged the leading features of Freud's thought in the lecture's opening, so now he rushes through a quite general list of Freud's most antediluvian unearthings: the totem feast and the "very realistic view of blood communion as identity of substance" on which it is grounded; the primal crime of parricide; "this whole ghastly and culturally very fruitful morbid world of incest dread and murder remorse ['Mördergewissensnot'] and yearning for salvation" (260; 171–72). He mentions such subjects, he insists, only to celebrate Freud's attitude toward them. Mann's marginal notes and underlinings in *Totem and Taboo*'s discussion of the ram as totemic substitute and animal sacrifice confirm this intent; psychoanalysis's posture toward these murky subjects is always, Mann claims, on the side of reason's ultimate triumph over its origins.[19] Freud's account develops from his roots in the "nineteenth century's . . . opposition to rationalism, intellectualism, classicism" that advanced the "night-side of nature and the soul" as the life-giving forces, but differs from it in his therapeutic refusal to isolate those powers from the mind and understanding. Like Schopenhauer, he gives reason a rescuing task, and in doing so opposes the contemporary "fiction born of today's tendency" to separate mind and politics (263; 176). He concludes that Freud is unavailable for the machinations of reactionary forces.

But too many today forswear Nietzsche's lofty path, or even try to enlist him on the side of nationalistic reaction and romantic primitivism. Nietzsche, perhaps blinded by high-mindedness, did not see the danger: that we live in the "waves" of history whose countervailing flow persists in spite of larger understanding, and whose overcoming requires not only right ideas but activist politics. Dramatic moments of choice occur for persons and for nations, and the members of the Democratic Club stand at such a juncture now. Mann must "reduce" and "clarify" ("eine reinliche Klärung") this "confusing" tangle of ideas for his students so that they can choose rightly (264; 177). Nowhere is Mann's penchant for converting a political situation into an interpretive and pedagogical one more evident. His sense of politics always involves ethical issues and appeals to the super-ego: " . . . a kind of manifesto in which I appeal to the conscience of the young people whose ear I have."

What makes possible the choice of "right revolution" and right politics is the proper shaping of the will: "I know no other way" (265; 179). This simplifying scenario marks the pedagogical turning point of the essay. All confusions vanish once this fundamental truth stands revealed. Its fulfillment requires an arduous journey that replicates those of Nietzsche and Freud — and the speaker before them, who places himself squarely in the patriarchal line of blessing from his forebearers. Students must move through anarchic "phases of dissolution" ("Auf-lösung") in order to reach the awareness of a free, unified existence in a culture directed toward "complete self-consciousness" (265; 178). The revolutionary of the future must be at home in those subterranean worlds but never make common cause with them or love them for their own sake. The journeyer can then press on through, or return to them as a liberator of their treasures, without falling victim to the abominations of their dungeons ("Verliese").[20] So loyalty to the grander Enlightenment and German romanticism leads to the development of "complete self-consciousness" and political self-confidence. He enlists Novalis — another deliberately surprising example — as one more enlightened prophet of his revolutionary principle. The Nazis on the other hand really offer only the confusions of unself-consciousness; they return us to the primitive darkness of murder and incest and leave us there without the scalpel of reason which makes youth potent and free.

This is admirable pedagogy indeed. In this rich, clever argument, Mann offers Germany's young men alternative language for their restless, defiant, even their *völkisch* feelings. Each step goes the Nazis one better. In following the new path they are both loyal Germans and authentic revolutionaries. For true revolution arises out of the nation's culture and at the same time requires individual choice and action. True revolution is both aristocratic and democratic, traditional and creative. True revolution offers solidarity and the freedom of an open future, not submersion in the factitious, determinist unities of fascist tribalism. More damningly, the Nazis' so-called revolution is not only wrong, it's out-of-date, moribund, old hat: the last sort of movement that a forward-thinking, up-and-coming young man would pin his star to. Fascists valorize the collective will of the state, but at the expense of invaluable individual choice. Even the timing of the argument — the way in which the subjects follow one another — appeals to the audience's self-estimation. The conclusion — "I know of no other way" except the education of the will — marks not desperation but optimism; the exercise of individual will is no half-hearted, last resort for young men, but confirmation that their "temperaments and intentions" will make all the difference for the nation's future.[21] As he instructs, Mann keeps his double position — mentor and fellow learner — before his audience: "One must say this to youth today" (265; 178). The German penchant for the impersonal pronoun serves him well here: Mann both "says things to youth" and separates himself from any autocratic, Jupiteresque position.

The self-influential force of the *Joseph* and "Kleist's *Amphitryon*" runs throughout this crucial section. The action is epic: a great journey must be taken by each of us, one with perils and tempting stopping places — before our goal of full self-consciousness can be attained. We must climb out of the "Verliese" — the bottomless well of the past, the abasement before inferiors (Eliphaz), the trickery and degradation in Laban's house — and we can only do so via the willed enactment of a morality grounded in self-knowledge. Freedom resides only here, not in the blindness of primitive blood-sacrifice (Laban's first-born buried in the cornerstone of his house), or the *oubliette* of literal castration (Potiphar and his parents). We must will a society that draws strength from the depths (libido) without lingering in their embrace. This is the patriarch's promise of the blessing reinscribed as Freudian purpose, and Mann enlists these elements of the *Joseph* novels to construct the pedagogical and political Freud he needs. And the placing of the creative, moral will at the center of politics brings to a national scale the choice of the "confused" Amphitryon, whose identity-saving loyalty to the Alkmene he loves is now extended — far beyond the specifics of Kleist's play — to the broader loyalty to authentic German culture necessary for sustaining civic life. As Mann meditated on loyalty throughout the *Joseph* story, his original account of Amphitryon's individual "temperament and intention" expanded and deepened. Freud and Kleist have been gently torqued into the service of liberal democracy.

But even this elaborate structure of containment does not satisfy Mann; more of Freud's potentially destabilizing views cannot be broached in any detail until he has affirmed psychoanalysis's fundamental purpose. That purpose is ethical, and Mann hammers home this conclusion to his charges. Psychoanalysis's therapeutic goal, its radical commitment to human betterment, justifies its existence as a cultural practice.[22] Moreover, he claims that psychoanalysis has become, indisputably, an established, mature mode of therapy. It has "triumphed" everywhere, growing from its roots in medicine to became a force in any number of fields: "science, history of religion, prehistory, research in literature and art, mythology and folklore, pedagogy, and so on" (274; 190). Such widespread cultural acceptance validates psychoanalysis as a new, powerfully interdisciplinary way of reconstituting self-understanding and political action. And not only has psychoanalysis become a cross-disciplinary "world movement," it has done so to its founder's "surprise." This shows that psychoanalysis, unlike the Nazis, has no ulterior motive or conspiratorial purpose. Inherently ethical, it overturns stultified academic psychology in a revolutionary spirit always welcome to a young audience. In this sense psychoanalysis, rather than fascism, is authentically youthful and in tune with the proper aspirations of youth. Its mission is to do away with disguises so that we come to know the unconscious of the self and the species, and can ally that knowledge to youth's natural drive toward the future. Further, it grounds its ability to instruct and influence in narrative re-formation and recapitulation. Psychoanalysis remains loyal to its narrations of the past and helps its patients to narrate the proper kind of loyalty to theirs. This loyalty empowers the will to choose cultural and political narratives that lead to still more freeing choices. In sum, Mann seeks to perform a psychoanalysis that contains the dark sides of the psyche and of German history without erasing their necessary power — the mistake of those who follow only the French Enlightenment — just as it is his artistic and political task to narrate a worldview of this psychology's relation to archetypal human truths in the *Joseph* retelling.

    In the same spirit Mann glosses Freud's statement in his autobiography that "As a psychoanalyst I must of course be more interested in affective than in intellectual phenomena." The gloss patently speaks to his student audience. Freud acknowledges what every young person feels: the power of emotion and impulse over mind. Then, says Mann, he refigures that feeling into a scheme that permits rational honor rather than regressive glorification of the buried life. Freud, like a good pedagogue, "never confuses." He stands beyond the "wave play of the time." He has traveled alone — a romantic isolato leading the way — and he has done so "entirely independently," apparently ignoring the German literary and philosophical tradition that might have supported his task (277; 194). Some of this is selective amnesia: Mann "forgets," for example, Freud's canny use in *Totem* of Schopenhauer in his discussion of the "omnipotence of thought" (XIII, 87). Mann apparently knew little about his life or education, as Freud, in his delicate, dry way, pointed out in his letter of 23 November 1929.[23] At the same time performative and pedagogical motives may have influenced Mann's claim; just as Freud's strong will overcame his putative ignorance and gave him focus and power ("Stoßkraft"), so many independent-minded yet ignorant students may follow in his wake.

The section ends with Mann's wish "to speak of unconscious tradition, of transpersonal relations" ("von unbewußter Überlieferung, überpersönlichen Beziehungen zu sprechen") (277; 195), and to affirm the cultural, textual, and perhaps unconscious transmission of meaning. The immediate debt is to *Totem and Taboo:* "No one can have failed to observe . . . that I have taken as the basis of my whole position the existence of a collective mind, in which mental processes occur just as they do in the mind of an individual" (SE XIII, 157). Mann deftly uses Freud's own thesis to analyze his unrecognized affinities with German humanism. In doing so Mann intimates a psycho-narrational theory of intertext; traces of Nietzsche and Novalis appear in Freud much in the way that Freud himself appeared in Mann's earlier narratives, before he had read him carefully. (This situates such collective knowledge firmly within Freud's provenance and lessens the necessity for, and perhaps the importance of, using Jungian terms in reading *Joseph*.) And what Mann means by "collective mind" differs radically from the fascists: it marks the beginning, not the goal, of political action. Claims for collective mind inevitably raise a host of questions. Mann does not pursue them here, both for pedagogic reasons and because his fuller answer lies in *Joseph*'s elaborations of the sphere.

With all his larger strategies of containment finally in place, Mann launches into the final, brio movement of his performance (277–80; 195–98). In less than five minutes he broaches his third fast-moving catalog of Freud's subversive subjects: the death instinct, libido theory, narcissism, the "fatality of drives" ("Triebschicksale"), sublimation and repression, and the theory of neurosis. This rapid summary may seem intellectually hasty and reductive, but it is rhetorically and artistically necessary, and in its own way subtle. For each of these has the potential to undermine Mann's "Enlightenment" Freud.

First, Mann asserts that Freud's formulation of these ideas follows the German romantics, but as an oxymoronic "independent dependency" ("selbständige Abhängigkeit") rather than a causal derivation. A clever sleight-of-hand: Freud's analyses that make so much of origins are themselves kept free of their regressive taint. Mann reuses the sentence structure of the incest and "Mördergewissensnot" paragraph we looked at earlier, when he first unveiled a number of unsavory impulses and then contained them in the Freud-as-surgeon metaphor (X, 260).[24] Here he lists several particularly destabilizing remarks: on the "primary human impulse to return to the lifeless"; on the interplay of Eros with the death drive; and on the "essentially conservative nature of that impulse." He concludes his catalog by terming all these claims a mere "paraphrase" or "rewriting" ("Umschreibung") of a Novalis aphorism: "The drive of the elements that compose us is towards de-oxidation. Life is *compelled* (*erzwungene*) oxidation" (278; 195: emphasis in original). Once again Mann gives us the belated scientist Freud who has just now arrived at these well-integrated radical eroticisms and long-pondered theories of "drive." Freud's text has, in this important sense, already been written, and its darkest corners already well illuminated by German artists. And for Mann readers, including the young men in the audience who were up on their contemporary fiction, the frame has yet another level. In *The Magic Mountain* Hofrat Behrens answers the eager Hans Castorp's big questions about "life and death" in this same "uncanny" (comic yet unsettling) way; they are both "oxidation" (III, 371; *MM*, 262). Ideas that muddled Hans might well do the same to his brethren in the auditorium, so Mann here dispels the "uncanny" from their minds and wills; these unsettling insights are really familiar, he reassures them, not "verwirrend." Similarly, what is Freud's libido theory but "to speak briefly, natural science stripped of mysticism and become romanticism" (278; 196)? Again, the doubleness of Freud's view of love and death gives to sexuality a "revolutionary" significance that may disturb some orthodox Christians, but not those who understand its place in the tradition and welcome the future such understanding promises. And to cement his point, Mann repeats, as in a rondo, his main melody: psychoanalysis's interest in the irrational and anti-intellectual is confined to the realm of knowing, and so cannot "encroach upon the will" and become "reactionary" (278–79, 196).

The essay's final paragraph, all but swaddled in its protective wrappings, risks declaring the full brunt of Freud's pessimism to the bearers of Germany's future. Freud teaches us that our whole culture "literally and actually . . . stands in the sign and image of the substitution-neurosis" (279; 197). The apparent harmony we perceive in civilization is in reality "thoroughly unstable, thoroughly insecure." Chilling words, except for the immediate turn Mann gives the argument. This unstable condition is all but identical to the unstable, scrambling position of a particular category of neurotic: "a neurotic person, *without a will to recovery*, [who] comes to terms with and manages his symptoms" (279; 197: emphasis mine). This is, Freud says, not an inevitable but a specifically pathological "state of existence [Lebensform] which neither can nor deserves to continue." Mann takes this passage from the second chapter of *The Future of an Illusion* (1927) and quietly alters the context. For at this point in *The Future of an Illusion* Freud is discussing neither general instability nor neurotics without will, but rather class divisions and the consequent social unrest they produce. He alleges the understandable and unrelenting hostility of the "underprivileged classes" in "all present-day cultures," since none has moved past the stage of "suppressing" a large segment of its people. Freud contrasts this class-driven, overt anger in the lower orders to the often overlooked "latent" hostility in the upper classes, and concludes "that a civilization which leaves so large a number of its participants unsatisfied and drives them into revolt neither has nor deserves the prospect of a lasting existence" (XXI, 12). Mann spins this in such a way that the "latent" hostility in the dominant classes resembles that of the weak-willed neurotic; they therefore need only choose to make a better world in order to avoid the deep-seated conflict Freud describes. Here, Mann claims, lies the "root of Freud's socialism" (279; 197). This is an ingenious take on Freud but not a very plausible one, and certainly not one underwritten by the somber text Mann chose to cite. "The will to recovery" turns out to be the psychoanalytic version of the choice of loyalty and the future that Mann wishes Freud to endorse. The essay ends by celebrating such a future, the "dawning-of-consciousness philosophy" of Novalis, of *Morgenröte*, of all German Romanticism, that forms "one of the most important foundation stones . . . of a free and knowing humanity." A final example of self-influence: Mann's evocative use of Novalis before a youthful audience is a repeat performance. He had used the same material and tone near the end of "On the German Republic" seven years earlier (XI, 849–52). His climactic sentence, a final review for the students, is italicized in the original, and presumably received similar emphasis in delivery: "*It is that manifestation of modern irrationalism that stands unequivocally firm against all reactionary misuse.*"[25] The emotional tone comes closer to the charged atmosphere of "Kleist's *Amphitryon*" than anything else in the lecture. Mann devotes all his emotional and textual resources to creating the "will to recovery" which Germany so desperately needs.

What else is *not* here in this reconstruction of Freud's worldview? A number of things, but at heart this sentence from *Totem and Taboo:* "At the conclusion of this exceedingly condensed inquiry, I should like to insist that its outcome shows that the beginnings of religion, morals, society and art converge in the Oedipus complex" (XIII, 156). Another summary — and representative — sentence from near the end of *Totem and Taboo* yields a pithy example of how Mann tries to negotiate this deliberate and glaring omission. Freud is elaborating his long-anticipated conclusion that all religions spring from the original effort to assuage filial guilt over causing (or desiring) the death of the father by offering "deferred obedience" to the totem animal, or other, more refined substitutes. Freud describes these attempts as varying "according to the stage of civilization at which they arise and according to the methods that they adopt; but all have the same end in view and are reactions to the same great event with which civilization began, and which, since it occurred, has not allowed mankind a moment's rest" (XIII, 145). Mann happily accepts, throughout the *Joseph* and the 1929 essay, the notion that civilization has stages, and that religious figuration is always appropriate to the stage in which it occurs. These claims fit with his conception of the Enlightenment, and with the dynamic revolutions of the sphere that join the upper and lower worlds. Freud's Comptean, fanciful "stages" of human thought in *Totem* — the animistic or mythological, the religious, the scientific — roughly correlate with the development in *Joseph* from Eliezer and Abraham-Isaac to Jacob to Joseph.[26] Freud's conclusion — that men, via remorse and totem substitution, in effect convert their fathers into gods — encouraged Mann in his more convivial account of mutual self-creation between gods and men.

Freud's aggressive atheism, his deliberate attempt in *Totem* to "cut off, cleanly, everything that is Aryan-religious,"[27] did not, however, suit Mann's novelistic purposes nearly as well as Kleist's exploration of love and loyalty. He also resisted the reductive claim that all these stages commenced, could only commence, from this one beginning and remained partial prisoners to it. He did use this idea for some of *Joseph*'s minor, less enlightened characters, but the entire "Prelude's" relativizing of beginnings, and its consequent pluralism, implicitly deny Freud's claim. And Freud's concluding notion — that this conflict can only be partially ameliorated by religion and "has not allowed mankind a moment's rest" — is simply ignored. Mankind may sometimes be "restless" in Mann's anthropology, but not because of the imperfect success of totemic substitution. So Mann elided the single-minded explanation that Freud offered for the origins not only of religion but of morality, art, even society itself: the Oedipal conflict. In some ways *Totem and Taboo* was a little too clear for Mann's taste, or for his artistic and pedagogic requirements. His marginalia confirm his demurs: Mann noted opposite a particularly assertive passage that "perhaps" the slaying of the father is the beginning of everything (Lehnert 1965, 482). He says the same thing in his account of Esau's anger against Isaac and Jacob (215; 141), where Esau's naive shock at the idea of father murder makes the passage so funny that any force it might bear disappears. And he rejects the repetition of this origin in the life of each individual, where the Oedipus site is the "nucleus of all neuroses as well."[28] As we shall see in chapter 5, Mann gives his Joseph almost no childhood. He moves from birth to seventeen; there is no Oedipal subject, no developmental construction of Joseph's subjectivity around the imperfect resolution of that conflict. Only Benjamin the "baby" has a developed childhood in the novels, and he is comically kept a baby by his father and brothers well into middle age.[29]

In *Totem and Taboo* Freud treated the Oedipus complex's connection to totem animals as uncontroversial, even obvious: "in substituting the father for the totem animal in the formula for totemism (in the case of males) . . . there is nothing new or particularly daring in this step forward. Indeed, primitive men say the same thing themselves, and, where the totemic system is still in force today, they describe the totem as their common ancestor and primal father" (XIII, 131). He adds that, unlike the anthropologists who have backgrounded this substitution, "Psycho-analysis . . . takes it as the starting point of our attempt at explaining totemism." The last thirty pages of *Totem and Taboo* devote themselves to showing how several subjects — *Joseph*-related subjects such as sacrifice and the origin of God — derive from the basic substitution of the totem for the beloved yet fearful father. But while Mann occasionally quotes Freud's text directly (e.g., the "Blut- und Bundesmahlzeiten" of 259) he makes little use of Freud's analysis because its determinism — this conflict necessarily produces suffering and cannot in principle be fully resolved or overcome — is exactly the negative determinism, the Splengerian drift, that he explicitly rejects. Here again we see that Mann uses a premise of Freudian psychology but not the conclusions that seem to follow from it. He can readily accept the band of brothers uniting against the father, and portrays the sons of Jacob as acting out a later but still dangerous version of this primal event. But it does not enter the lives of the major male characters in any decisive way. Instead he refigures the narcissism that precedes the Oedipal conflict in personal development and constructs a very different primal scene out of his revision. Mythically speaking, we begin as Amphitryon, not Oedipus.

IV

[Freudian psychology] offers to each and every individual a convenient means to hoist himself up on to the plane of tragedy, by conceiving of himself as a new Oedipus.

— Michel Leiris, *L'Age d'homme* (1972)

Like *Joseph and his Brothers, Totem and Taboo* is an elaborate intertextual meeting ground. Freud's broad reading in contemporary anthropology interweaves with psychoanalytic theory, both his own and his colleagues'. Freud openly acknowledges most of his intertexts, as the protocols of science require. *Totem* also has many features of good storytelling; hidden mysteries await unraveling, and an increasingly complex but forceful plot line propels the reader forward. Seen formally, Freud's sources are either friends or foils; they provide support or somehow got things wrong. Anthropologists have unearthed invaluable material, but their interpretations are incomplete; only psychoanalysis can illuminate its full significance. Able forerunners (Darwin and Frazer) and misguided peers (Jung) either prepare the way for, or fall short of, the master narrator. Freud and his loyal band of brothers treat most of their forebearers with respect, but with a steady eye on their deficiencies of explanation and theory. They have a sense of the blessings which the psychoanalytic future holds, and they work toward it with patriarchal diligence.[30]

Totem and Taboo in turn entered the *Joseph* narrative in several different ways. It provided Mann with anthropological information that supplemented Jeremias, Horowitz, and his other principal sources, and at the same time spun an unsettling narrative about that information.[31] Mann found it easier to ignore unwanted conclusions in his theological and historical sources than those he found in *Totem*; Freud's new role as champion of the anti-Nazi enlightenment made him as much partner as precursor. As a result *Totem* appears in *Joseph* in a whole series of ways: direct citation, imitation, paraphrase, inversion, parody, and discreet omission. The opening sections of the fourth chapter of *The Tales of Jacob* ("The Flight"), which concentrate on Isaac, Rebecca, and the events leading up to Jacob's "theft" of the blessing, ably represent this wide-ranging intertextual encounter. "The Flight" contains both specific reenactments of Freud's text and the crucial organizing motif of the sphere which helps control *Totem*'s dispersive power. The former shows the local operations of intertextuality; the latter pushes toward an overview of the entire tetralogy.

The narrator's brisk foreshortening of Isaac's character throughout *The Tales of Jacob* provides an instructive way into the complex containment of Freud's anthropology. Genesis's account of Isaac's adulthood receives short shrift and strange focus. At times the patriarch hardly seems to figure in his own narrative. His journey to Gerar to seek relief from famine and, especially, his not-quite-private fondling of his "sister" Rebecca interest the narrator largely because of the droll dilemmas they produce for their observer, King Abimelech (126; 80–81). The narrator also passes over the several stories concerning wells and fertility, tales that could easily have enriched one of *Joseph*'s major symbols. Jacob persistently compares his experience to Abraham's, rarely to Isaac's.[32] The only two narrative paragraphs devoted to the adult, active Isaac emphasize the primitive, imitative nature of his ego (127–28, 185–86; 81, 121). The theoretical discussion of egos "open at the back" lumps the patriarchs together as instances of one another, but the novel's practice differentiates between them; it individualizes Abraham and of course Jacob but leaves Isaac in the shadows of the communal past.

The Tales of Jacob's alter-narrator, Eliezer, "could not say enough" about Rebecca's charms (122; 78) but elaborates few tales about his master to Joseph. The *Joseph* narrator too finds Rebecca far more interesting than her husband. He relates Ishmael's dubious "trifling" ("scherzen," from the Luther Bible: 192; 126) with the young Isaac largely from Abraham's point of view; Isaac the true son is little more than the beautiful boy-object who occasions Ishmael's expulsion. Also a pawn in his most celebrated scene, the near-sacrifice on Mount Moriah, Isaac has no voice in Jacob's narration of his trial. Nor does he gain any obvious self-conscious insight from his trauma and rescue. There are plausible artistic reasons for all this — the need for economy in an already crowded canvas, the wish to foreground Jacob's remarkable spiritual development — but it still surprises. In Joseph's cosmopolitan imagination Esau and Eliphaz, even Nabu the go-between and Nergal the fox, play larger roles than his own grandfather.

Finally given a tongue in the hoaxing scene, Isaac speaks as a blind, baffled, and barely conscious old man, not a self-knowing bearer of the blessing. He has always clung to the more primitive line of the elder son's absolute priority, even though he and Rebecca "knew" that Jacob was the true son of the blessing (197; 129). This half-sensed contrast between the ancient law of inheritance and the "larger myth" of Jacob's appropriateness for the blessing produced his blindness (198;

129–30). He retreats into the darkness of his tent, blind "like the dying moon," in order half-consciously to perform his necessary role; this passive withdrawal leaves far behind the high-minded wrestling with the idea of God in both Abraham and Jacob. Isaac's blessing of Jacob contains old formulas and figures — "the dragon of the waste," "the bringer of the equinox" — that he speaks "mechanically" and that neither he nor Jacob understand (211; 138). It is a literally mindless performance, one chanted out of tribal memory and at odds with the performative modernity that Rebecca brings to her own repetition of primitive mantras (207; 135). Indeed Rebecca, by sacrificing her love of her favorite son to flight and the blessing, seems thematically more in line with Abraham and Jacob than Isaac; through her the fertile blessings of double sexedness reenter the patriarchal line.

So, to emphasize, Mann's wish to harness Freud's disruptive anthropology within the *Joseph* narrative shapes, in no small part, this curious treatment of Isaac. Within the tradition of the patriarchs and the blessing, Isaac embodies and then contains one aspect of the Freudian portrait of primitive man. Before the sons can band together to kill the father (*Totem* IV), they must feel the threat of the father's murderous violence against them. Isaac incarnates this corner of the Freudian primeval that others in the tradition have largely left behind: the agon of near murder by his father. He was not thrown into a pit but elevated on a mountain, and then on the altar of God, and his elevation ironically turned out to be a falling, a psychic freezing and fixation. Neurotically trapped, as *Totem* might have argued, by primal reality-turned-fantasy, he cannot escape its net.

Isaac's brief death narrative makes this even plainer (185–86; 121–22). It occurs in *Joseph*'s narrative before the hoaxing and hence influences our reading of that scene. It also offers the most graphic illustration of *Joseph*'s artful containment of *Totem and Taboo*. Haunted by the near violence of the sacrifice, Mann's Isaac becomes the substituted sheep that had once saved him, transformed at the moment of death into the totem animal:

> "A god shall they slay," he babbled, in ancient and poetic language, and went on with his head bent back, his eyes wide open and fixed, and his fingers spread out, to say that they should all hold a sacrificial meal with the flesh and blood of the slain ram as he and Abram, the father and the son, had once done, for whom the god-and-father beast had intervened. "Behold, it was slain," they heard him rattle in his throat, he went babbling and rambling on, they not daring to look at him, "the father and the beast instead of the man and the son, and we ate. But truly I say to you that there shall be slain the man and the son

> instead of the beast and in the place of God and ye shall eat." Then he
> bleated again, in an entirely natural way, and died. (186; 121–22)

These final prophesies, gnomic and terrifying to his audience but clear
enough to modern readers, evoke the bloody origins of religion: the
devouring of the father-god in his totemic substitute. It is a measure of
how far the patriarchs' culture has already advanced that the onlookers
are so horrified by Isaac's primitive evocations. Nearer in time to the pit
of religious sacrifice and devouring, their recoil at the same time protects the modern reader. Armed with anthropology and comparative
religion, we readily interpret their fear, and in doing so we take further
distance from it. Even the potential horror of the primitive that might
flow through Isaac's liminal language is mitigated by the persistently
comic cast of his performances and self-blindness. Like one of
Nietzsche's "little waves," Isaac remains an eddy in the current propel-
ling mankind into the future and its blessings.

Still, the slaying of the father and its later inversion — the slaying of
the son in myths of the dying-rising god — do take us to a yet deeper
level of the well of the past. Frames within frames: we catch this brief
glimpse of prehistorical violence which itself was already a substitution
of the totem animal for the father-god. Beyond that substitution, the
narrator claims, we cannot go. But if we accept Freud's account in *Totem and Taboo*, we can go a good deal further. The divine father is a
substitution for the oppressive, dangerous father of the Oedipal conflict, and Freud, citing Frazer and Darwin along the way, goes to some
lengths to establish this origin for sacrifice and totemism (XIII, 128ff.).
Joseph's Isaac shows the outcome of identification with the totem object; like Freud's "little Hans" he "identifies himself with the dreaded
creature," and like "little Árpád" he abandons human speech for the
voice of the totem animal (XIII, 129–30). There is even a layer below
the Oedipal drama: its "narcissistic precondition, the fear of castration"
and an account of its substitute, blinding (XIII, 130). So Freud offers
an explanation of Isaac's behavior and his blindness that the *Joseph* narrator, like the anthropologists Freud chides, has "been glad to keep in
the background" (XIII, 131). The outcome replicates the 1929 essay;
neither the Oedipal explanation nor this Freudian account of narcissism
will be permitted to "throw a light upon the origins of totemism in the
inconceivably remote past" (XIII, 132). The father-narrator of the *Joseph* novels sacrifices Isaac once again, this time to the larger good of
containing that disquieting account.

Isaac's burial in Abraham's double cave-tomb at Hebron — his dark
tent made permanent — completes his regression. He returns to the
earth in the fetal position, a literal infant without coherent speech or

developed consciousness. But his figure in the tetralogy is not entirely silenced. In a remarkable revolution of the sphere, Isaac acquires a mature voice in the death scene of his Egyptian counterpart and variant, Mont-Kaw (990–1000; 657–663). Potiphar's steward knows Isaac's story better than the patriarch himself; the sphere has rolled, and Joseph's ersatz, worldly father, blinded by renal failure, knowingly blesses his successor as worthy substitute for his own long-dead infant son.

The narrator ends his account of Isaac's entombment with a mythical analog from another tradition:

> Together they sewed Yitzchak in a ram-skin, with his knees pulled up, and thus gave him to time to devour, to time who devours his children that they may not set themselves over him, but must choke them up again to live in the same old stories as the same children. (For the giant cannot tell by feeling it that the clever mother gives him only a thing like a stone, wrapped up in a skin, and not the child.) (187; 122)

The narrator connects Isaac's burial to the tale of the child-devouring Kronos and his son, the saved sacrifice Zeus. Rebecca repeats this reference in her chant over Jacob before he, wrapped in a bag of skins, enters the dark cave of his father's tent as a substitute for hairy Esau: "I anoint the child, I anoint the stone, the blind eat; at your feet, at your feet must fall the brothers of the depths" (207; 135). It is a complex, asymmetrical reference (and not one that Freud uses in the relevant section of *Totem*). It both affirms the transparent meaning of the Kronos legend — the child Jacob-Zeus saved by the substitution to inaugurate a "new beginning" — and retains the darker allegory: the devouring of every child, of every new beginning, by time. Even the vomiting forth of the young leads to endless repetition of the same story. Only characters who defy perfect repetition, the endless simulacra, develop a new sense of self. Jacob and Joseph — and Amphitryon — so defy and so acquire. In the Greek myth the vomited stone became the omphalos, center of the world and benign totem marker at Delphi from which the god spoke of the future. Just so, Elohim "swallowed" the literal substitutions and magic of the ur-religion, and gave forth not another identical beast-god but a new beginning of the spirit in the marriage of himself and the people of Israel (186–87; 122). It is one more of the small but telling intertexts that weave through the *Joseph* narrative.

Unquestionably one of the master motifs of the tetralogy, the revolving sphere is at once a structural principle, a thematic subject, and a nascent theory of narrative. It appears more than sixty times over the course of the novels. Mann probably developed the idea from his early reading in Alfred Jeremias, but its roots run deep in his own work.[33] All the tetralogy's symmetries between myth and psychology, the general and the individual, derive from its operations.[34] That the sphere raises problems of time and form long familiar to philosophers from Schopenhauer to Cassirer does not detract from the originality, or the intellectual drama, of the narrator's very literary account.

By the time we arrive at "The Red One," the sphere has already been deployed in several different ways and become familiar. The "Prelude's" master myth of the soul, spirit, and matter introduced the idea of descent and ascent between upper and lower worlds, as well as the idea of a future of potential reunion and blessing. Earlier sections of *The Tales of Jacob* used preliminary figurations of the sphere — Jacob's sons and the zodiac, the "spheres" of both space and time into which Eliezer's permeable ego flowed, Jacob's meditation before Shechem on the "circular descents and ascensions" of his twenty-five years of exile — to explore the circulation of types and images. Now the narrator generalizes:

> Here our tale flows freely into mystery, and our reference points lose themselves in the endlessness of the past, where every origin proves to be only an apparent stopping point and inconclusive goal whose mysterious nature arises from the fact that its essence is not that of the straight line ("Strecke") but the sphere. For a straight line has no mystery. The mystery is in the sphere. But the sphere consists in completion and correspondence; it is a doubled half that forms a whole made by joining together an upper and a lower, a heavenly and an earthly hemisphere which complement one another, so that what is above is also below, and what happens in the earthly repeats itself in the heavenly sphere, and the heavenly in the earthly. This complementary interchange of two halves which together form a whole and a closed sphere makes for actual change — namely, revolution. The sphere rolls: that lies in the nature of spheres. Top is soon bottom and bottom top, if one can speak at all of top and bottom in such a situation. Not only do the heavenly and the earthly recognize themselves in each other, but also through the sphere's revolution the heavenly can become the earthly and the earthly the heavenly, from which it is clear that gods can become men and conversely men can become gods again. (189–90; 124)

The generalized account of the sphere offers not only the anticipated overview, but a finer-grained account of its enigma. Both details and the general view matter greatly: the specifics of the narrator's description show the subtleties in the sphere's operations, and the narrator's way of elucidating its mystery is itself archetypal for the entire project. The revolving sphere imparts motion, enabling a much wider variety of connection between hemispheres, and it also imparts a paradoxical double view: it permits the divine and human, or the past and the present, to develop sequentially (or to exchange places sequentially), and simultaneously to mirror each other from afar. They can both become one another over time and recognize each other instantaneously in space.

Several interconnected threads clarify, and maintain, the mystery of the sphere. The first of these is already familiar: unlike a *Strecke*, a finite mathematical line, the sphere itself has no locatable beginning and so does not privilege any source. The most ancient figure or tale is already a copy of an unknown — and unknowable — earlier version. Every putative origin remains a provisional stopping point in its continual revolution, and every assertion of simple, straight-line historical progress creates a tunnel vision that lops off the heights and depths of experience. At the same time the sphere provides a structure in which the infinite regress of the "Prelude's" descent and its own apparently endless revolutions can be contained. It is finite and formed — yet unbounded. This even includes its own invention. Even though the sphere began as a constructed figure for clarifying change and repetition in the world, this origin in the mind of a narrator neither diminishes the mystery of its revolutions, since the sphere antedates any description of its workings, nor contributes to the explanations of variation that it empowers. The sphere's relativity extends to all descriptions of itself.

Next, the narrator explicitly distinguishes the three-dimensional sphere ("Sphäre," "Kugelrundheit") from a flat circle such as the one that framed the lingam at Beth-el. In effect, this constructs a spatial archive: the sphere is "filled" with gods and men. This leads to the sphere's greatest and most patent mystery: the complementary motions of incarnation and elevation. The archive empowers incarnation and elevation in two ways: by image and by narrative. Men and gods "behold" one another and hear each other's stories. The sphere not only juxtaposes divine and human images, but is itself both a narrative and a "statue with the name 'at the same time'" (439; 292).[35] Perceived as narrative or drama, the sphere aligns the tales of gods who have become human with those of humans who have ascended to divinity. Both statue and circulating cosmic library, the sphere reembodies its images and narratives in current human readers, or releases them into the divine.

Further, the sphere has a marked theatrical quality, as we have come to expect in *Joseph*. It shows gods and men the correspondences between their performances, those preserved in both image and script, form and action. Men and gods move across "stages" in every sense. Gods and men reenact the performances of their predecessors at varying levels of awareness; Osiris imitates his earthly prototype, and Esau struggles not to be the castrating son of Kronos. Human actors may fathom the sphere's scenarios poorly (Cain), or partially (Ishmael), or expertly (the mature Joseph). Gifted, self-conscious performers can grasp events simultaneously in time and in space; knowing the scripts and their variants leads to the general knowledge that things revolve, and will revolve again in partially predictable ways. But this insight does not yield control over the sphere's revolutions. For part of the sphere's mystery arises from its revolutions' independence of human awareness. Neither Joseph the playwright nor his most recent narrator can dictate the precise turn of events. The most successful performers introduce their subtle alterations in the sphere's patterns only after aligning themselves with its forms and momentum.

The sphere also expresses, as the narrator tells us repeatedly, the "unity of the dual" (e.g., 581; 389). Just as it permits and contains unbounded repetition, it permits and mediates dualism. Seen at rest, the correspondences between upper and lower hemispheres give form and meaning to single, isolated events. Events, figures, tales stand separate from and yet can integrate with their corresponding other. But the sphere simultaneously both revolves, shifting those relationships, and rolls, expressing the forward, "once-for-all" motion of time. Either view without the other is ultimately one-sided. If a character sees only sameness in his divine counterpart, or a narrative repeats its precursor exactly, a kind of paralysis ensues. In the 1929 essay the spiritual nostalgia and death-honoring art of a Pfitzner exemplifies such fixity. In the novels this happens, briefly, to Joseph in the well after his brothers' attack, when after seventy-two hours of deprivation he could no longer distinguish the heavenly from the earthly and for a time lost himself "in the dreamy arrogance of death" (584; 391). This was also the moment when his body and soul divided (571; 383). If, on the other hand, a character sees only the rigid duality of the upper and lower spheres, or ignores all duality in the name of the forward progress of linear time, then his existence narrows or fragments in a way that forecloses both human and divine development. For this reason it remained the "great certainty guiding [Joseph's] life" that the sphere did in truth revolve

(581; 389), and that events in the "lower world" could not even occur, let alone be understood, without reference to their heavenly counterparts. This visceral belief is anchored in his "flesh and blood" (581; 389). Life requires both the "unity of the dual," and "the doubleness of the unity."

The sphere's mystery also derives from the truth that no one can know it in its totality. There is no place to stand outside all of its revolutions; the place of the observer within its many fields both enables and limits any understanding of its operation. The wealth of "completions and correspondences" keeps any sense of final meaning in suspension. The sphere stays endlessly the same and endlessly revolves: "that lies in the nature of spheres." And since it is not a simple spherical object but a generalized geometry, it revolves in several ways at once, creating revolutions within revolutions (e.g., Jacob in Laban's country), smaller patterns within larger. To emphasize, one can imagine standing outside any particular sphere and watching it revolve, but this does not place the observer outside all the sphere's operations: there is no such "outside." No one in the novel, including its narrator, can master the mystery of the sphere.

Both microcosmic and macrocosmic, the sphere's versatility shapes every level of the *Joseph* novels. The small, rolling eye-spheres of Joseph's guardian angel direct us to the upper and lower spheres as readily as great cosmic transformations. The moon, the round stone over the well, the breeding cycles of Jacob's sheep, the wrath of the brothers, even the comic horror of flip-flopping "nausea" produced in Isaac's people by his reversion to the ram (186–87; 122) — everything from local objects and incarnations to the deepest patterns of recurrence interconnect in the sphere's dynamic form. The world may be seen from the aspect of cosmic harmony and equally from the highly relativistic "many spheres" of human vision that Joseph describes to the Ishmaelite (671–72; 447). So the sphere accommodates not simply the double but the many (see XI, 665; "Theme," 17). Multiple yet all-inclusive in its various aspects, the sphere gives Mann's performing narrator a way to organize his material at every level even as he maintains its polyvalent nature.

Predictably, a paradox of time interweaves with the sphere's unity and multiplicity. Seen one way, events happen first in one hemisphere and then descend or rise to the other: "events do not happen all at once, they develop according to pattern . . . the stages of a tale" (203; 133). But from another vantage point they happen in both simultaneously. Esau is the successor of earlier Esaus; at the same time he is Edom the Red. This enigma of time fascinates the young Joseph, and, turning pedagogue, he patiently instructs his logical little brother Benjamin in its mysterious complexities (e.g., 453–55; 302–3). Joseph's prized illustration for this paradox is the "feast," which ceremonially repeats in all its "hours" a culture's defining event, making the past present and so structuring time without compelling it. The feast's reincarnation of the past simultaneously portends a future; this hour of the feast will return, preserving continuity and coherence even as knowledge of its revolutions makes possible allotropic changes in its practice and fresh readings of its meaning. Joseph's understanding of the feast's hours literally enables him to survive when he is thrown into the pit (583–85; 390–91).

The narrator carefully distinguishes between this conception of the feast and another, more stultifying version of repetition: Freud's primitive totem feast and the "very realistic view of blood communion as identity of substance" on which it is grounded (X, 260; *PM*, 171–72). This includes the primal crime of parricide, briefly evoked in the 1929 essay: "the morbid world of incest dread and murder remorse," whose effects determine rather than free. In the tetralogy even the primitive characters have moved beyond literal repetition, but not very far. The two short sections "Die Nachahmung" ("The Imitation") and "Das Gemetzel" ("The Slaughter") offer a none-too-subtle Freudian variation and blood bath (177–84; 115–20). The slaughter of the Shechemites by Jacob's sons, the all-but-primal band of brothers, at the wedding feast of their sister Dinah taps the primal energy of father hatred and turns it against other rival males. The scene appears right before the account of the sphere and is, so to speak, answered by it. Not quite willing to slaughter the dominating Jacob, the brothers displace their uncontrollable fury onto the entire male population of Shechem. They impose sexual sacrifice (circumcision) and then strangulation and castration on not only Dinah's actual ravager but all his kin and comrades. Foreign leaders substitute for the father, and the abducted sister for the father's women; the original Freudian blood feast remains very visible.[36] And Jacob's Isaac-imitating blindness in the affair arises not only from his aestheticizing of the scene — his excessive pleasure in the patterned repetition of Abraham's circumcision command — but also from his half-conscious awareness of the real object of the brothers' hatred. He speaks of the brothers' justifications, and of his secret pride in their "craft and virility," but beneath these lies his unfathomable dread. While the brothers are looting Shechem, Jacob sacrifices a lamb to God and receives, he says, a divine command to travel to Bethel, the great scene of his original uplifting. Strengthened, he denounces his victorious sons in language that makes their crime one against him, not the men of Shechem. Their actions have threatened his death and the death of the blessing; Jacob sees the substitution without quite seeing it fully. A few pages later comes the "answer" of the sphere, perhaps *Joseph and his Brothers's* most subtle containment of Freud's cultural determinism. It adds the knowledge that no catastrophe stands alone but is always part of a wider narrative that does more than repeat itself. Neither fall nor rebirth is permanent. Freud's violent tale, in which the catastrophe of father murder is internalized and helplessly reenacted in every succeeding generation, is in this sense a truncated story, a primal scene within a larger, more hopeful drama that both the *Joseph* and Freud's therapeutic ethic construct.

The use and containment of *Totem and Taboo* in the *Joseph* has still further refinements. The sphere is both "revolving" ("drehende") and "rolling" ("rollende").[37] The narrator does not consistently distinguish between the two terms, but a rough pattern of difference emerges. The revolving sphere is a stabilizing principal in that it regularizes the movement "between the earthly and the heavenly." Each figure or event connects to a template, and each template to an instance; this organizes difference within the perfect containing form of the circle, and gives every image or narrative a corresponding companion elsewhere in the sphere. No person or tale stands alone; everything begins and ends in relation to its counterpart. "For what is above comes down; but what is beneath would not know how to happen and could not, so to speak, occur on its own account, without heavenly image and counterpart" (423; 282).

So conceived, the revolving sphere explicitly contains — but does not erase — the two dangers that threaten it: indeterminacy and a paralyzing determinism. Spherical revolution can augur determinism because it can only repeat itself and so risks rendering all development illusory, even meaningless. This is, as per the "Dinah" narrative, the reductive menace of *Totem and Taboo*. It can also augur a radical indeterminacy because it begs the question of origins. Its revolutions might well produce endless variations — variations in image, in narrative, in divine incarnation — like those in evolution: ceaselessly unfolding without limit, origin, or goal. And once again no single viewpoint exists from which the course of the sphere — progressive or endlessly multiple — can be definitively determined. Because there are "many centers" to the world, as Joseph affirms, spheres (and spheres within spheres) may roll in incalculable directions.

The model meets these threats by adding the fourth dimension to this revolving, synchronic model: the rolling sphere. The sphere rolls through time — "men become gods, and gods men *again*" — and in doing so creates another set of patterns, and indeterminacies. Time both moves and stays the same: the final element in the mystery of the feast. Most especially, the patterns formed by the rolling sphere can chart the development of personal and ethical self-consciousness in the individual and the species. The complicating geometrical figure that expresses this development is the spiral or helix, that is the path formed by the intersection of any part of the rolling sphere with the median line it periodically crosses. The narrator does not explicitly use the word "Spirale" in his exposition, but the term does fit exactly with his descriptions of the rolling sphere.[38] These points of intersection mark the ascent or descent of the "lower" or "upper" world into its companion opposite. The coiled spiral incorporates both the endless circular motion of the sphere and the linear "progress" of succession. It gives further form to both repetition and change, making it commensurate with the stages of development that Mann regularly attributes to both divine and human self-consciousness. At the same time the spiral denies the final authority of any definitive center; it confirms the openness and mystery of origin. The spiral substitutes for the certainty of a definitive origin story the qualified affirmation of patterns recognized, variations incarnated. Its action does not entirely remove the instability that the absence of origin generates. But it does give an alternative structure to both form and change that preserves both open-endedness — the future — and the meaningfulness of repeated structure. It illuminates the sense of potential and expectancy in each image, each action. The possibilities created by the careful reading of events is emphasized, not simply the recognition of a single, long-established Truth. The spiral formed by the rolling sphere rescues the *Joseph* tetralogy from all premature completions, and sculpts its endlessly playful ambiguities. It fulfills the Nietzschean claim, cited in the 1929 essay, that revolution is at once conservative and progressive.

In the opening pages of *Totem and Taboo* (XIII, 4n) Freud affirms a view of origins that may well have figured in the "Prelude's" making (and which is at some odds with the reductive aspects of his anthropology). Describing his theory of totem, he readily acknowledges the difficulty of obtaining hard facts:

> There is scarcely a statement which does not call for exceptions or contradictions. But it must not be forgotten that even the most primitive and conservative races are in some sense ancient races and have a long past history behind them during which their original conditions of life have been subject to too much development and distortion. So it comes about that in those races in which totemism exists today, we may find it in various stages of decay and disintegration or

in the process of transition to other social and religious institutions, or again in a secondary condition that may differ greatly from the original one. The difficulty in this last case is to decide whether we should regard the present state of things as a true picture of the significant features of the past or as a secondary distortion of them.

Mann took up Freud's account of the bottomlessness of the past — it coincided with some of his other sources and his own speculations — but carefully contained the implications that Freud drew from it. "Decay and disintegration," "transition to other . . . institutions," "differ greatly from the original," "secondary distortion" — all four of these phrases mark paths that the narrator occasionally takes in *Joseph*, but always within the broader, more integrating rhythms of his spiraling sphere. *Joseph* resituates both poles of Freud's text — the reductive and the open-ended — into a complex and always dynamic literary structure that preserves their force without granting ultimate explanatory power to either. *Joseph* displays no wish to resolve these tensions; neither the heights nor the depths alone can sustain the narrative. Its conception of meaning requires mystery — the spherical sublime. Skeptical readers may say Mann believed that all divinity originated with the human. But all this shows is impatience, even discomfort, with *Joseph*'s inexhaustible complexity. Both the sphere and the intricacies of intertext oppose such a reduction. The perpetually revolving sphere allows its narrator always to have "one more version," a version that contains runaway variations or one that breaks free of life-denying replication. *Joseph*'s dichotomies are easily recognized permutations of Mann's life-long artistic obsessions: the relations between art and life, form and matter, death and love. The richness of the "sphere" figure gave his newest work unprecedented flexibility — and therefore unprecedented subtlety — in plumbing their relationships.

The sphere also revolves within this latest retelling of the story itself. Mann returns repeatedly not only to the tales of Genesis and their elaboration in commentary but to his own earlier formulations of the material; he refigures his own figures. His Adonis-hero can become an all-too-human, upper-echelon bureaucrat without entirely losing the spark of his divinity. In the same way the sphere illuminates *Joseph*'s playful use of literary modes. The up-close view of realism, the comic irony of partial knowledge, the overarching sweep of myth — each has algorithms and a history in literary practice that the narrator manipulates for particular effects. The sphere also underwrites intertextuality and self-influence. The open and self-conscious "return" of *Tristram Shandy* in *Joseph the Provider* or the "descent" of the *Koran* or Firdusi into *Joseph in Egypt* situates the tetralogy both structurally and historically in the ever-evolving cosmos of narrative. The "Kleist" and "Freud" essays are not only important inaugural points for the tetralogy, they are also outcomes of its performance and ethical vision. Both essays depend upon the sphere's dynamic in their own beginnings: *Amphitryon* re-creates earlier dramatizations of the hero and Mann re-creates his first passionate encounter with its performance; Freud's revolution turns out to be the latest incarnation of the higher sphere of German humanism that can confront the reactionary monolith of fascism. The 1929 essay clearly takes its shape not only from the political pressures of the day but from the Freud *Joseph* had already created for Mann, the Freud he required to underwrite his fiction.

The sphere also models the act of reading *Joseph and his Brothers*; we too are simultaneously in our own era and Joseph's, and take much pleasure in how the two draw together in the final volume. More particularly, the sphere foregrounds intertextual reading. We do not simply absorb the text in a linear way but constantly move back and forth across its enormous tapestry. Every narrative requires this, of course, but most do not foreground or thematize the process; in this sense reading *Joseph and his Brothers* necessitates, and dramatizes, self-conscious rereading. We come to see the dangers of monophonic or one-way reading: the reductive perception of similarity that blinds us to the subtle changes in reincarnated archetypes, uncritical projection of our own desire, a lazy or scattered memory. Intertextual threads weave our path, both in colors we can easily see and in muted shades we can barely detect. The "Kleist" essay is both suspended in time near the beginning of the *Joseph* and incarnates itself in succeeding scenes when identity, loyalty, and ethical decision are at issue. *Totem and Taboo* and the 1929 "Freud" essay circulate through the text, and the tetralogy maintains a middle path between the reduction of the one and the excessive control of the other. In this way Mann draws out the ethical entailments and responsibilities of reading.

Throughout his public performances of his "Freud" essays Mann remained silent about his opposition to the master from an earlier generation. Part of that opposition was conscious, but an equal amount, I believe, was not. The 1929 essay is not so much a simple misreading of Freud as a complex reconstruction shaped by both literary and political desire. The same complexity applies to their personal relationship, at least as Mann performed it. Freud as forgetful student receiving reminders about German humanism, Freud as colleague and fellow searcher for truth, Freud as all-knowing father — the relationship of the two men echoes uncannily in the exchanges between Jacob and Joseph at the well. Each plays a different part at a different hour of their relationship. Most typically, however, Mann dramatizes Freud as the stern elder of law and science who is yet loving and permissive, while he plays the youthful scion who turns every narrative — the theological, the psychoanalytic — into thread for his own spinning.

"The Red One" does not, however, end with a celebration of the sphere and its manifold virtues. It ends instead with the second geometric figure that will play an increasingly larger role in the novels to come: the triangle. The narrator describes this figure in an ominous way. The rival pairs of father-son and brother-brother, who battle and "castrate" one another, often have a further relationship in which one member of a pair stands between two others. The narrator cites Ishmael, poised between Abram and Isaac: "to one he is the son with the sickle, to the other the red brother" (194; 127). Had he succeeded in seducing the young Isaac into homosexual love, the father would in effect have been castrated and the fertile future promised his people foreclosed. The choice of this example inevitably forms a subliminal triangle for Mann's readers who know his own story: a person poised between Katia and a beautiful boy (not only Klaus Heuser but his precursors in Lübeck and Venice). The triangle, with its welter of cross-relationships, will frame several sections in *Young Joseph*: "The Grove of Adonis," the confrontation with the brothers, the Pit. It plays an even larger role in *Joseph in Egypt*: in the immemorial theology of the city of On; in the silenced history of Huia, Tuia and their castrated son; and in the novel's central, tangled relationships between Joseph, Mut-em-enet, and Potiphar.

As the last two examples remind us, the triangle is first of all the figure of Oedipus. The elaborate containments of the 1929 "Freud" essay and *The Tales of Jacob* are not enough to silence those final pages of *Totem and Taboo*. The specifically ethical outcomes of the two alternatives are still not worked out in the fiction. But the triangle also encodes the figure of Amphitryon poised between embodied wife and his endlessly repeating, divine simulacrum. Beyond both of these, it also expresses the figure of Narcissus, poised between the echoing voice of the disembodied beloved and the endlessly repeating figure in the water's lower sphere. The interplay among these three triangles will inform everything that follows. Triangles and the sphere: *Joseph and his Brothers* struggles to construct a narrative ethic and a discourse of subjectivity that can confront the terrible personal and political losses of the 1930s, and contain their hour within the larger feast of European art and humanism.

Notes

[1] Lehnert 1965, 477. A few earlier traces support Lehnert's view. For example, the 24 May 1921 *TB* entry notes an arresting "essay on a new book of Freud's that I found stimulating in that it confirms certain historical tendencies. The end of Romanticism, of which I am still a part, expresses itself in all kinds of ways, including for example a weakening and dying of the sexual symbolism that is virtually identical with it (*Parsifal*)." Reading about Freud leads Mann into his typical autobiographical speculation; he expresses little interest in reading the book itself.

[2] Dierks 1991b, 113ff. Whether these connections arise from Mann's own reading of the "Gradiva" or from more dispersed sources remains uncertain. Dierks's specific claims for actual textual parallels seem to me inconclusive, but intertextual weavings certainly do typify Mann's work from "Death in Venice" forward, and structural parallels between "Gradiva" and "Death in Venice" are evident even to a skeptical eye.

There have been a number of studies of Mann's half-acknowledged relation to Freud in the years before his more careful reading of the actual texts. Jean Finck's book (1973) opened up this line of inquiry. He sees Mann's "misunderstandings" of Freud as having deep autobiographical roots rather than more specific artistic motives.

[3] "Mein Verhältnis zur Psychoanalyse" (XI, 748–49).

[4] "Bekenntnis zu Siegmund Freud," *Neues Wiener Journal*, 8 May 1936 (*Frage und Antwort*, 223).

[5] Krokowski's lectures borrow from *Three Essays on Sexuality* but subvert their intent. Mann later said that the "bißchen komisch" portrait of Krokowski was "compensation ("Schadloshaltung") for the deeper concessions which the writer makes to psychoanalysis in his works" ("Mein Verhältnis zur Psychoanalyse" [XI, 749]).

[6] See, among others, Harpprecht 1995, 642.

[7] Lehnert 1965, 478. This chapter's information on marginalia comes from this essay. Lehnert's careful and thorough account of them remains the definitive summary. See also Lehnert 1993, 216.

[8] Mann could even be quite cutting in his containment of psychoanalysis: see his letter to Alfred von Winterstein, 6 Dec. 1947 (*Briefe* II, 573).

[9] For example, in his letter of 25 February to Helen Lowe-Porter, Mann says that he will soon have completed about four hundred pages of manuscript and that he was approaching the end of Jacob's "Lebensgeschichte." See also Hayman 1995, 374–77; *DüD* 14/II, 103. Harpprecht, citing Albert von Schirnding for support, believes that any exact dating for this period is impossible (1995, 663).

[10] This tone also typifies Mann's other explicit messages to youth: he opens his Lübeck "Ansprache an die Jugend" in his own home school, the

Katharineum, with a gemütlichen tale about how students from these very halls had visited him in Munich for "a delightful hour. We drank a glass of beer and chatted" (X, 316).

[11] In *Joseph the Provider* Mann defends the "indivisibility" ("Einheit") of religion and politics in this same spirit (1373; 908–9).

[12] Letter to Charles Du Bos, 3 May 1929 (*Briefe* I, 291–92: emphasis mine).

[13] Ricarda Huch's *Blütezeit der Romantik* (1899), and a speech she gave in 1924 (*Essays* III, 417), are widely regarded as Mann's source for this reading of Novalis. In 1924 he termed her, perhaps in a moment of holiday hyperbole, "die erste Frau Deutschlands . . . es ist wahrscheinlich heute die erste Europas" ("Zum sechzigsten Geburtstag Ricarda Huchs": X, 429).

[14] This makes for a small citation problem. Giving three references for each quote or paraphrase makes the text lumpy and pedantic. On the other hand, some important material is not in the *GW* version. I give the "*Essays* III" citation for those passages but use only the *GW* citations for those passages — the great majority — that are identical with the *Essays* version.

[15] Herbert Lehnert conjectures, plausibly, that there was little need to keep a separate script for the speech, since the essay was already in print. If such a script was saved, it was probably destroyed during the war along with other manuscripts and papers that were in the office of Mann's attorney, Valentin Heins (E-mail to the author, 3 Aug. 1996). Also see Harpprecht 1995, 1481.

[16] About half of these passages reinforce or develop a point already made in the lecture; Mann evidently wanted to make sure that his students were with him. He also offers a small aside to the audience about the pace of the lecture. Larger, more consequential additions include the opening two pages, more thorough explications of German romanticism and Novalis (*Essays* III, 135–36), and a lengthy quote from the end of the "Research" chapter of *The Magic Mountain* (III, 398; *MM*, 281) followed by a passage from *Beyond the Pleasure Principle*. The opening section and the material from *The Magic Mountain* will be discussed below.

[17] That Mann was happy to adjust this manuscript to different audiences is confirmed by his almost casual comment to Joseph Warner Angell, editor of *The Thomas Mann Reader* (1950): "I am leaving it entirely up to you whether you prefer to include 'Freud's Position in the History of Modern Thought' or 'Freud and the Future.' I am inclined to believe that 'Freud's Position' is more important as a critical essay than the celebration-speech, 'Freud and the Future.' However, 'Freud's Position' has definite lengths, which you will be quite aware of and which you can easily remove." Letter of 13 Sept. 1948 in *DüD* 14/II, 362 (original in English). Mann also gave the lecture — the same version? — in November for the Society for Medical Psychology in Munich, and again in Paris in May 1931 for the Germanistic Institute of the Sorbonne.

[18] Mann had second thoughts, apparently, about celebrating Freud's literary virtues quite so enthusiastically in the August version of the lecture. This is

borne out by another circumstance; in a few months he would support Freud for a Nobel prize, but in medicine, not literature (Gay 1988, 456).

[19] Lehnert 1965, 481. See also Lehnert's 1993 review of this material in the Reclam "Interpretationen" series.

[20] Helen Lowe-Porter offers the more graphic "*oubliettes*," which foregrounds the motif of the "pit" from *Joseph*.

[21] Once again Hitler, another champion of the German will to victory, sounds like Mann's dark opposite, an Alberich to his Wotan: "For the liberation of a people more is necessary than an economic policy, more than industry: if a people is to become free, it needs pride and willpower, defiance, hate, hate and once again hate" (13 April 1923: Baynes 1942, 43–44).

[22] Mann emphatically repeated the same point a year later in an interview in the *Neue Leipziger Zeitung* 15 June 1930 (*Frage und Antwort*, 165).

[23] *DüD* 14/II, 361n. See chapter 5 for a full discussion of this letter. Without making too much of it, it is worth noting that Freud's Jewishness, a subject which the *Joseph* intertexts might have carried into the foreground, is never mentioned: a discrete pedagogical silence in 1929?

[24] The English version in *Past Masters* (172) moves the metaphor higher up in the sentence, muting this effect.

[25] Mann's Novalis, drastically trimmed to serve his purposes, is another product of "the Magician's" art. For some reason the italics do not appear in the English version, though they appear in both *Essays* III (154) and the *GW* (X, 280).

[26] Freud credits this typology to "the authorities" in anthropology and uses it uncritically throughout *Totem*: see particularly the "Preface" and the "Animism" chapter (esp. XIII, 77).

[27] Freud to Abraham, May 1911: Gay 1988, 326.

[28] In 1928 Mann wrote a brief introduction for his frequent *Joseph* readings. In it he carefully limited repetition to the general, mythical level. He noted that the associative time scheme of *The Tales of Jacob* exemplifies "myth as the timeless ever-present," and the idea of repetition "an obedient succession on well-worn mythical paths." He connected it to "people who do not quite know who they are." The introduction first appeared in print as "Ein Wort Zuvor: Mein *Joseph und seine Brüder*" in *Neue Freie Presse*, 31 Oct. 1928 (*GW* XI, 654–69).

[29] Another revisionist (and student of Max Weber), Branislaw Malinowski, accepted much of Freud but explicitly rejected the Oedipus complex (the lead article in *TLS*, 28 June 1996 gives a helpful summary). In *TLS*, 21 May 1996, in a review of Edith Kurzweil's *Freudians and Feminists*, Juliet Mitchell observes that "By definition of the way it operates there is not much for psychoanalysis to say about its own discovery — the center point that it was able to formulate by looking from the edges; it has never had very much to say, that

is, about its own key formulations — the Oedipus complex and the castration complex — which are the figures in its own carpet" (12).

[30] Dierks (1972, 161ff) elaborates the evidence for Mann's own long-standing allegiance to the "patriarchal."

[31] See Lehnert (1965) for the complete catalog.

[32] Only at the very end of his life does Jacob return to Isaac, likening his descent into Egypt to his father's and self-consciously mimicking his blindness in the blessing of Joseph's sons (1718, 1765, 1781; 1140, 1172, 1182). But even here he reflects very little on his father's religious acumen; that is reserved for Abraham.

[33] Lehnert 1965, 469. See also Berger 1971, 48–49, where the connection to the Osiris saga is emphasized, in good part because Mann's discussion of that tale follows directly after his first general description of the sphere's operation. Lehnert cites the specific sentence in Jeremias's *Das Alte Testament im Lichte des Alten Orients* that caught Mann's attention: "Im Kreislauf können in den Wendepunkten die Eigenschaften des einen auf den anderen übergehen, da ja der Kreislauf repräsentant in der Oberwelt oder in der Unterwelt sein kann" (316). Lehnert, and, especially Berger, trace other roots of the motive to *The Magic Mountain*, particularly the "höhere Wirklichkeit" in the portrait of Hans's grandfather and the "Steigerung" motif.

[34] "Myth and psychology — the anti-intellectual bigots want to keep them well separated. And yet, it seemed to me that it might be amusing to attempt, by means of a mythical psychology, a psychology of the myth" (XI, 137; *A Sketch of my Life*, 68). These distinctions also lie at the heart of Mann's reading of Wagner in the 1933 essay and appear in any number of letters and writings about the *Joseph*: representative are the November 1942 Library of Congress address entitled "The Theme of the *Joseph* Novels" ("*Joseph und seine Brüder*. Ein Vortrag": XI, 654–69), and the letters to Ernst Bertram (28 Dec. 1926: *Briefe* I, 262–63), Jakob Horovitz (11 June 1927: *Briefe* I, 270–73) and Karl Kerenyi (20 Feb. 1934: *Briefe* I, 352–54).

[35] Helen Lowe-Porter very freely renders this climactic phrase of *Young Joseph*, chapter 2, "das Standbild mit Namen 'Zugleich'," as "the image that resolves the riddle of time."

[36] The narrator takes further distance from the near father murder by inserting the Egyptian diplomatic reports on this far-off border skirmish, and by recounting the "comic" effect of their stilted Babylonian prose on court officials (183–84; 119).

[37] The narrator occasionally uses "schwingen" ["swinging"] to describe the sphere's more violent motion (e.g., 194).

[38] The term has a well-known place in European modernism. Wyndham Lewis's definition of "Vortex," despite obvious differences, is apposite: "A shaped, controlled and heady circling, centripetal and three-dimensional, around a funnel of calm." And Yeats's system of interlocking gyres move in

spirals, with each turn bringing both a heightened self-consciousness and a potential scattering. Here I emphasize its particularly literary, rather than philosophical ("Hegelian"), function. See also Ferris 1980, 160ff.

4: Revisionary Narcissism and Performance in *Young Joseph*

For talent, my friends down there in the audience, talent is not anything easy, not a trifle; it is not mere ability. At bottom it is a necessity, a critical knowledge of the ideal, a dissatisfaction, which rises, not without suffering, to the heights of its powers.... To be known — known and loved by all the people of the world — you might call it selfishness [Ichsucht], you who know nothing of the sweetness of this dream and yearning!

— Thomas Mann, "A Weary Hour" (1905)

Narcissism! There is not narcissism and non-narcissism; there are narcissisms that are more or less comprehensive, generous, open, extended. What is called non-narcissism is in general but the economy of much more welcoming, hospitable narcissism, one that is much more open to the experience of the other as other.

— Jacques Derrida, *Points . . . Interviews*, 1974–1994

Nircississies are as the doaters of inversion. Secilas through their laughing classes becoming poolermates in laker life

— James Joyce, *Finnegans Wake*, 526.

I

AMONG ITS MANY SUBJECTS *YOUNG JOSEPH* contains a study of narcissism and its consequences: narcissism in God and the cosmos, narcissism in the development of human culture, narcissism in one seventeen-year-old who finds himself at the bottom of a dry well.[1] Each of its seven chapters takes up some aspect of the theme. The novel begins by exploring Joseph's irresistible, androgynous combination of youth and beauty — "the most beautiful among the children of men" — and the unself-conscious "arrogance" that his "proverbial charms" produce (395, 409–10; 262–63, 272). The narrator's tone is objective and his manner abstract, but the Heuser memories are just beneath the surface. The "Body and Soul" section generalizes this arrogance; Joseph's dreamy gazing at the moon confirms his unusual combination of "mind and beauty" (410; 273). The moon mirrors back both female and male divinities: the seductive Ishtar of the tetralogy's opening scene at the well, and Thoth, god of wisdom and writing. As he gazes at the moon Joseph does not think of himself as actually divine. That would be overt idolatry or self-dissolution. Rather he drifts toward a slightly more modest self-love in which the superior beauty of the Ideal Other exists to illuminate and honor its human counterpart. Joseph looks in the mirror of the moon and sees his own double-sexed, enchanting uniqueness. This self-illuminating unification of beauty and learning, male and female, "ravished his soul" just as the "narcissistic" allure of matter and incarnation ravishes God's original emissary to earth, the Soul (40; 24). This unification is the "Lieblingsgedanke," the "amorous idea," that "forms the source of his secret delight, and by which his vital sense of life is nourished and sustained" (411; 273).

Joseph's worship of both beauty (Ishtar) and mind (Thoth) in the moon sets the stage for chapter 2, the cosmic, sympathetic mirror-gazing of Abraham and God as they shape one another. The text carefully discriminates between this mutual development and that of Joseph's self-glorification. The novel's main narrative begins with the "Grove of Adonis" scene in chapter 3, in which Joseph's identification with the mangled young god comes under comic scrutiny. Then in "The Dream of Heaven," the most megalomaniacal of his narratives, Joseph tries to surpass his father's Israel-defining vision of the ladder at Beth-el. Chapter 4 begins with perhaps the subtlest scene of all, "The Coat of Many Colors." Here the ethical pitfalls of narcissism play out between the contending egoisms of father and son. The remaining chapters extend narcissism's consequences into the wider world: the "Dream of the Sheaves" narrative and its violent, beauty-marring consequences; the deflationary conversation with the sour angel assigned to guide Joseph to Dothan; the mangled Joseph's painful meditation in the stony pit. *Young Joseph* ends in a dark parody of its beginning: not a beautiful boy gazing on Ishtar but an old man's grief-driven, overweening wish to transform himself into the suffering mother-lover Ishtar and descend to Hades to rescue his son and beloved. As this overview intimates, the novel's study of narcissism blends features of the classical tale and Freud's analysis into an elaborate and specifically performative construction of the subject. Peter Heller argues that no single psychological theory of narcissism can suffice for understanding a major literary text (1995, 123). Mann's resistance to and incorporation of Freud into his own exploration of narcissism bear this out.

The "Echo and Narcissus" tale surfaces late in the history of classical mythology. The earliest surviving version appears in *Metamorphosis* III, and the subtleties of Ovid's androgynous love story rival Freud's. The story of the double-sexed prophet Tiresias, the patriarch of gender borders and the misdirected masculine gaze, frames the poem. Tiresias bridges the stories of Narcissus and Oedipus. Blinded by Juno for revealing that women gain greater pleasure from sex than men, the "kindly father" Jupiter compensates him with the gift of foresight. His prophesy concerning Narcissus establishes his reputation as a powerful seer, preparing the way for his role in Oedipus' drama.[2]

Even as a baby, Narcissus's beauty (like Joseph's) charms those around him. His name derives from the Greek *narkáo* (to grow numb). He is sixteen — almost seventeen? — when his fall occurs. Tiresias's prophesy that the beautiful boy will only live to old age if he "never comes to know himself" contains ambiguities the Delphic oracle might envy. Does his chaste refusal of all suitors produce a kind of self-knowledge? Is his delusion that the beloved image in the water-mirror is truly an Other a deception that makes self-knowledge possible? Or does he only know himself when, like a stymied psychoanalytic patient, he recognizes his delusion but cannot free himself from it? If he had recognized that Echo's plight mirrored his own, would that knowledge have saved him? The image that he sees in the water is both a discovery and a creation; the poet compares it to a statue (Pygmalion), a god (both Bacchus and Apollo), and a shadow. Even after death Narcissus continues to see only his own image in the river Styx. And so on: "self-knowledge" remains an elusive goal in the poem, with the "veil" of the water's surface barring the boy from his beloved just as Rachel's veil blinded both its giver and receiver, and interwove the wooer and the wooed. Like those who mourn Adonis, women of the river and the forest mourn his passing, and his transformation via fire into a lovely flower ironically renders him a permanent object of adoration who can neither see nor respond. It is a parable of Eros and Thanatos, and Joseph's own metamorphosis into Osarsiph, the dead Joseph, marks his perilous proximity to Narcissus's fall into his well of endless reflection.

Freud wrote about narcissism in several texts, most notably in the 1914 essay, and some of his claims have already appeared in earlier chapters. A brief review of those ideas should help us understand Mann's borrowings and revisions in his tetralogy. Many of them also appear in less systematic form in *Totem and Taboo*, the Freud text that Mann knew best when writing *Young Joseph*.

"On Narcissism" (1914) takes the familiar Freudian form of a journey of exploration.[3] Freud locates the etiology of narcissism not in culture but in individual development, and not in the literal pleasure of self-caressing but in a "wider field": "the libidinal complement to the egoism of the instinct of self-preservation." This is "primary and normal narcissism" (*SE* XIV, 74), a universal stage in development that precedes the Oedipal. (Curiously, while the classical drama actively shaped Freud's theorizing about the Oedipal conflict, he showed little interest in the nuances of the Narcissus myth [see Adams and Williams 1995, 1]). Primary narcissism — in which the ego and libido instincts "act in harmony with each other" — is "disturbed" in the child by the "castration complex" (92). From this disturbance arise libidinal cathexses of other people and objects in the world.

Drawing heavily on clinical experience with paraphrenics and hysterics, Freud defines "secondary narcissism" as the withdrawal of libido from persons in the world, in both reality and fantasy, after the initial choice of those objects (75). This process obscures, or entirely conceals, primary narcissism. But primary narcissism remains detectable in children and primitives, especially in their claims for "omnipotence of thought" in magic. So primary narcissism persists even after libidinal development turns the normal child toward objects in the world; nothing is ever quite lost in the Freudian psyche.

Clinical practice also led Freud to the crucial distinction between ego-libido and object-libido, a distinction which he returns to several times in "On Narcissism." Sexual energy can be directed to others, or to the self; this reflects our basic attractions toward hunger and love (78), and argues against any unified concept of psychic energy. But we cannot detect the differences between object and ego-libido until the choices are actually made. Further, "the sexual instincts are at the outset attached to the satisfaction of the ego-instincts" and even when they become independent they still show their roots because the first sexual object is the caregiver: the mother or her substitute (87: see also *CP* IV, 44). This is "anaclitic" (imitative or recollective) object choice, the normal route of development via unconscious recollection.[4] "The highest phase of development of which object-libido is capable is seen in the state of being in love, when the subject seems to yield up his whole personality in favor of object-cathexis" (76: IV, 33). But psychoanalysis has discovered a second kind: the choice of the self as first love-object rather than the caregiver: the narcissistic choice. Men, Freud claims, typically take the anaclitic route, idealizing their beloved, while women, by a tortuous route typical of his labored theorizing about female development, have a certain self-sufficiency which compensates them for the social restrictions placed on their object choices.

Freud develops this view in a passage (89) that Mann underlined (Wysling 1982, 97n): "Strictly speaking, it is only themselves that such women love with an intensity comparable to that of the man's love for them," and so prefer the most ardent lover. He adds that "it seems very evident that another person's narcissism has a great attraction for those others who have renounced part of their own narcissism and are in search of object-love." This accounts, among other things, for adults' attraction to the beautiful child — its narcissism and inaccessibility — and plausibly for Mut-em-enet's initial attraction to Joseph. In litera- ture, Freud avers, "great criminals and humorists [e.g., the trickster Jo- seph] compel our interest by the narcissistic self-importance with which they manage to keep away from their ego anything that would diminish it. It is as if we envied them for maintaining a blissful state of mind — an unassailable libidinal position which we ourselves have since aban- doned" (89). Similarly, parental love of the narcissistic child is a revival of their own buried memories of narcissism: "Parental love, which is so moving and at bottom so childish, is nothing but the parents' narcis- sism born again, which, transformed into object love, unmistakably re- veals its former nature" (91).

What happens to the ego-instincts once the object cathexes assert themselves? They are repressed along lines drawn by internalized social expectations that have formed an ego-ideal (the perfect self) for the in- dividual. "This ideal ego is now the target of the self-love which was enjoyed in childhood by the actual ego" (94). This locates one begin- ning point of the Freudian super-ego. Conscience operates as the "spe- cial psychical agency which performs the task of seeing that narcissistic gratification from the ego-ideal is ensured and which, with this end in view, constantly watches the real ego and measures it by that ideal" (95). Further, "[The ego ideal] binds not only a person's narcissistic libido, but also a considerable amount of his homosexual libido, which is in this way turned back into the ego" (101).

Freud has other, connected stories about narcissism, cultural stories widely shared by scientific and literary contemporaries of Mann. In his "Leonardo" essay (1910) he alludes to the Greek tale in connection with the painter's homosexuality and childhood autoeroticism but does little with its specifics (XI, 100). In the *Introductory Lectures*, part 3 (1916–1917) he asserts that object choice takes place according to two different types. In the narcissistic type, the subject chooses an ego as similar as possible to his own. In the "attachment" (anaclitic) type, the subject chooses quite different people who have become precious through satisfying the other vital needs (XVI, Lecture 26, esp. 426–27). In *Totem and Taboo*, as we have seen, he puts forward three stages of cultural development — the animistic, the religious, the scientific — and claims that they are paralleled by the first three stages of libidinal development: the autoerotic, the narcissistic, the choice of external objects (XIII, 88–89). The connection between this progression and Goethe's march "from a loving self-absorption via autobiographical confession to educative responsibility" must have both pleased and unnerved Mann. In both *Totem and Taboo* (88–89) and "A Difficulty in the Path of Psycho-analysis" Freud observes that scientific revolutions have nearly always undermined the "narcissistic illusion" of human beings (XVII, 140). This illusion empowered the anthropocentric conceptions of the universe which science has systematically exposed and destroyed. Freud goes on to argue that of all the cultural practices in the modern world, only art tries to preserve the narcissistic "omnipotence of thought" that characterizes the early stages of both personal and cultural development (XIII, 90). Narcissism proves culturally useful in that it can diffuse aggressive feelings within civilization, but this hardly compensates for the illusions it sustains.

Discussions of narcissism in Mann's work typically begin with an analysis of the author himself. It is hard to name another writer of comparable stature whose character has been so uniformly categorized; all four of Mann's recent biographers argue that narcissism anchors his character, and all (especially the triumphantly sour Hayman) judge him for it. They all turn to the recently published volumes of his diaries to support their view, and have little trouble finding abundant evidence of self-centeredness there. The diaries do indeed reveal Mann's petty side and inordinate self-regard; they also reveal many other, complicating things about his character, including selfless service, that the "revelations" of egotism currently obscure. The biographers go on to trace his narcissism's formation to events and patterns of his childhood, and to use passages such as my epigraph from Schiller's monologue in "A Weary Hour" to affirm its central place in his writing.

Critics have also explored its literary ancestors, particularly Mann's self-elevating imitations of Goethe, and in addition to the inevitable judgments have also found some compensating advantages for his art.[5] Manfred Dierks argues that Mann's account of the narcissistic personality, vacillating between self-grandeur and emptiness, far surpasses Freud's and anticipates the more recent theories of Kernberg and especially Heinz Kohut (Dierks 1991a, 34). Hans Wysling's excellent study of narcissism in *The Confessions of Felix Krull* emphasizes, more modestly, the combination of complexity and precision that Mann brought to his elaborations of Freud (1982, 92–3). He interweaves Krull and Joseph's late adolescent beauty — "a beauty that inclines to the feminine" — with their fluid crossing of gender borders (96). Hugh Ridley's discussion of Mann's "disturbed narcissism" (1994, 146–7) closely resembles Peter Heller's "oscillating narcissism" (1995, 130). In effect following the organization of the 1929 "Freud" essay, Heller carefully situates this understanding of narcissism in eighteenth century German writers and literary history. Then he shows how many of Mann's characters "oscillate" between feelings of "self-love and self-hatred . . . self-preservation and self-surrender, self-aggrandizement and self-denial, pathological and/or creative self-involvement," reflecting their creator's own "ambivalently oscillating egocentricity" (124, 129). Heller derives Mann's fondness for leitmotif and even his famous irony — " . . . the positive and negative affect toward the same object . . . [that] is a fundamental condition of his art from his earliest to his latest works" — from this oscillation (130).

Whatever *Young Joseph*'s construction of narcissism owes to Mann's much-maligned character, it reveals his extraordinary knowledge of its intricacies and consequences and his ability to take distance from its operations. One could say that Mann works out his narcissism, or even narcissistically improves his narcissism, in the novels. And narcissism unquestionably has positive features for both Mann and his fictions; without it, artistic creation might well never begin and characters never develop. But whatever its personal benefits, the novel conclusively shows that Mann is not simply a defenseless, self-indulgent victim of narcissism; both major and minor characters attest to his discernment. The comic, self-knowing cameo of Rimut, priest of the god Sin and oil-gazing narcissist who prophesizes Joseph's career to Rachel, offers a funny, sagacious instance (337–41; 223–26). And while the "oscillating narcissism" diagnosis may sometimes describe Mann, it does not easily fit his Joseph. In his great moments of doubt, downfall, and self-castigation he confronts his blindnesses and moral failures without self-hatred or self-denial. He never despairs of the ultimate success of God's plan for the future or his own lasting fame; Thomas Mann frequently despaired of both. All this is to say that Mann's demonstrated knowledge of narcissism — its types, its refinements, and its unavoidability — complicates his portrait considerably, and leads him to affirm narcissism as a necessary mixed blessing in adult life.

The dynamics of narcissism in *Young Joseph* connect to its interest in the performative and the ethical, and to the tetralogy's determined rejection of reductive origin stories. Narcissism too has multiple beginnings. Near the end of the 1929 "Freud" essay Mann paraphrases a passage from *Beyond the Pleasure Principle* — libido arising mysteriously from the attraction that holds body cells together — and reads it as a gloss on Novalis. He does so to nail down his argument concerning the romantic roots of Freud's materialism, and so to contain the leveling power of Freud's "organic substructure" explanations. It is an account congruent with the unity of body and soul, beauty and mind, that lies at the root of Joseph's character: not a materialistic anchoring of desire and mind in the flesh, but their mutual interweaving. The two are always together in Mann's construction, however dim that unity may seem in primitive men or divinities. True, Mann occasionally uses such explanations himself when they suit his needs; Rachel's "organic forgetfulness" of the pain of childbirth is a ready example (378; 251). But by and large he shuns definitive origin tales or couches them in the protective coloration of mythological narrative. By containing origin's reductive power to privilege the earliest stages of development, Mann further clears the way for his own supplementary conception of narcissism. He uses some Freudian constructions but steers a course much more amenable to his own political commitments and especially to the unfolding of the *Joseph* saga. The subtle triangle of relationships in the Narcissus story — the beautiful, arrogant boy who can only perceive his own image and echoed narrative in the world — seems ripe for exploration, and Mann will use much of the story to illuminate his hero. Finally, Mann's portrait of narcissism in *Young Joseph* will prove to be another informative instance of self-influence.

II
"The Grove of Adonis" and
"The Dream of Heaven"

What else is there but Narcissism I often ask myself.
— Lorrie Moore, *Who Will Run the Frog Hospital?*

Young Joseph unfolds a sequence of scenes that give purchase on the structure and subtle shadings of Joseph's youthful narcissism. In the first of these, "The Grove of Adonis," Joseph leads his eight-year-old brother Benjamin into what they call "our place," the sacred wood where the women of Hebron annually reenact the death and resurrection of Tammuz-Adonis (442; 294). There he retells the story of the lovely youth's fall and rise. Shortly after that visit Joseph narrates to Benjamin his impossibly extravagant "Dream of Heaven," in which he journeys to the throne of God and is glorified. The narrator places these scenes immediately before Joseph's more modest but nonetheless calamitous "Dream of the Sheaves" that leads directly to his own mangling and transformation. The sequence ends with Joseph's self-confrontation and narcissism-analysis in the "pit," the dry well in which his outraged brothers cast him.

Jacob disapproves of his youngest sons' frequent visits to the grove of Adonis, fearing not only religious contamination and devouring beasts but also more prideful overreaching by his beloved. Nonetheless the grove has become the two brothers' familiar hideaway, and they lead us into its labyrinthine recesses. We do not witness the women's ritual itself, but rather Joseph's elaborate reconstruction of it. He carefully elides any reference to the openly sensuous hours of the Adonis feast (probably preserved for us in the "Song of Songs"); that is not a stage he is ready to mount. As he narrates, he silently weaves himself a myrtle wreath — the garland of love and death's intermingling in sacrifice, and a symbol of intertextual play — betokening his identity with the dying-rising divinity.[6] The myrtle marks Adonis and also his mother, Myrra, who bore him after her own guilt-driven metamorphosis into the sacred tree named for her. So Joseph stages a scene in which Benjamin may hear the familiar tale, see its woven image, and gaze adoringly on its fleshly reincarnation.

Both studied and compelled, Joseph's theatrical identification with the Mangled One recalls the tetralogy's opening scene by the well, when he bared his body to Ishtar. Here again he flirts with the role of her beloved son and spouse. There the chanted babble of erotic religious ecstasy interwove itself with his witty paraphrases of myth. Here he narrates the story of the god in order to call up the divine reflection before his audience. The section's delicate interplay between Joseph's self-conscious, even smug dramatization and the subterranean blindnesses of his tale exposes his narcissism with precision.

Seen through the lens of self-influence, the dramatic situation of "The Grove of Adonis" draws not only from the mythic drama but from Mann's many performances before youthful audiences, certainly including the "Kleist" re-creation.[7] Here its effect permeates the scene, coloring its background and atmosphere, rather than directly shaping a particular line or action. The section comically inverts the erotic scene of 1927. There Mann renarrated *Amphitryon* under the gaze of his beloved, Klaus Heuser, and instructed him in loyal love. Here the beautiful lad moves from the audience to the stage, turns pedagogue, and tries to instruct an even younger boy in the mysteries of love and death. But Joseph must narrate before an equally adoring but garrulous and decidedly unerotic Benjamin. As Mann did with *Amphitryon*, Joseph has made two earlier visits to Adonis's sacred play. On those occasions his black eyes looked into the mirror of his alter ego, the beautiful wooden representation of the god with its "black glass eyes," and recorded the high ceremonies of entombment and release. Now in his "Wiedereroberung" of the sacred drama he must look into the loyal, and deflationary, gray eyes of his little brother. Again like Mann, he will play all the parts, male and female, as he restages the play for his worshipful audience. In 1927 Mann began by affirming loyalty to Kleist's absent drama as an intimate part of love; here his Joseph's renarration of the absent Adonis ritual shows us his narcissism in full relief. The comic incongruity reveals Mann's insight into the blindnesses of such performance even as it exposes Joseph's.

Joseph's presentation deftly epitomizes his everyday ambition; he sets out to make himself the divine youth of sacrifice and resurrection. Without some such appropriation and performance, he cannot enter the world as he wishes to be seen; without an audience and mirror, there can be no satisfying self-adoration. He affects a neutral, anthropological kind of pedagogic responsibility to his brother, but his real purpose is to teach Benjamin to behold divinity. Naturally Joseph cannot simply announce that he is Adonai, "Lord"; to convince, he must lead his brother to see the divinity in him. So he must combine image and narrative in order to create an acknowledgment, a revelation, that will confirm his godhood. His silent weaving of the myrtle wreath throughout his reenactment indicates the ambivalence in which he is enmeshed: he can point toward but not declare his divinity. The inhibitions, the comic blockages, that interrupt his performance illuminate his narcissism's cul-de-sacs.

Joseph's reconstruction of the hieratic drama captivates the reader, but no more than the reactions of his brother. Benjamin's performance amalgamates knowing repetition and first-time eagerness. In looks and language he is indeed Klaus Heuser's inversion: chubby, articulate, an ironic putto rather than an erotic icon. Like the "Kleist" audience, Benjamin already knows the story of the sacred play, yet he loyally wishes to hear it yet again from his brother's lips. So as Joseph constructs himself in Adonis's image, Benjamin's "naive" questions form a kind of anti-narcissism trick mirror which reflects only the nuances of self-love in his elder brother's tale. Benjamin's noli me tangere status makes him perfect for these reflections, since it comes not from any blatant narcissism of his own but from the melancholy and shyness intrinsic to his character as "mother-slayer." Joseph's birth had torn Rachel, and Benjamin's had killed her; the brothers in effect both wear the touch-me-not myrtle but are sacrifices to different elements. Additionally, Benjamin's view of Joseph pinpoints the narcissism in Jacob's view of his son. Both see the lost mother in the double-sexed Joseph as well as the adored scion or sibling. But unlike his father, Benjamin keeps his head in the midst of his adoration, and tries to educate his brother even as he endures Joseph's disingenuous pedagogy. He is the only selfless admirer in the Grove of the Lovely Boy; his attempts to read his brother's secrets are acts of loyalty and love, not self-aggrandizement.

Joseph seems unaware of Benjamin's concentrated efforts to grasp his feelings. He does not see his youngest brother any more clearly than he sees his other siblings, and he thinks that "the little one" only takes a child's pleasure in the repeated story. But Benjamin listens equally for the tone and rhythm and subtleties "between the words" in order to sense the "secret thoughts" that are intermixed with Joseph's narrative "as salt is in the sea" (447; 297). Benjamin understands his brother far better than the brother troubles to understand him, and he struggles to maintain their fraternal relatedness that his brother's narrative threatens to erase. For example, when Joseph begins to narrate the lamentation for Adonis, he unconsciously withdraws his arm from his little brother — the perfect narcissistic gesture — and must be reminded that they have come to the grove together. Again Benjamin observes that Joseph now shaves, but he sees it not as a badge of adulthood but rather an attempt to hold on to his smooth-cheeked, adolescent beauty: the regressive side of narcissism. So Joseph believes that he is withholding things from his adoring younger brother "until his understanding waxes" like the moon, when the opposite is the case. Reading between the words, we see the barely suppressed and nicely ironic moon metaphor in "Dein Verstand ist im Zunehmen und wird bald rund und voll sein." (451; 300). "Your understanding waxes, and will soon be round and full" indeed: Joseph's ostensible "full moon" understanding is in fact eclipsed by his narcissistic shadow.

The complex mirroring in the scene extends well beyond the relation between the brothers. A shrine stands at the center of the grove (440; 293). It is a four-sided, Massabic pyramid taller than a man, decorated with "symbols of procreation," and surrounded by clay votives filled with earth and new green sprouts. The women also lay out fertile green images of the god on stretched canvas screens, sew them with sprouts, and trim them to an even shape. These three form the triangle of images — the pyramid, the phalluses, the fertile god-images — that the grove mirrors back to Joseph. Each of them reflects a threatening image for Joseph that, blinded by his insight, he cannot see. The setting echoes Narcissus's pool, reflecting back youthful fertility that disguises a fatal embrace. The pyramid stands at the silent center of Joseph's narrative, the death marker surrounded by the multiple images of the god. He sits directly on the base of Ishtar's altar surrounded by the images — no loyal devotee would do this — and weaves the wreaths of myrtle and narrative that will create his divinity. Joseph thinks he can, in godlike fashion, renarrate that death tale without entangling himself in its net.[8]

As narrating performer, Joseph happily assumes all the roles. It is not enough for his brother to see him as Tammuz-Adonis. He must be both player and narrator, both the double-sexed god and the insulated observer of his ceremonies. We presume that on his two previous visits to the grove he also let his selfhood flow into the cult statue and felt the women's mourning as tears for his own "mangling." Now, with an audience he narcissistically takes to be only an extension of himself, he once again tests himself with the trial of Adonis. Both Joseph's half-conscious borrowings from "The Testing" section and, for the reader, the subliminal self-influence of the "Kleist" lecture resonate through the scene. In "The Testing" we saw how Joseph's spontaneous refigurations of the Abraham and Isaac story always called attention to his narrative cleverness. He brashly resituated his father into God's position as narrator, testing God's servant Jacob with the trial of Abraham. He made everyone's voice, even God's, into a likeness of his own: the quintessential expression of his narcissism in narrative. Here too he wants to be everyone, and his studied mastery of Near Eastern tales extends his power. He wants, in other words, to be like the Jupiter of Kleist's drama, or God the omniscient creator and master dramatist.

All this makes plain that Joseph enacts a narcissism not of oscillation but incorporation, of taking all parts and all voices into himself. Narrative expansion marks his narcissism, not a helpless passivity before the mirror. Its precariousness requires all the different mirror images of the god: the black eyes of the statue, and symbols shaped from both nature (the sprouts) and art (the pyramid and its carvings). Joseph chooses also to perform the song of the maiden "of delicate countenance, specially chosen and named anew each year," who sings out the song of resurrection at the moment of the god's rebirth (452; 301). Rereaders know that this will reappear as the song of Serah, Asher's child, to Jacob at the end of the tetralogy, but what Joseph gains from his reenactment is the additional pleasure of double-sexedness; he can be both goddess and girl in the course of his tale. So the scene reveals the dynamics of an active, narrating, inexhaustible narcissism, its dangers and necessities; this Narcissus must not only see the other as himself, but multiply the others and even help to construct the mirror. In the "Kleist" lecture Mann did much the same thing in part for narcissistic reasons, but also to honor the art and extend the fame of his predecessor. Joseph has no such ambition for Adonis or his worshipers.

Despite all its uses of multiplicity, Joseph's Adonis story depends on narrative reduction. He admits differences only insofar as they point toward the figure at the center of the stage. The young Joseph finds himself in many gods and god-stories, but what he finds always turns out to be the same: a dreamy, floating sense of self-divinity. This is another feature of the narcissism of omnipotence, the desire for there to be only one story, one narrator, and one adoring audience. Like Kleist's Jupiter, Joseph cannot imagine that others do not love him better than they love themselves or anyone else. This shows itself both in the overall narration of "The Grove of Adonis" and in many of its details. So, for example, Joseph patronizes Adonis's worshipers, who know that the god will be resurrected yet lament full-heartedly. He names, but does not understand, the truth that those "mindless" mourners easily perceived — that the future the ritual portends can only be a repetition of the past. Joseph's narration may be about the future and the resurrection of the god, but only the timeless moment fills his immature imagination. His projected universe is a plenum. He knows "nothing of the rules of the imagination," its art of divining the emotions of others and even of preserving the self with that knowledge (485; 324).

Joseph grandly asserts that the mystery of substitution itself, while part of the sacrificial story of Abraham and Isaac, is "greater than that: it resolves the whole stellar position of man, god and beast" (449; 299). So what Joseph knows surpasses the knowledge of his predecessors; neither Isaac nor Adonis knew that he was a sacrifice, and so neither could deliberately offer himself as such — but Joseph can. In "The Testing" he called it "the advantage of these latter days." Yet this sweeping knowledge blinds Joseph as much as it frees him. He can't imagine that his reenactment anticipates his own immediate future. This focuses his narcissistic oblivion; he sees only the insulating beauties of self-elevating, self-conscious repetition. And when Benjamin points out the difference between the Adonis of this ritual and the "Adonai" of Abraham and Jacob, Joseph dismissively disagrees: "he is the son and the beloved and the sacrifice" (451; 300). (Mann's frequent insertion, throughout this retelling, of intertexts from the gospels reinforces our awareness of Joseph's pretensions.) With that sentence Joseph finishes his weaving of his myrtle wreath and prepares for self-crowning, the literal narcissistic capstone. It follows his explanation of the relationship between God and the image. "I almost believe you think that because the image is not the god, the god is not the image. Take care, it's certain! For the image is the instrument of the present and of the feast. But Tammuz, the Lord, is Lord of the feast" (453; 302). Joseph may wish Benjamin to read this aphorism as theological orthodoxy, but it is patently one of an aggressive Narcissus who wills that the image and the god, the self and the ideal other, be one. With that Joseph evokes the finale: the rejoicing, dancing and feasting which end the women's ritual.

By now the lineaments of Joseph's narcissism are plain: not a single reflected face but multiple figures and mirrors, and a self-love large enough to embrace them all as personae in his dramatic repertoire.[9] It requires not passivity and absorption but active and unbounded self-construction. Joseph the storyteller claims to know everything, and to practice the godlike art of representing another completely. His knowledge is divided from his character, and he cannot see past the self-pleasuring of auto-incarnation. He steadfastly resists every attempt of Benjamin's to relativize the ritual: "Not 'again,' . . . it is always the one and only time" (454; 303). To which Benjamin wittily replies, "'As you think, dear brother, so it is.'" Joseph's actual myrtle-crowned death lament is about to begin.

Benjamin presses further, asking first about the heavenly, then the earthly origin of the tale. Joseph, more interested in the "heavenly version" — the descent of Ishtar to her beloved — offers Adonis's conception and birth narrative. The story parallels the Oedipus legend, and its nuances further illuminate the psyche of its narrator. Still sitting at the base of the Ashtaroth pyramid, Joseph spins the tale of King Gabel, whose kingdom lay at the base of snowy mountains. Joseph directs Benjamin's attention to the sexual symbols on the sacred pyramid as he narrates. The king had a beautiful daughter, Myrra. The goddess Ashtaroth filled Gabel with passion, and he impregnated his child. Rage and remorse seized Gabel when he realized that he would be the father of his own grandchild, and he planned to kill his victim. But the goddess hid her in "a tree."[10] Joseph demurely refuses to name the tree, despite Benjamin's prodding, and a brief debate between two styles of narrative ensues. Joseph mocks Benjamin with all the other details he also "doesn't know," making fun of the wish to have myth narrated in a realist mode. Benjamin's desire to live in a world where recognizable similarities between self and other render the latter familiar and empirical perfectly illuminates Joseph's narcissism, the unself-conscious conviction that the world exists only to reflect the voice and coloration of the narrator.[11] Benjamin sees his mother in Joseph without subsuming one into the other: the equipoise that still eludes Joseph (458; 306). At points Benjamin sounds like a precocious Georg Lukaçs defending the balanced historical view of realism against Joseph's transcendental subjectivism.

The tree opened in ten months, and Adonis emerged as both son and brother to Gabel's daughter. Smitten by his beauty — again the fatal gaze — Ashtaroth-Ishtar immediately took possession of him and secreted him in the underworld. But the Queen of Hades, Ereshkigal, also desired him, and a struggle ensued between the goddesses. Ereshkigal compelled Ishtar to descend into the underworld to rescue her beloved boy. The queen treated Ishtar as an ordinary entrant to the underworld, forcing her to remove an article of clothing at each of the seven gates until she arrived naked before her throne. When begging failed, the two queens fought, and Ishtar was soon locked up and afflicted with diseases. In her absence the earth languished. Finally God intervened, consigning Adonis to the underworld for one-third of the year, to the earth for the same period, and to a place of his own choosing for the remainder. That "third place" is hard to name, according to Joseph, especially since both male and female divinities desired Adonis and seduced him. This inaugurated, says Joseph, the tale of absence, mourning, and return that the women celebrate in the grove.

Joseph's performance of the Adonis story not only incarnates his narcissism but shows how the *Joseph* tetralogy extends Freud's analysis. Had Freud chosen to use the classical tales in his 1914 essay, his Adonis-Narcissus would plausibly resemble his Oedipus, an isolated figure victimized by powers beyond his control. A Joseph drawn as Freud's hypothetical Narcissus would be little more than the rent boy of goddesses and fathers, and the prisoner of his own desire. This helplessness is of course one thread in the novels: Joseph cannot refrain from tattling on his brothers or seducing his father by exploiting his love. In this way Mann forms a bridge between the myth of Narcissus and Freud's clinical ideas. The seventeen-year-old Joseph stands between the paralyzed boy and his own mature self who refigures narcissism into ethics.

This makes for a literary psychology that augments Freudian abstraction in concrete ways. Narrative multiplicity, its prismatic reflections, take us further into narcissism than the generalizations of even avant-garde psychoanalysis. Mann does not claim that because Joseph is a narcissist he narrates in such and such a way, but rather that Joseph continuously expresses his narcissism in narrative, and that we can know it best through his narrativizing. It has no definable, controlling origin, though many of its intertexts and inaugural points can be seen. Mann's ample fiction permits a reconstruction of Joseph as developing from his father's idealization of his character, but that particular Freudian narrative is backgrounded.[12] In this way the *Joseph* novels, like the 1929 essay, connect to the mainstream of German humanism without, in effect, submitting to analysis.

So we come to understand Joseph's narcissism as that of a particular kind of overreaching narrator. Like Kleist's Jupiter, even the renunciatory Jupiter, young Joseph has no narrative but autobiography; he cannot move to "educative responsibility." His pedagogic duty to Benjamin has been compromised, or is impossible. He takes erotic pleasure in being the virgin consort of Ishtar and even entertains a painless mangling, but he feels no authentic empathy for either the god or his mourners. Joseph here has little loyalty to his brother or his tradition; he can only narrate first-person, and cannot speak as anyone else even as he vainly tries to assume their divine mantles. Joseph directly quotes the Tammuz-Adonis ritual's lamentation of the goddess for "the adored god, my spouse and son." It replicates the novels' opening scene, right down to the "Höhle," the nearby hollow which is used as a symbolic grave for the image (446–47; 297). The voice of the goddess in the chant speaks for the moon that was alluring but silent before: "No one loved you more than I" (449; 299). But that voice only gives back his own, and has no love to offer but reflected self-admiration; the rituals of self-construction prevent him from breaking out of his narrative cocoon. Psychically speaking, he is still before the well, worshiping the goddess, and has — can have — no idea that the feast may become existential for him. He tries to make the grove of Adonis his own private garden or laboratory; appropriation is central to his narcissism. For narcissism is always a mock relation, not simple isolation; there must always be a reflection in the pool, a voice in the woods, the delusion of an admiring other. Benjamin loves his brother and is loyal to him; Joseph loves himself as he appears in the divine images and narratives that surround him in the garden.

Immediately following "The Grove of Adonis" comes Joseph's longest speech in his entire life-performance: the "Dream of Heaven" (459–69; 306–13). Benjamin has heard this particular narrative "more than once"; in fact, Joseph obsessively relates a whole series of "most shameless" dreams to his little brother (458; 307). Joseph knows enough not to repeat them to all his siblings — his narcissism isn't quite that blinding — but he cannot ignore them or simply keep them to himself.

By having Joseph narrate his own dream, the narrator again forgoes the privileged position of the omniscient novelist and stays within the more limited — and psychoanalytic — frame of presenting the dream remembered, and inevitably altered, by the dreamer. This shifts the focus away from the dream images themselves to the way in which they are told and retold. Many things in Joseph's retelling — his posturing, his analytic interjections, his intertextual thievery, his moral cover-ups — underscore that this is no strict replaying of a dream tape. Yet neither Benjamin nor the reader can confidently distinguish the actual dream from all the embellishments and extensions that accompany it. As a result Joseph's narrative narcissism shows itself equally in his natural propensity for such dreams, in his artful dream enhancements, and finally in his repeated recreations of them.

Benjamin already knows well the narrative trance Joseph assumes: closed eyes, fists pressed to his chest, melodramatic voice. His posturing helps maintain his delusion that his loving brother is both entranced and unknowing. He looks into the mirror of his one-boy audience and sees only a worshiping reflection. His performance swings back and forth between the real, compelled "moving emotion" ("Herzensbewegung") of narcissistic flight and theatrical calculation. Nothing inhibits him.

All this focuses the scene's narrative intricacy and layered rhetorical effects. We read with and through Joseph's narration just as Benjamin does, carried along by its excitement even as we note its rococo excesses. At the same time we double that process by intermixing our sympathetic awareness of Joseph's need to perform — his narcissistic core — with our critical distance from his prideful usurpation of other narratives, especially those of his father. Self-revelation, religious vision, heady performance, multiple plagiarisms — the section achieves a parodic modernist epiphany of its own in its multileveled yet unified narration. In doing so it models precisely the kind of revelation that our narrator prefers, and requires, for Joseph's narcissism: not Freudian stages of unconscious emotional development or causal explanations of Joseph's dream, but a narrative performance that enacts and exposes narcissism's dynamics and consequences.

A comparison of Joseph's dream fabrications to the whole project's narration highlights the effects of these narrative choices. We may not know just what *Joseph*'s narrator borrowed from his many sources, but whenever he claims literal truth for his amplifications of the story — conversations quoted verbatim, tradition "corrected" — we know that he is fictionalizing. His claims of all-knowing authority unravel, deliberately, as soon as he announces them. The narrator's many voices and shifting angles of vision keep his aesthetic and ethical critique of narrative omniscience before us, and further expose Joseph's attempts to, in effect, speak for the entire universe.

Everything about "The Dream of Heaven" narrative is over the top, impossibly hyperbolic. The dream doubles, even triples the identifications and blindnesses of "The Grove of Adonis." The dream's surface is all self-glorification — Joseph rising past circles of adoring angels to receive the blessing of a grateful God — and its latent text all pastiche and undercutting. Its ironic reservations are nearly as excessive as its excesses are ironic. Joseph counts on Benjamin's ignorance of Babylonian tales, but the reader knows that Joseph's journey is a rehash of Eliezer's narrative of Etana and the eagle which bore him to Anu's heaven to retrieve the symbols of his kingship. Joseph had recently written down that tale — a narcissist's paradise — and memorized it (408; 271). For the reader (though not for Joseph), it inverts the "Prelude's" Manichaean narrative of *Adam qadmon's* grand descent through the seven spheres of the planets (39–40; 23–24), and mimics God's command to the angels to bow down before Adam (47; 28).

The overt textual borrowings from within his own tradition reveal even more; Joseph once again seeks to outdo the achievements of the patriarchs at every point. In "The Testing" and "The Grove of Adonis" Joseph sought to surpass Abraham's sacrifice; here he self-consciously exceeds his father's dream-vision at Beth-el. Jacob's dream had its own extravaganzas; he could, for example, only tolerate its brilliance through closed eyelids. The narrator underlined its psychological, compensatory function — a dream "which his soul, humbled yet smiling privately in its abasement, erected for its own strengthening and consolation" (141; 90) — and stressed its intertextual and multicultural root stock: the Gilgal and phallic stone, the ramped pyramid of Babel that models his umbilical ladder to heaven, the Egyptian and especially the Babylonian iconography. But all these features intermingled seamlessly in the dream and required no audience except the dreamer himself. Jacob's dream generated meaning in and of itself, and was narrated as a psychic event, not a reconstruction. Joseph's acquires meaning only when retold with an interpretative slant before an adoring auditor. Mann ingeniously uses this shift in narrative stance to pinpoint narcissism's dynamic.

There are many parallels between the two dreams — so many in fact that the sheer weight of their number mirrors the all-consuming nature of Joseph's narcissism from yet another narrative angle. Jacob's visionary journey was harmonious, comprehensible, and comparatively swift; Joseph's exceeds all measure. Jacob's few extravagances were organic; Joseph's are self-consciously enhanced. Jacob's dream compensated;

Joseph's dream aggrandizes. Jacob remained anchored to the earth even as he glimpsed "the most noble Face"; "he dreamed himself not away from the place" (141; 90). His vision traveled up the ladder, and to the fiery arch to behold the face of the Lord, but he never imagined his own bodily ascension. The winged animals and angels of Jacob's ladder "stared straight ahead"; the angels praising God cast their eyes down and grow silent as Joseph soars past them. In Jacob's dream beautiful messengers of indeterminate gender danced in measured tread, and gracefully flowed up and down the ladder. In "The Dream of Heaven" only Joseph ascends, and those angels who accompany him prove to be either obsequious or petty in their jealousy. Jacob felt blessed to overhear the music of the spheres, "one mighty wave of harmonious sound"; Joseph is the center of the cosmos and hears the waves of sound rebound through heaven only to his own glory. Jacob's God sat upon a golden throne; Joseph's occupies a mountain-top palace built of sapphires' light, and the "pillared Hall" at its center is measureless in its depths (465; 310). The throne of Joseph's God is surrounded by seraphim, who cannot contain their curiosity and peer out at the Chosen One. Jacob's God wears a "robe woven out of moonlight" (143; 91); Joseph's God covers Joseph's new throne with "a tapestry woven out of pure brilliance, light, glory and splendor." Jacob' God spoke to the humbled, still-supine dreamer and repeated Adam's creation by breathing new life into his creature; Joseph's God becomes a worshiper and elevates the lad to the status of vizier, commander, and Child. No heavenly creature bowed to Jacob; all — and not just the sun, moon, and stars of Genesis — bow down before Joseph. Jacob's God announced that Jacob's seed would be blessed; Joseph's God elevates him "beyond all words" in the timeless present, and makes him the intercessor, even for angels, with Himself. Jacob awakened to tears of joy and paced the circle of the Gilgal precinct in wonder; Joseph's dream ends in a cosmic orgasm ("my flesh was on fire, my veins glowed bright, my bones were like a fire of juniper-wood, my lashes turned up like a flash of lightning, my eyeballs rolled like balls of fire, the hair of my head was a glowing flame, my limbs were fiery pinions, and I awoke" [468; 312–13]).

Joseph's extended performance makes for a hard-to-absorb, even irritating narrative in the silent theater of the mind, but read aloud, with all its dramatized ironies and blindnesses, its foreboding yet comic arrogance, it plays beautifully. Oral performance also brings to life Joseph's propulsive, breathless style; his dream narration can't stop. Each description, word-bound and narrated in time, fails him as soon as it is told; it cannot meet his insatiable need for elevation, for ekphrastic ecstasy. Like a symphony with cadence after impossible cadence, the dream can't will its own end but must keep on soaring. This unveils an unresolved paradox at the center of Joseph's character: the wish to surpass the father, to be all-powerful in deed and all-knowing in narration, and the equally powerful wish to honor the father-God, the loyal font of love and security. Narcissism's insatiable demands, its endless rebounding from glory to glory of self-reflection, leads Mann's Joseph to appropriate his father's narratives, exploit his love, and substitute in his father's soul a kind of infinite Joseph, one who incarnates everything that Jacob ever loved: Rachel, God, his chosen son. Only the self-unraveling of this grandiose fantasy can uncover its counter-image of the Other. Joseph has not murdered the father but rather usurped his self-constructing narratives. He tells Benjamin that he would, "after a little while," have returned to his family and exalted them with his new powers. But this is only an intuition of the chastened man he will become, not an acknowledgment of his narcissistic excess.

At the end of his brother's seemingly endless narration, Benjamin again comments on Joseph's razor — his attempt to preserve his androgynous, godlike youth — and warns him once more against telling the others of his "eternal glorification." He urges Joseph to keep his little brother's image in mind when tempted, but Joseph is not yet ready — or able — to choose loyalty to the loving fraternal face. Benjamin can only do battle against Joseph's narcissism with his small ironies of overpraise and innuendo, and Joseph cannot acknowledge the brother's independent love any more than he can see into his deeper union with his father-God.

Finally, "The Dream of Heaven" fully expresses Mann's intertextual refiguration of primary and secondary narcissism. Psychoanalysis's story of narcissism remains detectable throughout; Freud's claim that primary narcissism evidences itself in our belief in the "omnipotence of thoughts" (88) takes on prodigal life here, and Joseph lingers long in this territory. Again, primary narcissism — the ego and libido instincts acting in harmony with each other — plausibly describes the root of the dangerous harmonies of Joseph's late adolescence. Interweaving the particulars of the scene's narrative levels with Freud's generalities yields a more rounded portrait of narcissism and its vicissitudes.

With these preliminary connections to Freud in mind, we can now revisit the question of origins. Both Genesis and *Joseph and his Brothers* maintain a silence about the psychic beginnings and the childhood development of Joseph's narcissism. The tetralogy devotes itself to filling in the numerous gaps in Genesis's narrative, but not that one. The God of Genesis shows little interest in infancy and childhood, but we may well expect the author of *Buddenbrooks* and "Tonio Kröger" to do so. The opening phrase of *Young Joseph* — "Now it is said that Joseph, being seventeen years" (393; 261: Genesis 37:2) — slyly uses Biblical authority to set aside the question. Eliezer has been Joseph's teacher from the beginning, but the narrator dramatizes only the lessons at age seventeen and summarizes the rest in the parodic conservatism of the mentor's "grand style" that has little to do with childhood (400, 405; 266, 269). The narrator claims that our actions arise from our "fundamental tastes and sympathies," but the example he cites for the thirty-year-old Joseph comes not from early childhood but his seventeenth year (1501–2; 994–95). He gives us no cameos of the child in Laban's house, no tales of him composing sagas for his elders' entertainment, managing the Canaanite equivalent of a puppet theater, or even grieving for his dead mother. When they brought him to Rachel at the end, "she did not know him." We know that he looked on her, but his reaction is not recorded (388; 257). We know that he stopped and poured oblations at her grave on his way to Shechem, but he is too caught up in his "childish foolishness" to feel anything (532; 357). Of his emotion at the moment of her death the text is silent. Put figuratively, he cannot behold her face.

I am of course not suggesting that Mann has somehow failed his readers here, or missed some splendid narrative opportunity. His reasons for silence were deliberate. As we shall see, it continued his strategy of containment of Freud, and yielded yet another way to highlight the central features of Joseph's narcissism.

Two brief, parenthetical passages provide snapshots of Joseph at nine. In the first and more important he experiences the double bind of tattling on his brothers; he enjoys the pleasure of saying whatever he wishes but dislikes the abuse his indiscretions earn him (85; 52). He can only compulsively repeat his behavior, not understand it. This expresses his narcissism, but neither explains it nor begins a pattern of development since he behaves in exactly the same way at seventeen. Second, on the return journey from Laban's land the nine-year-old dazzles villagers with his beauty and brags about his place as favorite in the family (383; 253–54). It provokes "pedagogic irresponsibility" in his admirers "because of his physical and spiritual charms," a pertinent grace note in our understanding of Joseph's psychic journey toward educational responsibility. This occurs just before Rachel's death, when he inherits all of Jacob's overweening feelings for the dead mother: an endless supply of fuel for his self-regard (376–77; 249–50). Except for these sidebars, all the acting out that could reveal young Joseph's buried life is left unacted. Mann lets us infer that there were many adoring paternal gazes such as the one in the novel's first scene (79; 48), and that the opening of the ego to precursor and archetype went on from the beginning. But the narrator does not tell us so directly.

His silence sets in relief a moving passage in *The Tales of Jacob*: the first gaze of Jacob upon the true son. In terms of the literal narrative, Joseph's hermetic identity seems to come from that gaze alone:

> And yet Jacob saw something he had not seen in Leah's children nor detected in the sons of the maids, saw at first glance what filled his heart, and the longer he looked, filled it to overflowing with reverent rapture. There was about the newborn something unutterable, a glow of clarity, loveliness, elegant proportions, sympathy, divine favor, which Jacob, if not to grasp, yet thought to recognize the essence. He laid his hand on the child and said: "My son." But as he touched it, it opened its eyes, which then were blue and reflected the radiance of its birthday sun shining high in the heavens; with its tiny, perfectly formed little hand it took hold of Jacob's finger. It held it in a gentle clasp as it fell asleep . . . . But Jacob stood there bent, a captive of his tenderest feeling, and gazed upon the brightness of his little son, perhaps an hour. (348–49; 231)

The narrator comes no closer to naming a definitive origin for his hero's psyche. It is the "primary" moment for both father and son, bathed in the echoing father-light of the sun, drinking in each other's image in the pool, touching and being held. Both literal imprint and symbolic symbiosis, the gaze seems a direct descendent of the first narcissistic fall, that of the soul into matter, and of God's "sympathy" with the soul's plight (46–47; 27–28). Jacob re-creates the moment again for Joseph shortly before his final blessing and death (1772–73; 1176). The narrator also returns to the image in several parallel scenes. For example, shortly after Joseph's rebirth as Osarsiph in Egypt, Potiphar's kindly dwarf Bes looks into his newborn face. Struck silent, his mouth falls open, and his angry countenance "smoothed itself out and took on an expression of self-forgetful inquiry" (794; 530). He then points his finger toward Joseph — not quite touching him — and names him his name: a lovely elaboration of the gaze motif. Potiphar does the same when he names Joseph his new steward (995; 660). And Pharaoh employs the image in his story of Joseph-Hermes, infant and god at once (1421; 940).

This inaugurating moment picks up a thread from the climax of *Amphitryon*. What it reweaves is obviously not a direct imitation of the scene, but Mann's firm loyalty to its ethical insight. The loyal gaze that rescued identity in Kleist's play now has a genesis within the *Joseph*, one which resembles a psychoanalytic beginning point but avoids its reduc-

tive outcome. The self-influential power of the 1927 performance anchors the ethical vision of the tetralogy in this gaze while paying due
honor to psychoanalysis. The *Amphitryon* drama offered a way out of
narcissism's dead end without sacrificing artistic energy — Mann's old
fear — or analytic insight. With the *Amphitryon* you can have both
your gaze and your ethics; in fact, you must have your gaze to have
your ethics.[13] That "primal scene" fathers the secondary flowerings of
narcissism à la *Joseph*. Ovid's mesmerizing infant Narcissus reappears,
but unlike his classical counterpart who only accepted adoration,
Mann's Joseph gazes back and grasps a finger. At the same time
Freud's pessimism — that is, the gaze's dark side — does not disappear
from Mann's stage entirely; its traces remain in Joseph's falls, Jacob's
suffering, and the father's ultimate sacrifice of his chosen one.[14]

So the "reverent rapture" in Jacob's heart reappears transparently in
the eagerness of God in Joseph's dream to elevate His son.[15] And Mann
gives us virtually no trace of the intervening stages of Freudian development: no permanent tainting of infant love with the loss and pain of
maternal withdrawal; no decisive Oedipal opposition and rivalry that
disrupt the loving gaze. The mother does not play a central role; Rachel's love for Joseph hardly figures in Mann's retelling. In Joseph's
case the psyche begins not with maternal care nor early trauma, but
with sustaining fatherly love intercalated between narcissism's fluctua-
tions; the gaze of Jacob fell upon the infant Joseph, and for good and
ill he loved him.

The gaze also inaugurates Jacob's second act of overweening love,
the transfer of his bond with Rachel to his son. At Rachel's death Joseph is well past the age of unconscious Oedipal conflict but not the
reach of his father's imaginative reconstruction. The narrator does not
dramatize the moment, but his narration gives us ample grounds for
inference and elaborates the gaze's doubleness as both ethical ground
and narcissistic trap. Jacob now also loves the son because he "is" the
mother as well, both the Rachel-image and her reincarnation. This
eroticizes Joseph for his father, and foregrounds the son's femininity
and therefore his double-sexed nature. It gives him an all-encompassing
and idealized, yet death-shadowed and ephemeral, mirror in which to
see himself: as beloved spouse and chosen child.[16] Repeating their primal scene, the son in turn absorbs "die Vaterimago," the image of the
father, and interlaces it confusedly with his own self-love; instead of
competing with the father for the mother's love, he narcissistically becomes her. Under his father's gaze Joseph becomes not only the "heavenly youth," but Mami-Adonis, beloved of all. His own capacity for
selfless love and imaginative empathy are smothered under his father's

adoration; he does not recognize the mother as Other, but absorbs her. "I and the mother are one" he announces to Reuben as he openly manipulates his sensitive brother with the power of his godlike gaze: all-receiving, all-absorbing, beaming the father's construction into Reuben's soul (500; 335: see also John 10: 30). This calculated frightening of his sympathetic eldest brother shows the unsavory side of Joseph's narcissism. In that appropriation lingers an emptiness, a doubt, a death shadow: he is both the son and a simulacrum, a stand-in who is and is not the mother. He is, and is not, the chosen one. It is like the emptiness that Narcissus gazes on: the other which is no other who points to a self which is no self. Mann detected the same emptiness in public performance: the ego both commands and disappears into the simulacra it calls forth.

The continuities between this pacific beginning in parental adoration and his complacencies at seventeen help us see that Joseph's youthful psyche forms itself less around an Oedipal battleground than the deceptively serene absence of conflict that a sustained narcissism produces. The tetralogy will chart meticulously how envy and hate, then sex, unmask that narcissism, and how it finally sets itself right in the political and playwriting responsibilities of a public life. Like *Amphitryon*, one of its founding fathers, *Joseph and his Brothers* repeatedly works toward defining moments in which the characters, and even God, perform acts of will grounded on loyalty. According to the 1929 essay, psychoanalysis ultimately promotes similar acts of will. But Freud's story about growing up traces the trajectory of unconscious emotional conflict; *Joseph*'s, like *Amphitryon*'s, traces the journey to the conscious moral decisions — and their often uncontrollable emotional frames — that form human character. For the Oedipal triangle *Joseph* substitutes the study of narcissism and its vicissitudes, and does so in such subtle and manifold ways that it exceeds its great predecessor in resourcefulness. Narcissism cannot be eradicated, but neither is it omnipotent, and Mann's accounts of it in the tetralogy show how deep his understanding penetrated. According to the "Prelude" to *Joseph the Provider*, the God of Abraham profited from the self-knowledge the "mirror" of his creation provided him (1278; 845). Once again it seems to me that Mann continually confronted his own narcissism in this sixteen-year reexamination, and that he broke through its confines where he believed it mattered most: in autobiography, in narrative, and in "educative responsibility" to his countrymen. Even a determinedly Freudian version of Mann's personal journey — for example, that he merely imposed a fantasy marriage of narcissism and loyalty on his story — does not undermine the power of his artistic achievement. For

Mann, narcissism both supports and suborns creativity; it fuels artistic confidence but requires unmasking because it narrows imaginative empathy and subverts ethical vision.

The multiple implications of the gaze are the microcosmic counterpart of the tangled web of mythological narratives that it evokes. Oedipus, Amphitryon, Narcissus, Adonis/Tammuz/Osiris: as our summary of Ovid suggested, an almost inexhaustible number of parallels connect these ancient tales (and their Freudian reconstructions). The permutations are kaleidoscopic: each tale contains elements of all the others in endlessly shifting relations. The Amphitryon and Oedipus tales, for example, can easily be read as variants on the Narcissus story. Seen this way, Oedipus portrays the blindness narcissism engenders: neither the father nor the mother was recognized by the overconfident, self-important ruler, who confused clever riddle-solving with self-understanding and the desperate love of his stricken Theban subjects with personal greatness. Similarly, the Oedipal conflict in Freud's version can be constructed as a kind of narcissism gone bad — the son as blind rival for the mother's love — and this narcissism's defeat as leading to an internalized, insatiable conscience. Kleist's Amphitryon, another father (in-law) slayer, is plausibly a Narcissus figure, a brash and unreflective general who contends with his own image. As we saw, much of the play reenacts the Narcissus drama with a hero who cannot be fully embodied and who seems an echo to Jupiter's incarnation of him. In this sense it is rather like having the Narcissus story as seen by the image in the pool. Again, the triangle that encodes Amphitryon, poised between embodied wife and his simulacrum, also encodes Narcissus, poised between the echoing voice of the disembodied beloved and the endlessly repeating and rebounding figure in the water's lower sphere. Oedipus found a stranger within, and Amphitryon a perfect simulacrum without; Narcissus arguably makes both these discoveries. At the climax of their stories both Oedipus and Amphitryon seem the ghosts of their former selves, and then come into their true natures through heroic moral decision. We already explored some of these similarities in the "Kleist" chapter, and a final sorting should clarify the intricacies of Joseph's intertextual reconstruction.

The tales of Adonis and Narcissus, who both die in the arms of their beloveds, mirror each other in several ways. The Adonis myth positions itself between the Oedipus and Narcissus tales. The product of father-daughter incest, Adonis is, like Narcissus, a victim of his own beauty. He captivates god and goddess alike; his image makes him an entrancing pool to all his worshipers. The great-grandson of Pygmalion is molded into an erotic object by divine lovers and human suppliants who love him better than they love themselves. Joseph at seventeen is lured by that worship, even of the mutilated, suffering body, and is blind to the moral consequences of such repetitive, regressive suffering. Ample traces of that same regression remain visible in the seemingly opposite extravagances of "The Dream of Heaven."

Microscopic and macroscopic, a memorable gaze also links Joseph's boyhood and maturity. Looking far ahead, the thematic climax of the tetralogy arises from this doubleness of the gaze: the "tam" of *Joseph the Provider*, the balanced "yes-no with a final yes" of Urim and Thummim, light and dark, life and death, in the mature Joseph.[17] "Sympathy with life and death": is it not cut from the same cloth as these early interweavings of the gaze and Oedipus, Kleist and Freud, ethical hope and determining prehistory?[18] In the "Urim and Thummim" section the narrator also makes explicit the precariousness of Joseph's memory and, by extension, of self-influence's half-conscious, extraordinary power. The occasion is Joseph's recollection of another formative gaze, as he stood atop the hill above Hebron and looked down on the tomb of Abraham set against the bustle of the city: "It may seem bold and arbitrary to connect such early feelings in his breast, which after all were matters of the moment, with the considered conduct of his present age, and probably still more rash to make the latter depend on the former . . . . [Yet] that was entirely characteristic of Rachel's eldest, though he scarcely knew it himself" (1503; 995–96). His receptive feeling for the balance of life and death, the "double blessing" (1504; 996) comes from this moment. The narrator affirms that such "fundamental tastes and sympathies . . . color our whole existence and dye all our doings" (1501; 994), including, it turns out, the construction of the narrative that records this truth. But what will matter most is how Joseph acts, what he wills into being as a result of his sympathy.

III
From "The Coat of Many Colors" to "The Pit": Narcissism on Stage

For the shadow of faintness which the thumb without a nail had cast had deepened now, at the back of her brain (which is the part furthest from sight) into a pool where things dwell in darkness so deep that what they are we scarcely know. She now looked down into this pool or sea in which everything is reflected — and, indeed, some say that all our most violent passions, and art and religion are the reflections which we see in the dark hollow at the back of the head when the visible world is obscured for the time.

— Virginia Woolf, *Orlando*

"The Coat of Many Colors" both invites and thematizes oral perform-ance. These are patently pages written to be heard: the sumptuous in-ventory of Jacob's tent, appealing to all five senses; three interconnected dramatic exchanges that build on one another, creating a storyteller's suspense even when the outcome is already known; Jo-seph's climactic monologue of temptation and seduction. The short experiment of reading the section silently, and then out loud, will con-firm its orality. If frequency is any guide, it was Mann's favorite section in the novel to perform.[19] One can easily imagine his voice lingering over the little incense burner, or climbing higher and higher in the closing monologue as Joseph, with calculation and innocent enthusi-asm and cruelty, worms his way into the *ketonet passim*.[20] His preference may also connect to the scene's critique of performance's excesses, confirming the speaker's pedagogic responsibilities even as he indulges in its pleasures.

Joseph's performance hypnotizes his father, an all-too-willing spec-tator of his son's magical transformation. We know from "The Red One" how susceptible Jacob is to this kind of intense double vision. Throughout the scene Jacob fears literal repetition and return: of mur-der and cannibalism as the origin of sacrifice, of the Avenger on this Passover night, of the fateful substitution of Leah for Rachel. Put in the language of the 1929 "Freud" essay, he fears and seeks to displace the primitive dramas of *Totem and Taboo*, and the substitution emerging before him uncannily evokes those sacrifices. Along with Jacob the audience witnesses the reappearance of Rachel. From the metonymic finger-biting gestures of concentration at the board game that opens the scene to the final pale incarnation in her bridal veil, "she" emerges like an image on a developing photograph, a ghostly palimpsest rising in and through the son's performance. The scene dramatizes the in-cremental stages of Joseph's self-transformation and, as drama requires, denies us any direct access to his thoughts until the climactic mono-logue. Like Jacob, we must watch his surface, his metamorphosis into an object of irresistible desire for his father. Morally, the scene draws on the corrupt spectral reappearance of Joachim Ziemssen in *The Magic Mountain*.

Concurrently the narrative spells out Jacob's fearful thoughts, his blindnesses, and welds them to his rebellious, all-but-sexual love of the beautiful revenant emerging before him. So he "forgets" that he himself had once thrown board games to Isaac to curry favor, and beyond that forgets entirely his own hour of performance and seduction in his father's tent. There Isaac's blindness had allowed the "right" son to earn the blessing; here the "wrong" son trades on the love that makes Jacob such a worthy, and gullible, father. Will Jacob imaginatively waste his seed, that is the future and the blessing, on the "wrong woman"? His ethical loyalty to the blessing and his love for his favorite are at odds.

Replicating his facility in "The Testing" and "Of Oil, Wine and Figs," the son conjures a little allegory to soothe his father's religious anxiety about Passover's bloody beginnings. In other contexts the tale shows Joseph's native tolerance for "the depths beneath" (e.g., 880–81; 587). But here it forms a narcissus-pool which mirrors back the self-adoration of its narrator:

> "Behold, there is a tree," he cried, and pointed with outstretched hand into the interior of the tent, as if he could see there what he spoke of, "magnificent in trunk and crown, planted by the fathers for the delight of those coming after. Its tips stir and gleam in the wind, its roots cling in the stones and dust to the kingdom of the earth, in darkness. Does the serene tip know much of the filthy root? No, for it has come out above it with the Lord, sways in the air, and thinks not of it. So, in my view, it is with tradition and indecency." (475; 317–18)

Joseph's cleverness masks the alienation and superficiality of his performance. To appease his father he creates a split between the buried roots and the soaring treetop, suppressing the fact that what the "fathers" gave was the tree itself, not its "most advanced" or "most primitive" part. The tips ("Wurzeln") cannot exist without the trunk and the roots, nor they without their light-gathering tips. Joseph claims to see only the tips in this arboreal mirror, only the freshest and prettiest new aspects of the self, and to keep from his father's sight the forbidding tales of sacrifice and murder that hold him back. But we know already that Joseph's "deepest conviction" is precisely the opposite of this — that the uppermost and undermost, the heavenly and the earthly, are unified and must know one another. Here, like the blithe and arrogant treetop, Joseph sways above his father, pursuing what he desires and claims to deserve. The "roots" he buries yet preserves are those of his identity with the mother, and the death-touched love (e.g., 921; 613) his father bears him on her account. In this way his narcissism's triumph produces its unraveling; its successful performance threatens to undermine the tradition upon which its glory depends.

Joseph's virtuoso exhibition demonstrates all the things that Mann distrusted about performance: its superficiality, its self-blinding, its dilettantish indifference to the ethical. His performance takes up the hubris in "The Testing" and carries it through another perilous revolution of the sphere. This time he does not simply suggest God's narrative point of view to his father but presses him to act precisely as God in conferring his blessing ("I choose whom I choose, and show favor to whom I show favor"). Joseph first seduces his father into displaying the *ketonet passim* (Jacob explicitly calls him a "tempter" ["Unhold"]) and then, even worse, weaves the long monologue of his own allegedly helpless seduction by the beauty of Rachel's veil. Joseph knows both his father's vulnerability and his collusion in the metamorphosis, as he confirms to Reuben later ("It doesn't depend only on me" [496; 332]). From words to images to touch — Joseph intimately enacts the mother in a kind of narcissistic incest, winning the veil that embodies the spiritual blessing.[21] Like Achilles' shield in *The Iliad*, it displays the entire known universe, the zodiac of divinity. The drama climaxes with a spectacular metamorphosis: "It was the mother-goddess who stood there before him, smiling, in the boy's lovely guise" (483; 323). The onstage transformation of the lad into the goddess darkly fulfills the promise of "The Grove of Adonis." Paschal lamb, spectral wife, divine mother: Joseph narcissistically, and fatally, plays all the parts.

Joseph's final question, "I have put on my coat ["Kleid"] — shall I take it off again?," gives a final turn of the screw to Jacob's seduction. His response — an immediate, energetic "No, keep it, keep it!" — plainly marks Joseph's success, and he ends the scene by running out of the tent to take his bows before a wider public. Jacob cannot ask for the cloak back because he uncontrollably wants to elevate the true son, even if in so doing he creates a sacrificial lamb for the vengeful brothers. But the power of the substitution suggests a chilling second sacrifice, one fully in keeping with his repeated fears of primitive roots and violence that have haunted the whole exchange. To take back the "Kleid" would be to unclothe "Rachel," to reenact the bridal night. The narrator pointedly tells us that "thanks to the robe his similarity to the mother, in forehead and eyebrows, in the shape of the mouth and the glance, had never stood out so clearly," and he "thought of nothing else than when he saw Rachel in Laban's hall on the day of the fulfillment" (483; 323). The unacceptable sexual uncoverings involved in that "sacrifice of the lamb" make a lesser evil of Jacob's arbitrary favor; the avenging figure of double-sexed desire comes perilously close on this Passover. This is Heuser all but entering the embrace of the charmed older lover, with the thinnest of membranes separating Joseph

from the Rachel that Jacob loved on the day of their fulfillment.[22] Will
the father replicate Ishmael's "trifling" with Isaac? Mann here dramatizes the threat that certain kinds of performance and the unruly Freud
of *Totem and Taboo* posed for his novel and his politics: unmasking,
stripping, revealing, foreclosing the future. No wonder the scene ends
with Jacob lifting up his hands in prayer.

"The Dream of the Sheaves" and "The Pit" play out Joseph's narcissism in a more realist mode. When Joseph emerges from his father's
tent he is greeted by the barely disguised bitterness of Zilpah and Bilhah, the pleasure-fear of Benjamin, and some particularly opaque pro-
nouncements from Eliezer. Joseph, blinkered by his victory, misreads
all three. His vague, self-reassuring response to Eliezer is especially
telling, since the servant has just gnomically prophesied his pupil's imminent descent into the underworld. Eliezer calls attention to the naked Ishtar in the underworld and to the phase of the sickle moon, a
time of death that "takes the manhood of the father" and sends the
"harvest fruit of the sickle rolling" over the earth — a bleak moment in
the sphere's revolution indeed. The old servant immediately celebrates
the fertility of the cast seed and the emergence of life out of death, but
this dark image of castration and father-maiming names the present
hour. *Joseph and his Brothers* comes no closer to affirming the Oedipal
center of *Totem and Taboo*, and Eliezer's haste in moving to more
pleasant hours of the feast mirrors Mann's own.

All this prepares for the layered reading of narcissism that organizes
the final sections of the chapter. The surface reading is clear and important: Joseph will move from the private, tented performance before
his father to the more public swindling of his brothers. His naive confidence that everyone loves him more than themselves lets him see only
his own reflection in the faces and motives of others. Imaginative empathy eludes him, even though sympathetic words pass his lips. Joseph's
affected surprise in the "Dream of the Sheaves," when the brothers all
turn to see their sheaves bowing down before his, reflects this perfectly.
His surprise is phony because he and his brothers had learned this
dream-image from their father's tales: the final pronouncement in
Isaac's blessing (211; 138). The unacknowledged intertext confirms
Joseph's unacknowledged concealment. Like Kleist's Jupiter, Joseph
feels himself to be an untouchable god behind the mask, reducing all
love triangles and complicating emotions to a single adoration. Eerily,
the fascist allegory of the bound axe handle reinscribes itself in the biblical dream: the brother-sheaves bowing down — the submissive tribe
before its Führer — and bound to Joseph's unifying divinity.

Joseph's rebirth begins, as Eliezer prophesied, when the brothers throw him into the pit. But his recovery turns out to be as mixed and subtle as his descent. As in the "Foreword" of 1948, Mann seems to give us something clear and straightforward, and then like a composer he steadily complicates his gift as he proceeds.[23] The method creates an entangling suspense that draws on the rhetoric of public performance as well as the narrative curve of many of Freud's writings: first a bald claim, then the discriminating permutations. Here the narrator first puts forward a tripartite "orchestration" of Joseph's psyche that seems to confirm narcissism's superficiality in his character (572–85; 384–91). It has one beginning point in the master myth of matter, soul and spirit (582; 390), and another in the passage from "A Weary Hour" quoted at the beginning of this chapter. The top layer, from which Joseph's blindly arrogant deeds proceed, also prompts his pleas toward his departing brothers. But on the second, "soulful" level he has "never really believed" in his own superiority or others' unconditional love. These thoughts both preexist and stand apart from his overt narcissism. At this level his latent pity for his brothers and for his father comes into play. At the lowest or spirit level, as "in the shadows and bass-notes of a deep-flowing river" (573; 384), he resees all his experience as a great revolution of the sphere in which all the divine narratives of death and dismemberment reappear in him, and whose on-going revolution gives him hope in spite of the hopelessness of his present position. Here he has made Eliezer's grand version of events his own. So in this model all Joseph's youthful narcissistic behavior was superficial and conscious, and cordoned off from his deeper character. He discovers, as Amphitryon did, the destabilizing consequences of unmasking the public self. His more substantial self has been, as it were, waiting in the wings. A relief "almost like laughter" follows from this knowledge, the same laughter that his father experienced at Beth-el after his humiliation by Eliphaz (143; 92). On this analysis Joseph's character seems given and clear, and its surface self-indulgences little more than Nietzsche's "daily ebb and flow of the little waves" in the 1929 "Freud" essay.

Yet things aren't that simple in either plot or character; Joseph's relief suggests premature, compensatory rejoicing. As "The Pit's" analysis unfolds, the narrator leads his audience to rediscover narcissism in the lower, archetypal levels of Joseph's character. The nagging "riddle" of his actions marks its presence; why, if he really knew better, had he acted as he did? His "wits" ("Verstand") cannot grasp the reason. A time-honored question, and one with which the narrator slyly commiserates: none of us, he says, can answer this question about ourselves, though perhaps it gives us glimpses of the holy (579; 388). But far from dismissing the question, this bland generalization keeps it firmly before us. For the narrator himself— not to mention Freud — has tackled just this problem of conscious calculation and unconscious compulsion before and come to much more intricate conclusions. The firm borders in Joseph's tripartite psyche break down as the narrator elaborates the content of the lower two levels. The upper world "mirrors" his self-understanding; as in his manipulative parable, he sees only the tips of the trees. "And his concentration was very natural, as the [higher] allusions all had to do with being and selfhood, with the vista of his ego . . . which now was growing brighter and brighter" like the waxing moon (582–83; 390: see also 1289–92; 853–55). As his "Bor," his dry well, becomes a prison and the underworld itself, Joseph's tiered ego expands to encompass the wider stage before him. It replicates precisely the split in narcissism that Mann frequently noted in performance: Joseph experiences an abeyance of self, as characters in the cosmic drama appear in and through his life, and at the same time plays all the cosmic roles within his "brightening" ego. So Joseph's knowledge of his own foolishness indicates his real development and sense of limits, and at the same time shows how such self-knowledge enables narcissism to return. Freud reenters here: "we suspect that this narcissistic organization is never wholly abandoned" (XIII, 89). Psychoanalysis has found narcissism resistant to cure; the narrator thinks he knows why and gives us a remarkable example.

At the end of his pit meditation, his bodily misery "overseen by his understanding" ("Verstand") and his soul filled with his pity for his father and brothers, Joseph drifts into the "dreamy self-satisfaction of death." Intangible and oceanic, it "mirrors" only the unity between himself and the "heavenly archetypes" (584; 391). In his "Narcissism" essay Freud notes that sleep, like illness, implies a narcissistic withdrawal of the libido into the subject's own person (II, 40). Mirrors, unity, and death: a return of narcissism in all its tenacity, and an arresting image of Joseph teetering on the edge of Narcissus's "primary" pool. It recalls Ovid's Narcissus, seeing only himself yet again in the "Pit's" deeper pool of Styx.

The narration, with great precision, figures this return in terms of "the face" (585; 391). Joseph pities the father and imagines his suffering, but does not see his face. No face of the beloved appears before his gaze, but only himself in the pit and the Ideal Other revolving to embrace him. The saving image of the father belongs to a later phase of Joseph's self-understanding. At the same time narcissism does entwine itself with hope and fuel a sense of the future; the "deeper" Joseph believes that he will not die, and that knowledge indeed helps to save him. "Just between us," the narrator later confides in *Joseph in Egypt*, "the feeling of expectation lies at the very base of the world" and therefore of our souls (844; 563). Narcissism both blinds and empowers; Joseph indeed sees one aspect of his self-love, but that insight blinds him to its ineradicable, and necessary, life at his lowest level. The section ends with Joseph's sympathetic, soulful "second layer" feelings for his father, dramatizing his growth while at the same time preserving the self-enclosed quality of the feeling. It is one of Mann's most subtle strokes of characterization.

In this way "In the Pit" completes the narrator's performative account of young Joseph's narcissism. Freud's 1914 analysis can be discerned in its fabric — including the Freud of neuronal fatedness or the determining stages of early development — but his influence is carefully circumscribed. The text is woven of looser cloth: of primary and secondary narcissism as character structures expressed in narrative performance. "Ruins that are themselves restorations" from "Gradiva" and *Totem and Taboo* also remains a vital idea, but the ruins are not those of a toddler's rites of passage but of ancient narratives refigured: a "Wiedereroberung." Mann's unrepentant narcissists can only remain omniscient narrators, fixated megalomaniacs, and the difficulties Joseph has in arriving at the right stories for his loyalty and love mirror the difficulties that *Joseph*'s narrator has in performing his own "latter day" intertextual tale. What substitutions underwrite and what images sustain both a good story and an ethical life? The Freudian threads show through clearly enough; in the *Bor* Joseph has given over the most overt aspects of his secondary narcissism, but has yet to grapple with the libidinal mysteries of primary narcissism and its relation to the death drive. For this he will need Egypt, and Mut-em-enet. But the *Joseph* text, seeking even more precision, uses the family resemblances between the Oedipus, Narcissus, and Amphitryon stories to triangulate, in every sense, the intricacies of narcissism's operations. Joseph's narcissism, like that of Ovid's character, Kleist's hero, and Freud's construction, has always been structured around the dynamics of love. Over time Joseph will bring his narcissism from the well into the world, just as Mann brought his beloved Kleist into Potiphar's house and his political performances into his own exile. With this understanding of narcissism unveiled and reincarnated, we are ready to journey into Egypt.

Notes

[1] Robert Alter (1996, 20, 8–11) points out the speedy, sure-footed way in which Joseph's narcissism is evoked in Genesis itself. A character's first words are "revelatory" in Genesis, and Joseph's beginning to the Sheaves dream is as self-absorbed as can be imagined: "Listen, pray, to this dream that I dreamed. And look, we were binding sheaves in the field, and look, my sheaf arose and actually stood up, and look, your sheaves drew round and bowed to my sheaf." Joseph repeats *hineh*, "look," three times; Alter suggests that this marks his wide-eyed naïveté, and may also dramatize his brothers' resistance and turning away. The insistence of "actually stood up" is not too far from adolescent speech today.

[2] Ovid (1958, 95). In another version Tiresias is blinded for seeing his mother and Athena bathing in a stream: the male gaze, Oedipal desire and blindness, and Narcissus's inability to know himself interwoven indeed. See also Pausanius 9.31: 7–8.

[3] Peter Brooks, reviewing John Farrell's *Freud's Paranoid Quest: Psychoanalysis and Modern Suspicion*, describes Freud's rhetoric in this way: " . . . his unremitting though often genial suspicion combined with his commitment to an heroic irony in relentless proof of the absence of the ideal, which eventually makes of the investigator himself an ironic hero" (1996, 30).

[4] Strachey's translation of "die Anlehnung" as "anaclitic" is good, I think, though the word means imitation more in the sense of dependence than copying.

[5] In "Fantasy on Goethe" (IX, 716; *Last Essays*, 99), Mann describes Goethe's "von großartigem Narzißmus" — his type of "splendid narcissism, a self-contentment far too serious and far too concerned to the very end with self-perfection, heightening, and a 'distillation' ('*Cohobation*') of personal endowment."

[6] Joseph entered the novel wearing a myrtle wreath, and snatched it off his head when his father accused him of throwing kisses toward the stars (62, 99; 37, 62). In *Joseph the Provider* (1520; 1006) all the guests at Joseph's wedding wear myrtle leaves, signifying marriage's intertwining of love and sacrifice. The wreath also recalls Jacob's wedding, when he sat "silent and dreamy" with a "blossoming twig of myrtle in his hand" and kissed the small figure of Ishtar on Rachel's veil (300; 197). The moon-nun Mut-em-enet's own connection with the myrtle ennobles her (1002; 668).

[7] Kleist's famous "Marionette" essay offers a parallel narrative study of narcissism: the fencing bear who is never fooled by the narrator's feints.

[8] This whole scene intriguingly anticipates Mann's 1948 image discussed in the first chapter: the "pyramidlike" one-volume edition of *Joseph* surrounded by its mirroring, satellite scripts.

[9] From the beginning the narrator has campily complained about the exaggerated "radiant wreath of famous beauty" that rumor and poem had woven about Joseph's head (63; 38).

[10] In Ovid, *Metamorphosis X*, it is Myrra who is overpowered by a desire for her father, Cinyras, and tricks him into making love. Cinyras is the grandson of Pygmalion, and Ovid narrates the Adonis story right after his account of the narcissistic sculptor's successful construction of an ideal other. When he discovers Myrra's deception, Cinyras pursues her, and the gods shield her in a myrtle. Ovid's account of Adonis's death is more specific, and for Joseph more prophetic. A boar, revenging a spear wound, "pierced the boy's white loins / And left him dying where one saw his blood / Flow into rivulets on golden sands" (295). Venus causes a flower to rise from his blood: anemone, the color of blood, and in appearance like that of a pomegranate, the fruit which conceals its seeds under a leathery skin. But the enjoyment of the flower is of brief duration, for it is so fragile, its petals so lightly attached, that it quickly falls, shaken from its stem by those same winds that give it its name, "anemone" (296). [*Anemos*: "squall"; *anemou*: "to expose to the wind."]

[11] Again, when Benjamin tries to describe Adonis's beautiful "coffin-chest" as a mere "box," Joseph insists on the original word; he allows no realist deflations in his narrative.

In Adams and Williams's scheme, Benjamin's behavior might well be characterized as "mimetic desire," that is "a narcissistic wish to establish verisimilitude between self and others as an attempt to render reality knowable" (1995, 2). In Mann's characterization of Benjamin, however, the weight falls much more on his set-apartness than as a "normal" narcissistic foil to his brother.

[12] See the discussion of Jacob's "gaze" below.

[13] Mann uses this idea in several scenes, e.g, the brothers' reluctance to look into each other's eyes when they are planning Joseph's destruction: "bargains struck only by word of mouth and not also with the eyes seemed scarcely to have been agreed upon" (595; 398).

[14] Touching must also play a role for Freud in the infant's formation of narcissism, but he glosses over this contact in his theory. Seen this way, *Joseph* brings to light or "corrects" a suppressed subject in Freud.

[15] Compare Heilbut (1996, 347), who sees this only as a "re-enactment" of Mann's gaze on the adolescent Klaus. Heilbut also reads Klaus's story "The Father Laughs," in which an aggressive, "unfeminine" daughter seduces her father, as a grotesque payback for his own father's desire (548–49).

[16] Joseph describes the "pattern" of his life in similar terms to Potiphar (921; 613).

[17] "And thou shall put in the breastplate of judgment the Urim and Thummim" (Exodus 28:30: see also 1 Samuel 14: 41.) Urim and Thummim denote two essential parts of the sacred oracle which the early Hebrews used to

determine God's will. The terms are almost certainly pre-Mosaic. The most common conjecture is that they were two small stones in the shape of dice or tablets, one meaning yes and the other no. The stones were probably light (Urim: daylight) and dark (Thummin: darkness, the absence of the sun). Or perhaps the stones were light on one side and dark on the other: whichever, when both were dropped, various combinations occurred which could then be interpreted. Or perhaps devotees shook them in a hollow "Ephod" image (e.g., Judges 8:27) and then threw them onto the ground. The "tablet" idea comes from Babylon, where Marduk had two "tablets of judgment" in his breastplate: Exodus 28:30 possibly seeks to integrate that practice into Judaism. The words have their roots in the forms "urtu" and "ertu," which mean "divine decision." The Assyrian word for a prophesy is *tamu*; that for an oracle, *tamutu*.

[18] To elaborate, if Joseph "is" Klaus Heuser, and even the naked, "radiant" Klaus Mann that the father once gazed upon (*TB*, 17 Oct. 1920) like Venus glimpsing Adonis, then Jacob's love for the boy could have been paralyzing. But instead Jacob perceives the mother in the boy, and creates a love triangle that Mann pursues much more overtly in the Kleist lecture than he allows Jacob to do here. There is little trace of the overtly homoerotic in Jacob, though he has an abundance of double-sexed fertility. Mann's own adoring parental gaze, so far as we know, was bestowed far more freely on the baby Elizabeth than on Klaus (see Harpprecht 1995, 448, 453; Heilbut 1996, 310–11; Prater 1995, 113).

[19] *TB*, 1 Apr. 1933; 17 June 1933; 21 Feb. 1934; 9 Nov. 1933 ("I read my statement of thanks to Switzerland, which was also warmly received, then remained on my feet for an hour-and-a-quarter reading of the 'Coat of Many Colors' and the subsequent episodes with the brothers. It seemed to have an extraordinary effect, and the heavy, unanimous, and prolonged applause did my heart good" (*TB*, 9 Nov. 1933; *Diaries*, 180). Mann chose the same passage for one of his last public performances, in Lübeck in 1955 (see Herbert Lehnert's eyewitness account in chapter 1, vi).

[20] Or *ketonet pasim*: literally an ornamental tunic. See Alter 1996, 209. Tamar, when she seduces Judah, wears its sister garment: the *ketonet paspasim* of temple hierodules (1568; 1039).

[21] On the relation of incest and narcissism in Mann, see Wysling 1982, 92. Mann once told Katia (29 July 1921) that he contemplated writing a story of father-daughter incest in which the father was motivated by the image of the mother in the daughter. In the *Joseph*, Mai-Sachme's love for his "three Nekhbets" sublimates that idea into a subtle, and ethical, story of expectation.

[22] In *Joseph in Egypt* Joseph says to Potiphar that this overweening son-love of his father's was a love "no longer in the form of life but of death" (921; 613).

[23] It has long been recognized that the descriptions of Joseph's exile and "death" in the pit are taken, with little change, from Mann's 1933 diary entries, especially 15 March and immediately following, and from his resigna-

tion letter addressed to the South German Writers' League. He wrote both just after his exile began. A remarkable instance of self-influence: through using his personal writing Mann contrives to turn his own suffering, via displacement and inversion, into something quite independent of his own loss.

5: Narcissism, Performance, and The Face of the Father in *Joseph in Egypt*

The Nietzsche lectures turned out well in English (especially in London)
and even better in German in the Swiss cities. But the best thing after all
was reading from Faustus *in the Zurich Schauspielhaus; the situation*
tied in perfectly with the farewell celebration of 1938, when I read from
Lotte — so perfectly that the whole intervening nine years of life seemed
to have vanished. I did the Fitelberg chapter (the temptation by the
"world"), and there was great amusement and responsiveness. Opus 111
came at the end. When Zurichers really like something, they combine their
applause with a trampling which produces a kind of thunder. Erika was
ecstatic. Since then she insists that I must write a comedy with parts for
the two of us to act.

— Thomas Mann to Kitty and Alfred Neumann, 14 July 1947

Performativity describes this relation of being implicated in that which
one opposes.

— Judith Butler

I

THE SPRING AND EARLY SUMMER OF 1929 WERE bleak seasons for Sigmund Freud. At seventy-three, his productive thinking appeared to have dried up. He had written little over the past year. His angina and heart palpitations persisted, and his jaw cancer had noticeably worsened. Wilhelm Fliess had died the previous winter, and death seemed imminent for him as well. Like Mann an able performer and pedagogue, Freud had nonetheless refused an invitation to speak at the biennial International Psychoanalytic Conference in Oxford, where restorative praise for his achievements certainly awaited him. A frustrating succession of clumsy and painful prostheses had kept him from attending in 1925 and 1927, when he had very much wanted to go; now depression added its weight to the inertia of age, and refusal came more easily. Yet out of this miasma he had, by early July, somehow begun to write again, and to write quickly; the new book formed rapidly, and despite one or two "writing difficulties" was finished in a surprisingly short time. In a 28 July letter to Lou Andreas-Salomé — the day he finished the project — he commented in the midst of many complaints, "I wrote, and in doing so the time passed quite pleasantly."[1]

In the same letter he wrote that he had read "Freud's Position in the History of Modern Thought" while working on his new book. As we saw in chapter 3, iii, the lecture first appeared in print in *Die Psycho-analytische Bewegung* in Vienna in the May-June issue of 1929 (reprinted in *Essays* III). In August *Die Neue Rundschau* published an abbreviated version which later appeared in the essay collection *Die Forderung des Tages* (*The Order of the Day*) and in all subsequent editions of Mann's work. Mann sent Freud a personal copy of the book, and Freud, perhaps after a second reading, penned a warmer response than the one he gave to Andreas-Salomé in July. Even as he offers Mann a few "corrections" for the essay, Freud thanks him generously for resituating psychoanalysis in the history of German "Geistesleben."[2] He is polite about Mann's exaggerations — it would be "impossible" for him not to know something about Nietzsche — and takes no overt offense at the essay's pedagogic tone. It evidently pleased Freud to be read as an active participant in a long-standing cultural conversation, and he seemed especially gratified that Mann had so carefully separated his project from the "reactionary mysticism" that was soon to exile both of them.

Yet Freud's response is in other ways quite curious, ironic, even "Freudian." For in the midst of gratitude and declarations of common purpose that can only be read as sincere, he also announces that he will soon send Mann "eine neue kleine Schrift" (*DüD* 14/II, 362n). He makes the requisite gestures of modesty; the new text will require the reader's indulgence, and hopefully will be his last effort. This little book, an outgrowth of Freud's illness and exhaustion, is *Civilization and its Discontents*. It bears an altogether different message from his friendly letter: not merely "corrections" but implicitly a wholesale revision of the 1929 essay's sunny outlook. The gap between the sanguine, progressive Freud of Mann's lecture and the gloomier Freud of *Civilization* makes it hard to imagine either man's overlooking it. One example among many: Freud's carefully constructed claim that civilization is aggressive against uninhibited love but negative/passive against uninhibited aggression does little to support widespread political resistance to fascism. So Freud's two missives, letter and book, indeed send Mann a mixed message. The letter overtly applauds his cultural alliances and political purposes, even as the text puts in his hands a comprehensive story of civilization's beginnings that must dampen those purposes and complicate both the essay's and *Joseph*'s optimism. The famous last paragraph of *Civilization* (XXI, 145), with its hard-won, somber hope that "eternal Eros" may again rise at least within particular individuals to maintain — only maintain — itself against its "equally immortal adversary," is more in keeping with the last paragraphs of *Doctor Faustus* than the *Joseph* tetralogy. The Eros-Thanatos struggle can perhaps be temporarily mitigated in a more liberal civilization, but it can never be resolved in Eros's favor.

Thomas Mann wrote some thirty thousand letters, of which nearly half are known to have survived. They range, inevitably, from the trivial to the magisterial. But few are more unintentionally revealing than Mann's reply, on 3 January 1930, to Freud's letter and his "neue kleine Schrift." Equally interesting in what it says and what it omits, the letter counterpoints enthusiasm and vagueness. Mann praises the book's extraordinary range and power: "*I read it at one sitting*, deeply moved by a courageous search for truth which, the older I grow, I see more and more as the source of all genius" (*Briefe* I, 296; *Letters*, 173: emphasis mine).[3] Mann does not, however, linger over the outcomes of that "courageous search." In fact, he doesn't discuss the book at all — a strangely attenuated outcome of such a riveted reading — but instead takes up his own search for truth in his familiar mode: autobiography. The slightly uncanny nature of his reactions continues, however, running like a ground bass through the fits and starts that comprise the rest of the letter. Grateful for Freud's emendations, Mann first says that he would have done better to contact Freud directly before writing the piece. Then he instantly cancels that wish, since "one seems as a writer better able to deal freely with a person who has not yet become a 'bürgerliche' reality, but remains somewhat in the mythical." It is hard not to conclude that his contact with Freud's latest manuscript reinforced his wish to keep Freud under the control of his own imagination. Mann may also have been nonplussed by the wealth of literary citation in *Civilization*: not only Heine and the several references to Goethe and Schiller (both Schiller's "diver" beneath the surface of things and his aphorism that "hunger and love make the world go round" receive marquee attention), but Twain, Swift, Galsworthy, Aristophanes, Rabelais. Such easy mastery of Western literature — Freud read several more languages than Mann — perhaps made him wince at the patronizing tone he had unconsciously adopted in reminding Freud about his place in the humanist tradition. Had he read Freud's candid letter to Andreas-Salomé, he might well have winced even more: "Thomas Mann's essay is no doubt quite an honor. He gives me the impression of having just completed an essay on romanticism when he was asked to write about me, and so he applied a veneer, as the cabinetmaker says, of psychoanalysis to the front and back of this essay: the bulk of it is of a different wood. Nevertheless, whenever Mann says something it is pretty sound" (*Briefe*, 407; *Letters*, 390). Freud was wrong about the essay's genesis and intent, but not about its organization.

Continuing, Mann's letter expresses "profound emotion upon reading of your years of isolation and ostracism" in spite of the "triumphal victory of your theory" and declares that similar, isolating misreadings of his own work by conservatives have made him an empathetic fellow sufferer.[4] Whatever we may think of the appropriateness of this parallel, Mann's determination to make common cause with Freud in their isolation against their fascist critics is apparent. This pushes into the background the common cause the 1929 essay put forward, which placed both men's opposition within the venerable and well-populated tradition of German humanism. But Freud had written of his feeling of alienation from Germany itself ("der ich für diese Nation ein Fremdkörper zu sein vermeinte"), not simply from fascism. So apparently following this lead, Mann redescribes the two men as lonely yet mutually sustaining allies against the Nazis.

As soon as a common cause has been intuited and more or less established, another reversal follows. Mann seems to say that he deserves, or at least cannot easily defend himself against, the crude negative reactions of "complex conservatives" because he himself came to Freud's work "shamefully late" on account of the inherent "slowness" of his nature in everything.[5] Is this merely polite regret for not reading Freud earlier? Or does he also wish that his own "courageous search for truth" had been more swift, and so acknowledge a sense of guilt that had he — and Germany — come to Freud earlier, these fascists might not be in a position to criticize either one of them? In a similar way the following sentence — "Everything must be very ripe in me before I can communicate it" — pulls the reader in contrary directions. On the one hand, it seems to take back the apology — I can't help being who I am — yet on the other suggests a reason for Mann's silence over *Civilization*: its chilling complexities must ripen in me — and my novel, perhaps — before I can respond fully.

These ambiguities lead to even more revealing ones. Freud's letter, its mild corrections aside, is anything but aggressive, yet Mann's response — confessional, apologetic, conciliatory — suggests that Freud, like a stern father, has pronounced judgment on him. His belated honoring of Freud's "triumph" seems to lead Mann back, associatively, to something close to his prewar view of Freud: the threatening unmasker of art and artists. His letter continues in a playful, almost bantering tone. We "Dichter" were all born to be the objects of your investigations, "myself foremost among them, if it doesn't sound conceited."

This leads to the wish to talk with Freud about this subject "and kindred themes"; Mann, the guilty latecomer, apparently wants to become a face-to-face(?) on-the-couch(?) object of Freud's "inquiry." He ends by saying, in what amounts to a Freudian joke, that he might come to Vienna later in the month to attend a murder trial, and then immediately equivocates, citing excessive recent travel. Though Mann does not mention it, the trial concerned a young man accused of murdering his father by pushing him off a mountain. In the event, he did not go. Instead, he spent the latter part of the month writing *A Sketch of my Life*, his autobiographical monograph; the pressure of his Nobel responsibilities coincided with a wish that Freud's letter and book also fueled.

The letter's subtext lies very near the surface; Mann becomes something of a guilty son who earlier should have honored, and been loyal to the father. At the same time Mann perpetuates his disloyalty, since he resists — indeed must resist at least until his reactions "ripen" — the power of Freud's latest book. His resistance and anxiety appear unguarded in this little psycho-narrative: Freud is both colleague and master, fellow isolated writer and father-on-the-mountain, constructor of myth and mythic construction. At the same time Mann's on-going response to Freud remains true to form. He always knew how to choose — by temperament, by artistic imperatives, by political need — what he required from Freud. It was a selectivity driven by a "mythical" Freud, one that *Civilization and its Discontents* itself theorized and that therefore posed yet another threat to the political and artistic tasks before him. "One sitting" indeed: Mann might well have been riveted by this melancholy essay that strongly qualifies, even undermines altogether, the chastened optimism of his project.[6] Just what and how Mann made his selections should take us further into the self-influential layering of *Joseph and his Brothers*.

II

For northern wizards were they [Ibsen and Wagner] both, crafty old weavers of spells, profoundly experienced in all the arts of insinuation and fascination wielded by a devil's artistry as clever as it is refined; great in the organization of effects, in the cult of detail, in all sorts of ambiguities and symbolic figurations, in the celebration of imagination, the poetizing of the intellect — and musicians they were as well, as men of the north should be.

— Thomas Mann, "Ibsen and Wagner" (1929: X, 229) and "The Sufferings and Greatness of Richard Wagner" (1933: IX, 367)

The artist's devotion to richness and many-sidedness, properly understood, was not the pretext for abstention Mann had previously made it, but a reluctance to accept anything less than truth.

— T. J. Reed, *Thomas Mann*

Like the *Joseph* novels, *Civilization and its Discontents* reconstructs the earliest experiences of humanity with the purpose of clarifying "the nature of man" (IV, 54; *JHB*, 33). Mann's self-observation that "everything must be very ripe in me before I can communicate it" applies to the author of *Civilization* as well. His book too ripened slowly, with roots not only in *Totem and Taboo* but in his "'Civilized' Sexual Morality and Modern Nervous Illness" essay of 1908 and even his 1890s correspondence with the now-dead Fliess. Freud worried throughout its making that the book was "banal," "common knowledge," "said nothing new"; most of its ideas were so familiar to him that he feared the same would be true of his audience. As the book progressed, however, its analysis became more involved and the originality of his "banal ideas" more evident.

There were many things in Freud's new work to attract Mann. *Civilization*'s opening epic gambit, which launches the reader on a descent to the beginnings of our common life, must have seemed to Mann a simulacrum, perhaps even an imitation, of the *Joseph* "Prelude." The frame of its first chapter — putative letters to a scientist and a poet — seemed to continue their friendly correspondence on a more general level. The content of *Civilization's* opening letter — an inquiry about the "oceanic feeling" in religion and early childhood — resonated fully with Mann's lifelong attraction to the boundless immensity of the ocean: from his own early childhood at Travemünde right through Diotima's "border of the great sea of beauty" at the end of "Death in Venice" to the opening of chapter 6 of *The Magic Mountain*. The letter could very nearly have been his own. And Freud's running dialogue with his reader, whose queries are repeatedly described and even given direct voice, placed him in a long-familiar narrative tradition and in a performance mode congenial with Mann's own. A good deal of *Civilization* reads like a staged conversation, an enacted, before-the-fireplace dialogue with a friendly yet skeptical auditor: very like the audience that Mann projects in his own discursive passages. Freud's demurs and reservations about his claims made any omissions and disagreements easier to legitimize, and Freud's fondness for autobiographical insertions obviously accorded with Mann's own essayistic practice. The normalizing account of bisexuality may also have given

Mann both private reassurance and further support for his portrait of double-sexedness in *Joseph*.

Beyond these connections lay a deeper assumption — now conscious, now subliminal on Mann's part — that linked the two texts. Freud reconfirmed his materialistic, conservatory view of the mind in *Civilization*: all experience is encased in memory, and no memory is permanently lost. Freud constructs the unconscious as an infallible and inexhaustible storehouse of the personal and cultural past, with each of its memories potentially available to dream-work and, via interpretation, to the considering conscious mind. Even Freud's cautionary demurs reinforce his conviction; he acknowledges the safer claim that perhaps what is in the mind "*may* be preserved," but sees it only as a possible "exception" that confirms the "rule" of complete conservation (XXI, 71–72; italics in original). Freud returns yet again to his favorite archaeological image: the ruins of Rome, themselves restorations of earlier civilizations, are preserved within the modern city just as the buried past remains in the mind's geography. These analogies finally fail of literal truth, Freud admits, because they cannot imitate the mind's capacity to hold both old and new in precisely the same space, but even with this scruple Freud still establishes a metaphoric connection between the archaeology of the individual and the city that takes us to the heart of *Civilization*'s greatest subject. It is his "Gradiva" essay rewritten on a larger scale, as though Pompeii had reformed itself out of its ashes.

Mann, as we have seen, does not finally accept the mechanistic aspects of this model of the psyche. Even when he seems to accept it, as in one section of the 1936 essay or in delineating some of *Joseph*'s minor characters, he invariably offers a more humanist-friendly version. The psychic intertextuality of egos "open at the back" is far less deterministic than the Lamarckian biology that haunted, and limited, Freud's enterprise. More important is another humanizing parallel between the Freudian psyche and a central structural principle of the *Joseph* novels. Motif writing, which Mann absorbed not only from Wagner but from several nineteenth century novelists, creates an aesthetic equivalent of Freud's conservatory. No image, no idea, no action is lost to the novel, which produces meaning through their return in ever-evolving but still recognizable forms. The Wagnerian leitmotif generates a conservative economy, a storehouse of material that can produce endless new variations. Many of these returns are calculated; others appear unbidden, even unnoticed, "from the depths" in the act of composition. As a rough visual equivalent the narrator uses the kaleidoscope ("Guckrohr") and develops it carefully in connection with

Joseph's "richer and more involved" life patterns (834; 557). Out of its finite number of "little glass splinters" arise an inexhaustible number of formal combinations.[7]

In "The Sufferings and Greatness of Richard Wagner" Mann puts forward an ingenious formulation of the leitmotif: a "[symbolic] formula — more, it is a monstrance; it lays claim to an almost religious authority" (IX, 366; *Essays*, 309). On this account individual motifs resemble the divided host; they are consumed, recombined, remade into different bodies and forms, yet retain their "divine" integrity. For Wagner, says Mann, their power to allude, associate, and emphasize enabled his two great subjects: psychology and myth. He describes Wagner's music in a pair of images that interweave motif writing and Freud in an arresting way:

> The texts around which [Wagner's music] entwines itself, and fills out their dramatic content, are not literature — but the music is. It seems to shoot forth like a geyser out of myth's pre-cultural depths — not only seems: it actually does do so — and in truth it is conceived, calculated, with high intelligence, with cunning shrewdness, in as literary a way as the texts are conceived in a musical way . . . . Psychoanalysis claims to know that love is put together out of sheer perversities. Yet even so it remains love, the most divine phenomenon in the world.
>
> (380–81; 319–20)

Mann smoothly shifts Freud's economy of the mind to art, where "ruins and restorations" can also occupy the same space as they do in mental life, and where the "perversities" of primitive origins capacitate, rather than determine, the formal beauty and elegance that flow from them. Literature and music can virtually change places in Wagner's productions in the same way that the unconscious, precultural impulses of the mind arise from myth and are reshaped by conscious making.

Joseph and *Civilization* seem in these ways texts produced from common cultural soil and narrative pattern, almost from a common mind.[8] All the more threatening, then, are the other sides of *Civilization*: the implacable death drive and its permanent entanglement with Eros, and especially the doubtful ability of civilization to maintain even a precarious balance between the contending energies that empower it. In these claims the originary "perversities" cannot be belled quite so easily. *Civilization*'s pessimistic drift makes for neither a novel of reunion nor, just as important, a sustainable antifascism. Freud's resituation of aggression and destructiveness at the heart of human life is very different from Wagner's alluring portrait of love-death, the self's ethereal merging into the infinite. The death drive leaves little space for mystical release; it threatens instead the overthrow of the humanistic art and progressive politics which make the *Joseph* novels possible. As Schiller's diver knows, "Who breathes overhead in the rose-tinted light may rejoice" (XXI, 73); the plunge into the depths remains dangerous.

One might well expect that a book read so breathlessly would have made an immediate, dramatic impact on the *Joseph* project. In January 1930, however, Mann was deep into *The Tales of Jacob*, which he would complete the following October. The novel by now had its own momentum, and Freud's book did not create some decisive new turn in its direction. *Totem and Taboo* and his many other sources had already provided him with the anthropological frameworks he needed to write the last pages of Laban's story, and the death of Rachel. Perhaps *Civilization*'s account of the irresolvable conflict between Eros and Thanatos added a layer to Rachel's death scene and Jacob's mourning. Its account of narcissistic enjoyment in the regressive satisfaction of the death drive (chapter 6) — the return to the feelings of omniscience that launched Freud's meditation — plausibly gave darker shadings to "The Dream of Heaven" and "The Pit." It may also have expanded Mann's vocabulary for analyzing Levantine civilizations, and he knew that the large-scale complexities of ancient Egypt awaited him just over the horizon.

But in the summer of 1932, when he began *Joseph in Egypt*, Freud's essay reentered the novel in force. As we shall see in detail, *Civilization* appears everywhere in *Joseph in Egypt*: in the anthropological decent to Thebes, in the comic but dangerous phallic strutting of Dudu, in the castration of Potiphar, in the repression of Mut, in the witch Tabubu's bloody rituals of conjuring, in Joseph's primary narcissism. Mann, in effect, gives Freud his freedom in the novel to say everything he can say about human origins and human depths. Mann's first face-to-face meeting with Freud in the same year may possibly have abetted this turn. But whatever the cause, Mann's reflections on Freud had matured and deepened notably since 1929–1930. There both political exigencies and his own reluctances produced a hypercontrolled misreading of Freud. But "misreading" is not, by itself, the proper term for *Civilization*'s presence in *Joseph in Egypt*. Misreadings and a willful harmonization continue, but in a more knowing, dialectic relation with Freudian pessimism. Mann does not attempt to mummify *Civilization* in the elaborate wrappings of the Munich lecture. It is another example of deferred self-influence; Mann needed — and was ready — to face the bleaker consequences of Freud's essay and resituate them in his own recreation of Egyptian civilization. Ancient Egypt, amply removed in both time and space, gave Mann the distance to close with Freud's most troubling ideas; they had indeed "ripened" in him.

Civilization and its Discontents, despite its pessimism, also helped Mann rethink the actual social context of his political vision: not nineteenth century liberalism, but the new mass culture and mass politics of twentieth century Europe. These were familiar and much-debated subjects throughout Weimar culture; in fact, we now recognize the new concept of "the mass" as one of the defining marks of European modernism. Mann had already broached these subjects in earlier essays, from Whitman's "social eroticism" and the defense of democratic politics in the second half of "On the German Republic" on through "Culture and Socialism." The similarity between the menace posed to individuality by the sheer size of political populations and the sheer depth of the Freudian cultural unconscious required framing and control. Mann acknowledges the claim that psychoanalysis, anthropology, and, increasingly, political science were advocating: that vast impersonal forces shape individual consciousness, including even its experience of individuality and its wishes for separation and privacy. Yet given full authority, this truth could obviously threaten the ethical and political decisions central to his work; neither Amphitryon's loyal love of Alkmene nor each young German's willed opposition to Nazism seem compelling when confronted with its power.

Mann's characteristic response had been, and continued to be, double. As before, he contains large impersonal forces, internal and external, by assigning their effects primarily to minor characters and by showing, à la Schopenhauer, how individual knowledge of their power can be liberating. He uses this strategy throughout *Joseph in Egypt*: Dudu, Huia and Tuia, Beknechons. But the mass society of Egypt and the unstable family triangle of Potiphar, Mut, and Joseph make confinement of these forces to minor characters impossible. So Mann's complementary strategy, from the beginning, undertook to show how the modernist decentering and fragmentation of the self could also enhance individuality. They can do so by multiplying the strains of the ego rather than simply making it the victim of contending forces. Mann wishes us to see how much larger our individualities become when grounded in scores of mythical narratives and patterns, and how the corresponding multiple social roles and alliances of mass society can free us from its stifling uniformities.[9] He decides, in other words, to show how the "mass" both stultifies and contributes powerfully to a refigured, open-ended individuality. Our individuality coheres around our recognitions, acknowledgments, choices, and relationships; these require the honoring of difference and the other in order to exist at all. Similarly, a group achieves cultural identity by acknowledging, not ruthlessly dominating, other groups. This matches precisely the democ-

racy and pluralism that Mann develops and defends in his lectures and
his tetralogy. It finds artistic counterparts in the kaleidoscopic voice of
his narrator — a voice unified and multiplied at once — and in his rejection of assumed omniscience as an aesthetic, and ethical, option.

III

*Was an oracle by its nature the unveiling of a future in which nothing
could change, or was it like an instruction to prudence and a warning to
human beings to act so that an announced misfortune did not come
about? That presupposed that the decision and the destiny were not fixed,
but that it was given to men to influence them. Yet if this were the case,
then the future was not external to man, but within him, and how then
could one read it?*

— Jacob to Laban, after Rachel's visit to the oracle at Harran

*What affects me most strongly and most immediately in a work of art is
the quality of its silence. The silence is more than an absence of sound, it is
an active force, expressive and coercive.*

— John Banville, *Athena*

*A son's picture of his father is habitually clothed with excessive powers of
this kind, and it is found that distrust of the father is intimately linked
with admiration for him.*

— *Totem and Taboo*

The sheer number of performances in *Joseph in Egypt* makes virtually
every section of the novel relevant to our discussion. The novel depends almost entirely on staged confrontations between two or three
people: Joseph's performances before his Midianite master and before
Potiphar in his garden, the Huia and Tuia one-act with Joseph as frozen audience, Mut-em-enet's pas de deux with her husband and then
her beloved, Joseph's ritualized trial. The Freud of *Civilization* and
Mann's comedic vision test each other in each of them, as we can see in
several particularly striking scenes.

Joseph's descent into Egypt has well-demarcated sections: the dialogues with the Ishmaelite and the angel-guide, the central rumination
on the desertion of Jacob, and the archaeological travelogue down (or
up) the Nile into the Underworld. The journey opens with easily recognized repetitions which the narrator entertainingly develops. Once
again Joseph is posed — and poised — before an older man and tested
on his suspect views. The site is not a well but the Ishmaelite's tent,

and Joseph's newly-formulated relativism replaces religious backsliding as the opening subject. A pragmatic skeptic shaped by worldly experience rather than a sense of providence, Joseph's latest fatherly examiner treads cautiously around his new purchase. Less blind than Isaac — he converses with Joseph at the entrance to his tent, not within its darkness — the Ishmaelite is wary of the "mysteries" of death and resurrection which he senses in the young lad. He steers clear of any attempt to possess his new slave's slightly disturbing nature. Joseph's proclamation to the Ishmaelite's son Kedema that there may be millions of centers in the world both amuses and alarms the old man:

> But see, the world has many centers, one for each being, and around each one lies its own circle. You stand but half an ell from me, yet around you lies a universe whose center I am not but you are. I, on the other hand, am the center of mine. Therefore both are true, according as one speaks from your center or from mine. For our circles are not so far from each other that they do not touch; rather hath God moved and folded [*verschränkt*] them deep into each other, so that you Ishmaelites do indeed travel quite independently and according to your own ends, wherever you will, but besides that you are the means and the tool, in our interconnected centers, by which I arrive at my goal." (671–72; 447)

Both the Ishmaelite and his son immediately read this as just another kind of youthful narcissism; they are right about the narcissism but not about its immaturity. Joseph's chastened new character has indeed forsworn his juvenile self-centeredness. The single great circle of his dream-domination over his brothers has shrunk to a modest circumference, no larger than that of any brother or merchant traveler. Comically, Joseph's professed new ego-boundary replicates the unassuming "but uncommonly good" pancakes that he serves his new master during their exchanges: many small circles of equal excellence and value. At the same time, however, this little philosophical exemplum continues the tripartite reinscription of narcissism analyzed in "The Pit": surface modesty masking lower-level alignment with cosmic tales of sacrifice and resurrection that his sense of destiny merits. This contrast creates a new psychic space, in effect a bigger stage, on which Joseph can be both performer and silent observer of his own performance. Narcissism now draws more of its satisfactions from the dramatist's mastery of scene than from the spontaneous charm of youthful beauty. So an enlarged theater of self-awareness has opened within Joseph, whose surface self-deprecations before his new master humorously sustain the more general or primary narcissism that undergirds them.

The Ishmaelite's clever, bantering dialogues with his new scribe must have pleased the audiences who first heard them. Patently written to be read aloud, they form the surface outcrop of the more important inner drama, the one that Joseph returns to repeatedly and which challenges his well-being: not playful repetitions of "The Testing" with his new, substitute father, but an all-too-real testing of his desertion of Jacob. The question of escape and return to the father obsesses Joseph. He broaches the subject again and again, long after it has been "settled decisively." It obsesses Mann as well, since it is both an obvious plot problem in his inherited tale and perhaps a reflection of his own torn feelings over his "forced desertion" of his fatherland. The overdetermined ruminations on the subject gather together the central ethical questions of the novel, and probe them at the dramatic and the formal level.

In the beginning of *Joseph in Egypt* the narrator reviews Joseph's symbolic death and rebirth (674–75; 449). The whole passage has a slightly overwrought tone. He emphasizes the "deep cleavage and abyss" between Joseph's past and present and declares that past irrevocably gone, silenced, inaccessible. He also stresses that Joseph's suffering became harder to bear the longer it continued. Then he immediately launches a self-reflexive account of the matter: "We set great store by this point, for it seems to us urgent to defend Joseph, now and later, from a reproach that has often been leveled against him in historical reflections" (674; 449). (The narrator frequently raises a "long-standing historical question" when he wishes to say something more about a subject.) A distinction between the "outwardly and inwardly possible" leads to the conclusion that Joseph could have done nothing other than what he did; any return would betray his brothers and deny the lessons of "The Pit." He is indeed dead, and his father's grief appropriate and inevitable. Yet in the midst of this QED analysis the narrator adds an odd, recondite point about our emotional life: our empathy with those who grieve for us is "harder and colder" than that we feel for strangers. Perhaps, but its place amidst all the authoritative reasons puzzles; it seems more an excuse than a contribution to the narrator's definitive explanation. It tempts us to query the firm conclusions themselves, as perhaps concealing ambivalence within their inevitability. But the section ends crisply, and the narrator turns to one of his wittiest and most charming performances: Joseph's long, information-gathering dialogue with the Ishmaelite. At its end Joseph announces his new name: Osarsiph, Joseph-as-Osarsiph, the dead Joseph.

But what follows is yet another section outlining Joseph's further reasons for resisting the "temptation" to flee east to Hebron. Each day, as the Midianite traders head south, Joseph anticipates the moment when he will be due west of his father's camp. It preoccupies him in the midst of his bookkeeping duties. Several times he nearly capitulates to its power. As the moment grows closer "his heart beat[s] anxiously" ("ängstlich-versuchungsvoll"), and he repeatedly takes imaginative journeys over the succession of ever-higher hills to Hebron. He envisions the actual reunion, and overpowering feelings carry him away. His "Rachel-eyes" inflame the portrait: "Up there sat Jacob, despairing, worn down by tears, in dreadful God-sent suffering, the blood-spotted sign of Joseph's death and mangling in his poor hands" (702; 468). The face of the suffering father makes the temptation all but irresistible; he would dry his father's tears with the magical phrase of his youthful divinity, "Here am I." He comes so close to flight that the narrator specifically compares the drama to the greatest temptation of his life — to embrace Potiphar's wife. But even this resemblance proves inadequate, and the narrator returns to the subject several more times, most notably with the parable of the cow and the silent calf (823–25, 958; 550–52, 637).

What finally enables Joseph to resist the temptation is not "harder and colder" emotional distance at all, but the deeper reaches of his narcissism. The text gives us the pith of Joseph's reformed self-love in four interconnected ways. First, he renounces the naive self-indulgences of earlier days. It would be "distinctly evil" to resist God's plan, since this would repeat his adolescent wish from "The Testing" to "The Dream of Heaven" not merely to be the center of things but to be wiser than God. Instead he now incarnates the sacrifice; he is the set-apart one who suffers in order that elevation may follow and God's plan be fulfilled. The play-acting of the "Grove of Adonis" has now been made flesh; there can be no more lifting up without actual sacrifice.

Second, the narrative connects Joseph's narcissism to his particular, rational sense of sin: not a deep ontological flaw or hopelessly warped will, but sin as a mistake, a foolish violation, a blunder. Joseph admits to no central or permanent flaw — a helpful attitude for sustaining narcissism's positive qualities. Third, he is now the real "center of the present and the Feast," and a deeper "longing and dreaming" supplant the vivid fantasy about flight over the hills. How could he take flight in order to become a mere shepherd again? That would be the pastoral version of a galley slave: a dead end, a refusal of a leading role in God's story. The only other alternative is the regressive, dreamy self-satisfaction at the end of "The Pit," the psychic equivalent of the galleys. Elevation in defeat: to return would be to lose his place in history.

Fourth, and decisively, the narrator reinterprets the tell-tale division within his hero that becoming Osarsiph, the dead Joseph, requires. The "temptation" to return has been one "of foolish fleshly desire" not of the spirit, where the pull of God's deeper plan holds sway (704; 469). Joseph's agonizing turns out to be another variation of the ur-parable of the soul, matter, and spirit, one that dramatizes the cost of this stage of his maturation. For it compels Joseph to renounce the unity of body and soul that he has always intuited as fundamental to his nature. Here he must split his "flesh" and his "fleshly feeling" from his spirit. The rift echoes his self-serving distinction between the tips of the tree and its roots, but with a difference. Here he divides himself internally but holds on to the larger unity of the revolving sphere in his new role as sacrifice and redeemer.

This disunity of body and spirit extends itself throughout the underworld of *Joseph in Egypt*: in Potiphar's divided body, in Huia and Tuia's fearful sacrifice, in Mut-em-enet's awakening, in the seduction itself. It also describes the new divide between the "fleshly" father and the plan of God. Both Joseph's primary narcissism and the promise of the blessing require, for a time, a division at the heart of love. "Osarsiph" becomes possible because Joseph turns away from the face of the father; the tearful mien of Jacob must be sacrificed. The price is a division at the center of Joseph's empathetic, and ethical, life. No wonder Osarsiph so actively creates father-substitutes — the Ishmaelite, Montkaw, Potiphar himself — and no wonder that these relationships all center on loyalty. Osarsiph's fidelity to his Egyptian fathers draws its compensatory energy from his life's fundamental, character-making loyalty that he left behind in the hills of Hebron. The "Kleist" essay — self-influence at its most significant — shapes this particular way of representing Joseph. The essay dramatized the inseparability of Eros and loyalty, of "loving without seeing." Joseph-as-Osarsiph can neither fully acknowledge nor entirely forget the face of his father, so he "sees" it again and again in the Egyptian faces that enter his circle. He now also thinks about Elohim largely in terms of loyalty and disloyalty, and connects disloyalty with death (e.g., in "Joseph becomes Visibly an Egyptian"). Not until Jacob's reappearance at the great temptation which closes the novel can Joseph's flesh and spirit, father and Father, reunite.

This central core of *Joseph in Egypt* interweaves with Freud's companion story of father murder and the development of civilization. Seen through *Civilization* and *Totem*, *Joseph in Egypt* narrates a sublimated father murder that resembles the Oedipal drama of psychoanalysis. Suppression of the wish to kill the father creates a space of memory and remorse, and leads to the half-measures and compromises of Joseph's psychic life in Egypt. It also offers only a meager hope of reconciliation. In the Freudian narrative there can only be a return to the father of memory: substitution is inevitable and barely satisfying. For Freud, to repeat, an even lower layer sustains the Oedipal drama — its "narcissistic precondition, the fear of castration" (XIII, 161 and 111–12) which Joseph barely escaped in the pit. *Civilization and its Discontents* has its own name for Osarsiph's struggle: "In this way the [death] instinct could be pressed into the service of Eros, in that the organism was destroying some other thing, whether animate or inanimate, instead of destroying itself" (XXI, 119). Joseph is finally a force for life, for Eros, yet Eros is always interwoven with the death instinct and "shares world-dominion with it" (XXI, 122). But, as we shall see, *Joseph*'s alteration of this Freudian script will be one in which the story of Amphitryon overlays that of Oedipus. It nurtures the possibility of a loyal return to the absent face of the father. Jacob's face remains frozen in Joseph's memory, sacrificed and preserved in his mock death, and its living expression searched for in those of Mont-Kaw and Potiphar. Joseph's Amphitryon-hope in the blessing is that the father's image may again appear before him not as memory or substitute, but in spirit and body.

In these ways "The Temptation" section models the divisions that preoccupy the novel. It may have also been an ideal platform piece for its creator. Without the diaries for 1932 we don't know if or when Mann performed this piece, but a section written to rebut a long-standing historical reproach must have tempted him to do so. Probably composed at his seacoast retreat at Nidden, "The Temptation" gave Mann the chance to perform some of his time-honored favorite subjects: time and the boundless sea, the emotions of travel and exile, launching the listener into a magical world. As a coda to the highly entertaining "Night Conversation," it makes for a well-paced sixty-five-minute reading. Further, its prose seems shaped as much by the requirements of hearing as reading. For example, Mann breaks up his opening paragraphs into small, accumulative units. The German is heavily punctuated, even by his standards; this makes for a propulsive reading with a discernible beat, as though we were actually walking south with Joseph and his companions. The rhythm pauses in the second paragraph's opening, which conjures the timeless immensity of the sea in smooth, long-running constructions. But in the paragraph's second half, where travel and scenic detail become the subjects, the beat returns. The punctuation diminishes somewhat in the latter part of the section, where the narrator evokes the emotional urgency of Joseph's dilemma. Formally the passage moves from outer to inner, from timeless immensity and suspended action to the most time-bound, acute

specific feelings — which can only enhance their poignancy. A performer might well emphasize the accounts of Jacob's imagined suffering and the rhetorical questions that organize the last two paragraphs.
The ending's ambivalence — the ringing affirmation of the living "Joseph in the feast" intermingled with the sacrificial "Osarsiph, the
swamp-born dead Joseph" — sustains both the promise and the divisive
loss. It requires just the right tone to convey the balance. Joseph's internal debate persuades most powerfully when we hear it in our mind's
ear or, for a fortunate few, in lecture hall or private study from the Joseph legend's most loyal narrator.

IV

Joseph's exemplum of the many circles has its cultural analog in the
many centers of ancient Egypt that lie before him on his journey. By
training and instinct he sees them as another kind of temptation; his
skeptical pluralism and narcissistic surety combine to form his distanced, rather superior perspective. Repeatedly Joseph finds himself
alone on some high ground in a new city, looking down toward its
shrine as he once looked down toward the double tomb of Hebron,
and judging the local culture. The urban scenes of chapter 2, "The
Entrance into Sheol," become increasingly complex and "advanced" as
we travel south. The cities are both ancient beyond memory and recently reorganized into "administrative districts" (Gau) of the Kingdom (726; 484).[10] Each exhibits more size, liveliness and cultural
sophistication than its predecessor. *Totem* and *Civilization* accompany
us like familiar guides on our anthropological tour of the land of Uto
the serpent, Lower Egypt. They appear, sometimes wittily, sometimes
ominously, in every stop.

   Goshen's fens surround Joseph's first stop at Per-Sopd, a city so old
that its priests and prophets wear lynx skins for unknown reasons and
always stare at the ground. Avoiding face-to-face encounter, its inhabi-
tants wander in a self-pitying withdrawal. They no longer know
whether their god, an impotent deity without identity or feast days, has
the head of a pig or a hippo. Per-Sopd's civilization avails little against
death's dispersive power; the city has almost disappeared.

   The caravan next stops at Per-Bastet, the comic City of Cats and a
higher rung on the ladder of civilization. The city and its citizens reek
of catnip, and also of an archaic, compulsive gaiety. Every year their
three-day feast attracts Egyptians from downriver, who lose their inhibitions, dance and gesture lewdly, and bawl like female cats visited by
males: a sort of Nile Karneval. The open-armed temple grounds of the

city's goddess promiscuously welcome visitors, and the temple portraits show Pharaoh surrounded by reddish-brown animal-headed gods who touch his shoulder in a friendly way. Raw Eros and Thanatos rule the city and, like the overmastering smell of valerian, urge its citizens to "let go," to abandon themselves laughingly in mind-erasing riot. Joseph harshly refuses this superficial resolution of civilization and its discontents. Like the heroic Freud of *Totem* who brought analytic clarity to the morbidities of the primitive world, Joseph, though "a small figure among giants," "stiffened his back" against unreflective excess (733–34; 489).

With Joseph's midwinter arrival at the sun-city of On (Heliopolis), we have descended to a much higher plane of theological and cultural sophistication. Though nearly as old as its northern neighbors, On bustles with life, more of it than Joseph has ever seen in one place, and its priests cheerfully instruct strangers in their theological discoveries. The city lies at the apex of the Nile delta, the point where the seminal river branches, and the thinkers of On draw every sort of entertaining conclusion from this. Their triangular city stands at the center of the river-body, the fertile triangle of the world, and worships the repeating birth of Merwer the Bull, famous for his "powerful hanging testicles." Anchored in fecundity, On also stands at the most abstract point of refinement and speculation, and worships the sun in its three-in-one phases, the center of the universe. The calendars, sun-dials, and city planning of the wise men of On firmly order time and space. Gilt covers the sacred buildings, reflecting sunlight everywhere and all but blinding citizens and travelers alike.

The points of the "phallic sun-spear" obelisk and the triangle dominate, and the Euclidean theology they generate seems a liberal version of Joseph's own tradition. The flaming golden tip of the four-sided obelisk at the center of the city marks the ineffable point at which the material and spiritual worlds meet. It symbolizes the syncretic theorizing of the priests: aspects of the sun may be found in every other god from cat and crocodile to Osiris and Re. Everything drives toward the point where sun and reflected sun permeate one another. The base of the triangle, on the other hand, symbolizes the multiplicity of gods and the world, which the tolerant, savvy priests of On have no desire to absorb or erase. The broad base has ample room for all the multifarious gods of the people, and its sides rise to form a "gathering place" ("Zusammenschau") which reconciles differences between them until they meet at the tip as One: Atum-Re (741; 494).[11] At the tip of the world the four-sided and three-sided figures of obelisk and triangle disappear into one another. Atum-Re's world-friendly benevolence and humor contrast with the aggressive younger sun god of Thebes, Amun, who conquers competing divinities and erases differences in a self-aggrandizing unity. The city basks in its sun worship, in the unvarying repetition of the seasons, in the pleasures of endlessly repeated discourse on the endlessly reflected sun. Tellingly, it shares a geometry with Joseph's "Dream of the Sheaves," where the brothers all make obeisance to the "point" and apex of Joseph and his standing sheaf.

Joseph's faith stands in between this kindly tolerance and the totalitarianism of Amun. On's homogenizing doctrines offer no sense of the future and the blessing; its timelessness and claims to permanence render it vulnerable. Even its fertile bull god never changes. (When he becomes vizier of Egypt, Joseph marries Asenath, daughter of the sun priest of On, and her family's hilarious portrayal of her as the eternally ravished bride epitomizes the city's mythic paralysis.) Amun, while also "chosen," has only a regressive ambition to turn the future into an imagined past. But between the two, Joseph's worldliness has much more in common with the people of On, where the depths of the river and the heights of sun speculation overlap one another.

Read through self-influence, the theology of On has roots in the 1929 "Freud" lecture, roots that extend the opposition between the city and its younger, conservative competitor to the south. It expounds some qualities of the German humanism that essay celebrates: syncretic, inclusive, unified but not uniform. Its priests are strong analysts of double states and double meanings, and their worship of sun and bull together mimics Novalis and Freud's "romantic-biological daydreams" (X, 278; *PM*, 196). Blending reaction and progress, enlightenment and romantic traditions in its "Zusammenschau," they also practice illuminating pedagogy, ready to perform at any opportunity. Joseph, ever the good pupil, listens without making righteous objections and absorbs their point of view. An enlightened city in every sense, its values of tradition, incorporation, and beauty are under siege from the rising fascist state religion emanating from the south. The 1929 essay's account of Christianity — primitive roots yet enlightening vision — finds a new incarnation at On. The tangled metaphor for psychoanalysis's spread in the essay's last pages — the "kernel's aura" — has its playful simulacrum in the tip of the On obelisk: fertility and enlightenment together.[12] On's theology epitomizes "reason's triumph over its origins," the outcome Mann claims for the Freudian project. It has none of Per-Bastet's "hostility to mind," and its theology and politics are one.

But the enlightenment of On comes at a price: the blindness of its insights. Like politically naive humanists, the priests of On imagine that their clever, combinatory theory will achieve unity while preserving diversity in the real world. Mann's gentle critique of Nietzsche in the 1929 essay applies directly to On: blinded perhaps by his high-mindedness, Nietzsche did not see that the "waves" of history whose countervailing flow persists in spite of larger understanding require not only right ideas but activist politics and pedagogy. The blitheness and laughter of On's citizens seem to extend Mann's kindly parody to Nietzsche's sense of joy. Unlike the Freud of 1929, who can contain the dark side of the psyche and of German history without erasing their necessary power, On lacks the ethical will to oppose Amun. Its strategy of democratic tolerance finally proves too quietist and innocently narcissistic to overcome the challenge from the south.

So Joseph struggles to remain loyal not only to his father's face but (like Freud) to narratives of the past. On's approximation to, and distance from, his inherited faith is subtly presented in the countenance of yet another patriarch: the "mild, laughing face" (Angesicht) and "fatherly" head priest of the sun cult (743; 495). His priests kiss Joseph and the Ishmaelites farewell "in the name of the father." The priest, looking rather like a beneficent Sarastro, blesses his children and sends them on their way.

Our analysis of the 1929 lecture highlighted Mann's silence about Oedipus before his youthful audience, indeed in all his public and private writing. But by October 1932 that silence was harder, and less desirable, to maintain in his novel.[13] As we saw in "The Temptation," nearly everything in *Joseph in Egypt* required more direct confrontation with Freud's cheerless intuitions about the psyche. The impotent incoherence of Per-Sopd and the bawdy vaudeville of Per-Bastet in some ways extended Mann's policy of containment: comic distance overrode any real peril in their raucous primitivism. The sphinx, however, was another matter; it embodied the violent, devouring qualities of the underworld that Joseph, and his maker, shunned. It was, in several senses, too big to be overlooked.

The sphinx's immemorial age figured briefly in the "Prelude" (21–22; 11), and the question of its sand-hidden gender arose well before Joseph arrived at Giza. Chapter 2, the journey chapter, opens with the Ishmaelite's chatty overview of the trek before them. Normally a tolerant absorber of travel tales, Joseph takes sharp offense at the old man's offhand reference to Hatchepsut, the queen who "wore the beard" (727–28: 485); he "listened only with difficulty" and "had no ear for her doings." Hatchepsut, Thutmose's I eldest daughter, first co-ruled with her half brother and husband, Thutmose II. When he died and Thutmose III came to the throne, Hatchepsut declared herself pharaoh and donned male clothing and the "beard of wisdom." Joseph actively disapproves of this practiced double-sexed duplicity, not entirely removed from his own. But what most signifies for us is Hatchepsut's recurring portrayal as a sphinx.[14]

"The Sphinx" section (743–52; 496–501) inverts the sunny, timeless optimism of "Edifying On" in nearly every way. The huge triangles of the Giza pyramids dwarf those of On. From a distance they too glitter in the sun, but up close their decaying, crumbling condition breaks up their surface brilliance. The "desolation" of the surrounding temple buildings testifies to the deeper power of time and death over all pretensions to immortality.[15] These tombs, "world-famous erections" ("Austritte"), contrast vividly with the protruding fertility of Merwer the bull (745; 497) and remind the awestruck Joseph of the tower of Babel. According to the Ishmaelite (who comically quotes Herodotus), their building required enormous sacrifices: thousands of slaves, but even more striking for Joseph, the daughter of King Khufu, an unsaved sacrifice prostituted by her father to pay for his crypt.[16] The long survival of the pyramids, "Great junk-piles of death" ("Großgerümpel des Todes"), makes them seem more monstrosities than immortal monuments. The most telling inversion of On's theology lies in the narrative relocation of the pyramid's apex. The long paragraph of description narrows down not to the pyramid's sun-greeting tip but within, to the little twig of mimosa which the dead Khufu clutches in his mummified hand: from Eros to Thanatos indeed.

Like the story of Hatchepsut, Joseph sees the pyramids and especially the sphinx as a direct challenge to himself and his father. The stone tablet between the sphinx's paws commemorates Prince Thutmose's "dream of the promise." Atum-Re "turned his face to his son and deliverer," commanding him to clear away the covering sands from his statue and receive the kingship as his reward. Joseph stands before the Ishmaelite as he reads the tablet, a silent yet inwardly defiant pupil. Angered by the story, he privately thinks this promise a paltry sort of fulfillment, as far beneath his own tradition as the unsaved sacrifice-child of King Khufu. After all, he reasons, the young prince would have become king anyway, and the sands are already obliterating this record of their removal. The great Harmakhis may be old beyond measure, but it promises only a sterile, repetitive future rather than the mutual development and expectancy God offers his people.

Yet his triumphalist comparison does not satisfy Joseph. "The sight of the sphinx . . . put his young blood in an unrest against which mockery did not prevail, and which did not let him sleep" (750; 500). The great creature stirs none of the Ishmaelites or native Egyptians in this way. The old man takes the same skeptical attitude toward the monument and its legends as Joseph did toward the priests of Per-Sopd and On. Later that same night Joseph's indignant critique "astonishes" Kedema, the Ishmaelite's son. Such compelling unrest and overreaction strongly suggest acts of suppression; Joseph's energetic defense of father and faith cannot contain his anxiety.[17] Driven, he braves the night and the distant howl of jackals to stand alone before the "giant idol" and question its "monstrosity." The extraordinary monologue that follows takes us into the center of nearly all our subjects: Freud and Oedipus, Kleist and self-influence, the ethics of loyalty and relation, Joseph's narcissism and sexuality. The narrator chooses not to quote Joseph's thought but to narrate it, giving us direct access to his conscious and half-conscious reactions.

Joseph begins by backgrounding the empirical mysteries about the sphinx — its size and origin — and foregrounding another: "How did the riddle go?" What riddle? The sphinx impresses the Ishmaelites but does not puzzle them, and the ancient Egyptians (either in this fiction or in fact) tell no enigmatic tales about the statue.[18] But for Joseph, the riddle lies in the monster's "arrogant" silence in the face of its interrogator; it neither responds to his questioning nor puts a question of its own. Like the "mysterious" lion that Jacob feared would devour his favorite (90; 55), its riddling allows for no relation. Unmoved, it only looks past Joseph in its "calm-drunken silence."[19] Inevitably the reader thinks of another roadside sphinx, sometime bane of a city, who did put a riddling question to a young traveler standing before it. *Joseph*'s construction of the sphinx begins in Egypt but ends in Greece; Egypt's monument metamorphoses into the Riddler of Boiotian Thebes.[20] The long-withheld story of Oedipus, unwitting father slayer, rises near the surface of Joseph's involuted monologue. We sense its lineaments in the hero, and particularly in the monster, which like a stone palimpsest opens to reveal a second sphinx within its precinct.

Oedipus's questioner traditionally sits high on a rock or pillar, its lion's body and eagle's wings denoting its power, and its unambiguously female head its gender. The encounter is archetypal, more a rite of passage than a unique event. In a number of sixth- and fifth-century Greek vase paintings a young, naked youth stands before the sphinx, or flees her pursuit, or is carried off in her talons to be devoured.[21] Other vases portray the moment of capture, with the sphinx either leaping against the chest of the youth to knock him down or crouching triumphantly over his fallen body; in the Getty 85.AE.377 the youth appears to be already dead. In the epic *Oidipodeia* the sphinx kills Creon's loyal/disloyal son Haimon. In Sophocles' play we do not hear the famous riddle as such — the earliest surviving account comes from the fourth-century mythographer Asklepiades — but for Freud, Mann and most contemporary readers the two are inextricably connected. The sphinx's legendary question concerns the nature of man, *Joseph and his Brothers*'s self-proclaimed subject (54; 33). The sphinx's three sun-names, Khepri-Re-Atum, correspond to the rising, midday, and setting sun, and therefore parallel the three stages of life the Greek riddler puts to Oedipus. Oedipus's overconfident answer — that he alone knows all life's stages — will be unmasked; Mann's corresponding scene unmasks the deepest threat to Joseph's ability to script a God-story that will sustain the promise. [22]

For Freud, the riddle of the sphinx is the riddle of the endlessly reflecting family triangle, the enabling-disabling desire of the son to supplant the father. Joseph's much-meditated refusal of the "temptation" to return to Jacob makes possible his God-story, yet does violence to his father. Joseph's narcissistic absorption of the mother has put a gender-tangling twist on the story, and he returns repeatedly in his monologue to the question of the great sphinx's sex. The monster's silence extends to its hidden sex that not even a hundred stonemasons could reveal. Its ambiguous gender goes all the way down, he avers, and can never be unearthed or resolved. In this way the sphinx, both Oedipal palimpsest and polished Narcissus stone, mirrors back to the double-sexed Joseph his permanently buried wishes: to erase his father; to yield to the polymorphous perversity and sex-death in the sphinx's embrace. It mirrors the devisiveness of the maturing narcissist's internal battle between self-love and object choice. In other words, it mirrors back Joseph as Freudian subject, as young Oedipus fresh from father slaying before a female sphinx of his own half-conscious devising. [23] *Joseph in Egypt*'s almost audible subtitle is "Joseph in the Freudian Sheol:" not the relatively benign, politically efficacious Freudian humanism of 1929, but the Freud of *Totem* and especially *Civilization* at his most pessimistic. Mann's Joseph must, like his Aschenbach, go all the way to the tigers and be tested.

The Egyptian sphinx, the Greek sphinx, the sphinx as slayer of youth, the sphinx as emblem of the bottomless "calm-intoxicating" love-death of primitive desire — Joseph's well-wrought, silent monologue keeps all these allusive but unmistakable threads before us. As a lad he thought that just naming the lion would solve its riddle (90; 55), but not now. He fantasizes his Greco-Giza sphinx as "wild, with lion's paws, lusting after young blood . . . with the claws of a dragon-woman . . . would not the terrifying creature [*Unwesen*] lift its paw from the sand and snatch the youth to its breast?" (751; 501). Like the disturbing Hatchepsut, the "mistress" and queen, the sphinx's passion will overmaster and devour him; to succumb to [woman's] timeless, overpowering passion is to be blind and blinded, castrated, eaten alive.

So Joseph stands before the sphinx, "trying his heart" not with the trial of Abraham, but with the trial of Oedipus. And what rescues him from its grip? Not the consolations of the sphere's revolution that occupied the "lowest layer" of his psyche in "The Pit," but the image of the father. The wording reveals the self-influence: the sphinx of Giza still casts its unswerving, sterile glance far above Joseph's head, but nonetheless he thinks: "Eye to eye with the forbidden, one who is the child of the spirit senses, and stands, with the father." "Eye to eye" with the saving image of the father: the Kleistian ethic of the face-to-face recognition that enables loyal love makes one of its most powerful returns. The scene contrasts vividly with Freud's description of Oedipus in *The Interpretation of Dreams*: "Like Oedipus, we live in ignorance of these wishes, . . . and after their revelation we may all of us seek to close our eyes to the scenes of our childhood" (*SE* I, 263). As we proceed through *Joseph in Egypt*, this primal scene returns again and again. It stands opposed to the strife and immobilizing power of Oedipus's rite of passage, in both its Greek and its Viennese versions. Freud at his darkest would freeze us in the unchanging stare of the primal scene which we can only repeat in narrow variations. The "Kleist" lecture's vision develops from a different exchange of glances and a different naming of names.

Oedipus is a hero of language, a champion who attacks and defeats a monster with words, not brute strength or a magic sword. Joseph's uncharacteristic silence before the sphinx suggests the temporary nature of his victory; this time he stands with the loving father and the fruitful promise, but the issue is still in doubt. To reinforce this, the Sphinx reappears in Joseph's dream at the end of his long night vigil, and speaks without riddling from his unconscious: "I love you. Come to me and name me your name, of whatever nature I am!" Joseph answers with a question of his own, revealingly balanced between the rhetorical and the real: "How shall I commit such an evil and sin against God?" (752; 501; Gen. 39: 9).[24] He has passed this test, yet the issue remains in doubt. This trial of course anticipates Joseph's extended trial before Mut, who becomes over time not only a Cleopatra but a sphinx and dragon-woman (see esp. 1136, 1141–42, 1162, 1202; 752, 756, 769, 795). At the climax of that trial the image and the silence return. The sphinx of unbridled desire cannot be defeated by words, but only by self-knowledge and acts of will. This is the conclusion of the 1929 essay as well, and one that *Joseph in Egypt* puts to the test.

The remainder of Joseph's tour-descent — Menfe and Thebes — can pass quickly for us. Menfe, "older than the pyramids" yet "teeming with life and awakened modernity," incorporates features of each earlier site and gives us civilization's discontents in their happiest possible form (752; 502). A city of irony and mediation, Menfe sports whole avenues of guardian sphinxes, and also a living bull god, whose point of view we comically enter as he watches his celebrants hop and shout in his honor. From the sphinx's impenetrable mystery to this most un-mysterious of totem figures: Menfe's citizens joyfully honor both sphinx and bull, and do not think too deeply about the theological im-plications. When Joseph, propelled by his theological training and his unnerving encounter with the sphinx, presses a local baker for answers about graves and gods, the man cheerfully walks away. In contrast, Thebes, 'The City of the Dead" and "navel of the world," is a multi-cultural metropolis yet much more monolithic in culture. Just begin-ning its great period of expansion, it appears to have a great future. But its theology and its aristocracy are frozen, and the city is falling under the sway of the new god Amun's storm troopers, who shoulder Joseph out of the way on its narrow streets (523; 783).

Looking back, we can see that Mann constructed his hero's journey in epic "ring structure," the performing poet's great mnemonic. We began at a dry well, with the Ishmaelites and Jacob's sons negotiating a crosscultural sale; we close with the Ishmaelites selling their wares around the Nile-fed well of Sippar Court in international Thebes. There are five intervening narrative rings. The outer rings match the vacant primitivisms of Per-Sopd and Per-Bastet with neoconservative Thebes. The inner rings parallel reconciling On with mediating Menfe. At the center of the construction stands Joseph's great scene before the sphinx, anchoring the journey in both Joseph's psyche and in the cen-tral intertexts that shape its outcome. Descent (and ring) completed, Joseph leads the Ishmaelite's camel out of the city the next day toward Potiphar's house.

V

Who can separate out the interplay of those sweet and happy chances to which life, groping here and there among inherited traits, adds the one unique thing that forms the gracefulness of the human face? It is a charm suspended on a knife-edge, it hangs, one may say, on a hair; so that if only a tiny trait, the smallest muscle, were placed differently, though but little were changed yet the heart's delight, the whole haunting miracle, would unravel.

— *Joseph and his Brothers* (228; 149)

Three of Joseph's mini-performances during his early time in Potiphar's suburban mansion epitomize the ways in which our subjects help to form the fabric of *Joseph in Egypt*. The narrator once again reminds us that each "represents" a number of other occasions, emphasizing Joseph's will to self-presentation. These performances before Potiphar mirror Mann's own onstage career; his self-consciousness together with his abandonment of self, his pleasure in and suspicion of roles, his ethical empathy, and his observer's distance all appear in them.

Joseph's opening "Prüfung" in the date-palm garden is the most dramatic. The narrator dips into both quoted and narrated monologue to show us, vividly, the new psychic space that Osarsiph occupies (889ff.; 593ff.).[25] As Potiphar approaches, Joseph gazes on his new master and thinks "Behold, there he walks in the garden in the cool of the day." The difficult balance of parodic intertext and authentic loyalty to the father sets the stage for the entire scene. God in his garden before his submissive slave, and the young god before the dazzled eunuch — we read the scene in both directions and in both tones at once.

As soon as Potiphar pauses before him, Joseph looks down. Proper obeisance, of course, but also thematic: the novel calls attention to, and then defers, a face-to-face encounter. Joseph evaluates his first moves with the newfound coolness of a professional actor — "Only middling," he judges — yet he is on edge; there can be no dress rehearsals for this act of his God-play. Seducing with his humble yet graceful postures, he speaks to the ground until Potiphar asks if he loves his work and is anxious to please. Then he raises his head and looks into the master's face. Jupiter before Amphitryon, Mann before Heuser, in a strongly refigured variation: Potiphar sees in the young god an entrancing hope of recovered potency, and Joseph beholds an Egyptian whose countenance may substitute for that of the forsaken father. Joseph's last thought of Jacob before the renunciation was of his tearful eyes; here in the first moment of this new meeting his "deep, black-Rachel-eyes, blank and deep . . . met the master's gentle and somewhat sad ones, long-lashed and brown like a doe's" (891; 594). These are very like the eyes of God in "The Dream of Heaven" (465; 311), who in turn has the eyes of Jacob (e.g. 68; 41). As soon as they gaze on one another, the narrator drops all Joseph's critical asides and commentary, and lets his face-to-face scene play. He positions us with Potiphar, and we follow his cautious but growing enthrallment; Joseph we only watch from the outside, as in a drama. This highlights the emotional and ethical effects of his performance.

Joseph ends this captivating scene with a Whitmanesque rhapsody on double-sexed fertility and the virgin birth he has wittily claimed for himself (898–903; 598–602). It is a paean to God the Father of the world, who creates with seed and the wind but most importantly with the Word. The maimed Potiphar needs to hear of the spiritual potencies of wind and word, but the speech depends as much on Joseph's divided character in the underworld as it does on his calculation. It succeeds brilliantly, of course, in seducing Potiphar precisely because it repeats, in an elevated and elevating style, the split between the fleshly and the spirit. The scene ends with a subtle turn of the Kleistian scene of naming and affirmation: Joseph once more, after a "pause that could not have come from reflection . . . solemnly looks up" and pronounces his uncanny name: "Osarsiph," the dead Joseph, who is now very much alive for his new master. His speech praises the "virtue of giving," and his face confirms the love and loyalty that his words promise. The isolated Potiphar, like Joseph's isolated God, requires loyalty (e.g., 919–20, 1056; 612, 702), and with it he can remake himself within Joseph's story. With his glance Joseph can satisfy both his self-love and his loyalty to the father, and the reader can see both the blessing and the ominous divisions that sustain it in this hour of the feast.

The next scene, in which Joseph and the fatherly steward Mont-Kaw make their pact to serve and protect Potiphar, elaborates that loyalty. It begins with an overlay of two face-to-face encounters. Quickly elevated to the position of waiter and reader to the master, Joseph asks after the fate of the reader he will replace. Politics motivate his question as much as empathy — no underling, however chosen, can afford enemies in the great house — but Mont-Kaw is alert only to the thoughtfulness. "Do you love the master?" he asks, and the two look into each other's eyes:

> The question was strangely moving, and shot through with memories familiar to Joseph since childhood. Just so had Jacob asked, whenever he drew his favorite on his knee; with just such painful searching had

his brown eyes with the delicate pouches beneath them looked into the face of the child. Instinctively the sold one answered with the formula appropriate to the ever recurring situation, and whose terms did not offend his inner life:

'With my whole soul, with my whole heart, with my whole mind' (907, 604; see also 976 and 993–94; 648 and 659).

This childhood flashback is a rare event in Joseph's characterization, and one which self-evidently matters. Joseph looks into the eyes of Mont-Kaw and sees the face of the father. And, in one of Mann's most ingenious uses of a proleptic intertext, Joseph utters a famous love-promise not from the Pentateuch but from the synoptic gospels. He does so "instinctively" ("unwillkürlich"), as though it indeed came from a prophetic intuition "open at the front." Joseph affirms loyalty in the present via the remembered face of the father and the future's vow of loving loyalty to God. This small epiphany keeps the Kleistian moment of recognition and acknowledgment at center stage.[26]

Arguably the most entertaining and witty exploration of performance in the entire *Joseph*, the small section "Joseph is Reader and Body-servant" completes our triptych of scenes. It presents two separate theaters within the space of reading. As in the scene of the "Kleist" lecture we have the youth and the older man, but with roles reversed: here a precocious Heuser, in effect, shows his loyal love by performing long-familiar texts for the vulnerable master — particularly a story of lovemaking that neither can quite countenance.

> Joseph, his feet drawn up under him or standing at a kind of liturgical lectern, performed splendidly: fluent, exact, seemingly unpretentious, moderately dramatic, and with such a natural command of words that the most involved literary style took on an aura of improvisational ease and informal conversation. He literally read himself into the heart of his listener, and these reading hours cannot be ignored in our understanding the fact of his well-known rise in the Egyptian's favor.
>
> (916; 610)

Imagine Mann at his own "liturgical lectern" or leaning forward in a family salon chair, reading this scene to an enthralled audience. A sixty-year-old performer may no longer "draw his feet up under himself," but in every other particular Joseph's style mirrors precisely his creator's gifts. He reads as Mann read, levitating his sinuous language into the air. Right breathing and intonation reveal his famously involved style to be a clear and supple script. Mann too made virtually no mistakes, dramatized his characters' voices, and conveyed his feeling for the story. Mann too sought to "read himself into the heart of his listener," for both self-gratifying and ethico-political reasons, and at times counted that achievement as vital to his standing among his contemporaries as his "pyramidenhaften" books. We "hear" Mann reading a narrative about right performance of a narrative: an imaginative layering as intricate as that in the "Kleist" performance. The narrator generalizes about Joseph's excellences as a reader but does not dramatize or imitate him reading; such an imitation of an imitation would have interfered with Mann's own performance of the section.

Long familiar with all his scrolls, Potiphar hears them as music as well as words, as scores to be performed. He anticipates their pleasing repetitions, and even dozes off to their soporific rhythms. Silent reading to him would be an oxymoron, like unheard music. Literature that aspires to the condition of music: long a Mann ideal, and one here familiarly tied to music's evocation of "letting go" and death. Mann naturally would prefer that his audiences hear his prose-music with attentive concentration, but he knows the hypnotic power of the musical reader, and is not above a little self-parody.

What follows this wry self-description takes us further into our web of subjects. Joseph performs the romantic first-person lyric of the little "Vogelstellerin" who longs for a beautiful youth (918; 611). The two together overcome death, "wandering hand in hand with hot cheeks through the flower garden of their bliss." Potiphar supposes that Joseph's perfect imitation of the lovers' voices comes from personal experience, and expresses his sympathetic approval. But Joseph's dramatizing, like Mann's in the "Kleist" lecture, serves both a higher and a lower purpose. He wishes to seduce Potiphar into seeing him as a youthful saved sacrifice, a beautiful person who models a sanctified state in which asexuality can take on a spiritual significance and even, paradoxically, promise a future. No-sex can become, by narrative sleight of hand, double-sexed, and a childhood maiming the means to a godlike elevation. Joseph reaffirms his empathetic link with Potiphar through narcissistic self-abnegation and sacrifice.

The irony, of course, is that his ability to imitate the lovers' voices does not by itself allow him to understand the power of the "flesh" he has turned away from.[27] In the little essay-dialogue on literary theory that follows, Joseph speaks only of the pattern of the story, its general form, and (unwisely) turns his back on its loving details. To see only the pattern without desire, or without the especial face of the beloved, mockingly inverts the "simplicity" Joseph finds in the little love story. The young Egyptian lovers overcome death; Joseph's Osarsiph-renunciation remains in it. In one way he knows this, even as he knows his new name; he retells with captivating allusiveness the death-driven transfer of his father's love from the mother to the son. But in another he does not; the particular arrogance of his primary narcissism still shelters him from passion's vicissitudes. The "garden" of the lovers he renames as a "demonic realm" guarded by shame, guilt, and mocking laugher ("Spottgelächter"). But he himself will shortly enter the same garden, bringing only the ignorance of passion his elevated set-apartness disguises. Joseph, so to speak, thinks he is Freud, but at this moment he is more like Parsifal, another motherless innocent.

From narrated performance to performing narrative, the chapter distills the right practice of Mann's twin passions. Intertextual disruptions abound; all the cited titles and texts in Potiphar's library are real,[28] and Joseph refigures his own tradition's tales in new, Potiphar-enticing forms. He transforms Adonis into the consecrated son-sacrifice of Judaism, and Potiphar into a god who must bear the suffering of his sinful people. The purpose of right reading and many-layered text alike is to delight and "sustain" ("unterhalten") the master, and to justify Joseph's characteristic mix of calculation and sincerity while maintaining perspective on his remaining blindnesses. "For we may also ask if sincerity without artful calculation and sophisticated technique can ever achieve practical results" (923; 614): Mann's artistic and ethical commitments come together perfectly. We move from writing to reading to writing again, now interwoven modes. We listen, as we read, to Mann's reading of Potiphar listening to Joseph reading — intricacies enough to suspend the reader and listener well above any simple binaries of ephemeral speech and permanent writing.

VI

God was there, and Abraham walked before him, consecrated in his soul through his outward nearness. They were Two, an I and a Thou, both of whom said "I" and to the other "Thou."

> — *Joseph and his Brothers* (431; 287)

For Levinas, "ethics" describes neither ontic nor deontic categories, which generalize theories of reality from subjective experience; ethics, rather, originates from the opposite direction — from the other to me, in the sensible experience of the face which he or she presents to me.

> — Adam Zachary Newton, *Narrative Ethics*

Mut-em-enet proved to be a godsend for *Joseph in Egypt*. One of Mann's great case histories, she recapitulates in finely filigreed detail the dilemmas of many of his doomed characters: the shocking awakening to passion, helplessness before its dark and invasive gods, exaltation interwoven with self-disgust, the fatal allure of "letting go."[29] Her family, once aristocrats of the nome, backed the wrong foreign protectors and lost their land holdings in Middle Egypt to upstart "petty kings" of Thebes. This repeats a familiar Mannian tale of aristocratic decline and upstart: "Hagenström" usurpation transmuted to Egypt. They did manage to retain positions in the court bureaucracy — her father was city prince of Wese, the Theban city of the dead — and arranged a class-appropriate marriage for their child. But her civilization cannot provide her with any means to balance the passion and honor, aggression and affection which striate its contours. Mut is not only a temple-virgin, condemned to a life of empty form, she is a story-virgin as well. She has no self-shaping or redemptive tales to draw on, no narrative history or exemplary forebearers. Mut comes to Joseph's story with no stories of her own. She is in effect the "Dora" of *Joseph in Egypt*, a blank slate on which earlier narrators have inscribed only callous summaries, and her latest interpreter is determined to provide her with the legend she deserves. At the same time her fall has a fortunate side, not only for the "pride of life" it leaves with her (1493; 989), and not only for Joseph and his God-story, but for a storyteller in need of her dignity and passion.

The narrator frames her downfall with a haunting paragraph evoking another of his fiction's familiars, the Dionysian "stranger god" (1082; 718).[30] In a paragraph shifting between the authorial and the general "we," he says that our earliest mental experience, just as we enter into civilization, is one of "sympathy with the affliction" ["Heim-suchung"] and annihilating forces that so often erupt into a peaceful life and sweep away its underpinnings.[31] Primitive man faced the same eruption, and in recognizing that we realize our kinship with him and so with human life's larger unity and "unchanging sameness." "All this was there from the beginning." At first we may take delight in this solidarity across time, but a little reflection dampens our pleasure. For the idea endorses an anthropological fatedness; Mut's tragedy reseen through this lens becomes another Freudian tale of beginning in loss and deprivation. The paragraph suggests how far we have come from the machinations of 1929, and how much Mann felt he could risk in his portrait of Mut. It explicitly counters Amphitryon's story of rebirth: no loving face and loyal calling of a name, only empathy for a shared, crushing "visitation." Just a little later the narrator adds that only with great difficulty can our higher thoughts hold their own against "eternal nature," and that our honor and civilized agreements can achieve little "against the dark, deep silent knowledge of the flesh" (1084; 719). Mut's heroism in the face of her bleak beginnings and the sterility of

her culture forms the basis of the narrator's case history. He "saves" her
not only from the reductive one-liner of the Genesis narrative, but also
from reductive pathos. "In short, if she is made seductive, is she therefore a seductress?" (1003; 668): a one-sentence encapsulation of her
innocence and victimization in the Eros/Thanatos wars. She does not
remain just another Freudian casualty. Her doomed struggle ennobles
in spite of (and in part thanks to) its failure. Though hardly a feminist,
Mann can expose patriarchy's cruelties even as he keeps the image of
the father at the center of his narrative.

Seen from the vantage of the God-story, however, both Mut and
Joseph enmesh themselves in doubtful pedagogy. An oblique, glancing
look defines their first encounter; Joseph only sees her Bovaryesque
white arm and her profile, and she does not distinguish him at all (822;
549). Years pass before they actually look into one another's faces.
Early reports of her verbal subtlety, carried by the faithful dwarf Bes,
also charm him; Joseph narcissistically admires in her what he prizes in
himself (948; 630). Though an innocent, she wears a sphinxlike wig
(912; 608) and carries out his sex education, a required course in his
deeper self-apprehension.

His learning has two interrelated parts, and Joseph requires both to
see all the way into his narcissism. Only by facing "the dark, deep silent
knowledge of the flesh," that is desire's power and the limits of the self
it reveals, can he grasp the deeper self-deceptions that his narcissism
fosters (and requires). In the salad days of his Adonis imitations, sexuality was safely distanced. Adoring women remained on the rooftops,
chanting his name, and the sexual mishaps of others were objects of
amusement, not self-revelation. No longer: Joseph has a great deal of
information about sex, from the behavior of sheep to the tales of Gilgamesh and Ishtar, but no experience. He tries to control passion with
the comparative innocence of his self-love. His chastity may take inspiration from his general love of everything in the world (1132; 749),
but that sort of broad experience proves feeble in the crucial moment
(1236; 817).

Second, his pedagogic performances with Mut expose narcissism's
subtle gradations; Mann's long-meditated understanding of this subject
lets him show how even a lecture on Moorish corn can achieve titillat-
ing self-satisfaction (1098; 728). Joseph tries to see only his own testing and a threat to his self-mastery in Mut's allure, but testing itself has
become just one more form of temptation. Gradually this blinding mirror dissolves. For example, the reworked rationalizations in his conversations with the panderer Dudu and the good dwarf Bes in the "Three-
fold Exchange" section pinpoint just how Joseph's revised ambition —

the wish to have everyone bow down to him in order to honor God —
backslides into self-aggrandizement.[32] Irony riddles each of his constructions. He misreads his desire as a flattering freedom of choice. He
misreads her desire as an instrument of God's elevation. In a lovely
Kleistian twist, he defends the blamelessness of his "blind loyalty" to
his mistress (1079; 716). He rereads his history in Potiphar's house as
one of triumph even as he slips into defeat. He even reviews his own
history as a self-lover, as though that could save him (1081–82; 718).

Perhaps the most subtle of all his blinding illuminations comes in
seeing his relation with Mut as a reenactment of Gilgamesh resisting
Ishtar (1130; 748). He had already decided that his first glimpse of her
in her carriage was that of "a boy looking up as if at a goddess, blinded
by awe" (1078; 715). Now he goes a step further. He muses smugly
that he once spoke as Gilgamesh without recognizing the words, but
now that he does he is protected as poor, ignorant Mut is not, for "in
him I see myself, and through myself I understand him" (1130; 748).
But all he actually sees is Gilgamesh's "discontent" with his mistress's
power; Joseph's quoted monologue dramatizes exactly how his knowledge of mythic pattern can derail self-inquiry. He has flashes of insight
into his culpability before the end (e.g., 1157; 766), but they alone
cannot save him. Every survival strategy promotes his blindness; he tries
to valorize the surface of their relationship — as he did with his three-
tiered consciousness — because he can't control the lower layers.

Besides the irony of "blind loyalty," their long courtship narrative
plays on (or inverts with moral purpose) the "Kleist" performance at
nearly every turn. We know that the play was on Mann's mind. Irritated
one afternoon by a "stupid" movie on Amphitryon that followed hard
upon newsreel images of the Nazi Nuremberg Celebration, he read the
Jupiter-Alkmene scenes out loud to Katia, Hans Reisiger, and his son
Golo. This was in late September 1935, just as he was writing the Mut-
Dudu-Joseph section and launching into the crucial love narrative (*TB*,
24 and 27 Sept. 1935). But even without that knowledge, the presence
of Mann's "*Amphitryon*" performance remains in view. Mut makes Joseph into a god, mimicking Alkmene's dilemma (e.g., 1167; 773); Mut
as "mistress" seeks the mastery that Jupiter willfully executed against
his servant and "idol" Alkmene. In *Joseph in Egypt*'s section "The First
Year," the "Kleist" essay's affirmation of loyalty as "loving without
seeing" is replaced by the fear that passion will disappear without constant "seeing" of the beloved (1089; 723). The couple's disguised conversations, shifting identities, and "apparitions" all draw on the
conversations of Jupiter and Alkmene. Jupiter's uncontrollable self-
disclosures offer a prototype for Mut's, and "The First Year's" psychol-

ogy of blindness in love elaborates the unseeing in *Amphitryon*. The "confusion of feeling" that the "pedagogue and humanist" Goethe condemned in Kleist — and that Mann defended in 1927 on the grounds that the psychological and pathological permeate one another — are explored exhaustively now.

In "The Second Year" Mut's agony over her inability to control Joseph's spirit as well as his body has its obvious counterpart in Jupiter's limited mastery over Alkmene. "Mut" in ancient Egyptian is a goddess, wife to Amun, and an "Urmuttername" ("archaic mother-name" [1083; 719]). So Mut transforms herself into "Rachel's sister," dressing herself in "Asiatic costume" and creating a parodic Oedipal drama (1083–84; 719). In disguise she becomes a grotesque of Jacob's beloved: Rachel as child-bride, lover, and overmastering mother. She appears before Joseph in her Canaanite regalia, seated on a wide armchair covered with a lion's skin, with the lion's jaws pointed out at Joseph's feet — the questioning-devouring sphinx indeed (1123; 744). As a goddess-mother, Mut assumes the prerogatives of an omniscient narrator, ironically taking over Freudian tales because she has no sustaining ones of her own. Mann returned to and "read in" *Civilization and its Discontents* in April 1936, while working on the final sections of *Joseph in Egypt* (*TB*, 16 Apr. 1936). At several points Mut seems to quote *Civilization* directly (e.g., 1044; 695), and her long, free-associating monologue to her ersatz analyst Dudu offers an extraordinary instance of "Freudian" characterization (1062–66; 706–8). To Joseph she not only affirms that every man desires his mother, she offers to slay the "father" Potiphar to make that possible (1170–72; 774–76). In the toils of passion every story refigures into the same story. The connections to the "Kleist" performance continue as well; her sly claim that "worship encouraged becomes desire" (1103; 731) could well be Jupiter's. Instead of constructing his own God-play, Joseph must take the part assigned him in Mut's script (1129–30; 748). Like Amphitryon, he nearly disappears in the goddess's appropriation of his name.

Each section gives the screw another turn. "On Joseph's Chastity" ends with Joseph's "self-confident cockiness" and his desire to be a "virtuoso of virtue," temptations that lure him to his "black eye" and fall (1143; 757). The playscript of "The Painful Tongue" offers a kind of anti-*Amphitryon*. Made disloyal by passion, Mut becomes now the lisping child-victim, now the voluptuous mistress, now the "beautiful witch," now the infuriated goddess in a cascade of metamorphoses and role changes that obliterate her dignified identity. The characters' long, halting speeches would make for tendentious stage drama — like *Fiorenza* — but they perfectly suit the drama of the author's public read-

ing. Like the crown in *Amphitryon* with its tell-tale *J*, both Mut's hi-
eroglyphic message and Joseph's abandoned outer garment are objects
that silently speak the truth. Even the abrupt biblical phrase "lie with
me" fits perfectly with Joseph's Narcissus-blindness; it echoes the last
independent phrase that Ovid's hapless Echo called to her beloved as
he deserted her.

Joseph in Egypt closes, as *Amphitryon* does, with scenes of unveiling
and judgment. In Mann's 1927 re-creation of Alkmene, "One name
breaks out of her deepest heart . . . Amphitryon!" (IX, 228; *Essays*,
239). *Joseph in Egypt* inverts that celebrative greeting. Mut's operatic
"Osarsiph!," like Kundry's "Par-si-fal!," summons Joseph to cross the
threshold and embrace her in her garden of enchantment: the garden
of shame, guilt, and mocking laugher. "Osarsiph!" and "Amphitryon!" — the two calls echo and rebound through Potiphar's twilit
halls and Mann's open text, one calling forth self-affirmation in loyalty
in love, the other the love-death of bodies divorced from self. One enables selfhood; the other explicitly rejects it in the name of Jovian con-
quest and submission. They exchange all manner of duplicitous glances
in and around their equally duplicitous conversations, but never one of
direct confrontation. And so on: Mann's retelling draws on the Kleist
drama and lecture at every turn, inverting, refining, varying, until we
are immersed in the parallels and ready to read the affair's denouement
aright.

The climactic section, "The Father's Face," opens with the story itself becoming silent, "drawing the veil" over the couple's final, ca-
cophonous duet in which all exchange disappeared and both talked at
once (1255; 829).[33] The narrator reminds us that his tale is being
"performed before a large audience" ("vor einem großen Publikum ab-
spielt") and requires pedagogic restraint. Playful humor perhaps, but
not mock modesty; Mann writes to perform and once again imagines
his audience in a hall, not a private study. So we listen as Joseph crosses
the threshold ("die Schwelle": comp. *schwellen*, to "swell"), fulfilling
his death-name. His stream of talk is dammed by his swelling erection.
Veiled and yet unveiled, the image of the phallus, like that of Narcissus
in the pool, deceives; Mut reaches out for it but comes away only with
"the upper garment" as Joseph, in extremis, chooses flight. Mut's last
triumphant cry, "I have seen his strength" (1256; 830), remains hollow; what she has seen is his weakness and self-division, his penis stiffened autonomically like that of the dead Osiris, rather than the face of
her beloved Joseph. Joseph had long meditated the parallel between his
life and Osiris's (e.g., 1082; 718), but that knowledge avails him
nothing now. Like Mut, we see only the image and not the flesh. Then,

in a stunning reversal, another carefully constructed image rescues Joseph from Osarsiph:

> But what enabled Joseph, in that uttermost extremity, to tear himself away and flee, was this: he saw his father's face (*Vaterantlitz*). All the more precise versions say so, and may here be confirmed as the truth. It is so: when, despite all his eloquence he was almost lost, the image of his father appeared to him. Jacob's image? Yes, certainly, Jacob's image. But it was not an image with definitive personal features which he might have actually seen somewhere in the room. Rather he saw it in his mind and with the spirit; it was an image of memory and admonition [*ein Denk- und Mahnbild*], the father's image in a broad and general sense. Jacob's features mingled with Potiphar's fatherly features, with those of Mont-kaw the modest departed one, and above and beyond these resemblances were other, even more powerful features. Out of brown and shining father-eyes with delicate tear-sacs beneath them, it gazed on Joseph with an anxious look.
>
> This saved him, or rather . . . he saved himself, in that his spirit brought forth the image [*sein Geist das Mahnbild hervorbrachte*] (1256–57; 830).

This is the decisive moment of Joseph's story, and the culminating self-influential moment of Mann's retelling. As a seventeen-year-old by the well, Joseph had looked into his "god-like" father's "countenance" ("Antlitz") as his father looked upward into the countenance of God (102; 63). Here the gaze of the father supplants the gaze of the sphinx.[34] The paragraph has at least four separable strands. In the "original," that is in Mann's imagined elaboration of the scene as it really happened, Joseph and Mut go on talking at one another until his body speaks for itself. In the "more precise" ancient commentators, that is those that supplement Genesis's silence on this point, Joseph does indeed see the face of his father — and the Father: "Peniel." He calls it forth just as Abram called forth, and recognized, God, and as Jacob saw the face of God at Beth-el: "for I have seen God *face to face*, and my life is preserved" (Gen. 32: 30).[35] The narrator emphasizes ancient authority for this scene, then elaborates with his own greater exactitude what Joseph saw.

Third, a welter of roughly symmetrical triangles connect the final threesome of "Kleist's *Amphitryon*" to Joseph, Mut, and the father's image. A self-influential reading steers us through these ambiguities to thematic clarity. It both includes and looks through the Oedipal conflict and the narcissism that have occupied so much of *Joseph in Egypt*. Joseph and his saving image stand at a midpoint between the narcissism of seeing only self-glory in the other, and the Oedipal father who threatens castration and sacrifice. As always, the father's image both rises from within him and is willed by him (50; 30), another erection but one from Joseph's deepest psyche and consciously obeyed.[36] The narrator is specific: the image bursts forth from within Joseph yet is the face of the other, not a reflecting pool. The face of the father does admonish, but it expresses anxiety rather than violence. Enabling rather than disabling, the beloved father's countenance empowers Joseph literally to re-cover himself.[37] Mann singles out this performative account of the psyche's structure and ethical ground as the heart of his tetralogy's central subject, "the nature of man." Joseph's ego opens not only at the back, but also at the front to a face and a future that simultaneously anchor and reanchor its unity.

"Kleist's *Amphitryon*" and the *Joseph* project work together to elaborate Genesis in yet another way. Joseph remains loyal to the tale in which he appears, just as Mann remained loyal to Kleist's play in its absence. The face of the father is emphatically no specter, no ghostly simulacrum of Jacob's specific features summoned to haunt a corner of the room as Joachim Ziemssen's summoned image once did. To cite Villon again, "the dead depend entirely on our loyalty," not our mindless or selfish needs. No frozen icon evoking idolatry, the father's image performs and empowers performance. It gives shape to fatherly anxiety. It gathers together Joseph's several fathers and the specific loving loyalties each of them called forth in him, just as Mann lovingly reenacted each of Kleist's characters before Heuser. Jacob is there and not there: what saves Joseph is not some miraculous incarnation, but loyalty, "loving without seeing," "saving (the) face," giving an ethical center to both the present and the future. The face of the Other requires response. Like *Ulysses, Joseph in Egypt* searches for the "fatherland," the resting place and anchor of the psyche.

So the image narrowly rescues Joseph from all the tales that would put him in Mut's embrace and undermine the God-story: Joseph-Osarsiph, the god potent in death; Joseph-Oedipus the father slayer and mother polluter who finds a stranger within his psyche; Joseph-Narcissus, who loves his own well-crafted, beautiful self-image in the arms of the goddess and who knows nothing of good and evil; Joseph-Noah, shaming with his drunken nakedness; Joseph-Jupiter, who thought himself omniscient in love-knowledge and in narration. The Joseph who proclaimed to Jacob "I and my mother are one," and who later entered Potiphar's house with the thought that he and his father were one (825; 551), now resees the father as his significant Other, whose history bears a blessing his own only approximates. In this way Joseph undergoes the trial of Amphitryon; stripped by Jupiter and an uncomprehending woman, he recognizes and calls forth the face of the beloved and is renewed. Parsifal saved himself by calling his mother's name, but Joseph stands with — not within — the father. The "silence" of "The Father's Face" comes not only from its purported modesty over Joseph's nakedness, but also from the silent images that arise in Joseph and in the folds of the text itself: fathering tales of loyalty and sympathy that shape its prose in silent but sustained dialogue.

When Mann finished *Joseph in Egypt* on 23 August, 1936, there was a family occasion: champagne, a celebrative poem written by Erika and performed by Elizabeth — and of course a reading from the final chapter by its weary creator. The daughters may divide the artist's functions, but their father does not; he writes in order to perform.

VII

This chapter began with an exchange of letters between Mann and Freud, and now ends with a brief epilogue: a letter from Freud written several months before Mann began "Freud and the Future" in 1936. Like that lecture, it is a birthday greeting, though an extraordinarily somber one. Freud writes as follows:

> Please accept a heartfelt message of affection on your sixtieth birthday. I am one of your 'oldest' readers and admirers; I could wish you a very long and happy life, as is the custom on such occasions. But I shall refrain from doing so; the bestowal of wishes is trivial and seems to me a regression into the era when mankind believed in the magic omnipotence of thought. My most personal experience, moreover, tends to make me consider it a good thing when merciful fate puts a timely end to our span of life.
>
> Nor do I consider it worthy of imitation when, on a festive occasion such as this, affection overrides respect and obliges the hero of the day to listen to speeches that overwhelm him with praise as a human being and analyze as well as criticize him as an artist. I don't want to be guilty of such arrogance. But I will permit myself something else: in the name of countless numbers of our contemporaries I wish to express the confidence that you will never do or say anything — an author's words, after all, are deeds — that is cowardly or base, and that even at a time which blurs judgment you will choose the right way and show it to others. (*Letters*, 426)

Did Freud have his approaching eightieth celebration in mind when he penned this death-haunted set of instructions for proper birthday cards? If so, Mann did not heed it; in fact he followed the "arrogant" practice of overpraise and analysis, and added another characteristic kind of his own: autobiography. But Mann undoubtedly took heart from Freud's laconic literary theory and the praise that followed from it. An author's words are truly deeds, equally those that condemn "the times" (and the leaders) who "blur judgment," and those that retell interwoven stories of Jewish and German beginnings in the ethical. Freud confirms Mann in his deepest wish to be great artist and teacher, aesthetic inspirer and moral example. It is in one way "overpraise," of course, since Mann's mission to German youth had not prevented Hitler's rise or his own exile, but it is well-tempered in another: such performative deeds, however quixotic, keep both brilliance and bravery constantly before us. To quote him, "we should not cease respecting the cherished hopes of more high-minded men because history did not honor their cause" (IX, 514; *Essays*, 361).

Notes

[1] Freud to Lou Andreas-Salome, 28 July 1929 (*Briefe*, 1873–1939, 407–8.; *Letters*, 389–91).

[2] 23 Nov. 1929; reprinted in *DüD* 14/II, 361–62n.

[3] It is possible, of course, that Mann exaggerated the intensity — even the quantity — of his reading of *Civilization*. This seems unlikely, however, given the pressure of both political events and the evolution of the *Joseph* novels. Nor was this his usual way of disguising a quick reading. With fame came many unsolicited manuscripts, and those from acquaintances required especially delicate handling. Mann perfected the polite and clever strategy of skimming a manuscript, then reading a small portion on which he could make some specific comment. That comment implied a careful reading of the whole.

[4] Compare Mann's "Vereinsamung und Verfemung" to Freud's "Vereinsamung und Befeindung": the root verb *verfemen* means "to proscribe or outlaw"; *befeinden* means "to show enmity or be antagonistic to." Mann makes himself and Freud "outlaws," not merely objects of antagonism.

In a 1932 interview, given the day after the first face-to-face meeting between himself and Freud, Mann repeated his claim for Freud's "triumphant life-work" to a reporter from the *Neue Freie Presse* in Vienna, and added that the "seed of Freud's work, planted years earlier, has today grown into a world-shading tree" (*Frage und Antwort*, 189).

[5] "Es war nicht wohllautend, aber ach, ich habe wenig Grund, stolz darauf zu sein. Ich bin beschämend spät gekommen — *langsame* Natur, die ich durchaus und in allen Stücken bin. Alles muß sehr reif in mir werden, bevor ich es mitteilen kann" (*Briefe* I, 296; italics in original).

[6] Mann's optimism, of course, is never naive or categorical, and his Nietzschean "courageous search for truth" always entailed facing its darker discoveries.

[7] The kaleidoscope image contains pitfalls of its own. It is, on reflection, more mechanistic that the narrator seems to notice. He uses it to illustrate the line of descent from Jacob's Laban-time to the more complicated, "difficult and dangerous" life-patterns of his son in Egypt, and to speak of the problems involved in knowing the entire story beforehand. But the kaleidoscope's more complex patterns appear randomly, not in any order of development or predictability. In that sense, for all their repetitive, self-reflecting structure, they defy sequencing in their endless play: a deconstructive turn that supplements Mann's on-going struggle to honor and contain Freud.

[8] By 1940 Mann writes easily, though with a careful vagueness, of the sympathetic relation between the *Joseph* and Freud: "[Freud's] psychological interpretation [of myth] had a number of points in common with my view of the meaning of the mythical and of the role which it occupies in the life of the title character" ("On Myself," XIII, 164).

[9] Michael Tratner, in *Modernism and Mass Politics*, insightfully works this out for the English and Irish high modernists. He argues that modernism — including especially all its ways of portraying individual consciousness — began as an attempt to "write in the idiom of the crowd mind. Modernism was not, then, a rejection of mass culture, but rather an effort to produce a mass culture, perhaps for the first time, to produce a culture distinctive to the twentieth century . . . . The contest between modernist and realist literary forms was thus not a contest between literature for a coterie and literature for the masses, but rather a contest between different ways of speaking to and from the mass mind, a contest based on different conceptions of how the masses think" (1995, 2). Mutatis mutandis, this illuminates Mann's self-described shift in artistic focus from the individual to the typical, and from political detachment to political performances aimed at reproducing German humanism. Tratner amplifies (11): "The debate between conservative national unity and socialist international multiplicity turned a debate about class relations into a debate about cultures," particularly in Mann's case the cultural narratives known as myth.

[10] "Gau," is the old word for tribal districts and no doubt for that reason impressed the Nazis, who adopted it to designate administrative regions; the connections between Egypt and Hitler's Germany begin early.

[11] The narrator picks up this theological thread in *Joseph the Provider* when he contrasts God's gift for combing many names in one person with Baal's multiple titles, which only scatter and weaken that "faceless" god's power (1728–29; 1146–47): a compact allegory of relativism's shortcomings?

[12] This connection may seem arbitrary without a little elaboration of its self-influential history. In the 1929 essay Mann uses the metaphor to characterize the starting-point of psychoanalysis's world movement: "the . . . enthusiasm

of disciples [Adepten] who have situated around its medical and psychological kernel this aura of influences ["die um ihren psychiatrisch-medizinischen Kern diese Aura von Wirkungen gelegt haben" (X, 274; *PM*, 190). He uses the same metaphor in the 1929 companion lecture on Lessing, where he borrows it from Otto Ludwig (IX, 235–36; *Essays*, 193–94). He also took it from the Novalis fragment "Das Allgemeine Brouillon," which he quotes in "On the German Republic": "Absolute Abstraktion — Vernichtung des Jetzigen — Apotheose der Zukunft, dieser eigentlichen bessern Welt: dies ist der Kern der Geschichte des Christentums" (*Essays 1919–1925*, 150). A less subtle version of it also appears in chapter 2 of *The Future of an Illusion* (XXI, 10), a text which Mann also quotes near the end of his essay. And in Freud's 1919 essay "A Child is being Beaten," Mann underlined the sentence in which Freud claimed that the archaic legacy of man developed from a "kernel" of the unconscious, "and whatever part of that inheritance has to be left behind in the advance to later phases of development, because it is useless or incompatible with what is new and harmful to it, falls a victim to the process of repression" (*CP* 2, 201). Lehnert sees this as a possible influence on Isaac's death scene (1965, 478–9); its range may be even greater. The 1929 essay itself grew from a "kernel" passage — III, #197 of Nietzsche's *Morganröte* — and the conception of a light-giving kernel resonates with the image of the father that ultimately rescues Joseph. Pharaoh develops a similar image when he compares himself to a theological "gold-washer" "testing" and purifying the "Körnchen" of truth out of the "absurdity" of comparative religion (1419; 938).

[13] Mann finished the "Sphinx" section in late October 1932 (letter to Hans Reisiger, 30 Oct. 1932: *DüD* 14/II, 126).

[14] The Metropolitan Museum of Art has a fine example in its collection. See also the excellent collection of photographs in Tyldesley (1996). I follow her English transliteration of the queen's name.

[15] Mann deftly ignores the traditional account of the pyramids as expressions of the Egyptian creation myth, in which life arose from the ocean of chaos in great mounds of earth (like islands appearing as the flooding Nile recedes). His pyramids are tombs and nothing else, in keeping with the death confrontation that orders his scene.

[16] *Histories* II, 166.

[17] See Eckhard Heftrich's excellent discussion in "Potiphars Weib" of the use of the Freudian "Es" in connection with the sphinx (1991, 70): also see Heftrich 1993, 113ff.

[18] I am grateful to Egyptologist Douglas Bowman for confirming this claim. Not only do the Egyptians tell no stories of riddling or even fortune-telling in connection with the sphinx, its name never even appears in the hieroglyphs of the Pyramid Texts. Egyptologists generally agree that the head represents Pharaoh Khephron, Cheops's son, as "Horus of the Horizon." Its placement between the two great pyramids most plausibly signifies the noonday sun, and

the head framed between the two pyramids may form the hieroglyph for "horizon" and the rising sun. The placement obviously mattered a great deal, since three of the four types of natural rock at that site erode easily; no sculptor would have preferred it. Only the head contains hard stone, as the most recent restorers of the statue have lamented. Lions regularly represent guardians in Egyptian iconography, and often appear in pairs, or in long rows like sentries. See Silverman 1997, 186–87 and Grimm 1992, 414–15.

[19] Several of the characters connected to the sphinx — Mut, Potiphar, Beknechons — also "gaze past men and things" (944; 628; see also 1024–25; 682).

[20] The Greek "sphinx" may derive from the Egyptian " shesep-ankh," "living image": quite a different connotation (Silverman 1997, 186).

[21] Gantz (1993, 495ff.) offers an excellent summary, which I use in what follows.

[22] Jacob's witty dream-conversation with Anubis comically anticipates Joseph's encounter. The jackal-headed "slender youth" leads him through the wilderness, then poses charmingly on a rock and takes questions from his creator, the dreamer (288–93; 188–92). The unsolved riddle here concerns Jacob's obscure intuition that Leah will be substituted for Rachel. Anubis crudely links the face [Angesicht] with individuality, and sees the body as generic: "For one woman's body is like another" (291; 190). Anubis's pose is, famously, that of a classical Hermes statue in Naples (*Gespräch in Briefen*, 41 [20 Feb. 1934]); another figure whose origins are mysterious. Not even the sanctity of the countenance can escape parody entirely.

[23] It also echoes Nietzsche's account of Oedipus as a man who gains intellectual powers by committing a "monstrous crime against nature," incest (*The Birth of Tragedy*, chapter 9).

[24] Parenthetically, it also illustrates Mann's revision of Freudian dream theory: "What is entirely unknown to the waking mind, what is simply locked away from it, the dream does not know either. The border between the two is fluid and permeable; there is *one* soul-space, through which the soul uncertainly moves" (1013; 675: italics in original). Mannian dreams are indeed wishes, but barely disguised ones; they usually express what the ego dare not make public rather than what it cannot accept unmediated into consciousness.

[25] On types of monologue, see Cohn 1978, "Introduction." One of the narrator's most playful, omniscience-avoiding uses of quoted monologue follows Joseph's first glimpse of Mut-em-enet. He drafts a *hypothetical* stream of consciousness, affecting to guess at what Joseph might well have thought (831; 555). This has the dizzying effect of fictionalizing how Mann's fictional composition of Joseph's voice actually took place.

[26] A philosopher might query Mann's easy linkage between a character's openness to the pluralism of mythic archetype and his more phenomenological anchoring of individual identity in recognition and loyalty. For Mann's literary sensibility, however, the two views complemented each other effortlessly. Mann's familiarity with phenomenology came chiefly through his

reading of philosopher and sociologist of knowledge Max Scheler (e.g., his letter to an unknown correspondent, 8 Jan. 1932: *Briefe* I, 311).

[27] In this same vein, Potiphar has Joseph read the Egyptian "Tale of the Two Brothers," whose story of seduction gone wrong closely replicates his own. Plainly Joseph does not absorb the lesson, and Joseph's next mentor, Mai-Sachme, has him copy out the tale again — this time in a deluxe edition (1327; 877).

[28] See Grimm 1992, 269ff., and Simpson 1973, esp. 302ff.

[29] Lehnert (1993, 188) takes up a lesser known and fascinating self-influential text in Mut's making: the unhappy love story in Mann's early unfinished novel "Maja."

[30] Mann thanked Karl Kerenyi for his treatise "Thoughts on Dionysus" and credited him with helping to shape the "Dionysian, maenadic" passion of Mut (Mann and Kerenyi 1960, 29 Sept. 1935). The phrase goes back to Aschenbach's terrible dream in "Death in Venice."

[31] On "Heimsuchung," see chapter 3, ii.

[32] Mann uses Dudu at every turn to sharpen our sense of loyalty by perverting its meaning. The dwarf uses the word constantly, especially in his big scenes with Potiphar and in the love messages he contrives as go-between (e.g., 1189–92; 787–88).

[33] For "face" Mann uses "das Antlitz," an older, more poetic term also used by Kleist and quoted by Mann at the climax of his reconstruction of *Amphitryon* (IX, 225; *Essays*, 237). He uses the word at other crucial points, from Joseph's first meeting with Mai-Sachme (1303; 862) to the climax of *Joseph the Provider*.

[34] In "Written Right Across their Faces: Ernst Jünger's Fascist Modernism," Russell Berman's analysis of fascism's reliance on the image over writing illuminates this juxtaposition of image and text (Huyssen and Bathrick 1989, 61–69). Mann's writing of the image, especially the image of the father, as central to Joseph's character can be read as a riposte to the fascist erasure of text.

[35] See also Genesis 4:5–6: "but for Cain and his offering he had no regard. So Cain was very angry, and his face fell. The Lord said to Cain, 'Why are you angry, and why has your countenance fallen? If you do well, will you not be accepted? And if you do not do well, sin is crouching at the door; its desire is for you, but you must master it'." Joseph too is commanded to keep his face up and overcome the crouching animal across his threshold.

[36] Just so, God first responded to Abraham because he was "touched" by his striving to serve the Highest (426; 284).

[37] Even though I vowed early on not to draw out parallels between the *Joseph* and several contemporary thinkers, I cannot resist citing a passage from Levinas: consciousness is "the urgency of a destination leading to the Other and not an eternal return to the self, an innocence without naïveté, an uprightness

without stupidity, an absolute uprightness which is also absolute self-criticism, read in the eyes of the one who is the goal of my uprightness and whose look calls me into question. It is a movement toward the other that does not come back to its point of origin the way diversion comes back, incapable as it is of transcendence — a movement beyond anxiety and stronger than death. This uprightness is called *Temimut*, the essence of Jacob" (48).

6: "The Performance of My Life": The 1936 "Freud" Lecture and *Joseph the Provider*

Myth is the timeless schema ... into which life flows when it reproduces the traits of the unconscious .... Significant life is the reconstitution of the myth in flesh and blood. For life in the myth, life so to speak in quotation, is a kind of celebration; in that it is a making present of the past, it becomes a religious act, the performance by the celebrant of a prescribed procedure; it becomes a feast. For a feast is an anniversary, a renewal of the past in the present.

— Thomas Mann, "Freud and the Future"

Freud's best legacy is his struggle to understand what moves him, a struggle which attests to the critic's violent desire and the object's power, a struggle in which the subject is impelled by a drive that cannot afford to be respectful since the questions raised are disturbingly intimate .... To think about art is to encounter an other, a beautiful but unsettling one, over whom I do not have easy mastery.

— Juliet Mitchell, *Psychoanalysis and Feminism: Freud, Reich, Lang and Women*

In his powerful essay on Freud and the Future, *Mann comes very close to Nietzsche's dark essay on the right use of history .... Mann gives us a twentieth-century version of Nietzsche's overcoming of the anxiety of influence .... Mann's essay ... seems to me unique in our century's attitudes towards the sorrows of influence.*

— Harold Bloom, *The Anxiety of Influence*

If I have aimed at making people laugh (as I also do in The Holy Sinner), *that may likewise be connected with the need to placate. My "humor" is really skepticism toward myself. "Thou comest in such a questionable shape."*

— Thomas Mann to Caroline Newton, 14 Apr. 1952

I

Mann drafted "Freud and the Future" in April 1936, working hard through most mornings and afternoons and refashioning the typescript in early May (*TB*, 1 May 1936).[1] This lecture had a specific occasion: the gala celebration of Freud's eightieth birthday on 6 May in Vienna. The invitation coincided with the crafting of "The Second Year" of Joseph and Mut's relationship, perhaps the most overtly Freudian of *Joseph in Egypt*'s sections (*TB*, 16 Jan. 1936). Mann fussed a little about the additional responsibility, until it became clear that he was primus inter pares among the nearly two hundred dignitaries who signed Stefan Zweig's brief congratulatory "Address."[2] It placed him at center stage in Freud's Vienna in his own "festive drama of homage," a kind of choryphaeus for his fellow artists and antifascist comrades throughout the civilized world. In the terse style he typically reserved for positive statements in his diary, he termed the opportunity "important, interesting" (*TB*, 20 Jan. 1936). He discussed some of his ideas, especially the "astonishing" connections between Freud and Schopenhauer, with pastor Kuno Fiedler (*TB*, 22 Apr. 1936ff.); the actual lecture allowed for no onstage dialogue, but conversation did play a part in its making. He "rehearsed" the final draft for both content and timing before family and friends (including Erich Kahler and Franz Beidler, Wagner's grandson [*TB*, 4 May 1936]) and was pleased with both. Brimming with confidence, he wrote to Alfred Neumann about the rehearsal's success (*Briefe* I, 416–17).

Mann had met Freud briefly in March 1932 when he was in Vienna to deliver one of his two new Goethe lectures. This second, honor-packed visit, however, had much more significance for both men. It fulfilled the made-and-cancelled offer in Mann's January 1930 letter to speak seriously with the patriarchal Freud on his own turf. In 1930 the writing of autobiography substituted for a face-to-face meeting with Freud; here the two happily coincided. No supplemental excuse, such as an Oedipal murder trial, was required this time.

Freud's heart was too unsteady to tolerate the gala evening fete, which fell on 8 May, so Mann brought a portfolio with the tributes from his fellow artists and a copy of his manuscript to 19 Berggasse that same morning (Jones 3 [1957], 202). He left with "moving impressions" of the meeting. He termed the evening lecture in the "overfilled hall of the Konzerthaus" a "tumultuous success" (*TB*, 13 May 1936), and repeated the triumph twice in the succeeding week in Prague and Brno.[3] In early June, Mann traveled to Budapest to give the "Freud" lecture yet again, followed by the "spontaneous talk" to the League of

Nations "Committee on Intellectual Co-operation" that he would later discuss so warmly in the 1948 "Foreword" (see chapter 1, vi). Immediately thereafter, he returned to Vienna, in part at the behest of Freud's family. He gave a reading on Saturday the 13th from the garden scene in *Joseph in Egypt*. The hall was not full this time, but the "superb" audience more than made up for it with the "warmest reception" (*TB*, 14 June 1936). Then he meet again with Freud and a small circle of friends the following afternoon for a private performance of the lecture. This meeting took place not in the city but at Freud's rented country house at Grinzing, with its lovely gardens: "beautiful as a fairy land," Freud termed it (Jones 3, 189). The actual performance took place indoors, with the "young" Thomas Mann reading to the elder master of the house: Joseph and Potiphar in another revolution of the sphere. Freud had his copy of the talk from Mann's first visit, but apparently had not read it; what moved him to tears was hearing Mann's rendition.[4] He wrote to Freud the following December that the afternoon "belongs among the most lovely memories of my life" (*Briefe* I, 431). Mann went to a musical comedy that night: a fitting theatrical close to a sequence of treasured, very successful performances.[5]

In his diaries Mann specifically mentions only one Freud text that he reread for the lecture: *Civilization and its Discontents* (*TB*, 16 Apr. 1936). In the address itself he mentions by name only Freud's talk "The Dissection of the Mental Personality" from the *New Introductory Lectures on Psychoanalysis* of 1933 (*SE*, XXII). It puts forward Freud's general theory of character structure — id, ego, superego — and their intertwining development. Both *Civilization* and "Dissection" concern themselves, at the cultural and individual levels respectively, with the precariousness of the ego. But Mann brings a hard-won optimism to his readings of them, one earned in *Joseph in Egypt*'s struggles with these stark accounts of human life.

Read strictly as a critical essay, "Freud and the Future" only partially satisfies; Mann once remarked that it was more of a public performance, and the 1929 essay more substantive (*Düd* 14/II, 362). It begins by querying its own authority, then meanders from topic to topic, aside to aside, in an unpredictable pattern. It moves at a level of abstraction that passes over nearly all of Freud's writings, and develops a timely but general argument. It mentions no case histories, a surprising omission for a lecturer committed to narrative and to the moral importance of therapeutic practice. The *Joseph* tetralogy receives far more attention than any Freud text — it is quoted verbatim and dominates the last half of the lecture. Its focus on autobiography might also surprise listeners unfamiliar with Mann's practices. Neither Freud nor the future garners as much overt attention as the speaker himself; self-narration in both first and third person seems to upstage any self-abnegating praise of the honoree.

But critical essay and autobiography comprise only portions of the lecture's magic brew. Heard as an intertextual performance, the blend of elements in "Freud and the Future" produces a fascinating, coherent exhibition. It is an extension of *Joseph* by other means, a companion text that both summarizes the evolution of the central drama and points the way toward its future. Mann celebrates not only Freud's eightieth birthday but *Joseph in Egypt*'s long journey through the underworld of passion and blindness. The essay counterbalances Mut-em-enet's tragedy of repression and outbreak with an optimistic reconstruction of Freud that anticipates the unity, if not the comedy, of *Joseph the Provider*. It offers the highest tribute Mann could pay to Freud: not that Freud somehow echoed or even anticipated his own work, but that his own work finally arrived at a point at which the great Freud could be more fully assimilated into its forward-looking politics and epic retelling. Mann no longer wishes to push Freud off the mountain, as he did in 1930; instead he has climbed to the summit with him.

The audacious title sets the stage. Freudian analysis naturally focuses on the past, revisiting and revising each patient's narratives or culture's beginnings in light of its developmental model. But Mann's Freud looks the other way, toward analysis's promise for the future. He becomes a patriarch of blessing and hope for those with ears to hear. "Freud and the Future" configures a psychoanalysis that Mann believed serves civilization with heroic determination and sympathy shaped virtue. Though Mann still skirts certain subjects, this second essay drops much of the defensiveness and uncertainty of its 1929 forerunner. The intervening years of work on the *Joseph* had given Mann far more confidence in his Kleistian counter-story to the deterministic, universalist aspects of Freud's doctrine. The intervening years of steady performing have also strengthened his command of the stage despite the fact that his political cause has been defeated by his nemesis-performer, "Bruder Hitler." Mann stood still neither as a novelist nor as a declaimer of his texts. But some omissions and ambiguities remain, as they must, and highlight the precarious elements in *Joseph the Provider*'s celebrative synthesis.

Once again, Mann adopts different yet complementary personae on the stage of the Konzerthaus. "Der Zauberer" slips in and out of as many roles as did the dramatizer of Kleist's play. These, however, are his own roles, subtle self-transformations that testify to his seasoned stage prowess. He speaks as "Thomas Mann" — Nobel-prize winner, heroic antifascist exile, arbiter of culture, and spokesperson for hundreds of famous artists. He speaks as Freud's mentor in philosophy and cultural history, as Freud's companion seeker and equal in unmasking the psyche's mysteries, and as his dutiful follower and pupil. At points an Olympian ironist and late-middle-age bearer of mythic wisdom, he can also be a faux-naïf autobiographer and youthful reader. One intertextual vein in this polyphonic monologue comes from *Joseph*'s urchapter "The Testing," which dramatized the son's instruction of the father by reshaping his narratives. Mann half-consciously places himself in the Joseph role, the scion to "dem alten Freud" who stages a celebrative performance of the father's most fruitful ideas (*TB*, 15 Jan. 1936 and 14 June 1936). Freud promises a future blessed by the illumination of the unconscious, the same blessing extended to the audience of *Joseph and his Brothers*. Father and son, Abraham-Isaac-Jacob and Joseph in modern dress, Freud and Mann carry forward from their great forebearers a tradition that leads to "a future freed from fear and hate, and ripe for peace" (IX, 501; 428). The two have unknowingly been companions all along.

Like the *Amphitryon* performance and the *Joseph* "Prelude," the speech opens with a rhetorical question. The question this time concerns the legitimacy of the speaker; why should a narrative artist like Mann be chosen by the Academy for Medical Psychology to be the spokesperson for Freud, "a great research scientist?" The logical response of a research scientist would be to inquire. But Mann instead veers into his own speculations, in effect saying that the actual motives of the Academy are not the actuality that interests him. In this way he immediately declares the Freud of this lecture to be his Freud, not the Freud of scholars or professionals. An artist stands before you, he continues, because artists know how to celebrate feast days. They also possess a knowledge of "dream-like penetration" that coincides with the "alpha and omega of all psychoanalytic knowledge": the mysterious interweaving of the knower and the known (IX, 478–79; *Essays*, 411–12). So this festival honors Freud's eightieth with a professional celebrant, but even more it makes public the "long-standing but unperceived" connection between artistic and psychoanalytic ways of knowing. The "profound sympathy" between psychoanalysis and literature has tonight finally come out of the closet. The claim must have startled the author of "Gradiva" or the loyal readers of *Imago*, but Mann carries it off with aplomb.

The essay's opening declared Freud to be a great scientist, but psychoanalysis's imaginative way of knowing extends scientific epistemology well beyond its disciplinary borders. Similarly, Mann's Freud has begun to metamorphose into a more complex figure that only an equally protean storyteller can construct. He is, as in 1929, a "researcher" in a second, complementary sense: not only the leader of an international group of scientists, but also an explorer, a solitary seeker, a patriarch who labors alone. This brings back into focus the original "dreamy" image of Freud that first crossed the narrator's "field of vision" ("Gesichtskreis") many years earlier — the solitary "knight between death and the devil" who "conquers the unconscious for humanity" (480; 413). Freud the wanderer opened a dialogue with the Other — the unconscious — and in so doing overturned all preceding psychology (Mann apparently devalued the work of Charcot and his many peers). Mann loyally preserves this "intuited image" of Freud, an isolato artist-analyst who takes us deeper into the psyche than the "knowing, discriminating" empiricists. The image preserves Mann's complex attitude toward Freud and also bears marks of intertextual self-influence. Though a father and true revolutionary, Mann's Freud also remains an innocent nomad, and hence primitive in the way that Abraham and Jacob remain "primitives" and Joseph "infantile" (498; 426). Freud's dialogue between ego and unconscious roughly parallels the mutual self-creation of Abraham and his divine Patriarch; each fathered the other into a higher self-consciousness (490; 314). This greater self-consciousness of role constitutes the "Gelebte Vita," the "lived life," that a knowledge of mythic pattern enables (492; 422) and on which both psychoanalysis and the art of *Joseph* depend. Had Mann known that Freud was completing what he termed a "historical novel" on Moses, he would have nodded without surprise.

These moves continue Mann's familiar reading, and misreading, of Freud from 1929 forward. He repeats his claim that Freud paid little attention to Nietzsche, Schopenhauer, and a host of literary precursors, despite Freud's explicit denial of this in the November 1929 letter examined earlier (chapter 5, i), and despite the overwhelming number of literary citations in his writings. In one way Mann was right; while Freud bought a set of Nietzsche texts in 1900, he read him only fitfully because he feared both the anticipations of his own work and the confining "predetermined point of view" he associated with philosophy (Gay 1988, 45–46). Freud did read some Schopenhauer in 1919 in connection with his emerging theory of the death drive, and cited him in the preface to the new edition of *Three Essays* in 1920. But he preferred to develop his theories from the data of actual analysis, a position quite different from the isolated disregard that Mann confers on him. Freud certainly knew enough of his forebears to have long recognized the connections Mann (among others) pointed out to him.

Mann adds to this, however, a paragraph which shows his explicit interest in intertextual reading as well as source studies. Not only do we
read Schopenhauer and Nietzsche in Freud, but when we reread either
philosopher after reading Freud our perceptions of them are altered in
the "strongest and strangest" way (487; 418). Reading intertextually
leads Mann to his discovery of the "mysterious point of contact" between Freud and Schopenhauer which lies at the intellectual center of
his composition.

Mann's idiosyncratic Freud-image serves a number of necessary
purposes. It maintains the autobiographical parallels between the two
men that Mann claimed in his January 1930 letter. He and Freud have
taken solitary paths and shared ostracism (a parallel all the more poignant now, three years into Mann's exile). Mann's own "latent, already-
existing, 'pre-conscious' sympathies" — note the deliberately redun-
dant elaboration — show him that psychoanalysis has "always" been
congenial to him even when he knew nothing of it (483; 415). The
"friendly interest" of certain "young" critics has shown Mann that he
"practiced" Freud long before he read him (482–83; 307–8), just as
the comparatively youthful Mann shows how Freud unknowingly reenacted much of Schopenhauer and Nietzsche. Mann is "youthful" here
in the same sense that Joseph and his brothers, though of great age,
always remain young before Jacob in *Joseph the Provider*. His canny
young interpreters seem successful graduates of the interdisciplinary
curriculum Mann proposed in 1929, scholars who have learned how to
read with and through their master's labyrinthine texts.

The two men's similarities also form a precedent for other bonds
between the artist and the scientist. Mann spends several minutes
summarizing the book of an unnamed "Viennese psychologist of the
Freudian school" who cited the *Joseph* novels as clinching evidence for
the shaping power of received tales in traditional biography (491; 421).
This scholar (actually Ernst Kris [*TB*, 14 June 1936]: was he in the
audience that night?) crosses the border between analysis and literature
from the psychoanalytic side. Most important, the common search for
truth among artists and therapists turns out to be the search for the
"mysterious point of contact" (487; 418) between two texts or two
figures. What undergirds these points of contact and half-perceived
symmetries that produce truth? "Sympathie" (IX, 491; 421).

The essay offers an impressive catalog. Sympathy not only opens the
border between art and science; not only participates in the reciprocity
between known and known, object and subject; it shapes the "precondition of receptivity" necessary to grasping art or psychoanalysis in the
first place (481; 414). Sympathy comes to consciousness but also oper-

ates in the preconscious, behind the scenes. Sympathy makes common cause among the lecture's contrasts: between Mann and Freud, between the diverse factions in the hall, between the young Mann and his life-altering encounters with Nietzsche, and between Freud and his unrecognized philosophical precursors. Without its "sensitivity and receptivity," the "love of truth" and "clarity of vision" that art and psychoanalysis share would be impossible (480; 413). Bound up with imagination but not identical to it, sympathy lets us discover coherence in our half-known lives, the patterns we have chosen and experience as destiny. Sympathy is the modern, psychological expression for the patriarchs' open-at-the-back, receptive egos, and their history may be described as a growing awareness of its dynamic. It anchors our understanding of the subliminal life of the individual and the species; psychology reveals one, mythology the other. It also underwrites intertextual interweavings, both conscious and otherwise; texts, like egos, open at the back. Further, if the knower and the known are inextricably interlaced, then autobiography becomes an especially valuable genre. This justifies, even seems to require, Mann's forays into his life story in the lecture. Sympathy's imperatives also underlie the ethical choice of loyalty and faithfulness; this echoes the discussion of attitude and will in the 1929 essay.[6] Sympathy enables mediation — the *Joseph* subject par excellence; Freud and his 1936 celebrant share not closed, omniscient egos but open, relational ones.

The intellectual climax of Mann's sympathy-celebration comes in a remarkable passage on fatherhood:

> The bond with the father, the imitation of the father, the father-play, and the transference to father-substitute images of a higher, spiritual type — how decisively, how formatively these infantile traits work upon and shape the life of the individual! I say 'shape,' for the most humorous, most joyful [*freudigste*] definition of what we call education [*Bildung*], is to me in all seriousness just this powerful influence of admiration and love, this childlike identification with a father-image *elected out of the most inward sympathy.* (498–89; 426: emphasis mine)

These two sentences distill the reshaping of psychoanalysis in the *Joseph* novels. Self-formation begins with a sympathetic attraction to the father-image, and self-formation unfolds as other relationships elaborate that beginning.[7] The pun on Freud's name, common and unremarkable in most contexts, resonates here; Mann's Freud does indeed enable this joy because he places "admiration and love" at our beginning, and because he brings us to knowledge of the patterns that underwrite our individuality: "Gelebte Vita."[8] Substitution here fosters gain, Bildung, not loss; the knower prizes the original image-formation in part because he has helped to construct it. We immediately recognize the passage's debt to *Amphitryon*'s tale of love, identity, and loyalty, and hear it also as a rehearsal of the climactic paragraph of *Joseph in Egypt* — the image of the father — which Mann will elaborate in four months' time. Freud has become one of Mann's own "father-substitute images of a higher, more developed type," one who provides psychological acuity, an anthropology of myth, and even political vision. In this sense "Freud and the Future" modeled Mann's future as well.

At the same time our speaker remains silent — yet again — about Oedipus, Freud's central myth for figuring the father. It must have struck at least the psychoanalysts in the Konzerthaus as an amazing, audacious omission in this panegyric to Freud and paternity. The fact that it plays an important part in Freud's own discussion of the "father image" in his "Dissection" lecture makes the omission even more glaring. Mann says that sympathy is "decisive" in the development of the individual: in the opening of the "Dissection" (and many other places) Freud unequivocally says it is repression.[9] But what has happened, we know, in the intervening time is that the Oedipus model — that is, the whole notion of constructing human identity around confrontation, internalization, and repression — has been backgrounded by a story of beginnings loosely organized around Oedipus's mirror-figure, Amphitryon: relationship, sympathy, response to the countenance and naming of the Other, loyalty, and steadfastness. Mann's emphasis on this view of the father makes the change explicit. Mut is a child of Oedipus and the sphinx — the narrator's last description of her repeats the monster's "stony stare into the infinite" (V, 1493; 989) — and Joseph finally is not.

In keeping with this reconfiguration, the unconscious has also become a hybrid construction that expands the common ground between analysis and literature. Unencumbered by any disciplinary or scientific need to develop a fixed model, Mann devises the unconscious that he needs. Still composed of Schopenhauer's will and the omnivorous, desiring id of Freudian pessimism, it also enfolds narrative (not Jungian) archetypes of myth.[10] From id to archetype to the face of the father: the unconscious has expanded to become a repository of formative texts, an archaeological treasure site of personal and cultural images. Put figuratively, it embraces not only Freud's witch-metaphor of the "swirling cauldron of desire," but *Joseph*'s master trope of the revolving sphere, the archive of recollected image and story. This yields formulations such as "the typical is already the mythical, insofar as it is the fundamental pattern and form of life . . . into which life enters by reproducing its traits out of the unconscious" (XI, 656; "Theme," 7). The

Joseph performance confines the Freudian id to sexual desire and the repressions it specifically evokes. This models Mann's union of psychoanalysis and literature perfectly, with the id's power enlisted yet contained and narrative's power extended to the deepest regions of the psyche. Mann's confidence in this construction shows itself in some sly humor. He claims that the analyst's "rational morality" prevents him from saying that the ego sometimes makes more progress by submitting to the forces of the unconscious rather than controlling them (486; 417). Here we have Mann the cautionary pessimist liberalizing Freud's Enlightenment restraint, an entertaining reversal of what the essay actually achieves. The sphere revolves, bringing Schopenhauer, Nietzsche, and even *Joseph*'s ideas of patriarchy into the present, and supporting the interplay between knower and known. Mann knows what he is making and declares it good.

The emotional climax of "Freud and the Future" comes just before the essay's final, epiphanic section on the "future" of its title.

> The Joseph of the novel is an artist insofar as and especially as he plays upon the unconscious with his imitation of God. I know not which feelings of presentiment and joy in the future [*Zukunftsfreude*] seize me when I lose myself in the amusement of this kind of play, in this reclamation of a festive living production, in this narrative meeting of psychology and myth which is at the same time a celebrative meeting of literature and psychoanalysis. (499; 426–27)

This conjures an engrossing image: a highly self-conscious, ironic artist given over to a sympathetic sublime that he cannot articulate, and confessing his childlike abandonment before a grand assembly. Joseph has precisely the same feelings just before his own God-play begins (1588–89; 1053–54). Anticipating the linguistic frolics of *Joseph the Provider*, the passage offers more word play on Freud's name, and a declaration that the "celebrative meeting of literature [Dichtung] and psychoanalysis" has been achieved in the making of the *Joseph* (and perhaps on the stage of the Konzerthaus as well). This sublimity sustained Mann; as he neared the end of *Joseph the Provider*, he wrote that he had such fun writing the novel that he could scarcely wait until the next morning came round and he could begin again (*Briefe* II, 257). A little earlier he penned a much-quoted line: "Your last question, about the 'real purpose' of my work, is hardest to answer. I say simply: *Joy* [*Freude*]."[11]

"Freud and the Future" ends with a description of a "cheerful suspicion" ["ein heiterer Argwohn"] that characterizes the psychoanalytic revolution and the "modesty" its unmaskings necessarily produce in each of us. *Joseph and his Brothers* may be said to do the same thing; its own playful skepticism about origins, and its unmasking of both the repressed and the narcissistic, also leads toward "the more objective and peaceful" world that analysis may one day empower. Freud predicts, says Mann, that psychoanalysis's long-term contribution to humanism will be as a science of the unconscious, not a therapy, but Mann rejects the separation of the two; neither psychoanalysis nor literature must give up their moral, and therefore political, persuasiveness.

In his lecture's last, hectic minute Mann crowds the famous quotes from the end of "Dissection" and *Totem and Taboo* into his performance. The "Dissection" essay's "Wo *Es* war, soll *Ich* werden" and culture's work of "draining the Zuider Zee" (XXII, 80) seem phrases tailor-made for Joseph's family reunion and social engineering in Egypt. In these declarations Freud and his eulogist grow closer together: a matched pair of modest, knowing constructors of "lived lives" and new, healthy societies. But Mann does not end by elaborating equalities; finally his Freud remains — must remain — a father-substitute and half-mythic figure. The sphere revolves, and one more archetype appears in and through the patriarchal Freud that the speaker has put before us. *Totem and Taboo* ends with Faust's "In the beginning was the deed," which Freud uses to summarize primitive man's uninhibited unity of thought and action.[12] Mann substitutes for this rather chilling conclusion one of Faust's *good* deeds: "the traits of the venerable man merge into the lineaments of the gray-haired Faust" confining the ocean to free new land for a new "Volk" (IX, 501; 428). This Freud-Faust, the venerable scientist-as-savior, embodies the common cause of literature and science that the 1936 performance has put forward from the beginning. Rereading the lecture in its light, we can see that Mann has always discerned Faust's image in Freud's fatherly countenance. Diary entries confirm that this particular ending occupied Mann's mind from the beginning; reflections on Faust, Nietzsche, and Freud occur in January (1/16) and especially April (4 and 22) of 1936, just as the drafting commenced: "Began the composition of the lecture today . . . Faust-thoughts for the lecture . . . to stand with a free people on free ground." "Free us from fear and hate, and ripe for peace": the right confluence of artists and scientists holds out hope for a humanistic politics and the overcoming of tyranny. Across the border in Germany other unions of artists and scientists are taking place which exacerbate the "fear and hate" of a soulless, antihumanistic future. In their place Mann offers his audience a Faustian yet limited Freud whose powerful knowledge exposes culture's dark secrets, and whose "modesty" merges with the final overcoming of narcissism and false omniscience that the narrator and newly modest protagonist of *Joseph the Provider* will chronicle.

In "Freud and the Future" Mann has, in effect, conducted a friendly psycho-literary analysis of his subject. He has again brought to Freud's consciousness his own half-known fathers and his buried connections with the best in German thought and poetry. He has, in other words, illuminated for Freud his true "Gelebte Vita," and led the patriarch to the same level of self-awareness that his several "mythic" examples — Cleopatra (the Tamar of the lecture), Napoleon, Jesus — discovered before him. He has done the same for the audience, showing them how the current festival in which they participate draws from the "theatrical performances" of antiquity and from Schopenhauer's conviction that we are each the "secret theater-manager of our own dreams" (487; 418). "The feast is the dissolving [Aufhebung] of time" (497; 425). He urges an open, receptive ego on Freud and the audience alike, while offering Joseph's witty, "infantile" nature as a fiction of self-understanding that produces personal and political integrity.

"Freud and the Future" is now read silently as a prose monologue, but at the cost of underestimating its content and flattening its celebration of sympathy. Helen Lowe-Porter, determined to make the lecture a formal essay, removed the several "meine Damen und Herren" salutations from her translation. But even silent readers half-consciously project a voice of a narrator; when we read we also listen. And when the reader chooses to listen more attentively to that projected voice, the feeling tone and ethical force of the lecture move more into the foreground. Reading the piece out loud — replicating its first reception makes its ethical energy significantly more prominent. Heard as a performance piece, the essay actively promotes a dialogue with, and between, Freud and Europe's progressive artists. As Mann composed his lecture, did he imagine Freud in the audience of the Konzerthaus taking instruction as Heuser and his cohorts had done before him? He undoubtedly did imagine Freud in the audience, but taking instruction — yes and no. Mann does not want the patriarchal Freud to pick up his Nietzsche again. In this one sense he preserves his "ignorant" Freud in mythic amber. At the same time, he solicits Freud to bring forward the sides of his teaching that Mann finds celebrative and politically forceful. And the sphere's dynamic allows him to express both at once: to hold the patriarchal Freud in a fixed esteem, and also chronicle the traditions of thought and imagination that point toward a postfascist community.

Mann's several meetings with Freud at 19 Berggasse took place, appropriately, under the gaze of the patriarch's many Egyptian and Greek

artifacts. Mann probably did not see Freud's fiftieth birthday com-
memorative medallion of Oedipus before the sphinx, the one which so
agitated him that he nearly fainted at its presentation (Jones 2 [1955],
13–14). But a Greek sphinx did in all probability oversee their conversations; a photograph from the period shows the statue sitting high
atop the curio cabinet just behind Freud's desk (Ernst Freud et al.
1985, 271). The statue, its wings uplifted and its mysterious sex only
half-hidden, looks over the heads of patients and visitors into the far
corner of the room. The sphinx may well have traveled to Freud's suburban house at Grinzing, since we know he had artifacts with him during his six-month stay in 1935 (Jones 3 [1957], 196, 199). But sphinx
or no, the Grinzing house offered a lovely setting for Mann's private
performance of "Freud and the Future" — and for other futures as
well. This area so charmed the Manns that they briefly considered
moving there and looked at several houses (Harpprecht 1995, 895).
Strassergasse 47's terrace overlooking the beautiful gardens anticipates,
for my imagination, the setting of Joseph's long dialogue with Pharaoh:
the lovely "Cretan Summerhouse" ("Laube") in Pharaoh's "temporary
quarters . . . east of the sun-temple, and connected to it by an avenue
of sphinxes and sycamores" (1402; 927). The retreat's Minoan decora-
tions charmingly echo Freud's long-standing interest in the Knossos
excavations (e.g., Ernst Freud et al. 1985, 168). This little parallel extends to the Grinzing performance itself. Mann comes to Freud's
summerhouse and explicates his dream-work very differently from
Freud's companions and court interpreters.

To my knowledge, no detailed account of that face-to-face encounter at the Grinzing summerhouse has come down to us; the prin-
cipals' written recollections offer only sketches, and Gottfried Bermann,
another attendee, gives no details in his autobiography. But Mann must
have looked up many times from his script into the face of the old man,
and it is tantalizing to speculate about what they saw. Freud disliked
most ceremonies in his honor, yet spoke very positively of this one and
gave Mann a farewell embrace when the performance was over. Did he,
at least for a time, accept Mann's remaking of his vision, or were his re-
ported tears signs of painful demure as well as "Freude"?

II

For masterpieces are not single and solitary births; they are the outcome of many years of thinking in common, of thinking by the body of the people, so that the experience of the mass is behind the single voice.

— Virginia Woolf, A Room of One's Own

The writing of *Joseph, der Ernährer*. — Joseph ("increase" in Hebrew) the "Provider" or "Nourisher" (literally the "one who feeds") — was delayed, then interrupted repeatedly by travel, relocations, perform-ances, essays and articles, international correspondence, radio addresses, and other fictions, all at a frequency exceeding the already high rate of the tetralogy's earlier years. The two intervening novels took the most time: the Goethe-book *Lotte in Weimar*, and another set of variations on *Amphitryon*'s great themes of identity and substitution, *The Trans-posed Heads*. But the pace of every part of Mann's life accelerated for the simple reason that he had truly arrived: in America; as the repre-sentative of the authentic Germany in exile; as an artist of world stature; as a tireless combatant of fascism; as an effective rescuer of internees and fellow exiles trapped by the war. He had become, in other words, a kind of Provider himself, welcoming compatriots to their powerful new country and lending wholehearted support to FDR, its charming, far more savvy pharaoh.

Another, more literary reason contributed to the delay. Mann liked to mention his "late discovery" of Tamar as the "right female charac-ter" for the final volume (e.g., XI, 678; "Foreword," xi-xii), but gender balancing seems a lesser cause. Tamar's femininity is, from her own point of view, strictly biological. Men may shape her into an erotic icon, an Astarte luring them on, but Tamar feels hardly any attraction to them. Jacob's sublimated erotic pedagogy, his struggle "to be able to feel again" through flirtatious instruction, does draw her, but mainly because of his tale of Shiloh, the promise of the saving hero to come (1552–54; 1027–29). Tamar interested Mann as a figure of will,[13] more specifically as a kind of spiritual monomaniac whose humorless deter-mination to enter the blessing's line of descent contrasts with Joseph's genial pluralism. Perhaps he even wished some of her determination for himself, as the artistic energy he had gained from his Joseph's youthful beauty and gaze dissipated with time. The narrator complains that the fully mature, rather corpulent Joseph lacks the appeal of his seventeen- or even his thirty-year-old counterpart (1766; 1172). Seen in this light,

Tamar represents a comic-solemn muse — the tongue-in-cheek narrator had already prayed for a classical Muse (1319; 872) — willing a flagging storyteller on to his tale's final scenes.[14]

Two further subjects finally brought him back to the novel with the necessary commitment: language, that is the wit, the charm, and the bantering "Sprachsphäre" not of "Thomas Mann" but "of the work itself" (XI, 656; "Theme," 6–7); and the great subject of narcissism civilized and made ethical through the delights of performance. Joseph's masked performances before his brothers are more boyish and emotion-filled than his painful entanglement with Mut. The narrator adds a funny, self-knowing reason to these; his Joseph at fifty-five is "distinctly thinner" than at forty and looks more like his youthful self again (1766; 1172). It's an insider's joke on his own deepest erotic attractions and their relation to his art.

Performance is literally everywhere in *Joseph the Provider*. The novel explores all of its fine gradations: the royal baker's simple lying, Joseph's chutzpah in prison, Judah's despairing eloquence, Jacob's gnomic mystifications before Pharaoh, Joseph's hyper self-aware stagings that spill over into childlike celebration. Performance indeed provides. It feeds a nation and reveals the intricacies of the psyche; it fuels narcissism and shows the way through its labyrinth. Joseph offers his own "pretty clear" copper mirror to Pharaoh's baker and wine steward in prison (1336; 883); by the end of *Joseph the Provider* the faces of his brothers, then his father, will give him the clearest of self-reflections.

Of the novel's many scenes, Freud might especially have enjoyed — and resisted — "The Cretan Summerhouse" ("Die kretische Laube"). This "many-branched" chapter (XI, 662) of interpretation combines humor at Freud's expense with entertaining transformations of his ideas. One of the cleverest of these comes in the chapter's preliminary scene, the six failed readings of Pharaoh's famous two-in-one dreams that prepare for Joseph's triumph (1388–99; 918–25). Pharaoh's old manservant credits the dreams' content to the god's mental "overheating" from his endless speculations, while his mother tartly concludes that he must misremember his dreams, since they are too "monstrous" to signify anything. A court treasury official, cornered into analyzing the dreams, tries to substitute rhetorical flourishes for explanation, but his noninterpretation gambit fails. Pharaoh's professional dream explicators scorn these commonsense moves. Though they naturally read Pharaoh's dreams as prophetic rather than reflexive, the scholars proceed from Freud's basic assumption that dream-content masks dream-meaning. Nervous and hide-bound in their books, the first six offer successive ideas of substitution: the dreams as coded family tragedy; the dreams as a political and cultural allegory à la *Totem and Taboo*. A second group tries far-future dynastic readings along the same lines, and with the same result. Pharaoh rejects them all because their substitutions don't resonate with the feelings his dreams produced in him. Freud would of course interpret his resistance. But Joseph's reading — naturally the seventh — backgrounds resistance and asserts a continuity between manifest and latent content that only the dreamer can confirm (see also 1013; 675). This meshes with the sort of narrator and dramatist that the adult Joseph has become; interpretive meaning arises out of empathetic apprehension of the other, not universalizing schema or unbridgeable gaps between the known and buried life, the upper and lower spheres. He systematically refuses to be an omniscient narrator, and agrees with Pharaoh that the interpretation must come *before* the dream and resonate with the dreamer (1351; 893). Joseph's behavior throughout "The Cretan Summerhouse" — calculated and sincere, superior and sympathetic — dramatizes the balance he has struck between his vanity and his loyalties. His performances now serve both himself and others; in elevating himself he provides for both Pharaoh and God.

"The Cretan Summerhouse" play forms around the familiar triangle of three archetypal characters in dialogue. Tiy the queen-mother, Pharaoh the god/father, and Joseph the precocious slave offer a venerable variant of the family romance. But the Cretan designs on the tiled floor and the lavishly painted walls provide a second, more fluid structure for its drama: the arabesque. Trademark Minoan octopi swim across the floor; trademark Minoan women with open bodices move their long plaited hair across the walls; fantastically blooming grasses frame the young Cretan prince as he hunts. All the colorful Knossos treasures that Freud also admired appear here: bull-vaulting paintings, children riding dolphins, bull rhytons, chryselephantine reliefs (1407; 930–31). As though under their massed influence, the triangle grouping of the main characters (and Freudian orthodoxy) multiplies and destabilizes. Tiy the mother and protector is also the Tiy the sphinx, a male/female poised above Joseph on a "high stool" and ready to strike (1408; 931). This sphinx "with a political mind" reads Joseph's gnomic stories and omnicompetent conversation as nothing but self-aggrandizing attempts to make himself godlike before Pharaoh. She is partly right; traces of a Jupiter-like, narcissistic superiority linger in Joseph's judgments about Pharaoh. Indeed, without his narcissism his performance might well falter. Mann encourages us in this perception by presenting Joseph through the eyes of the royal family; we do not enter his mind but only watch his virtuosity in action. But when Tiy descends from her chair to deflate and devour this "spoiled child," it is he who unmasks her instead. Oedipus defeats the sphinx with language; Joseph deflects with simple silence her attempts to expose him, and wins her over with his vow to serve her dreamy, abstracted child. "I will never betray his kiss," he swears on Pharaoh's life (1467; 971), and that promise transforms the sardonic queen into Tiy the hopeful helpmate who actually proposes Joseph's role as state mediator to Pharaoh. She moves, in other words, from exposure to loyalty, from a violent Oedipal story to a relational, Kleistian one in which she and Joseph form a covenant. She repeatedly looks into Joseph's eyes (e.g., 1438, 1448; 951, 960), and at the conclusion puts her hand on his shoulder and becomes a willing player in his larger performance.

Despite his daughters, this Pharaoh hardly figures as a father at all but rather as Ikhnaton the son, a case study of an unsuccessful passage through Freud's Oedipal stage.[15] Mann uses the more reductive Freud to full advantage here, even more forcefully than in his portrait of Mut. Ikhnaton's pharonic ancestors were warrior-kings (156; 101), and his father an ambitious architect and builder whom he could never dream of supplanting or accepting (967; 643). The ensuing neurosis left Pharaoh with visionary powers, but with a fatal inability to incorporate the material side of life into his living or his theology. Jacob's son intuits that Pharaoh has no sympathetic, sustaining image of the father and so half-consciously struggles to construct one in the sun's disc. For this same reason Joseph labels as "masculine" the depths that Pharaoh has renounced (1450–51; 959). His substitute father-god Aton has neither a fleshly side nor guile, and hence neither passion nor humor to mediate differences. Pharaoh's theology is inventive, but these autobiographical roots determine its shape, and the compulsive way in which he elaborates it betrays his possession by his past even as he dreams of a new future. He wants to be another sort of omniscient narrator, one determined to erase anything — the claims of time, recalcitrant priests, even competing gods — that opposes his immaterial, compensatory sun-vision. For him life oscillates between self-regard and self-abnegation — that is, between narcissism and its opposite — and his visions remain detached from social realities. His blinding migraines nicely echo Isaac's blindness in his tent, seeing only what he wished to see. The example of Pharaoh reveals another way that omniscience and narcissism go together and lead only to a dead end. Joseph easily recognizes Pharaoh's narcissistic withdrawal, aristocracy, and hypersensitivity because it closely resembles his own at seventeen. His own hard-won discovery that "the ego and the world belonged together, were in a certain sense one" (1303; 862) lets him understand it as well.

The chapter, either taken whole or especially in its performance-enhancing subdivisions, shows its artistry most fully when read aloud. Joseph's dizzying array of improvisational roles in the scene — deferential slave, disinterested analyst, bardic poet, uncanny foreigner, Socratic theologian and pedagogue, loyal pact-maker — confirms its arabesque form; no one knows what curlicue is coming next.[16] This dialogical parataxis — Hebrew rhapsode and economic strategist cheek by jowl — ideally suits the sudden character and voice shifts preferred by a dramatizing reader. Few scenes in *Joseph* are more richly pleasing to hear. Mann performing Joseph performing: the oral performer and the dramatized performance constantly mirror one another and multiply our pleasure in each.

Joseph's education of Pharaoh very much resembles the interdisciplinary and crosscultural curriculum Mann touted for his "confused" student audience in the 1929 "Freud" lecture. In 1929 Mann's "third way" sought a curricular reunification of science with the arts, and hence the return of wisdom, emotion, ethics, and the tempered exploration of the primitive to formal learning. Egypt's confused boy-king prefers a narrow theological disciplinarity and a top-down pedagogy, seeking only to teach his mother and all his "weak" and "hopeless" subjects to think and feel exactly as he does (1445–48; 956–57). He says that as ruler he "must not think what he cannot teach" (1462; 967), but this cramped sense of "educative responsibility" only exacerbates his narcissism. Joseph tries to dissuade him from this self-defeating strategy without opposing "the father" directly. He makes masterly use of the subjunctive, thinking aloud without actually speaking authoritatively and letting his student "overhear" ideas that he can then claim as his own. Like Hermes before Sosias, Joseph metamorphoses into an indistinguishable alter ego who can guide Pharaoh toward greater fertility in both theology and economic policy. It is an extraordinarily subtle form of therapeutic suggestion.

So Joseph becomes the stand-in, the second Pharaoh in touch with, exemplifying, the "illumination" from the depths. He assumes the divine mantle outwardly, but for entirely different reasons: not to conquer, but to provide. He supplements Pharaoh's lightness with his knowledge of the pit, and precisely because of his self-awareness of his own performance, he keeps his own hard-won modesty intact. In the language of the 1929 essay, Joseph offers himself as an agent of Pharaoh's will, a will that must make the right moral (and therefore political and economic) choices in the face of the rising fascism of Amun-Re and his retrograde priests. So yet another youth takes instruction from a Mann manqué versed in antifascist theater and politics. The longish, meandering speeches of the two young men together create a "third way": multiplicity, a pluralism of affect and effect, a formal freedom which interlaces the organic and the spontaneous. Further, the transformation shows explicitly how Joseph's adult performances both preserve and transcend narcissism. From the dismembered god to the integrated, multivoiced man: Joseph at thirty has become the active, politically minded dramatist who can both put bread on the table and make a God-play worthy of the Highest. Magically, Joseph remains both adult moral instructor and the beautiful seventeen-year-old who incarnated so many of Mann's loves. Pharaoh may acclaim his new slave as a divine Hermes-come-to-Egypt, but Joseph now prefers the god's human face. From all-knowing Jupiter to mediating Hermes: in Kleist's play the same two gods come to self-understanding, but only Hermes does so without "losing face."[17]

"The Cretan Summerhouse" in turn forms one part of the large-scale mediation between complex oppositions — especially Eros and death — which run the length of the final novel. The narrator handles the outcome of these mediations with a care driven by his deepest themes. In one way the book's long-anticipated cadences and comedic vision drive it toward a powerful synthesis which gathers up all its loose ends in a triumphant finale. Mann once described his book as one that "seeks to blend many things, and because it feels and imagines the human as a unity, it borrows its motives, memories, allusions, as well as its speech sounds (*Sprachlaute*) from many spheres" (XI, 664; "Theme," 15). Organic unity subsumes differences, and the novel ends authoritatively with its title in italics: "*Joseph and his Brothers*" centered and set apart, a perfect revolution of the sphere. But seeing the text only in this single-minded way turns *Joseph the Provider* into just another example of modernism's coercive victory of form over wayward content. The context for Mann's comment in "The Theme of the *Joseph* Novels" points to an alternative sense of "unity." There he is describing how his novel is "a Jewish novel" only as "one style element among others"; its "unity" is composed of "many spheres," not any single, perfect one. So a longer gaze into the text reveals how it both constructs an overarching synthesis and at the same time actively resists its momentum. Reunions and re-visions dominate its telling. Voices and texts retain their separate integrity, and death does have its say. The "Cretan Summerhouse" chapter models this complexity; it both uses and playfully unravels modernism's love affair with the omniscience of form. *Joseph the Provider* offers an integration that preserves differences, and Freud's darker veins of thought are once again visible, yet contained. Its model remains the interwoven tapestry of triangle and arabesque, not the handle of the fascist axe. Both Joseph-Hermes and the text remain middlemen, their fragments on view, even as they weave an enchanting tale.

III

I don't know, Mai, what sort of man I am.

— Joseph to Mai-Sachme

All your eyes turn into a mirror
And bend the whole full beam upon me
Leading it up and down, from head to foot,
And say to me — speak, and answer my query:
Who am I?

— Kleist, *Amphitryon*, cited in Mann's lecture

A sense of mystery is a different thing from an ability to interpret it, and the largest consolation is that without interpretation there would be no mystery.

— Frank Kermode, *The Genesis of Secrecy*

Joseph's God-play, its several acts spaced over more than a year, reassembles our leading subjects for a final performance. Narcissism and its necessary vicissitudes; the ethics of loyalty grounded in face-to-face relation; intertextuality and self-influence; political and pedagogical responsibility; Mann's life-long love of drama, opera, and stage appearances: all these gather together for the delight and instruction of its several audiences, both inside and outside its telling. Parody and epiphany at once, Joseph's play stands deeply situated in its fictive time, in Mann's own historical and artistic time, in the reader's time of reception, and if not exactly "for all time," then certainly in the time of future auditors needful of its pleasures and its insight. Its long-drawn-out, suspenseful performance makes reflective moral knowledge possible. Though famous for their laconic style and gapped narratives, the "J" and "E" writers of the Genesis version also take their time (42–48) with the "original" God-play. Speedy self-revelation undermines moral effect; we need only imagine Joseph receiving the list with his brothers' names on it, traveling swiftly to the Fort of Thel, and saying straightaway, "I'm Joseph. It's OK." *Joseph's* extended, exhaustive narrative, like the God-play, produces blessings of its own.

We do know that Kleist's *Amphitryon* was once again on Mann's mind as he prepared to resume work on *Joseph the Provider* in 1940. Of all *Joseph*'s satellite essays, he singles it out for its "direct connection" with the tetralogy ("On Myself," XIII, 166). He loyally revivifies the *Amphitryon* in Joseph's (and Mai-Sachme's) dramaturgy. In 1927 he wrote of his willingness to "travel a long way" to see a "young director's" fresh performance of the play, and in the California writing of February 1942 he finally arrived at Joseph's version after a much longer journey than even he could have anticipated (*TB*, 1940–1943, 384ff.). Joseph as dramatist, stage manager, and protagonist rolled into one replicates and then inverts the position of Kleist's Jupiter. Like Kleist's god, Joseph the "vice-god" (1582; 1049) dons disguises and appears above the other players; Jupiter put on a perfect human guise, and Joseph wears a quasi-divine one. Just as the Thebans took Jupiter to be their general, the other players take Joseph to be a god and bow down repeatedly before him. *Amphitryon* ruminated on the layers and postponements of recognition; the difference between recognizing and knowing that — and whom — you recognize reappears in Joseph's God-play and underwrites its ethic. Kleist's drama required the stripping down and confessions of its victim-characters in order to test their loyal natures. Its dependence on humor and the artful jest gave Mann another precedent in German humanist writing for his own theological comedy. The reconciliation scenes in *Joseph the Provider* speak expressly against narcissistic withdrawal, aristocracy, and pathos: a straight line of descent from the critique of divine self-involvement in the "Kleist" lecture. Both plays celebrate the primacy of time-bound human love over divine perfection and omniscience. In a free-flowing intertextual sense, Joseph indeed read Kleist before he began.

Joseph's final understanding of his narcissism comes in making the God-play. He plans his drama with his jailer-turned-steward Mai-Sachme, and Mann presents their conversation as another mini-drama like "The Painful Tongue": all markers of the narrative mode disappear (1585–92; 1051–56). Though he needs his collaborator, Joseph (like Pharaoh) won't admit it, and Mai-Sachme quickly learns the art of making his invaluable plotting suggestions as though his master had already thought of them (e.g., 1618–19; 1073–74). Joseph confesses to Mai-Sachme that at seventeen he had been a "Grünschnabel," a little know-it-all full of "criminal over-confidence and blind nerve" (1585; 1051). But rereading the past constitutes only part of Joseph's final testing. The drama he devises tests not only his brothers but himself in every way. He can only complete his self-knowledge by performing its consequences; "man cannot know beforehand how he will act in his story" (1588; 1053). For making the right story and making self-knowledge are functions of one another. Imagine the alternatives —

Joseph the Hidden Rescuer, who provides for the Israelites but never reveals himself; Joseph journeying to Hebron to announce his survival — and their aesthetic flatness and ethical poverty become apparent. Performance keeps Joseph in the story even as he directs it, just as it kept Thomas Mann, dramatic reader and political pedagogue, immersed in the immediacy and the consequences of his productions. To be both author and performing character at once, making the story "already written in God's book" (1592; 1056) fresh and spontaneous, is performance's greatest blessing. In the words of the "Kleist" lecture, if we take ourselves too "heavily" the gods will "make light of us" (IX, 220; 232). But if, as Joseph says, we can make the solemn "light" (1593; 1056), we celebrate God's greatest gift and in so doing lead "God himself, the mighty Unanswering, to laughter" (1593; 1056).

Joseph deliberately appears before his ten brothers in an intimidating Narcissus-Gallery. He stands upstage center at the apex of an "open triangle" of tables that recalls the unifying theology of On (1651; 1095). He and his guests are surrounded by lavish, mirroring wall paintings of the Provider not as a sacrificial lamb but as a double-sexed Hapi, the fertile bull and river god in glory (1582; 1057: see also 760; 507). By assuming what appears to be the most narcissistically gratifying of all positions — the omnipotent god in his seat of judgment — he overcomes it. The scene reverses his youthful performances before his brothers; as he plays the role of the arbitrary, tyrannical Führer, Joseph constantly experiences the boundaries of his narcissism exactly when he appears to expand its range. The performance of a staged omniscience exposes its limits, and Joseph's shaky imitation of dramatic surety promotes the education of everyone: the brothers, the reader, and himself. Only his Egyptian retinue, Mai-Sachme excepted, remain baffled and therefore immune to the pedagogic layers of his performance. So precisely because the scene fulfills his earlier dream of submission and triumph, Joseph moves through his final narcissistic "Prüfung." Mann dramatizes self-influence at work in Joseph's own dramaturgy even as Kleist's play colors his own imagination: parallel textual mirroring devoted to exposing and containing narcissism.

From "The Testing" onward — through his adolescent scenes with his brothers, with Potiphar in the garden, with Mut, and even with Pharaoh — Joseph always kept a reserve, a Jupiter-like distance and calculation. Here his artistic planning aims toward full disclosure, and for the first time he has a bad case of nerves. Now the distance is all external, part of the act, and the calculation it requires to sustain it so intermixes with his celebrative, humbling emotions that its narcissistic coolness dissolves. Joseph comically struggles to remain a god, hiding his face behind his parodic handkerchief-veil. Several times he refers to bringing the brothers "before his face," but he keeps it covered (1602; 1062): a transparent use of *Amphitryon*. He must postpone the moment of his all-too-human incarnation as their brother until suspension between roles is no longer artistically pleasing or ethically necessary.

The brothers too expected to find themselves in quite a different play — the proper flattering of an unpredictable top administrator. They learned a few snatches of Egyptian to that end, only to discover that they stand in the dock at a criminal trial. Had it turned out to be an Oedipal trial — had they in fact slain their father — the God-story could have turned Freudian and tragic, and Joseph might well have descended on these aging sons like the sphinx, devouring and destroying (e.g., 1588; 1053). The first virtue that Joseph tests for, openly, is loyalty: loyalty to the father, to Benjamin, even — a trace of narcissism — to their guilt over his "murder." But in the God-play's opening act the brothers quickly come to occupy a position closer to that of Amphitryon than Oedipus. The divine judge dismantles their identities, and only he can name their true name. Jupiter's humiliation of Amphitryon — "before me he shall bow his face [Antlitz]" (220; 231) — repeats, then inverts itself here; the brothers bow down that Joseph may tell them who they are and raise them up. Judah in fact says "Bei deinem Antlitz" ("By your favor" in Lowe-Porter's version) when he announces that Jacob lives (1599; 1060). And when Joseph orders the brothers to return with Benjamin, he adds "or you will not see my face [Antlitz] again" (1610; 1068).

But once the brothers confess their guilt and their even deeper, Kleistian loyalties, Joseph can reveal himself as *not* divine. With this *Joseph and his Brothers* reaches its well-staged humanist epiphany: the god has become man. Kleist's Jupiter forswore his illusion about acquiring the warmth of human love and savored the bittersweet pleasure of such renunciation. But he did so to accept fully his nature as god, not to become, as Joseph does, "only an economist" (1682–83; 1116). What Joseph renounces, then, is not narcissism as such — no one can — but the blinding performances it occasions. The experience that Mann garnered from hundreds of stage appearances bore fruit in this triumph of comic self-reflection. His character's God-play is itself a montage, a modernist interweaving of narrative fragments that mirrors in miniature *Joseph the Provider*'s own construction, and has roots in Genesis's own four-stranded, self-quoting mosaic.

Joseph the Provider's narcissistic reflections have further levels. Before, in the pit at Dothan, we saw how Joseph experienced a loss of self, and at the same time replayed the elevating cosmic dramas of death and resurrection within his larger ego. There his recognition of his superficial narcissism both partially freed him and blinded him to its deeper strains. Now his hermetic cosmic model has metamorphosed into a human drama of relatedness. At seventeen he looked into his brothers' faces only to see a single, projected adoration, or a single violent hatred. He felt sympathy for their plight, but only as a group. Now he sees their individual faces and imagines how each of them separately must feel (1595ff.; 1058ff.).

Turning to the God-play's several audiences, the scene cleverly encapsulates each listener's reception of Joseph. The Egyptians believe they know their master and find his vulnerability perplexing; his brothers know only the threatening judge, yet find his performance mystifying; even literary adviser Mai-Sachme has a limited view, since he knows only Joseph's version of the past and lacks the ability to be surprised. But Mann's own audience, as in the "Kleist" lecture, occupies all these positions. At once before the curtain and behind the scenes, we see the drama through the eyes of all its participants simultaneously. Yet even our knowledge stops short of omniscience: we may know Joseph's secret, delicious agonies, and we may know how the story turns out, but we do not know how it will do so. That "how" — not the "act" but the "result" in Joseph's terms (1585; 1051) — comprises the final stage of our own education in love and loyalty.

As Joseph looks out across his great hall, he sees not only his individual brothers but his own absence among them. The bustling chamber, jammed with awed spectators and flattering god-portraits, disguises this lack. His perception signals his narcissism's refiguration; Joseph can only gain his full maturity when he images himself among his brothers, one among many. At the climax of *Amphitryon* Jupiter reveals himself, then withdraws to Olympus; Joseph withdraws from his assumed divinity in order to make himself flesh again among the sons of Jacob. This is narcissism both curtailed and rescued, narcissism put in service of artistic and ethical performance. Without his desire to perform, to receive the adoration from the many human and artistic mirrors in the audience, indeed without fulfilling his dream of his brothers' submission, Joseph could not be an artist and rescuer. Without these desires, the text suggests, there would be no stories for the future. Even more important, without a strong sense of the self's dignity, belief in humanity's dignity and ethical worth would be impossible (1716–17; 1139). So traces of his narcissism naturally, necessarily, remain. We have already mentioned his suppression of Mai-Sachme's role as co-author. He also refuses to give Reuben — himself a credible improvisational playwright at the dry well — independent credit for his wonderful speech (1617; 1073).[18] But these small blindnesses and vanities only make his new and larger self-insights more convincing, and morally more instructive for his future audiences.

Not only narcissism but its textual counterpart, self-reflexive narrative, also takes on a more complex role in the tetralogy's final novel. Like Joseph's rise in Egypt, it comes to rule over the story but only to reveal a hidden nature. *Joseph the Provider* uses the techniques of metafiction not to disable or relativize, but to enact the tetralogy's moral vision. The novel's "proto-postmodern" features (Heilbut 1996, 543) are themselves intrinsic ethical performances, as two theorists can help us see. In *Narcissistic Narrative* Linda Hutcheon formulates the process this way: "Historiographic metafiction, therefore, works to situate itself in history and in discourse, as well as to insist on its autonomous fictional and linguistic nature . . . . Metafiction teaches . . . that discourse is language as *énonciation*, involving, that is, the contextualized production and reception of meaning," freeing us from the authoritarian claims of omniscience. We have to become performers ourselves in the production of meaning (including ethical and political meaning) because we are forced to acknowledge the world as a human composition, and therefore to participate actively in its creation: "freedom through artifice" (Hutcheon 1984, xiv, xv, 70, 155).

Adam Zachary Newton's rich and subtle book *Narrative Ethics* offers a second, even more illuminating model for understanding Mann's narrative as ethical performance. He distinguishes between "moral propositionality, or the realm of the 'Said,' and ethical performance, the domain of 'Saying.'" Arguing that narrative "initiates responsibilities, alongside forms," Newton names the "intersubjective relation accomplished through story" as "what I will call ethics: narrative as relationship and human connectivity, as Saying over and above Said, or as Said called into account in Saying; narrative as claim, as risk, as responsibility, as gift, as price. Above all, as an ethics, narrative is performance or act — purgative . . . malignant . . . historically recuperative . . . erotic and redemptive." Narrative "is not merely a property of texts," but is itself an ethical act entailing "the ethical consequences of narrating story and fictionalizing person, and the reciprocal claims binding teller, listener, witness, and reader in that process" (Newton 1995, 5, 9, 7, 292, 11). This moves past Hutcheon's account of the reader's education via participation in metafiction's contextualizing. Newton's analysis ably theorizes how *Joseph*'s reflexive modeling of intertextuality enacts ethical vision within narrative itself. In all these ways Joseph's narcissistic focus on the process of narrative turns inside out to become an ethical performance.

Mann's repeated dipping into *Tristram Shandy* throughout *Joseph's* composition produced more than the arts of digression, linguistic frolicking, and "comic technique" (XI, 665; "Theme," 16) so often noted. He was once again rereading Sterne's novel as he wrote the reunion play (*TB*, 4 Feb. 1942). The unpredictable turns and swirls of Sterne's arabesques model both Joseph's improvisational art and *Joseph the Provider's* textual serendipity. The arabesque is *Tristram Shandy's* comedic trope for literary form, and the arabesques of Joseph's improvisations under pressure have their textual equivalents in the free-form expansions that mingle with the more formal structures of the Genesis tale. Just as Mann once amused his father with imitating the voices of Lübeck burghers, Joseph "does voices" both to distract his brothers and to amuse God, the story-loving father. The arabesques that the loyal Trim draws in the air with his stick marked for Sterne the freedom, personal and formal, of his text (*Tristram Shandy*, IX, 4); borrowing from Sterne gave Mann a narrative manner particularly suited to his ethical and pedagogical views: expressed limits, anti-omniscience, dialogic freedom.

The revelation scene itself draws openly on the climactic moments of *Amphitryon*, playing out the permutations of concealment and unknowability that so enthralled Mann in his 1927 performance. The split male figures of Jupiter and Amphitryon, the ideal and the real, come together in Joseph, who shares equally in the human puzzlement and the divine playwright's isolating knowledge of identity. Benjamin takes on the role of Alkmene, the loyal but baffled spouse who cannot recognize the face of her beloved (see also Heftrich 1993, 414). Benjamin too took Joseph to be a Jupiter, a "*metatron* and prince." He stares across at the face of the god-become-brother just as the deceived Alkmene and the loyal Amphitryon stared at one another. Alkmene may be a "cultured woman" ("gebildete Frau" [IX, 214; 227]) and Benjamin a father eight times over, but Mann emphasizes their childlikeness just beneath their adult surfaces. He characterizes both as "confused" (IX, 228 and V, 1661; 239 and 1102), his old term of choice for youth's malleable naïveté. He also relies on the same "indescribability" in their half-knowledge of the mysterious figure before them; following Kleist exactly, he builds his drama around what the characters cannot say.

Benjamin's unconscious loyalty to the absent face of his brother — Kleist and Freud together — leads to his two inarticulate cries of recognition. Unlike Alkmene, he does not name the beloved by his true name. The authority of Genesis and Joseph's self-knowledge require that he be the one to announce his full humanity. Just as Kleist's god metamorphosed from human lover to remote divinity, so the divine Joseph, undoing the final knot in his narcissism, metamorphoses into the beloved brother. Joseph's "Children, here am I" echoes Jupiter's "It was I" and "Give, give to the truth your voice, child" (221, 236) but with all the difference. Jupiter conceals his face, but Joseph, "heedless of the tears on his face," stands revealed before the "staring" brethren. The "somewhat heavy" man who comes down to meet them supplants the brothers' "truer" image of the young Joseph; Alkmene abandons her "truer" Amphitryon for the real husband's embrace. The brothers, like Kleist's Theban citizens, struggle to see Joseph as both prince and brother (1683; 1116), but Benjamin, like Alkmene, sees their unity at once.

Joseph's play unexpectedly creates the setting for Judah's great speeches (1637–38, 1674–80; 1086, 1110–14) that demonstrate his central place in the descent of the blessing. Nothing measures their independent strength better than the spontaneous compliment Joseph pays them as the God-play begins to pass out of his hands (1682; 1115): "Judah, that was a powerful speech. You made it for ever and ever." Judah's ego, honed by suffering, opens to the far future in a way that Joseph's cannot. For Joseph's brilliant play also shapes the first scenes in his final sacrifice, his displacement in the line of the blessing. His praise of Judah implicitly acknowledges that he will not be the lead player much longer.

IV

Denn was wahr ist, ist nicht die Wahrheit. Die ist unendlich fern, und unendlich alles Gespräch. (For what is true is not the truth. Truth is endlessly far, and all dialog is endless too.)

— Joseph to Pharaoh

In literature I expect to see a turning away from all extremes, experiments, sensational and exotic materials back to original and simple human matters; I see a new trend towards purity and the underlying myths of humanity, in other words a new classicism, recurring on a different plane.... Once more I find that man, and especially the artist, is much less of an individual than he hoped or feared to be.

— Thomas Mann to an unknown correspondent, 8 January 1932

Joseph and his Brothers ends with death: the death of its patriarch, and the self-conscious death of the narration itself. The story "fixes its eye on its last little hour, just as Jacob did .... Never in its most expansive days did it contemplate living longer than Jacob did — or at least only

so much longer as it would take to recount his death . . . . Old and sati-
ated with life, satisfied that there should be a limit to all things, it will
then place its feet together and fall silent" (1746; 1159). The narrator
has long thought of the "Joseph" story as self-knowing (e.g., 827; 553)
and now extends that knowledge to the end of his own retelling. The
idea connects to Mann's long-held double view of death as both a corrosive force in the heart of love and a preserving principle, setting the
limits that give art its formal closure and make life's future possible.

Once he has seen the face of his son, Jacob's wish to die (Gen.
46:30) dominates the final pages of the novel. The text dramatizes
Freud's conception of the death drive with a surety and confidence it
did not risk in earlier hours of the feast. Jacob joins, then supplants, Joseph as the playwright for the final scenes of the God-drama: the reunion scene, Joseph's three visits to his father's "death-bed" in Goshen,
the pronouncement of the blessings and the moment of death itself.
Joseph is left to stage the epilogue, the elaborate "Great Progress" of
Jacob's mummified body to the double cave at Hebron. The change in
playwrights foregrounds once more Mann's shadow title "Jacob and his
Sons," a story that necessarily closes with the passing of the father.

Central to this mixture of death and blessing is "Of Denying Love,"
the reunion scene between father and son (1731–41; 1149–55). It enacts the blessing-word "tam" ("uprightness"), but with its strong connotations of opposites yoked together, a yes-no that yields the darker
yes of the narrative's conclusions (1504–5; 996–97: see chapter 4, ii).
Highlighting the scene's performative side, the half-whispered adagio
duet between father and son takes us into their final, shared understanding of sacrifice.

The scene's intertextual revisions depend on knowing the Genesis
account:

> He sent Judah before him to Joseph, to appear before him in Goshen;
> and they came into the land of Goshen. Then Joseph made ready his
> chariot and went up to meet Israel his father in Goshen; and he pre-
> sented himself to him, and fell on his neck, and wept on his neck a
> good while. Israel said to Joseph, "Now let me die, since I have seen
> your face and know that you are still alive." (46: 28–30: RSV)

Joseph does not reply to his father's wish but speaks instead "to his
brothers and his father's household" (46: 31). So in the Bible Joseph
comes alone, presents himself before his father's face, and then silently
weeps, while Jacob speaks of the moment as the climactic scene of his
life. Joseph's survival enables him to die.

The narrator makes several sagacious alterations in this scene. On the one hand, Joseph rightly wishes to display his success — that is, his fertility — before his father, just as Jacob did before Esau. He has elevated the fecundity of striped and spotted sheep into national economic policy, a triumph that should delight the father. Our Joseph arrives not alone in his chariot but in a spectacular, Cecil B. De Mille display of his grandeur. "There was a glittering and a flashing, a shimmer of color; it rolled on swiftly and turned into chariots with teams of horses and shining harness, gay with feathers. Runners were at front and in between, and runners also in the rear and at the sides. They all fixed their eyes on the foremost car, above which were poles with fans" (1735; 1151). At first it seems too much, a regressive incarnation of "The Dream of Heaven" with Joseph now actually appearing in all his narcissistic glory before the father-god. Jacob at first may see his son's "magnificence" that way, as his funny, deflationary question to Judah suggests: "Who is that fairly thickset man dressed in the splendor of the world, just stepping down from his chariot . . . and his necklace is like the rainbow and his clothing altogether like the brightness of heaven?" (1735: 1151).[19] Would it not have been more seemly for Joseph to come alone in a chariot, and then walk or even run forward to greet Jacob and beg his forgiveness?

A little reflection leads us to understand Joseph's display as thoughtful, even wise; he intends that Jacob shall read his approach in both the right and the wrong way. The adult Joseph must know the double effect that such a garish display would have on his Egypt-scorning father. At the end of the earlier reunion scene with the brothers he said to the messenger Naphtali, "Now we must think of nothing but the father" and continued, "don't be hasty, for you may not run off alone, and no one shall have the prerogative to say to our father what I shall convey to him and what I planned to say long ago when I lay on my back at night and contemplated this story" (1684–85; 1117). He instructs Naphtali about the right pacing for the revelation, "clever and loving at once" (1686; 1118). For Joseph understands reunions, and in the midst of all his powerful feelings he knows what awaits him in this one. He will make his father's final sacrifice of his beloved as easy for him as he can. Had he arrived alone, on foot and unadorned, he would have appeared to Jacob's imagination as Rachel coming to greet him at the well many years before. He would have seemed unchanged to his father, Joseph-as-Rachel, and therefore as seeking the renewal of Jacob's overweening love. So this studied, hyper-theatrical entrance reveals itself as more in the service of loving self-sacrifice than narcissism. It proclaims to the father both Joseph's triumph and his ineradicable worldliness. It repeats "The Testing " yet again, with Jacob facing the high challenge of sacrificing his love in the name of the blessing, but with Joseph now helping with (not deflecting) the dramatic circumstances to complete the sacrifice. In *Joseph the Provider* Joseph's narcissistic youthful dreams are repeatedly fulfilled — the elevation and gilding, the brothers' obeisance — but only to reveal the dreamer's hard-won freedom from their power.

Reversing Genesis, Mann's Joseph first looks smiling into Jacob's face and "forms the word 'Father'" (1736; 1152). But Jacob does not speak; instead he makes the perfect theatrical gestures to proclaim himself playwright of the spiritual blessing and set the terms of the reunion. He limps dramatically as he approaches his lost lamb and gropes for him like a blind man. Then he holds him at arm's length and peers long into his face "with sorrow and love" until he can see some trace of Rachel's features. The gestures conjure the young Jacob before his blind father; Israel's performance sets the mythic, retrospective tone for the entire scene. The eyes and the tears reveal the mother and the son in this sophisticated, worldly man of power, and in another reversal of Genesis it is Jacob who falls on his son's neck to "weep bitter tears" as Joseph asks for forgiveness. Jacob replies, "God has forgiven us;" from the beginning of the scene both plainly understand the shared excesses of the past and the requirements of the present. This will not be a blessing of blindness and trickery or the groping embrace of the wrong wife, but a judgment made by one who now sees and knows. Recognizing Rachel's features marks both reunion and the necessity of separation. Joseph wants to say "little father" to the patriarch, but Jacob has control of the script now: only "Father" is allowed, and Joseph instantly understands this as well. "Of Denying Love" replays Jacob's wedding night in sunlight, with Jacob once again handing the familiar myrtle branch of sacrifice to his beloved.

Emotion sweeps through both men even as they knowingly play their parts. They speak specifically about life and death; Jacob proclaims his wish to die, and Joseph urges him to celebrate life after this long period of separation. Unknowingly, Joseph repeats the blessing-bearer Judah's words to Jacob that "life," not death, gave his beloved back to him (1713–14; 1137). With sincerity and calculation Joseph returns to his bantering tone in "The Testing." He cleverly theologizes their suffering as God's overestimation of man's threshold of pain; he wanted only to "prick us and dab us" ("und nur stupfen und tupfen"), not cause misery (1737; 1153). But Jacob, while once again smiling at Joseph's wit and allowing him "some truth," forbears. No longer does "half of the truth lie with you, and half with me, since I showed myself weak in self-confidence" (107–8; 67). The confidence has been won. He accepts the trial of Abraham and sacrifices his beloved — which entails sacrificing the excess of his own feeling. He now reorients his love within the larger, more high-minded and painful narrative of the blessing. Jacob does not withhold love from his son, but he no longer permits that love to overmaster the blessing's imperatives. They must bear the suffering that has always accompanied the blessing-destiny (14; 6–7).

So both father and son know from the beginning the outcome of this blessing scene in the God-play. Jacob interrogates the morals of his worldly son in a self-conscious, ritualized way that comically tempers his earlier disgust; when Joseph urges tolerance for Egyptian culture on his father, Jacob replies, "I know, my son, I know" (1740; 1155). And when Jacob finally pronounces his sacrifice and rejection, Joseph only says, "I hear and know" and "I know." Jacob stages his sacrifice by embracing his son and whispering into his ear what they both already understand. They turn aside their faces: from the image of god and the beloved to the voice of God, disembodied yet deeply intimate. This latest enactment of the father-and-son sacrifice turns private and inward; sacrifice no longer requires knives and blood, but the deliberate renunciation of self-centered love. No ram waits in the thicket. Hundreds look on from the parties of Egypt and Israel, but they can only see a dumbshow. Yet read aloud, perhaps with a microphone carrying the whispered voices across a room, the story's audience can hear — and feel — everything.

Love and loyalty may appear to split apart in the scene, but the performance shows us otherwise. Father and son have each shed their blindnesses — that is, their respective narcissisms of excessive feeling and excessive self-importance — and can see each other plainly. Jacob's renunciation differs markedly from that of Kleist's Jupiter. Both may have been arbitrary in their loves (e.g., IX, 212; *Essays*, 224), but the god magnified his feelings and enjoyed the bittersweet pleasure of dropping his mask and returning to omniscience. Jacob sacrifices his feelings and takes neither pleasure nor pride in the knowledge he now makes public. Saying "Father" and "my son," not the "Väterchen" and "Rachel-in-Joseph, the Bearer of the Blessing" of the "Coat of Many Colors" section, Joseph and Jacob name themselves aright and proclaim the loyalty consonant with clear-sighted love. Jacob will take Joseph's first two sons as his own and elevate them; Joseph will carry his father's body to Abraham's grave and keep faith with his brothers. "God has forgiven *us*": the relationship remains fundamental even as it is refigured. But like his pupil Pharaoh, Joseph finally was not "the right one for the way" of the patriarchs (1468; 971).

Jacob summons Joseph three times "to his death bed" in order to elaborate the new right relation between father and favorite. The three scenes taken together offer the novel's final and most free-ranging interweaving of Eros and Thanatos. In their first, very private visit ("Submission"), Jacob launches into his longest dramatic monologue, more than a thousand words in a single paragraph (1771–75; 1175–78) that displays its craft most fully in oral performance. In his narration Jacob achieves what he only threatened to do at Joseph's disappearance: to descend like Ishtar pursuing Adonis into the underworld where love and death commingle. But he knows now that he cannot enact his old, rebellious wish to rescue his mangled son from death and return triumphantly with him to the upper world; omnipotence and God-defiance no longer lure him. Nor can he return from the "underworld" of Egypt alone. Ostensibly his monologue seeks Joseph's promise to return his body to Canaan. But this connects to a deeper purpose: to descend one final time into the underworld of the past, and to place Joseph's beginning in relation to his own ending. This means descending not in the flesh but in memory to the scene of his primal gaze into the blue eyes of the infant Joseph-Dumuzi (348–49; 231: see chapter 4, ii). In that inaugural moment Rachel, nearly dead from Joseph's violent birth, "caressed [streichelte] his hair" as he looked from her eyes to the "glow of clarity, loveliness, elegant proportions, sympathy, and divine favor" in the face of the infant Joseph. Now, as Jacob utters that memory, Joseph spontaneously "caresses [streichelt] him soothingly as a sign of his love and loyalty" (1773; 1176). Jacob repeats the central phrase, "There I want to establish — on your love and loyalty [deiner Liebe und Treue] I base the request I make of you," to carry him in a human way out of the underworld of Egypt and bury him in the upper-world hills of Hebron (1773–74; 1176–77). From the gaze to the ethical, and from a death-touched birth to a renewal of love at the onset of death: the self-influential lectures on Kleist and Freud weave together in a final figuration. In this subtle way love and loyalty continue in and through death. Jacob will not be buried with Rachel; he accepts every consequence of his renunciation. Nor will he be buried with his sons; Joseph and his brothers will remain in Egypt, and the tomb at Hebron will be sealed. There can be no God-defying conquering of death. Instead he can give the "dead" Joseph the worldly blessing "of the heights above and the depths beneath," and depend on his favorite's death-touched love and loyalty to finish his story in the right way.

The dying Jacob has, in the words of the 1936 lecture, attained the greater self-consciousness of the "Gelebte Vita" (IX, 492; *Essays*, 422), the knowledge of mythic pattern on which both psychoanalysis and the art of *Joseph* depend. Jacob is the "father of the higher type," the promise-bearing fatherhood which at the same time requires sacrifice and death. Through his deep knowledge of the patterns he attained his final individuality and created a new, spiritualized form of son-sacrifice that will shape the future in a new and distinct way. Jacob's renunciation brings him close to Freud's somber proclamation of our "common unhappiness" even as it also affirms a future consonant with Mann's rational humanism: yes-no, with a final, darker yes. Jacob's peace with this final hour of the feast marks him as the best of patriarchs, a man who like Mann's "der alte Freud" paves the way for a future in which the brothers of all the tribes may embrace and honor one another in love and loyalty.

The scene ends with the tabloid Jacob scripted: the father and son sitting in silence on the deathbed of love and renunciation, the old man leaning his head on the shoulder of the younger (1775; 1178). From cradle to "Sterbebett" — the "depths beneath" of underworld and memory intermingle with the last expressions of love and loyalty and the imminence of death. From this meeting Jacob gains the strength to carry out his cross-handed blessing of Ephraim and Manasseh, to narrate Rachel's passing one final time, and to undertake the exhausting blessing of his zodiacal clan. The required trickery of the blessing aside, Ephraim's resemblance to Rachel makes him a natural favorite. In seeing him Jacob unknowingly fulfills Mai-Sachme's hope: to see his beloved Nekhbet incarnated one final time in the third generation (1314–15; 870).

The final two scenes are increasingly public. First Joseph's sons, then all the people of Israel gather to hear Jacob's judgments upon his descendants. Jacob's risk-filled artistry in constructing his final act rivals any drama his son has composed. The narrator's own artistry supplements the patriarch's; by surrounding the scene with the secular playfulness of *Joseph the Provider*, he actually magnifies the solemnity of the Blessing. The frame plays for laughs even as the teeming life of Israel gather in the death tent. Eliezer's bumbling son Damasek-Eliezer, who cannot learn his lines let alone perform them with any sense of timing or dignity, shows the virtual uselessness of an ego cut loose from "Gelebte Vita." His scrambled delivery of Jacob's summons leads directly to another round of humor about the "youthful" septuagenarians quaking before the anticipated anger of their god-like father. Even Joseph's tactful calming of the brothers with a little discourse on the "leniency" ("Nachsicht") the moment requires, has a we're-in-for-it-now tone.

In the play itself Jacob seems to pose himself deliberately on his deathbed, with his beard spread carefully over the obligatory sheepskin and the sacrificial headband in place for his final testing. His "blind" eyes track his sons into the room. It is "Schönes Gespräch" in a post-modern frame; the haunting quality of the blessing ritual's archaic syntax stands in higher relief because of the surrounding raillery. The text's dialogy at first seems to suspend us between performance and sincerity, and no one knows at first whether the patriarch's pose, or his pauses and mumblings, or even his exhaustion, are deliberate or not. But as the performance continues, we come to see that this binary is, like Damasek's mispronunciations, irrelevant; Jacob must self-consciously perform in order to make the blessings work, and he must speak uncensored all of his associations and memories in order to make the blessings authentic. Jacob has earned the power to bless not only because he wrestled the angel but because he has sacrificed, and here he sacrifices for one last time his narcissism of feeling. He had years to plan them, yet their delivery is spontaneous (an effect that Mann seemed to prize most highly). The textual border, abutting bustling life and hieratic finality, models the future: the bar Jacob must cross and the future that his blessings — indeed his passing — evoke for his people.

Narrative self-consciousness permeates the solemn blessing. Jacob makes plenty of blunders in his prophesies and wildly evokes a Shiloh-Christ proleptically intermixed with a Nietzschean Dionysus at the end of his extravagant blessing of Judah, the chosen one. The patriarch's "happy, yes, an artful and somewhat sad smile" before beginning the blessing of Joseph, the Virgin-Bull, shows the depths and the serenity his performing and the "Gelebte Vita permit. As in the reunion scene, Jacob whispers Joseph's double blessing — or rather "*almost* whispers it" (1798; 1194: italics mine) so at least some of the people Israel can hear and learn it. The calculated difference between the unhearing crowds at the reunion scene and this formalizing of Joseph's destiny within earshot shows how precisely Jacob has constructed his final act as both blessing and sacrifice, Eros and Thanatos. Joseph remains his storehouse of Rachel-love", but the father forswears the thrill of privacy and the gaze into the face of the beloved.

"Not without rapture will his name be remembered": the double negative lends just the right qualification to Joseph's worldly triumph. "And what is sweeter than the double and the doubtful?" Jacob asks, recalling *tam* and the "double face" of God (1125; 745). "Well I know that the double is not of the spirit" (1799; 1194); he marks the sadness within Joseph's life even as he celebrates its blessing. He ends by repeating his prayer for God's forgiveness: the final gift-lesson in narcissism's education. "He finished, and hesitantly drew his hand back from his head" (1800–1; 1195). Joseph is "sent away" as Rebecca had sent her favorite away once and for all (528; 354), and Jacob turns from life to his final vision of his future: the double cave at Hebron. Within that image he crosses the border. So even as Jacob passes into the final wanderings of the moments before death, staging and ritual and contemporary allusions remain, and remain vital; without them his judgments and his leniency lose their efficacy, and forfeit their responsibility to God to make a story that will last into our own time. Joseph closes his father's eyes (the promise of Genesis 46: 4), lays his forehead on his father's brow, and weeps; the first gaze between father and infant rounds into this unseeing yet face-to-face parting between patriarch and his half-saved sacrifice: death's power and love's loyalty together in the same gesture. It is a gesture calculated with great feeling by Joseph, master of the closing ceremonies, and the narrator, equally master of the moment when he will, hesitantly, draw his hand away from his final page.

V
Hitler, "The Great Progress," and Modernism

It [the brothers' fear] allowed me to finish the book with the sound of Joseph's cheerful voice — to let him speak *once more.*

— Thomas Mann to Agnes Meyer, 5 Jan. 1943
(emphasis in original)

But death is in life, and life in death, and he who has learned this truth has penetrated the mysteries.

— Eliezer to Joseph

[Fascism is] an ultra-nationalist movement with an exaggerated ethnicity, a lust for violence and war as regenerative and moral, a core belief in social and national renewal through authoritarian leadership, corporativism and party rule, and an aesthetic politics that emphasizes the organic nature of society and national culture and supplies the semiology to reinforce it.

— Richard Overy, in *TLS*, 15 Nov. 1996, summarizing
Stanley Payne's definition in *A History of Fascism, 1914–1945*

[The use of myth in the Joseph *novels is like] what happens in a battle when a captured gun is turned around and directed against the enemy.*

In this book, the myth has been taken out of Fascist hands and humanized down to the last recess of its language — if posterity finds anything remarkable about it, it will be this.

— Thomas Mann, "The Theme of the *Joseph* Novels"

Shortly after Hitler the conqueror rode triumphantly through Freud's Vienna in 1938, Mann the exile, in the midst of a lecture tour, rode through the streets of New York City with Mayor LaGuardia, saluting policemen along the way (*TB*, 19 May 1938). The drive created a pleasing, if insignificant, counter-parade to fascism's spectacle. But on New Years Day 1943, as Mann was writing the "burial chapter" (*TB*, 1 Jan. 1943), Hitler, in seclusion, received a funeral notice of his own: the ongoing retreat of Army Group Don from its failed attempt to relieve Stalingrad. On the day that Mann finished *Joseph and his Brothers* (4 Jan. 1943) he also finished rereading another story of recovery and blessing through loyal love after a descent into the pit: *Crime and Punishment.* In honor of the ending he once again poured champagne and read the closing sections to Katia, Elisabeth, and her dedicated antifascist husband, Giuseppe Borgese. Elisabeth was especially moved by what she heard. He ended his diary entry by celebrating the firm hold of Dostoevsky's countrymen on the precious Grozny oil fields — another nail in the Nazi's coffin. Perhaps the family also raised their glasses to the Russians, past and present.

"*Jacob and his Sons*" ends, just before *Joseph and his Brothers* does the same, with the "Great Progress" of the patriarch's body to Hebron and its entombment in the double grave.[20] Genesis says only that the "elders of Egypt" escorted the Israelites, and that "it was a very great company" (50: 7–9). This sparse account gave Mann his extraordinary cadence. "Der Gewaltige Zug" mimics with cutting, comic precision the political theater of Hitler's Germany by assuming a similar form, then turning its content inside out. Just as the tetralogy began with a counterstory to the fascists' fable of Germany's pure origins, it ends with a fascist-appearing but pointedly anti-fascist parade. The spectacles that allured the young men of Munich, or overawed the citizens of Nuremberg, color the pomp of the Egyptian Empire moving through its outlying territories. The elaborate order of march, with all the showy trumpets and full-dress soldiers, only magnifies the disparity in purpose and theme. The ruling princes "from all parts of the kingdom ('Reich')" (1810; 1202) — from unique friends to middle management bureaucrats to Pharaoh's wigmaker — trek not for the glory of their Führer or even their own delight, but to carry the foreigner Jacob-Osiris out of exile and into his homeland. Joseph's long-meditated motive — to humble the pride of Egypt in the name of his father (1813–14; 1204) — complements Mann's wish to expose the Nazi's moral bankruptcy with his novel. The dominant, racially pure Egyptians cross the Sinai not as they always have, as conquerors, but as servants to the dead Hebrew patriarch and his descendants. Hitler's genocidal anti-Semitism inverts itself into the empire-wide honoring of Israel. Fascism's well-known reliance on the image rather than the word is put to anti-fascist use; Joseph tricks the Egyptians with their own penchant for display. We don't look through this performance to see the substance; the performance *is* the substance, the moving image in narrative of fascism's self-unraveling.

The final scenes take *Joseph*'s wrestling with death's disintegrating power into the grave itself. Jacob's entombment is as stark and unspiritual as can be imagined. All the brothers "turn pale" as Jacob's people open the pit (1815; 1205). The patriarch's two eldest servants struggle to lower the ponderous mummy into its narrow, dusty passages. "Absolute indifference" ("unbedingte Gleichgültigkeit") reigns in the soundless grave. They drop Jacob's casket somewhere in its depths and hasten out of its "musty spell" into "the sweet air of life" (1815; 1205). There is no trace of the blessing, or any other sort of hopeful future in this silent emptiness; once sealed permanently, we feel that neither the Israelites nor our storyteller wish to ever open it again.

The book ends on this bleak ground but in life's sweet air, and their yes-no conjunction form the final yes of the brothers' reconciliation. The scene's emotions comes from *Totem and Taboo*; the sons of Leah and the maids have so internalized their guilt over Joseph's sacrifice that they cannot escape it unaided. The story of Jacob and his sons is over for them, and they know no familiar tale to help them enter the new world without the patriarch's protection. Forgetting Abraham's — and Freud's — promise that "the father is always with you," they fear that Jacob's passing frees Joseph to punish them. They turn their brother, now sixty-five, into the avenging father-god. "I and the father are one": the tetralogy makes its way up to this final, Freudian moment. Will the father-substitute, the brother-in-glory, kill his son-siblings? Their ancient Oedipal dread transforms the sixty-five-year-old Joseph into the Führer, a Lamech (547ff.; 367ff.) or a pharaoh-sphinx ready to devour them for their ancient crimes. A bemused Benjamin carries their message to Joseph, and the brothers gather in the moonlight like sheaves to fall down before him one last time.

Instead Joseph opens his arms and, as Jacob had once commanded him (526; 353), bows down to his "brothers, you old brothers!" The life-affirming performance focuses itself sharply. The ten are old in their fear and their primitive fixations, and they have temporarily forgotten that they are equally old as Joseph's brothers; they have never been anything else but his family. We recall Joseph's complete happiness at seventeen, working in the fields with his siblings and for the time preferring their company to the lessons and shelter of his father's tent (503–4; 337). Then his uncontrollable narcissism undermined his authentic love for his brothers; now they can recover their communal solidarity and fertile harvesting. He announces their proper name — brothers, not slayers — and proclaims them "saved." He stages his final unmasking in the open air before his tent, unlike his forefathers who remained inside in various stages of blindness, and unlike Kleist's Jupiter, whose narcissistic withdrawal from relationship Joseph explicitly overcomes.

Put in Joseph's *Amphitryon* language, the brothers still misconstrue their roles in the God-play (1817–18; 1207) and the godlike man behind the mask. But Joseph reminds them of the complete omission of brother murder in Jacob's cursings, and turns that silence into a principle for the future. The Cain and Abel archetype no longer has a part to play in their story. He forgives their suspicions, for "one can very well be in the story without understanding it," and magnanimously confesses to the opposite error of always knowing the script too well. This is one of the narrative's finest ironic touches; for most of its duration Joseph didn't "know the story too well." It's the last brushstroke of narcissism in his portrait, and the perfect stroke to preserve Joseph's imperfection. True to his own many-voiced God-play — one that extends beyond even his hero's knowledge — Mann gives us the reconciling emotions of the reunion but withholds uniform resolution. A shadow of blindness, of Jacob's grave and *tam's* tempered affirmation, must remain even here. Joseph offers the brothers a humorously understated version of his elevation — "I matured somewhat" — and begs their forgiveness for putting them in the villain's role. The alien gravepit provides the stage for a family reunion: as in *The Ring*, love emerges out of sacrifice and death, and a new order of brotherly camaraderie out of the old world of brothers' retribution.

The final intertextual intrusion into *Joseph and his Brothers* makes perhaps the largest claim of all: "For a man who uses power against right and reason only because he has it, he is laughable. If he's not yet so today, then in the future he shall be, and we hold with the future" (1818; 1207). Joseph's self-reference bleeds into the contemporary world of 1943, and Joseph-Mann wishes on his great nemesis and destroyer of Germany the most damning fate he can imagine: ridicule, insignificance, a bad joke. It is his version of Hannah Arendt's "banality of evil," a more demeaning end for the grotesque patriarch Hitler than even the tawdry immolation he in fact underwent. "Sleep in peace!" Joseph says, offering a benediction to his brothers as he stands among, not above them. Like Amphitryon and Alkmene they caress each other tearfully as the curtain comes down on the "beautiful story" and "Gotteserfindung," the God-invention of *Joseph and his Brothers.* "Sleep in peace!" — Mann's farewell phrase for his narrative as well, brought to conclusion on a California hillside not unlike Hebron in topography. Perhaps as he wrote the final "Brüdern" he reflected on the trace pun in "Der Gewaltige Zug": the powerful last stroke (Zug) of his pen, the last word. *Joseph*'s final performance both produces formal coherence and mitigates its reductive effects. Everyone has been caught in the act.

Mann's projected audiences — in theaters and lecture halls, in reading chairs, by radio receivers — are themselves caught up in the performances of the anti-fascist *Joseph* and its companion essays. The Nazis sought to create monumental works that overawed and, despite all the cheering, effectively silenced audiences. Their art aimed to make interpretation unnecessary; the Nation would once again be unified before the eyes of a grateful people who need only watch and believe. Thomas Mann countered with a monumental work which foregrounded plural voices, a kaleidoscopic narrator, palimpsestic styles, permeable egos, unlocatable beginnings, narcissism's anatomy, cultural loyalties, and the ethics of aesthetic performance. The novel's essayistic mode, far from instructing us in a single truth, contains virtually every kind of dialogic variation and therefore requires constant engagement and reinterpretation. *Joseph*'s saving image of the father stands against the text-erasing images of fascism. Mann avoids the dangers of art — repetitive or serial, industrial-mechanical or free-floating — which erase either difference or harmony; he struggles on every page to preserve both.

The monolithic term "modernism" reduces the great variety of artistic practice in the early twentieth century to a single abstraction, and arguments seeking to locate Mann either in or outside its confines risk the same reduction. Clearly many modernisms arose in the wake of the early twentieth century's new science, crisis in representation, last-gasp imperialism, and world war. Mann's anchoring in eighteenth-century German humanism and nineteenth-century haute-bourgeois life precluded him from practicing certain kinds of modernism, but they actively encouraged him to participate in others. Most visibly, his sense of artistic belatedness and his exploration of consciousness in the wake of Frazer and Freud place him in its company. Russell Berman aptly locates him among "liberal" rather than conservative or radical modernists, and includes among his reasons Mann's characteristic substitution of ambivalence for univocal identity, and the objectivity afforded by "essayism" for fictionalizing (1989, 67, 79). Liberal modernists and rhetoricians of irony such as Mann critique structures of representation and explore the immobility of the present. Mann puts forward the *Joseph* tetralogy as a self-knowing counter-voice to the immobilizing rhetoric of fascism's monologue. By showing the limits of any single discourse, and through self-consciousness about its own roots in narcissism, *Joseph* carries out its ethical enterprise. During the *Joseph* years Mann also became an engaged modernist, a political and cultural activist, even if his politics were sometimes naive and his culture unnecessarily patriarchal. Unlike those modernists who missed the vital distinction between flawed bourgeois institutions and the abiding values of liberal freedom, he placed his own narcissism in service and showed its political face.

Foregrounding performance and self-influence in *Joseph and his Brothers* has enabled us to discover richer connections between Mann's essays, fiction, and public appearances. We have learned more about the oral quality of his writing, both how projected performance shaped particular passages as he wrote and how literary form enhanced political speechmaking instead of isolating itself from its effects. Thematizing performance in *Joseph* allowed Mann to constantly test its values in fiction as well as before his many publics. Staging narcissism helped him to understand, and in part render ethical, narcissism's stages. The relations between lonely writing desk and public arena turned out to be reciprocal, not one-way; performance became more than an aftermath. And performance also laid a further ground for intertextuality, particularly self-influence, beyond the choices and momentum of writing itself: it preserved not only sentences and ideas but entire scenes and onstage emotions that made their way into succeeding texts.

In August 1955, one of the German obituaries for Thomas Mann declared that a "throne has been left empty" (Prater 1995, 509). But in truth Mann had long since abandoned all thrones for more modest seating. In 1948 he concluded his "Foreword" to *Joseph* by saying that his "pyramidlike" tetralogy had "a measure of durability." In his diary he described *Joseph*, "good and bad alike," as "a monument of my life . . . of *steadfastness* ("*Beharrlichkeit*"). "Durability" and "steadfastness:" those words evoke tradition and timeliness, loyalty and determination, and suggest how *Joseph and his Brothers* can continue to perform for Germany, and for human society, in succeeding hours of the feast.

Notes

[1] In the "Foreword" to the 1948 one-volume edition of *Joseph*, Mann places the 1936 "Freud" essay "in the orbit" of *Lotte in Weimar*, which he began shortly after finishing *Joseph in Egypt*. But the "Freud" essay was delivered in Vienna on 8 May, and he did not finish *Joseph in Egypt* until 23 August (*TB*, 23 Aug. 1936; Bürgin and Mayer 1969, 121–123). Since plans for *Lotte* did begin in the spring, it is perhaps better to say that the "Freud" essay orbits in the gravitational fields of both larger works, one nearing completion and one just beginning.

[2] *TB*, 3 May 1936; *Frage und Antwort*, 224; Freud to Stefan Zweig, 18 May 1936. Mann edited Zweig's draft. Perhaps because of that the "Address" anticipates the lecture at several points, including Mann's division of Freud into a "physician and psychologist" on the one hand, and a "philosopher and artist" — more Mann's Freud — on the other. See Jones 3 (1957), 205–6 for the full text, and Potempa (1992, 94) for an abbreviated version and a list of the signatories.

[3] Mann delivered the lecture several more times in Europe, and even gave it in English at Princeton in 1939. He noted in his diary that the American audience was very large and that it was "a good performance in spite of some nervousness" (no doubt because of the language). Christian Gauss told him, he records, that it was "'the most interesting lecture in my experience'" (*TB*, 13 Feb. 1939). Mann inevitably fell prey to occasional blunders in speeches given in English; at a 1934 gala dinner he called Alfred A. Knopf "not only a publisher, but a creature too" instead of a "creator" (Katia Mann 1975, 104).

[4] Freud to Marie Bonaparte (16 June 1936) and Arnold Zweig (17 June 1936). Mann recorded Freud's emotional reaction in an unpublished letter to Ida Herz (Bürgin and Mayer 1969, 123).

[5] Freud's eccentric response to Mann's reading deserves a section of its own. He first articulated it that afternoon and then, apparently forgetting that he had done so, expressed it again in a letter the following November (*Letters*, 432–34). He reread Joseph as the mythical prototype of Napoleon I, whose older brother and "hated rival" was named Joseph. (Mann mentions Napoleon in the lecture but makes no explicit connection to Joseph.) Internalizing and inverting this hatred, Napoleon idealized his brother, married "Josephine" largely because of her name, and remained loyal to her despite her "betrayals." He went to Egypt, *imitatio* Joseph, and in doing so not only tried to impress his older brother but opened up Egypt to European rediscovery. In this light both the statuettes at 19 Berggasse and the *Joseph in Egypt* that Freud had just finished owe everything to Napoleon's inversion — a true beginning indeed! Finally, writes Freud, the emperor elevated his brothers to be kings and princes, and then launched his own self-destructive downfall when he became "disloyal" to Josephine and marched off to Russia. The permutations of this reading boggle the mind. Did Freud think about Thomas's well-

known enmity with Heinrich? Is there aggression in this, especially since Freud acknowledged sadly (and rightly) that he would not live to read the final, reconciling volume? Was Freud "secretly" vexed with Mann once again trying to educate him, Napoleon-fashion, about his putative intellectual ancestors? Did Freud subliminally recollect his own father's name as he theorized (Jacob), and think of himself as a failing Joseph-Napoleon? Did his colleague and "provider," Princess Marie Bonaparte, great-granddaughter of another Napoleon brother, Lucien, play a role in this fantasy? These associations would require a *Joseph*-length manuscript to untangle. For an interesting discussion, see Heftrich 1993, 119ff.

[6] Sympathy also figured prominently in Schopenhauer's ethics, as Mann developed the subject in his essay on the philosopher two years later (IX, 552–56; 390–92). In the 1942 "Joseph" lecture to the Library of Congress, Mann specifically extended sympathy's role into the future, as the foundation of the new humanism's blessing: sympathy "will be only too necessary for the work of reconstruction" that will follow "the collapse of the accustomed world" ("Theme," 8).

[7] Mann's Freud connects here with several revisionist accounts of psychoanalysis, most intriguingly with Julia Kristeva's resituation of transference-love at the beginning of human development and analytic therapy (1987, chapters 1–2, and passim). In Kristeva's reconstruction Freud becomes the first thinker to make the love relationship the model of psychic functioning (14).

D. M. Thomas's fictional reconstruction of Freud in *The White Hotel* (1981) gives us a portrait uncannily like the one Mann is sketching. The case study of "Frau Anna G" purports to be a manuscript solicited by the Frankfurt City Council in 1930 as part of the Goethe Prize (129–30n). "It seemed appropriate on this occasion to introduce a case in which reason and imagination can be seen as partners in the search for truth, as they were in the heart and mind of the genius whom we honour. Disordered and sentimental though Frau Anna's journal is, I believe Goethe himself would have seen in it more of purity than coarseness; and that he would not have been surprised to learn that in the realm of the libido the highest and lowest are closely connected, and in a way dependent upon each other: 'From Heaven, across the world, to Hell.' *Long may poetry and psychoanalysis continue to highlight, from their different perspectives, the human face in all its nobility and sorrow*" (143n: italics mine).

[8] In his lecture on Wagner's *Ring* (November 1937), Mann opens with a highly charged panegyric on "Admiration" ("Bewunderung"), "the source of love, indeed love itself" (IX, 502; *Essays*, 353). The passage plainly draws energy from "Freud and the Future" and the *Joseph* novels, and in turn contributed to the intensity of the reunion scenes between Jacob and Joseph.

[9] Mann could draw some support from passages such as the "Gradiva" essay's comment on love (my chapter 2 epigraph), but the preponderance of evidence is against him.

[10] Mann cleverly cites the "somewhat ungrateful scion" ("etwas undankbar Sprößling") Jung as sharing the conception of "Gelebte Vita" and the complicity of knower and known with the patriarch he abandoned (IX, 488–90; 418–20). Mann makes Jung's "rebellion" seem more a matter of character than substance: a calculated comfort for Freud the abandoned father?

[11] Mann to Viktor Polzer, 23 Mar. 1940: *Briefe* II, 139. Italics in the original.

[12] The example also coincides with Mann's rising interest in his projected Goethe novel *Lotte in Weimar*, an interest which would soon suspend his work on *Joseph*.

[13] Letter to Erich von Kahler, 31 Dec. 1941 (*Briefe* II, 230).

[14] Harold Bloom offers a related account (1973, 55). "[His Tamar] stands, as Mann perhaps only partly realized (great ironist though he was) in some sense for Mann himself, and for any artist who feels strongly the injustice of time, at having denied him all priority. Mann's Tamar knows instinctively that the meaning of one copulation is only another copulation, even as Mann knows that one cannot write a novel without remembering another novel."

[15] Mann may have been tempted to use the ancient stories of the historical Ikhnaton's arabesques of incestuous relations. He out-Oedipused Oedipus at every turn, sleeping with his mother, his wives, and several of his daughters. But those tales did not fit well with his portrait of an abstracted, neurasthenic prophet whose characterization depended on deferment and substitution.

[16] Mann also used the arabesque metaphor in connection with Joseph's "kaleidoscopic" career (834; 557). For a fascinating, supplemental account of its meaning, see Heftrich 1993, 142ff.

[17] The Hermes of Mann's "Kleist" lecture is not a direct-line precursor of the Joseph-Hermes character in *Joseph the Provider*. Yet Kleist's Hermes, more trickster than mediator, does place the god's crafty, mimicking nature right at the beginning of *Joseph*'s making.

[18] Surprisingly, Lowe-Porter altered Mann's chapter breaks here, moving up the beginning of "The Money in the Sacks" to Joseph's exchange with Mai-Sachme. In the original the chapter does not begin until the brothers are reassembled before Joseph (1619; 1074).

[19] Jacob has apparently abandoned his fantasy from the early days of his Laban-time to build a "house of gold" for God (251–52; 165).

[20] A more modern rendering of "Der Gewaltige Zug" would be "mighty procession," but for me Lowe-Porter's more sonorous, antique phrase captures the occasion's self-conscious dignity, and its forecast of the Exodus ("Auszug").

Works Cited

Adams, Jeffrey and Eric Williams, eds. *Mimetic Desire: Essays on Narcissism in German Literature from Romanticism to Post Modernism.* Columbia, SC: Camden House, 1995.

Alter, Robert. *Genesis: Translation and Commentary.* New York: Norton, 1996.

Bakhtin, Mikhail. *The Dialogic Imagination.* Ed. Michael Holquist. Trans. Caryl Emerson and Michael Holquist. Austin: U of Texas P, 1981.

Barnouw, Dagmar. *Weimar Intellectuals and the Threat of Modernity.* Bloomington and Indianapolis: Indiana UP, 1988.

Barthes, Roland. "The Struggle with the Angel: Textual Analysis of Genesis 32:22–32." *Image — Music — Text.* Trans. Stephen Heath. New York: Hill and Wang, 1987. 125–41.

Baynes, Norman H., ed. *The Speeches of Adolph Hitler.* Vol. 1. Oxford: Oxford UP, 1942.

Berger, Willy R. *Die Mythologischen Motive in Thomas Manns Roman "Joseph und seine Brüder."* Cologne and Vienna: Böhlau, 1971.

Berman, Russell. "Written Right Across their Faces: Ernst Jünger's Fascist Modernism." *Modernity and the Text: Revisions of German Modernism.* Ed. Andreas Huyssen and David Bathrick. New York: Columbia UP, 1989.

Bermann Fischer, Gottfried. *Bedroht — Bewahrt: Der Weg eines Verlegers.* Frankfurt a. M.: S. Fischer, 1967.

Bertram, Ernst. *Friedrich Nietzsche: Versuch einer Mythologie.* Berlin: G. Bondi, 1920.

Bloom, Harold. *The Anxiety of Influence.* Oxford: Oxford UP, 1973.

Brooks, Peter. Rev. of *Freud's Paranoid Quest: Psychoanalysis and Modern Suspicion* by John Farrell. *Times Literary Supplement* 27 Sept. 1996: 30.

Bruhn, Gert. *Das Selbstzitat bei Thomas Mann: Untersuchungen zum Verhältnis von Fiktion und Autobiographie in seinem Werk.* New York: Peter Lang, 1992.

Bürgin, Hans, and Hans-Otto Mayer. *Thomas Mann: A Chronicle of His Life.* Trans. Eugene Dobson. University, Alabama: U of Alabama P, 1969.

Burns, Rob, ed. *German Cultural Studies.* Oxford: Oxford UP, 1995.

Cather, Willa. *Not Under Forty.* New York: Alfred A. Knopf, 1936.

Clayton, Jay and Eric Rothstein, eds. *Influence and Intertextuality in Literary History*. Madison: U of Wisconsin P, 1991.

Cohn, Dorrit. *Transparent Minds: Narrating Modes for Presenting Consciousness in Fiction*. Princeton: Princeton UP, 1978.

Cowart, David. *Literary Symbiosis*. Athens: U of Georgia P, 1993.

Craig, Gordon. "Under an Evil Star." *New York Review of Books* 5 Oct. 1995: 24–26.

Derrida, Jacques. *A Derrida Reader: Between the Blinds*. Ed. Peggy Kamuf. New York: Columbia UP, 1991.

——. *Points . . . Interviews, 1974–1994*. Ed. Elisabeth Weber. Trans. Peggy Kamuf et al. Stanford: Stanford UP, 1995.

——. *The Post Card: From Socrates to Freud and Beyond*. Trans. Alan Bass. Chicago: U of Chicago P, 1987.

Dierks, Manfred. "*Doctor Faustus* and Recent Theories of Narcissism." *Thomas Mann's Doctor Faustus: A Novel at the Margin of Modernism*. Ed. Herbert Lehnert and Peter Pfeiffer. Columbia, SC: Camden House, 1991a. 33–60.

——. *Studien zu Mythos und Psychologie bei Thomas Mann*. *Thomas-Mann-Studien* 2. Bern and Munich: Franke, 1972.

——. "Traumzeit und Verdichtung. Der Einfluß der Psychoanalyse auf Thomas Manns Erzählweise." *Thomas Mann und seine Quellen*. Ed. E. Heftrich and H. Koopmann. Frankfurt a. M.: Klostermann, 1991b. 111–37.

Draine, Betsy. "Chronotope and Intertext: The Case of Jean Rhys' *Quartet*." Clayton and Rothstein, eds. *Influence and Intertextuality in Literary History*. Madison: U of Wisconsin P, 1991. 318–37.

Editorial Board of *The American Scholar*. "Outstanding Books, 1931–1961." *The American Scholar* 30 (1961). 600–630.

Ferris, Timothy. *Galaxies*. New York: Harrison House, 1980.

Finck, Jean. *Thomas Mann und die Psychoanalyse*. Paris: Belles Lettres, 1973.

Freud, Ernst, Lucie Freud, and Ilse Grubrich-Simitis, eds. *Sigmund Freud: His Life in Pictures and Words*. Trans. Christine Trollope. New York: Norton, 1985.

Freud, Sigmund. *Briefe 1873–1939*. Selected and edited by Ernest L. Freud. Frankfurt a. M.: Fischer, 1960.

——. *Collected Papers I–V*. New York: Basic Books, 1959.

——. *Letters of Sigmund Freud*. Selected and edited by Ernst L. Freud. Trans. by Tania and James Stern. New York: Basic Books, 1960.

——. *The Standard Edition of the Complete Psychological Works of Sigmund Freud*. Ed. and trans. James Strachey in collaboration with Anna Freud, assisted by Alix Strachey and Alan Tyson. 24 vols. London: Norton, 1953–74.

Gantz, Timothy. *Early Greek Myth*. Baltimore: Johns Hopkins UP, 1993.

Gay, Peter. *Freud: A Life for our Time*. New York: W. W. Norton, 1988.

Grimm, Alfred. *Joseph und Echnaton: Thomas Mann und Ägypten*. Mainz am Rhein: Philipp von Zabern, 1992.

Hansen, Volkmar, and Gert Heine, eds. *Frage und Antwort: Interviews mit Thomas Mann 1909–1955*. Hamburg: Albrecht Knaus, 1983.

Harpprecht, Klaus. *Thomas Mann: Eine Biographie*. Germany: Rowohlt, 1995.

Hayman, Ronald. *Thomas Mann: A Biography*. New York: Scribner, 1995.

Heftrich, Eckhard. *Geträumte Taten: Joseph und seine Brüder*. Über Thomas Mann 3. Frankfurt a. M.: Klostermann. 1993.

——. "Potiphars Weib im Lichte von Wagner und Freud." *Thomas Mann Jahrbuch IV*. Ed. Eckhard Heftrich and Hans Wysling. Frankfurt a. M.: Klostermann, 1991. 58–74.

Heftrich, Eckhard and Helmet Koopmann, eds. *Thomas Mann und seine Quellen: Festschrift für Hans Wysling*. Frankfurt a. M.: Klostermann, 1991.

Heilbut, Anthony. *Thomas Mann: Eros and Literature*. New York: Alfred A. Knopf, 1996.

Heller, Peter. "'Narcissism' in Thomas Mann's Goethe Novel." *Mimetic Desire: Essays on Narcissism in German Literature from Romanticism to Post-Modernism*. Ed. Jeffrey Adams and Eric Williams. Columbia, SC: Camden House, 1995. 119–41.

Herodotus. *Histories*. Trans. Aubrey Selincourt. Harmondsworth: Penguin Books, 1972.

Hutcheon, Linda. *Narcissistic Narrative*. New York: Methuen, 1984.

Huyssen, Andreas and David Bathrick, eds. *Modernity and the Text: Revisions of German Modernism*. New York: Columbia UP, 1989.

Jones, Ernest. *The Life and Work of Sigmund Freud*. 3 vols. New York: Basic Books, 1953–1957.

Kermode, Frank. *The Genesis of Secrecy: On the Interpretation of Narrative*. Cambridge: Harvard UP, 1979.

Kleist, Heinrich von. *Werke*. Vol. 1. Ed. Erich Schmidt. Leipzig: Bibliographisches Institut. n.d.

Koelb, Clayton. *Thomas Mann's "Goethe and Tolstoy": Notes and Sources*. University, Alabama: U of Alabama P, 1984.

Koopmann, Helmut. "The Decline of the West and the Ascent of the East: Thomas Mann, the *Joseph* Novels, and Spengler." *Critical Essays on Thomas Mann.* Ed. Inta M. Ezergailis. Boston: G. K. Hal, 1988. 238–65.

———. ed. *Thomas-Mann-Handbuch.* Stuttgart: Kroner, 1990.

Kristeva, Julia. *Tales of Love.* Trans. Leon S. Roudiez. New York: Columbia UP, 1987.

Kurzke, Hermann. *Thomas Mann: Epoche-Werk-Wirkung.* Munich: C. H. Beck, 1985.

Lanham, Richard. *The Motives of Eloquence.* New Haven: Yale UP, 1976.

Lehnert, Herbert. "Fictional Orientations in Thomas Mann's Biography." *PMLA* 88 (1973): 1146–61.

———. *"Joseph und seine Brüder." Thomas Mann Romane und Erzählungen.* Ed. Volkmar Hansen. Stuttgart: Philip Reclam, 1993. 186–227.

———. *Thomas Mann: Fiktion, Mythos, Religion.* Stuttgart: Kohlhammer, 1965.

———. "Thomas Mann in Exile 1933–1938." *Germanic Review* 38 (1963a): 277–94.

———. "Thomas Manns Vorstudien zur Josephstetralogie." *Jahrbuch der deutschen Schillergesellschaft.* Stuttgart: Kröner, 1963b. 458–520.

Lehnert, Herbert and Eva Wessell. *Nihilismus der Menschfreundlichkeit: Thomas Manns 'Wandlung' und sein Essay 'Goethe und Tolstoi.'* Thomas Mann Studien 9. Frankfurt a. M.: Klostermann, 1991.

Lesser, Jonas. *Thomas Mann in der Epoche seiner Vollendung.* Munich: Kurt Desch, 1952.

Levinas, Emmanuel. "Four Talmudic Readings." *Nine Talmudic Readings.* Trans. Annette Aronowicz. Bloomington: Indiana UP, 1990.

Longus. *Daphnis and Chloe.* Trans. Christopher Collins. Barre, Mass.: Imprint Society, 1972.

Mann, Erika. *Briefe und Antworten I: 1922–1950.* Ed. Anna Zanco Prestel. Munich: Ellermann, 1984.

Mann, Erika and Klaus Mann. "Portrait of our Father." *The Stature of Thomas Mann.* Ed. Charles Neider. New York: New Directions, 1947. 59–76.

Mann, Katia. *Unwritten Memories.* New York: Knopf, 1975.

Mann, Monika. *Past and Present.* Trans. Frances F. Reid and Ruth Hein. New York: St. Martin's Press, 1960.

———. *Vergangenes und Gegenwärtiges.* Munich: Kindler, 1956.

Mann, Thomas. *Briefe I: 1889–1936; Briefe II: 1937–1947; Briefe III: 1948–1955.* Ed. Erika Mann. Frankfurt a. M.: S. Fischer, 1961, 1963, 1965.

——. *"Death in Venice" and Other Stories.* Trans. David Luke. New York: Bantam, 1988.

——. *Dichter über ihre Dichtungen*, vol. 14/II. Ed. Hans Wysling. Frankfurt a. M. and Munich: Heimeran/S. Fischer, 1979.

——. *Essays, Band 3: Ein Appell an die Vernunft, 1926–1933.* Frankfurt a. M.: S. Fischer, 1994.

——. *Frage und Antwort. Interviews mit Thomas Mann 1909–1955.* Ed. Volkmar Hansen and Gert Heine. Hamburg: Albrecht Knaus, 1983.

——. *Gesammelte Werke. I-XIII.* Frankfurt a. M.: S. Fischer, 1974, 1990.

——. *Joseph and his Brothers.* Trans. H. T. Lowe-Porter. New York: Knopf, 1948.

——. *Letters to Paul Amann*, 1915–1952. Trans. Richard and Clara Winston. Middletown: Wesleyan UP, 1960.

——. *The Magic Mountain.* Trans. John E. Woods. New York: Knopf, 1995.

——. *Notizbücher 1–6; Notizbücher 7–14.* Ed. Hans Wysling and Yvonne Schmidlin. Frankfurt a. M.: S. Fischer, 1991, 1992.

——. *Past Masters and Other Papers.* Freeport, New York: Books for Libraries Press, 1968.

——. *Reflections of a Non-political Man.* Trans. Walter D. Morris. New York: Frederick Ungar, 1983.

——. *Royal Highness.* Trans. A. Cecil Curtis. New York: Alfred A. Knopf, 1939.

——. *Stories of Three Decades.* Trans. H. T. Lowe-Porter. New York: Knopf, 1936.

——. *Tagebücher, 1921; Tagebücher, 1933–1934; Tagebücher, 1935–1936; Tagebücher, 1937–1939; Tagebücher, 1940–1943.* Ed. Peter de Mendelssohn. Frankfurt a. M.: S. Fischer, 1979, 1977, 1978, 1980, 1982.

——. "The Theme of the *Joseph* Novels: An Address to the Library of Congress," Nov. 7, 1942. *Thomas Mann's Addresses 1942–1949.* Washington, DC: Library of Congress, 1943. 1–19.

——. *Mann, Thomas — Agnes E. Meyer: Briefwechsel 1937–1955.* Ed. Hans Rudolf Vaget. Frankfurt a. M.: S. Fischer, 1992.

——. *Mann, Thomas an Ernst Bertram: Briefe aus den Jahren 1910–1955.* Ed. Inge Jens. Pfullingen: Neske, 1960.

——, and Heinrich Mann. *Briefwechsel 1900–1949.* Ed. Hans Wysling. Frankfurt a. M.: S. Fischer, 1984.

——. and Heinrich Mann, *Letters of Heinrich and Thomas Mann.* Ed. Hans Wysling. Trans. Don Reneau. Berkeley: U of California P, 1998.

——. and Karl Kerenyi. *Gespräch in Briefen.* Zürich: Rhein-Verlag. 1960.

Mayer, Hans. *Thomas Mann*. Frankfurt a. M.: Suhrkamp, 1980.

Mieth, Dietmar. *Epik und Ethik: eine Theologisch-ethische Interpretation der Josephromane*. Tübingen: Max Niemeyer, 1976.

Miller, Owen. "Intertextual Identity." *The Identity of the Literary Text*. Ed. Mario J. Valdés and Owen Miller. Toronto: U of Toronto P, 1985. 19–40.

Miller, William Ian. *The Anatomy of Disgust*. Cambridge: Harvard UP, 1997.

Mitchell, Juliet. *Psychoanalysis and Feminism: Freud, Reich, Laing and Women*. New York: Pantheon, 1974.

———. Rev. of Edith Kurzweil, *Freudians and Feminists*. *Times Literary Supplement* 31 May 1996: 12.

Newton, Adam Zachary. *Narrative Ethics*. Cambridge: Harvard UP, 1995.

Nietzsche, Friedrich. *The Birth of Tragedy*. Trans. Shaun Whiteside. London: Penguin Books, 1993.

Otto, Susanne. *Literarische Produktion als egozentrische Variation des Problems von Identitätsfindung und- stabilisierung, Ursprung, Grundlagen und Konsequenzen bei Thomas Mann: Analyse des novellistischen Frühwerks mit Perspektive auf das Gesamtwerk* . Frankfurt a. M.: Peter Lang, 1982.

Ovid. *Metamorphosis*. Trans. Horace Gregory. New York: Viking Press, 1958.

Phalen, James. *Narrative as Rhetoric*. Columbus: Ohio State UP, 1996.

Potempa, Georg. *Thomas Mann-Bibliographie. Das Werk*. Morsum/Sylt: Cicero Presse, 1992.

Prater, Donald. *Thomas Mann*. London and New York: Oxford UP, 1995.

Reed, T. J. *Thomas Mann: The Uses of Tradition*. Oxford: Oxford UP, 1974.

Reeve, William. *Kleist on Stage: 1804–1987*. Montreal: McGill-Queens UP, 1993.

Reiss, Gunter. "*Allegorisierung*" *und Moderne Erzählkunst*. Munich: Wilhelm Fink, 1970.

Renner, Rolf Günter. *Lebens-Werk: Zum innern Zusammenhang der Texte von Thomas Mann*. Munich: Wilhelm Fink, 1985.

Ridley, Hugh. *The Problematic Bourgeois: Twentieth-Century Criticism on Thomas Mann's* Buddenbrooks *and* The Magic Mountain. Columbia, SC: Camden House, 1994.

Scaff, Susan von Rohr. "The Dialectic of Myth and History: Revision of Archetype in Thomas Mann's *Joseph* Novels." *Monatshefte* 82 (1990): 177–193.

Scheid, John and Jesper Svenbro. *The Craft of Zeus: Myths of Weaving and Fabric.*. Trans. Carol Volk. Cambridge: Harvard UP, 1996.

Silverman, David, ed. *Ancient Egypt*. New York: Oxford UP, 1997.

Simpson, William Kelly, ed. *The Literature of Ancient Egypt: An Anthology of Stories, Instructions and Poetry*. New Haven: Yale UP, 1973.

Sterne, Laurence. *Tristram Shandy*. Ed. James Work. New York: Odyssey Press, 1940.

Sultan, Stanley. "Joyce and Mann: Citizen Artists." *Eliot, Joyce and Company*. Oxford: Oxford UP, 1987. 195–217.

Thomas, D. H. *The White Hotel*. New York: Viking, 1981.

Tratner, Michael. *Modernism and Mass Politics: Joyce, Woolf, Eliot, Yeats*. Stanford: Stanford UP, 1995.

Tyldesley, Joyce. *Hatchepsut*. New York: Viking, 1996.

Vaget, Hans, and Dagmar Barnouw. *Thomas Mann: Fragen zu seiner Rezeption*. Bern: Lang, 1975.

Williams, Bernard. *Inconvenient Fictions*. New Haven: Yale UP, 1991.

Wysling, Hans, ed. *Dichter oder Schriftsteller?: der Briefwechsel zwischen Thomas Mann und Josef Ponten 1919–1930*. Thomas-Mann-Studien 8. Bern: Francke, 1988.

——. *Narzissmus und Illusionäre Existenzform: Zu den Bekenntnissen des Hochstaplers Felix Krull*. Bern and Munich: Franke, 1982.

Wysling, Hans and Paul Scherrer. *Quellenkritische Studien zum Werk Thomas Manns*. Bern and Munich: Franke, 1967.

Index

Flaubert, Gustave, ix
Fliess, Wilhelm, 174, 179
Fowles, John, 5
Frazer, Sir James, 117, 120, 256
Freud, Ernst, 230
Freud, Sigmund, 2, 12, 23, 30,
35, 54, 73–77, 87n29, 95–
116, 119–21, 126–31, 133–
34n18, 157, 159, 167, 212n4,
213n8, 218–30, 232, 236,
245, 249–50, 256, 258–
59n5,7, 260n10; biography, 3,
83n1, 174–77, 211; works by:
Beyond the Pleasure Principle,
96, 133n16, 144; "A Child is
being Beaten," 214n12; *Civilization and its Discontents*, xii,
174–84, 188–97, 204–5, 207,
212n3, 220; "'Civilized' Sexual
Morality and Modern Nervous
Illness," 179; "A Difficulty in
the Path of Psycho-analysis,"
142; "The Dissection of the
Mental Personality," 220, 226,
228; "Dora" ("Fragment of an
Analysis of a Case of Hys-
teria"), 204; *The Ego and the
Id*, 96; *The Future of an Illusion*, 96, 113–14, 214n12;
"Jensen's *Gradiva*," 89n44,
95, 96, 132n2, 169, 180, 222,
259n9; *The Interpretation of
Dreams*, 3, 197; *Introductory
Lectures* III, 141; "Leonardo
da Vinci and a Memory of his
Childhood," 141; "Mass Psychology and Ego Analysis," 96;
Moses and Monotheism, 103,
223; "On Narcissism," 70,
139–42, 151, 156, 168, 169,
170n4, 171n14; *Three Essays
on Sexuality*, 132n5, 223; *Totem and Taboo*, xii, 1, 65, 66,
68, 69–70, 71, 96–97, 104–8,

111–16, 117–21, 126–31,
132n1, 134n26, 139, 142,
163, 165, 168, 169, 179, 182,
184, 190–91, 196, 228, 233,
254
Friedmann, Susan Stanford, 37n2
Frye, Northrop, ix
Galbraith, John Kenneth, ix
Galsworthy, John, 176
Gantz, Timothy, 85n17, 215n21
Gassner, John, ix
Gauss, Christian, 258n3
Gay, Peter, 134n18,27
Goethe, Johann Wolfgang von, 1,
2, 6, 7, 8, 9, 12, 23, 28, 30,
56, 85n15, 86n21, 142, 176,
207, 219; works by: *Faust*, 20,
42n34, 75, 228–29
Grimm, Alfred, 215n18, 216n28
Grimm's Fairy Tales, 28
Hamsun, Knut, 24
Hardt, Ludwig, 41n30
Harpprecht, Klaus, 132n6,9,
133n15
Hatchepsut, 193–94, 197
Hauptmann, Gerhart, 30, 95
Haydn, Hiram, ix
Hayman, Ronald, 40n26, 48,
132n9, 142
Heftrich, Eckhard, 37n3, 42n39,
84n14, 214n17, 259n5,
260n16
Hegel, Georg Wilhelm, 87n30
Heilbut, Anthony, 171n15, 242
Heine, Heinrich, 176
Heins, Valentin, 133n15
Heller, Peter, 138, 143
Herodotus, 85n17, 194
Herz, Ida, 258n4
Hesiod, 85n17
Heuser, Klaus, 44–47, 50, 60, 64,
74, 80, 83n7, 85n16, 99, 104,
131, 137, 145, 146, 165,
172n18, 199, 201, 210, 229